SILENCE

SILENCE

The Winchester University Press PREFACE SERIES

The Winchester University Press PREFACE SERIES stands at the intersection of creative practice and critical interrogation. Each PREFACE SERIES title consists of an extended piece of writing in a chosen form (prose, poetry, script) alongside a self-reflective commentary on the nature and construction of the piece, written by the authors themselves. Following in the tradition of writers such as Henry James, who produced insightful commentaries on their own works, PREFACE SERIES titles are both innovative, creative works and sophisticated reflections on the nature of the creative process.

SILENCE

Tom Masters

Published by the Winchester University Press 2010

First Published in Great Britain in 2010 by
The Winchester University Press
University of Winchester
Winchester SO22 4NR

British Library Cataloguing-in-Publication Data
A CIP catalogue record for this book is available from the British Library.

ISBN: 978-1-906113-03-2

Printed and Bound in Great Britain

CONTENTS

Preface **xi**

Hemisphere One - Poetry

Book One **3**

Book Two **65**

Hemisphere Two - Critical Reincarnations

Book One **107**
- **Cosmological Paradigm – Radiation Era** **109**
- **Theory** **110**
- **Practice** **183**

Book Two **203**
- **Cosmological Paradigm – Matter Era** **205**
- **Theory (Caravaggio, *Unstill Life*)** **206**
- **Practice (Caravaggio, *Unstill Life*)** **249**
- **Theory (Leonardo, *Anatomy*)** **264**
- **Practice (Leonardo, *Anatomy*)** **271**
- **Theory (Hieronymus, *Wilderness*)** **380**
- **Practice (Hieronymus, *Wilderness*)** **387**

Afterword **391**

Bibliography **395**

PERMISSIONS

By permission of the President and Fellows of Harvard College, extracts have been reprinted from *Ancient Mystery Cults* by Walter Burkert, pp. 5, 6, 10, 12, 15, 33, 93, 106, Cambridge, Mass.: Harvard University Press, Copyright © 1987 by the President and Fellows of Harvard College.
By permission of the Publishers and Trustees of the Loeb Classical Library, extracts have been reprinted from *St. Jerome: Select letters*, translated by F.A. Wright, Cambridge: Harvard University Press, Copyright © 1933, by the President and Fellows of Harvard College. Loeb Classical Library ® is a registered trademark of the President and Fellows of Harvard College.
By permission of the Publishers and Trustees of the Loeb Classical Library, extracts have been reprinted from *Nonnos: Volume 1*, Loeb Classical Library Volume 344, translated by W. H. D. Rouse, Cambridge: Harvard University Press, Copyright © 1940, by the President and Fellows of Harvard College. Loeb Classical Library ® is a registered trademark of the President and Fellows of Harvard College.
By permission of the Random House Group Ltd, extracts have been reprinted from *Caravaggio: A Life* (1999) by Helen Langdon, published by Chatto & Windus.
By permission of the Taylor & Francis Group, extracts have been reprinted from *Myth* (1997), by Lawrence Coupe, p. 1.
By permission of the Taylor & Francis Group, extracts have been reprinted from *Jerome* (2002), by Stefan Rebenich, pp. 4, 5, 6, 7, 8, 9, 12, 13, 14, 15, 19, 41, 210.
By permission of the Taylor & Francis Group, extracts have been reprinted from *Leonardo da Vinci* (2001), by Sigmund Freud, pp. 12, 24, 25, 52, 69, 73.
By permission of the Phaidon Press Limited, extracts have been reprinted from *Caravaggio* (1998), by Timothy Wilson-Smith, © 1998 Phaidon Press Limited, www.phaidon.com.
By permission of Gerald Duckworth & Co Ltd, extracts have been reprinted from *The Way of Hermes: The Corpus Hermeticum and the Definitions of Hermes Trismegistus to Asclepius* (1999), translated by Dorine van Oyen, Jean Paul Mahe, and Clement Salaman.
By permission of Little, Brown Book Group, extracts have been reprinted from *Leonardo: The First Scientist* (2001), by Michael White.
By permission of Guggenheim Museum Publications, extracts have been reprinted from 'Only the Perverse Fantasy Can Still Save Us' in *The Cremaster Cycle* (2003), by Nancy Spector.

By permission of Penguin Books Ltd, approximately 175 words from *Lives of the Artists Vol. I* by Giorgio Vasari, translated by George Bull (Penguin Classics, 1987). Copyright © George Bull, 1965.

By permission of Penguin Books Ltd, approximately 255 words from *Phaedrus and The Seventh and Eighth Letters* by Plato, translated with an introduction by Walter Hamilton (Penguin Classics, 1973). Copyright © Walter Hamilton, 1973.

By permission of Penguin Books Ltd, approximately 149 words from *The Symposium* by Plato, translated with an introduction and notes by Christopher Gill (Penguin Classics, 1999). Copyright © Christopher Gill, 1999.

By permission of Penguin Books Ltd, approximately 264 words from *Thus Spoke Zarathustra: A Book for Everyone and No One* by Friedrich Nietzsche, translated by R. J. Hollingdale (Penguin Classics, 1961, reprinted with a new introduction 1969). Copyright © R. J. Hollingdale, 1961, 1969.

By permission of Penguin Books Ltd, approximately 402 words from *Twilight of the Idols: Or, How to Philosophise with a Hammer; The Anti-Christ* by Friedrich Nietzsche, translated by R. J. Hollingdale (Penguin Classics, 1968). Copyright © R. J. Hollingdale, 1968.

By permission of Viking Penguin, a division of Penguin Group (USA) Inc, extracts from *The Odyssey* by Homer, translated by Robert Fagles, copyright © 1996 by Robert Fagles.

By permission of the Walter Kaufmann Copyright Trust, extracts from *The Gay Science* by Friedrich Nietzsche, translated by Walter Kaufmann (Vintage, 1974). Page 181 (67 words), pages 273-274 (196 words).

PREFACE

A SINGULAR BEGINNING TOWARDS A SINGULARITY

> Sing to me of the man, Muse, the man of twists and turns
> driven time and again off course, once he had plundered
> the hallowed heights of Troy.
>
> ~ Homer, *The Odyssey*

This project began inflamed with Promethean hubris. It was my initial intention to write an epic poem that would exceed the monumental weight of both *The Iliad* (c.720 BCE) and *The Odyssey* (c.700 BCE) combined; that would aspire to out-do the intellectual acumen of Lucretius' *On the Nature of the Universe* (c.50 BCE); that would be infused with the profound vision of Dante's *Divine Comedy* (1321); and that would transcend the textual breadth of Pound's *Cantos* (1917-1969). I envisioned writing an epic poem whose truly *epic* proportions would be matched by its architectonic innovation. Unlike Dante's *Divine Comedy*, which is composed exclusively in *terza rima*, or Milton's *Paradise Lost* (1667), which is composed in decasyllabic blank verse, I envisioned a poly-metrical structure that would form an abstract correspondence with the Big Bang theory of the Universe.

Formulated in opposition to Fred Hoyle, Hermann Bondi and Thomas Gold's 'steady-state theory', in which the Universe has no determinate point of origin and whilst 'expanding [retains] the same density at all times due to the continuous creation of matter', the Big Bang theory asserts that the Universe originated out of a 'singularity', a cosmic point initially predicted by Albert Einstein in his *General Theory of Relativity* where 'temperature and density [are believed to have been] infinite'. From this mysterious and mathematically unstable point of relativistic implosion (for here most cosmologists believe that the theory of general relativity 'breaks down', making 'it impossible from first principles to know what the Universe should look like in the beginning'), proponents of Big Bang cosmology, such as Roger Penrose and Stephen Hawking argue that the emergent Universe exploded outwards, undergoing 'a series of dramatic transformations known as phase transitions'. This incredibly 'hot' period of tumultuous metamorphoses, comprising the 'Planck', 'hadron', and 'lepton' eras, is collectively known as the 'Primordial fire ball' or 'radiation era', and led, through a process of gradual cooling, to the 'decoupling', 'recombination', and structural evolution of the 'matter era', ultimately going on to form the stars and planets observable today. Whilst the Big Bang theory 'is not complete', requiring, as the cosmologist Ian Ridpath observes, a 'satisfactory theory of quantum gravity', something which is essential in order to fully understand the condition of the Universe in the immediate wake of the singularity, it is nevertheless highly persuasive, accounting for such phenomena as 'Cosmic Background Radiation' and the fluctuating density of galaxies. In the context of my poem I intended to use this cosmological paradigm as a metrical framework. Thus, just as the Big Bang theory begins with a singularity, a point of infinite values and mathematical silence, so too my epic was to have started with a blank page symbolising this fundamental absence. Then a surge of raw, discordant sounds – a primitive ejaculation of phonemes – would have burst onto the page, representing the tumultuous, chaotic heat of the Primordial fire ball. This was to have been succeeded by the emergence of simple metrical configurations, relating to the gradual cooling and expansion of the Universe. Following the paradigm, as the poem progressed, these structures would have become evermore elaborate, emulating the complexity

of stars and planets. Indeed, it was my intention to have as many as three narrative sequences, each written in different metres, running concurrently, converging and diverging in what I foresaw as a restless ontological exchange. This would have been followed by a period of entropic decline in which the metrical structures that I had instigated would begin to break down, a gesture in accordance with the hypothesis that the Big Bang Universe will end with matter collapsing in on itself to a point of infinitude, a phenomenon which cosmologists have termed the 'Big Crunch'. In conformity with my paradigm, and in a desire to further distinguish my epic from those which had gone before, I wanted to have no single protagonist (like Odysseus in the *Odyssey* or Dante himself in the *Divine Comedy*) distinguishable from the whole, but rather sought to make the Universe my 'hero'. This, I thought, could be achieved not only abstractly through the metrical association outlined above, but also through a form of anthropomorphisation. It was my intention to fill these metrical structures with the cultural traditions of humanity; to create a fusion and fission of myth, history, mind and metre; to perform a Universe of human experience and culture in a myriad of incarnate forms. This literary 'pantheism' was to have seen figures such as Apollo, Krishna, the Buddha, Plato, Aristotle, Kali, Jesus, Newton, and Einstein engaged in an exotic exchange of perspective: a human complexity imitating an inhuman one.[1]

Not only would my epic poem represent a staggering feat of structural engineering it would, in addition to its astrophysical concerns, embrace the varied fields of theology, philosophy, cognitive psychology, and linguistics. It was my initial intention to use my epic to examine the cognitive functions of language, to test the limitations of thought, and through this, the human striving to express the inexpressible – namely God. One of the foundations of this enquiry was to be a theory of psycholinguistic hermeneutics which sees language as the totality of conscious thought and thus the only qualifiable constituent of the phenomenal

world. This line of thinking arose primarily out of two intellectual sources. On the one hand there was the later, language-based philosophy of Ludwig Wittgenstein, in which the systems that we perceive in the external world around us are 'ultimately [of] our own construction [and thus] the appearance of independent objectivity is only the effect of procedures which come naturally to us', procedures which are inevitably constructed out of 'language'. On the other there was the Critical Philosophy of Immanuel Kant, whose *Critique of Pure Reason* proposes a 'transcendental' divide between the world of 'noumena', or 'things-in-themselves', residing outside our spatiotemporal 'sensory experience' of objects and thus cognitively inaccessible, and the 'empirical', cognitively accessible world of 'phenomena'. Accordingly, I came to see language, through which the phenomenal world is understood, as the sum-total of being because it is our only point of cognitive reference, arguably constructing both our personalities and perceptions. Consequent to this position, there is a continuous dialectic between self, ideas, and objects (including other people), which is, by necessity, purely representational. Things-in-themselves cannot be known because they are a-linguistic and thus cognitively do not exist. Nevertheless, their existence is implied by their phenomenal presence as language, but must remain an implication because their actuality cannot be realised independently of thought.[2]

Having argued this position, I then wanted to move the discourse of my poem on to the problems encountered when we try and articulate that which is said to transcend the Universe of material phenomena. In light of the above, such 'metaphysical' discourse may be dismissed as being quite literally senseless, for being neither bound to linguistically constructed subjective phenomena, nor a-linguistic objective noumena, it is negative: devoid of all meaningful content. However, through its articulation it is, nevertheless, undeniably *present*. This presence through absence, or 'false' signification, is thus at once complex and perplexing, for the mind, conditioned to word-object correspondences, cannot comprehend nothingness. It is, therefore, beyond the beyond: outside of implication and actuality, and thus totally hermetic. Conversely, because the mind receives the metaphysical in the same manner in which it receives noumena as phenomena (i.e. linguistically), the illusion of meaningful signification is maintained.[3]

At this point it might well have seemed necessary to agree with philosophers such as David Hume, Bertrand Russell, and A. J. Ayer, each of whom came to reject any notion of a transcendent metaphysics as absurd, or else to follow the example of latter-day metaphysicians, such as Martin Heidegger or P. F. Strawson, and seek to redirect metaphysical discourse into a more 'reasonable' space. Nevertheless, in spite of the critical weight bearing down upon me, I remained undaunted, and felt that a reclamation of transcendent metaphysics was neither absurd nor needed to stand in contradiction with the above. The foundation of my posited 'solution' was what I termed *apophatic kataphasis*, or 'negative affirmation', and was heavily influenced by what is known as 'apophatic theology'. The concept of apophasis, or 'negation', appears to have entered Christian theology via the Alexandrian teacher Clement, who argues in the fifth book of his *Stromata* (c.200 CE), that 'God is ineffable, not susceptible of capture by the philosopher's categories, boundless [and] unknown', but arguably finds its most profound/attuned expression in the writings of a mysterious theologian known as 'Dionysius the Pseudo-Areopagite' (*fl.*500 CE), so-called because in his works he chose to commit a certain pious fraud by claiming to be the Dionysius whom the Apostle Paul had converted at Athens. Indeed, there is a marked difference between Clement's apophasis and the apophatic position adopted by Pseudo-Dionysius. Whereas the former's negation is moderated, and thus 'the necessity to deny a univocal application of human terminology to the divine is not allowed to undermine the truths as set out in revelation or philosophy, faith in which is [seen as] necessary for human progress towards salvation', the latter takes a far more radical stance, performing 'a negation which is posterior to both affirmations and first-order negations about the divine'. In other words, as the theologian J. P. Williams observes, '[Pseudo-Dionysius'] apophasis is the negation of both affirmation and negation and not merely of affirmation only'. I saw this as representing something of an epiphany, for in this mystical tradition I perceived the means of circumventing the positive/negative, phenomenal/noumenal dichotomy, and articulating the ineffable. As Williams remarks:

> [t]hrough its dialectical affirmation, negation, and subsequent negation of both proceeding stages, [Pseudo-Dionysius' apophasis] creates a contradiction which cannot be resolved in favour of either of the contradictory positions, or of a third position, even that of no-position. Now the mind can only 'hover' between the poles of the contradiction, affirming both and neither, negating both and neither. In thus despairing of the 'either-or' logic of dualistic thought, the religious subject is encouraged to divine a holistic method of approach to the ground of its being… Rather than attempting to subject the divine nonduality to violation by the dualisms of conceptuality and predication, apophasis therefore provides a framework within which speech may aspire to articulate a nondualistic vision of it.[4]

Equally inspiring was the manifestly poetic quality of Pseudo-Dionysius' language. Although not written in metre, his corpus is rich with the devices of poetry. Metaphor and simile abound, and it appeared that such devices were conditional for the articulation of transcendence. The line, 'the transcendently shining darkness of wisest silence', for example, from his *Mystical Theology*, embodies the mysterious theologian's dialectical technique in startlingly figurative terms. Darkness is shining and yet transcendent; wisdom, so often associated with lofty discourse is the provenance of silence; silence is affirmed as wisdom and simultaneously negated by its articulation. This poetic understanding of Pseudo-Dionysius' work was heightened by my concurrent reading of a psycholinguistic text, *The Poetics of Mind: Figurative Thought, Language and Understanding* by Raymond Gibbs which argues that, 'human cognition is deeply poetic and that figurative imagination constitutes the way we understand ourselves and the world in which we live'. If our reception of the phenomenal world is grounded in a poetic understanding, then it seemed logical that these poetic devices should help us towards articulating its transcendence.[5]

In addition to providing what I perceived as a theological solution to a philosophical debate, a variation of this poetical dialectic was to become the fundamental dynamic of my own poetic undertaking. My epic would not simply represent an anthropomorphised expression of the Big Bang Universe, but would go so far as to embody the counter-expression of an apophatic non-position. What was to ensue was to be a grand game of metaphor-contra-metaphor; of signification through antithesis; of form-versus-content-versus-concept. The kataphatic, or affirmative, dimension of the work was, naturally enough, to reside in the exoteric performance of the mythological and historical figures discussed above. Yet these, through both the aggressive juxtaposition of their a-historic interaction and the metaphorical dynamic of their conflicting perspectives, would draw the reader towards the primary negation, that of the poem's esoteric, metrical correspondence with Big Bang cosmology. With the first mask stripped away and the second made manifest, I envisioned the posterior negation, which transcends both the characters and the paradigm, deriving from the antithetical relationship between the kataphatic concept of the phenomenal Universe, performed as a language structure, and the essential inexpressibility of its transcendent other. In other words, I believed that the transcendent would be 'revealed' in antithesis. The precise means by which the reader would grasp this revelation was to be profoundly mysterious. Mindful of Williams' warning that apophasis should not be understood as merely 'a second-order discourse', concerned only with the limitations of 'human concepts and linguistic ability', but rather as a 'soteriological' exercise, an 'ascent…into silence' to use the Pseudo-Dionysian term, I believed that the attuned reader would achieve a form of spiritual enlightenment through an attentive meditation on the text, the precise dynamic of which would necessarily transcend rational articulation. Retrospectively, it would be fair to say that I intended to write a work for initiates.[6]

What was I thinking? With hindsight I should, perhaps, have heeded the warning of Aeschylus. Prometheus, that over-reacher *par excellence*, was chained to a 'bitter rock' for his transgressions against the power of Zeus, his reward for stealing fire the torment of 'a thousand years' beneath 'the sun's flaming rays'. Yet in my defence it must be observed that I was very young at the inception of my project. Twenty-three years old, and having just finished an epyllion inspired by the writings of the Roman poet Catullus, I was wedded to the notion of the big gesture, naively oblivious to the technical difficulties inherent in my conception; technical difficulties of which those around me were all too painfully aware. Indeed, my friends, invariably older and more experienced than myself, counselled me against it, saying that what I proposed to do represented a life's work and really ought to be undertaken by a more mature poet. I, however, 'struck by Apollo' as Hölderlin so succinctly puts it, was determined that I could not only begin my magnum opus in my early twenties, but that I could complete it within three years! Such an inflated opinion of my powers proved to be unfounded, and thus in a progression which ironically mirrors Big Bang cosmology, the wild heat of my initial intentions began to cool into a more stable, realistic structure.[7]

This is, of course, how it should be. As Janet Burroway has observed, '[the process of writing is one of] development and revision…a continuum of invention and improvement, re-seeing and chiselling'. In other words, it is a journey of refinement. Like the wanderings of Gilgamesh or Odysseus, or Dante's pilgrimage through *Inferno* and *Purgatorio* towards the beatific vision of *Paradiso*, it is the traumatic journey of experience that defines as it refines. During the writing process I found my poetic style changing as my practical knowledge broadened. Unsurprisingly, these creative metamorphoses slowed my rate of composition, and what became apparent as my epic progressed was that it would be, for the foreseeable future, a work in progress: my magnum opus would *not* be finished by the wizened age of twenty-six.[8]

Here it was comforting to remember that the monumental poets of the last century, such as Ezra Pound and Louis Zukofsky, had spent decades constructing their texts. The *Cantos* and *'A'* (1928-1974) respectively were 'born' before the Second World War and 'died' in the Space Age. Consequently, and reassuring for a young poet suffering from growing pains, they thus bear witness to the mutant influence of time, evolving, in the case of *'A'*, from Poundian inclined *vers libre* into a form which imitates sheet music. Additionally, their status as finished works, despite representing nigh-on half a century's labour apiece, is also open to debate; something which is embodied in Pound's repeated reference to his *Cantos* as 'drafts', regarding them, as Humphrey Carpenter has observed, '[as something resembling] a "half-time report" rather than necessarily the finished text'.[9]

Reconciled to the production of a work in progress, I then began to find that I had sincere misgivings about my original epic conception. As we have seen, it was my initial intention to use a metrical structure that would form an abstract correspondence with Big Bang cosmology, beginning with silence and then evolving through a primitive ejaculation of phonemes to a point of elaborate complexity, before entropically declining once more into silence. This framework was to be filled with figures from world history and mythology, and was to mysteriously engender, through its ingenious complexities and contradictions, a non-moment of apophatic transcendence. Whilst the chance to create a work of such technical virtuosity was highly seductive, I became increasingly concerned that its wilfully obscure character might, in fact, prove detrimental to its effectiveness. More and more this 'work for initiates' seemed destined, not to attain 'the transcendently shining darkness of wisest silence', but rather the dusty silence of the unread, engendering in those brave enough to breach its opening page nothing more spiritual than confused irritation. Thus, it became clear to me that I needed to rethink both my poem's architectonic design and the means by which it would relate to the dynamics of apophasis.

To this effect, I turned my attention to what is arguably the archetype of literary theory, Aristotle's *Poetics*. For Aristotle, classical epic poetry shares a strong affinity with 'tragedy'. Both represent 'an imitation in verse of admirable people' and both are 'constructed dramatically'. However, their differences traditionally occur in regards to 'length' and 'verse-form'. Whereas the action of tragedy is ideally confined to 'a single day', such as the events in Sophocles' *Electra* (c.418 BCE), the action of classical epic poetry 'is unrestricted in time' allowing the poet to create a work that is as vast as it is complex. Conversely, tragedy, for all its temporal restrictions, is afforded greater metrical freedom through the action of its 'chorus', whereas classical epic poetry, as 'narrative verse', is restricted to the uniformity of the 'heroic' dactylic hexameter. The archetypal epic poet, in the eyes of Aristotle, is 'Homer', and the Homeric epics are exemplified as possessing an outstanding 'brilliance'. What particularly impresses Aristotle as being remarkable about these works is the way in which Homer deftly controls both his 'plot-structure' and his treatment of 'character'. In the philosopher's conception, the ideal plot 'should be concerned with a unified action, whole and complete, possessing a beginning, middle parts and end, so that (like a living organism) the unified whole can effect its characteristic pleasure'. This being the case, it is in some ways ironic that Aristotle should have admired the Homeric epics so enormously, for Homer, 'in comparison to other poets', takes this paradigm in an unusual direction. Interestingly, whilst retaining the main imperative of Aristotle's structural principle, he simultaneously contracts his action whilst expanding his episodes. *The Odyssey*, for example, does not seek to represent the wanderings of Odysseus in a pedantic and voluminously linear fashion, narrating his adventures from the fall of Troy to his eventual return to Ithaca some ten years later in direct succession, but rather concentrates the Aristotelian dimension of his plot 'on the last stage of Odysseus' homecoming'. It is around this finely whittled sequence of action that Homer weaves a number of dramatic narratives, including Menelaus' account of the Trojan Horse, told to Odysseus' son Telemachus in Book IV, and Odysseus' account of his adventures to the Phaeacian Court of King Alcinous in Books IX-XII. Significantly, these episodes are close to a form of dramatic monologue, transcending the epic conception of narrative verse and encroaching closer to the character-driven forms of tragedy; a genre which the philosopher found, because it is more 'concentrated', altogether superior. Indeed, Aristotle was considerably impressed by Homer's ability to transcend his own voice, saying 'in person…as little as possible', thereby enhancing his power of 'imitation' and thus the dramatic intensity of his work.[10]

The Aristotelian argument and the Homeric epics certainly provided food for thought, presenting me with several creative possibilities. As we have seen, my reservation about my original epic conception was one of accessibility. By mapping my characters onto an abstract, and exacting, metrical framework I feared that any personality they might possess would be lost to the potentially disfiguring dynamic of the design. At the forefront of my mind was the consideration that, as the kataphatic dimension of the apophatic process, the figures from world history and mythology needed to be both tangible and *affirmative* – the positive charge, if you will, amid the double negative of the primary and posterior negations. What attracted me about the Homeric paradigm was precisely the tragic power of characterisation so vehemently praised by Aristotle in his *Poetics.* However, were I to abandon the rigorous metrical structure, and thus allow the characters more room to breathe, I knew that I would necessarily problematise the action of the primary negation which relied on the hidden structural correspondence to Big Bang cosmology. Additionally, I saw that this problem could not be circumvented by bringing the cosmological apparatus into the foreground as something resembling an Aristotelian narrative because its function was inescapably conceptual and *not* subjective. As attractive as these sources might be, I could not afford to lose sight of the fact that this was never intended to be a poem *about* astrophysics, but rather a poem which *uses* astrophysics to a very different end, namely the path to transcendence.

In my journey to find a solution to the problems which, like Odysseus, I had brought upon myself, I turned from Homer and Aristotle to another ancient poet of a very different temperament – Ovid. Indeed, Ovid's epic masterpiece, the *Metamorphoses* (c.8 CE), could not be further removed in spirit from either its Homeric antecedents or from the Aristotelian definition of classical epic poetry. As the classicist E. J. Kenney observes, '[t]he *Metamorphoses* conforms to the conventional pattern of classical epic in so far as it is a long poem in hexameters... That is as far as conformity extends'. Unlike *The Odyssey*, which retains, in concentrated form, a single, anchoring, Aristotelian plot-structure, the *Metamorphoses* is '*ex hypothesi* and of set purpose episodic'. It is also, as Kenney points out, 'of its nature anti-generic', embodying the character of 'pastoral', 'elegiac', and 'tragic' poetry as the occasion demands. Consequently, one might be tempted to go so far as to say that the *Metamorphoses*'s only consistency is inconsistency.

However, there is, of course, a unity belying the disunity and that is the poem's preoccupation with the theme of transformation and the central authority accorded to the Pythagorean doctrine of 'metempsychosis'. To be sure, Ovid's conception is very clever indeed, for the inconsistencies inherent in his epic's structure are consistent to his intent. The whole poem performs the instability '[o]f bodies changed to other forms', something which is not only reflected in the subject matter of the mythological narratives themselves, but also in the playful contradictions which permeate the text. For example, in the proem, Ovid proclaims that his work will be 'one continuous song from nature's first/ Remote beginnings to our modern times'. True, the poem does begin with the 'creation' of the Universe and ends with 'the apotheosis of Julius Caesar', however, the attribution of the singular to what is, in fact, a highly pluralistic exercise would seem, at least superficially, to be somewhat perverse. Yet this paradox, which draws our attention to the epic's *plurality*, simultaneously reminds us of the intellectual *unity* which informs the whole. As Pythagoras explains in his famous speech in Book XV, 'Nothing retains its form'. Nevertheless, despite the perpetual transmutation of the Universe, mirrored so effectively in the microcosm of metamorphosing bodies, there *is* a still-point at the eye of the storm – the soul, which, according to Pythagorean doctrine, retains its essence despite transmigrating between countless forms. Thus, it is testament to Ovid's genius that the intellectual 'soul' of the *Metamorphoses* retains its singularity even though (or perhaps because) it is seemingly inverted through the performance of a plurality of narrative 'bodies'.[11]

Be that as it may, Ovid's epic, for all its inherent unity, still retains the potential to be dissolved into its constituent parts without damaging the power of its individuated narratives. Ted Hughes, for example, in his *Tales from Ovid* (1997) presents 'twenty-four passages from the *Metamorphoses*', significantly without the Pythagorean material of Book XV. That the story of 'Pygmalion', for instance, or 'Echo and

Narcissus', makes perfect sense without this explicit philosophical dimension emphasises the structural solubility of Ovid's work. The stories function independently of the whole, being, in effect, whole unto themselves.[12]

This poly-formality intrigued me and seemed rich with creative potential, although at this point I remained unsure of precisely *how* it would affect my evolving structural dynamic. Thus, from the epic poems of the Greco-Roman world, I turned my attention to those composed in English, hoping to gain further insights from works that were written both nearer to my own time and in my own language. Indeed, given the theological qualities of my epic undertaking, it would have been reasonable to assume that Milton's *Paradise Lost*, a poem which creatively expands out of *The Book of Genesis*, would have proved an important stimulus. Alas, whilst I greatly admire the majesty of Milton's strangely inflected lines, there was nothing of practical significance to be gleaned from his epic masterpiece. Not only did I find Milton's affirmative treatment of theology to be completely antithetical to my interest in Pseudo-Dionysian apophasis, but I also found in his architectonics the same Aristotelian problems I had encountered in the works of Homer. Rather, it was in certain Modernist epics of the twentieth century that I alighted upon a development, in English, of that which had most captivated me about the *Metamorphoses* of Ovid.

To be sure, the affinities between these works are striking. Zukofsky, for example, in *'A'* writes, in what seems to be a deliberately Ovidian gesture, that his epic represents 'One song/ Of many voices', a reference both to the poem's unifying choral motif *and* to the plurality of the voices which make it up. Likewise, Pound's *Cantos* also display a certain debt to Ovid. In his *A Packet for Ezra Pound*, for example, W. B. Yeats recalls a conversation in which the poet outlined the conceptual character of his epic undertaking:

> There will be no plot, no chronicle of events, no logic of discourse, but two themes, the descent into Hades from Homer, a metamorphosis from Ovid, and mixed with these medieval or modern historical characters.[13]

Yet Pound owes more to Ovid than simply the theme of 'metamorphosis'. Once again we are witness to a form of epic that is profoundly modular in design; whose unity is reconciled through its disunities; and which is forever on the cusp of separation. Unlike the cantos of Dante's *Divine Comedy*, whose narrative imperative is one of linear progression, Pound's *Cantos*, like the mythological narratives which constitute Ovid's *Metamorphoses*, retain the potential for autonomous existences independent of the whole. To be sure, this broad-based, poly-formal structure is also manifest on an individuated level, for each *Canto* appears to occupy an intensely paradoxical position, to be caught between solidity and liquidity; lyricism and dissonance; personality and impersonality. 'Canto IX', for instance, oscillates between the lyrically evocative power of lines such as:

> One year floods rose,
> One year they fought in the snows,
> One year hail fell, breaking the trees and walls.
> Down here in the marsh they trapped him
> in one year...[14]

and markedly prosaic passages performing in the guises of letters:

> "MONSEIGNEUR:
> Madame Isotta has had me write today about Sr. Galeazzo's daughter. The man who said young pullets make thin soup, knew what he was talking about. We went to see the girl the other day, for all the good that did, and she denied the whole matter and kept her end up without losing her temper. I

> think Madame Ixotta very nearly exhausted the matter. *Mi pare che avea decto hogni chossia.* All the children are well. Where you are everyone is pleased and happy because of your taking the chateau here we are the reverse as you might say drifting without a rudder. Madame Lucrezia has probably, or should have, written to you, I suppose you have the letter by now. Everyone wants to be remembered to you.
>
> 21 Dec. D. de M."[15]

Similarly, in 'Canto II', we find, not only a formalistic disruption, but also an interruption of time and identity, as 'Robert Browning', 'So-Shu', 'Eleanor [of Aquitaine]', 'Homer', 'Schoeney's daughters', 'Pentheus', 'Tiresias', and 'Cadmus' (to name but a few) cohabit in a landscape of associate dissociation which might be a mythologized island of 'Naxos' but which is never fully defined. Akin to 'Beasts like shadows in glass/ a furred tail upon nothingness', the reader is both uncertain as to *who* is speaking and possibly even *why*. That the sequence is monumental, measuring some one hundred and fifty lines and grandiosely endowed with a plethora of references which exude the poet's learning (or at least his eclecticism), is certain. On one level it feels like a towering block of marble; it feels *epic*. However, on another, it feels very insubstantial indeed; light-headed and giddy. This diversity of signs, musical and strange, at once envelops and alienates – largely, I think, because through their performances these signs actually refuse to perform. Pound's depth arguably resides in his superficiality, in his apparent absence from his poem, and from his characters' absence of sustained coherence. As Hugh Kenner observes, '[Pound's poetry presents] an undisturbed surface which, as Eliot remarked of Ben Jonson's, "reflects only the lazy reader's fatuity"'. Undisturbed, perhaps, but not un-disturbing, Pound's seemingly inscrutable surface demands a level of reader participation previously absent from the epic tradition. Unlike classical epic poems, the *Cantos* offer us no proem, no rationale, no clearly stated intention. Here the muses have 'eyes like Picasso' and sing about nothing so straightforward as 'the rage of Peleus' son Achilles'. Rather, we are left to float, exiled on a wine-dark sea of 'enigmatic phrases', amid the driftwood of 'Ovid, Cavalcanti, Sordello, Sappho, Confucius, and Lincoln Steffens'. As Yeats remarked, it has 'no plot, no chronicle of events, no logic of discourse'. Consequently, 'the descent into Hades from Homer' and the 'metamorphosis from Ovid' can be seen, not merely as thematic concerns, but also as the reader's responsibility to penetrate that surface and, as Pound enjoined in his *ABC of Reading*, 'Make it New'.[16]

Indeed, Pound's depersonalised aesthetic of reader participation relies on the seemingly complete absence of the poet from the exoteric dimension of his work. As Kenner observes, '[unlike Eliot] in *The Waste Land* [where] we feel assured that the man is properly about his business…Pound's way…is to await with a vigilance of his own the exact events that will enter his purposes without modification'. This illusion of authorial absence is, of course, a profoundly epic concern, alluding back to Aristotle's epic conception in the *Poetics*. Epic is 'traditionally [an] impersonal genre', and Pound performs this impersonality, performs this *tradition*, throughout the *Cantos*. To be sure, although Pound is in the business of *making it new*, much of his poem's complexity can be understood, not only in relation to Ovid's *Metamorphoses*, but also in the light of classical Homeric epic and its historic affinities with tragedy. Pound's art echoes the Ancient Greek actor's adoption of the 'persona', or 'mask', the simulacrum of his performed identity, and in many ways the *Cantos* can be interpreted as inviting the reader to perform the tragedy of culture in a war-torn and rapidly changing world; a world where, with the old certainties gone, it is the role of the poet to impart to the reader the fragments which remain; to perform, or rather to get his reader to perform through the interpretative act, the pieces as both a gesture of remembrance and a means of remembering.[17]

Yet Pound's fascination with masks, something which reaches a state of near atomic fission in the *Cantos*, with identities flowing like molten lava between the lines, actually predates the poet's epic work. Early collections of his poetry, such as *Personae* (1909), *Ripostes* (1912), and *Lustra* (1913-1915) reveal a marked preference for writing in other voices. Significantly, in early works such as 'Piere Vidal Old', in which Pound assumes the persona of the twelfth-century troubadour Piere Vidal, he sustains a lyrical coherence throughout, and the work is rich with the idiosyncrasies of human speech:

> And conquered! Ah God! conquered!
> Silent my mate came as the night was still.
> Speech? Words? Faugh! Who talks of words and
> love?!
> Hot is such love and silent,
> Silent as fate is, and as strong until
> It faints in taking and in giving all. [18]

To be sure, reading Pound's early compositions *after* the *Cantos* is like rewinding a film of a smashing glass. The sharp and brittle shards reconfigure into a lucent vessel of communication, whose dramatic intensity is naturally accentuated through the singular clarity of its voice. Here Pound's impersonality reaches truly personal heights, for in poems such as 'Piere Vidal Old' the persona moves and develops from stanza to stanza in a linear manner precluded from the *Cantos*. However, these early works also represent a mask of another kind, behind which is not the face of Ezra Pound but that of Robert Browning. In many ways Browning prefigures Pound's metamorphosis, or, if one prefers a Homeric analogy, Browning is the blood-drained shade of Achilles haunting Pound's Odysseus in Hades. Works such as 'Fra Lippo Lippi' from *Men and Women* (1855), for example, show a marked correspondence, not only with Pound's pre-*Canto* compositions such as 'Piere Vidal Old', or 'Praise of Ysolt', whose dependency on the

Victorian master is manifest, but also with the spirit of the dramatic which pervades both tragedy and the epic tradition. Browning's 'dramatic monologues' have a power and intensity, born of their immediacy and vitality of language, of their scale and diversity, which spirals back through the literary continuum via Shakespeare and Chaucer to the pre-cognisance of tragedy in Homer.[19]

It was whilst meditating on Browning and the form of the dramatic monologue that I experienced a moment of near Joycean epiphany. The Renaissance scholar Marsilio Ficino, with his mind very much on Plato, wrote that inspiration is the provenance of 'divine frenzy'. It is certainly, in my experience, by turns osmotic and strange, for by cogitating on the above I suddenly arrived at a radical re-conceptualisation of my epic's structural dynamic. As we have seen, it was my initial intention to map figures from world history and mythology onto a metrical framework that would form an abstract correspondence with Big Bang cosmology, something which I came to fear would lead to a wilfully obscure work that would, for all its technical conceit, be ultimately unreadable and thus necessarily fail in its task to perform the kataphatic dimension of the over-arching apophatic process. The solution which now presented itself startled me with what I saw as the beauty of its simplicity, at once enhancing the affirmative dimension of the poem *and* providing a stronger dialogue with the epic tradition.[20]

My first bold move was to abandon the cosmological metrics, for, whilst theoretically an ingenious way of performing the primary negation, I could see that so rigorous a metrical framework would, in fact, finally prove disfiguring to my intellectual design. Instead, inspired by the modular structure of Ovid's *Metamorphoses* and Pound's *Cantos*, and by the techniques of Browning and his antecedents in the Homeric epics and their affinities with tragedy, I elected to perform the kataphatic dimension of my epic as a series of dramatic monologues. The originality of this move may be discerned when one considers that previously epics have, as we have seen, been either narrative or counter-narrative. *The Odyssey* and the *Metamorphoses*, for example, despite their technical differences retain a narrative framework, their dramatic episodes *contained* within this necessarily distancing structure. Works like the *Cantos* and *'A'*, by contrast, whilst disrupting narrative expectation, nevertheless retain a certain distance through their surface complexities, their method of engagement essentially contra-dramatic. Thus, whilst the potential of the dramatic monologue may be said to be *latent* in classical, Ovidian, and Modernist epic, it has not hitherto been foregrounded to such a radical degree.

The prime advantage of the dramatic monologue structure, as I saw it, was the playful duality of its nature. On the one hand there was the question of enhancing the accessibility of the kataphatic, or *affirmative*, dimension. As I have said, it had always been my intention to people my epic with figures from world history and mythology, and now I could focus on individual characters in sufficient detail, thus allowing them to properly breathe. In selecting my personas I determined to be mindful both of Aristotle's injunction in the *Poetics* that epic represents 'an imitation in verse of admirable people' and of the genre's historical affinities with tragedy. Consequently, the personas would be people who had contributed to human development – artists, scientists, philosophers, and saints – and their monologues would contain the essence of their thought. This is not, of course, to say that I wanted the monologues to be exclusively cerebral affairs – far from it. The personas I would select would rather have much in common with the suffering heroes of classical epic and tragedy, with Odysseus, Oedipus, and Ajax, with Chryses, Orestes, and Agamemnon; figures like Nietzsche, afflicted with syphilis, Caravaggio, a hunted fugitive running for his life, and St. Hieronymus, finding God in the white-heat of the wilderness. The monologues would be rich with the senses; the ideas would *live*. As this makes apparent, my treatment of apophasis was not going to be of the strictly *semantic* kind. Unlike writers such as Edmond Jabès, whose obsessive entanglement with 'the mysteries of the Book' pervades a near pedantic bookishness, or Geoffrey Hill, whose *The Orchards of Syon* (2002) contracts a heightened literariness to a point of excruciating density, I did not want the business of language to be the subject of my work. Rather, I conceived my relationship with the process of apophasis to be similar to the relationship of Michelangelo's *Sistine Chapel Ceiling* (1508-1512) with *The Book of Genesis* – a conceptual transformation through aesthetic form. Of course, it would *be involved* with language, for a poem is inescapably a language structure, and it would play with different modes of discourse (something that will become evident when we presently come to discuss the new dynamic I envisioned for the primary and posterior negations) but it would *not* be meta-linguistic in any *exoteric* sense. Instead, the kataphatic monologues would inhabit the seamless illusion of their presence, and on a superficial level the reader would be unaware that they related to a wider spiritual process. To this effect, I envisaged an unaffected style that would have something in common with that employed by Pound in his pre-*Canto* compositions – a lyrical clarity echoing Browning – and although the metrical forms I went on to employ have evolved with the project, from the onset I was determined to avoid wilful obfuscation unless it served the development of the character in question.[21]

That said, I also intended that the monologues should be mindful of their epic identity through both their monumental qualities, as understood in relation not only to their projected lengths but also in regards to the elevation of their themes, and in their marked divergence from any notion of authorial solipsism. I did not wish to cultivate anything encroaching on the Romantic conception of the 'egotistical sublime', as embodied by either Wordsworth's *The Prelude* (1798-1850) or Whitman's *Leaves of Grass* (1855-1892), but rather sought to encapsulate the impersonality through the projection of personality promoted by Aristotle in the *Poetics*, and practised, in varying ways, by epic poets as diverse as Homer and Pound. Thus, despite the monologues' desired accessibility, I also wanted the reader to be mindful of their artificiality, to be highly conscious of their performative character.[22]

In so saying I am fully aware that the use of the personal pronoun 'I', even in works which appear to be autobiographical, is not unproblematic. As Peter Wilson observes:

> [r]elatively straightforward syntactic theory as well as more sophisticated theories of discourse caution us against a simplistic equation between textual 'I' and an assumed writer. For example, in the sentence 'I went to the bank yesterday', the 'I' is a pronominal marker signalling a subject relation within a larger grammatical construct. The fact that the writer of this sentence, namely myself, did not go to the bank yesterday does not invalidate it as a textual entity. On the other hand, given certain mundane facts about my life, the sentence could have, probably has been, and most likely will be used to report a factual event pertaining to me.[23]

Consequently, when we read poems such as Larkin's 'High Windows', from the eponymous collection of 1974, for instance, we are potentially ambivalent about the relationship between the textual 'I' who guesses 'he's fucking her and she's/ Taking pills or wearing a diaphragm' and the poet composing the text. Given Larkin's age at the time of writing 'High Windows' (fifty-two), and what we know of his temperament from interviews and personal correspondence, the poem could very well be profoundly autobiographical. Then again, the assumed 'Larkin' of the poem could equally be a persona, in either a total or a mitigated sense. As Andrew Motion points out:

> Larkin…is careful to create a recognisable no-nonsense middle-class tone in his work – partly by adopting the terms of reasonable argument typified by a poem like 'Reasons for Attendance', and partly by a judicious sprinkling of throwaway phrases: 'I'm afraid', 'it seems', 'of course', 'Too subtle that, too decent too. Oh hell'. These are ways of suggesting a mind following a line of thought, and often of realising something plausibly 'true' for the first time, and they are also a means of registering the speakers' social position. [24]

As the above makes apparent, Larkin's no-nonsense middle-class voice is very much a cultivated affair, and accordingly strains after a pose. The astute reader, mindful of such textual strategies, knows better than to naively embrace a poem like 'High Windows' as being in any *literal* sense true, and thus Larkin's deft manipulation of the demotic may be seen as embodying a certain authorial distance. His 'depressed' sensibility, with its celebration of the 'unremarkable', is arguably as much a performance as Shakespeare's Caliban from *The Tempest* (1613). However, it is testament to the illusory power of Larkin's work that the ambivalence surrounding author-text identification remains for, in spite of the reader's sophistication, the 'I' *could* be Philip Larkin, Hull Librarian, marvelling at the changing state of youth, precisely because the poem's reality is not exclusive to that of its author's. We may think that we know better, but we can never know for sure.[25]

By contrast, in the case of the monologues which I planned to write, the divergence between text and author would be manifest. I am clearly not, for example, either Nietzsche or Caravaggio, I did not write *Thus Spoke Zarathustra* (1885), nor did I paint *David with the Head of Goliath* (c.1610), nor, for that matter, was I alive in either the nineteenth or seventeenth centuries. Subsequently, the masks I would be adopting would be self-evidently masks, their lies explicit through the authorial distance of their content. Thus, whilst performing the kataphatic dimension of the apophatic process, the monologues would simultaneously hint at negation through their self-conscious artificiality, without, of course, actually performing it. Like the simile of the 'cave' from Plato's *Republic* (c.370 BCE) they would seem like shadows on the wall, and although the reader would know that they were projections they would still be unaware of the precise nature of the sun projecting them. To be sure, what attracted me about the dramatic monologue form was its potential to stand concurrently for and against its epic identity, to be profoundly affirmative and yet self-consciously hint at the negative. On the one hand the monologues would be clearly in dialogue with the epic tradition, monumental in length and lofty in theme, conveying personality whilst retaining authorial impersonality; on the other, their heightened modularity would belie their hidden unity. Like the world of the senses to which the kataphatic dimension of the apophatic process may be seen to correspond, the monologues would appear multiform, their sequencing apparently arbitrary. Caravaggio, for instance, would follow Nietzsche, who would be followed, in turn, by Leonardo da Vinci and St. Hieronymus. Thus, whilst their proximity would imply cohesion, their sequencing would appear palpably random, thereby compounding the insistence of mystery. Initially the reader would be uncertain as to whether it was an epic that they were reading or just a collection of poems, as to whether there was a definitive meaning behind the monologues or just a profusion of disconnected interpretations. Consequently, despite their contiguity, the poems would stand like monumental monoliths, daring disjunction.[26]

Having defined my new conception for the kataphatic dimension of the apophatic process, we will now go on to discuss the reconceived dynamic of both the primary and posterior negations. As we have seen, it had been my original intention to execute the primary negation through the juxtaposition of the metrical correspondence with Big

Bang cosmology and the narratological figures from world history and mythology. However, the disestablishment of the cosmological metrics through the rise of the modular, dramatic monologue structure necessarily problematised this micro/macrocosmic relationship. Nevertheless, I still wanted the Universe to be an active element in the primary phase of negation, because I saw in it the potential to mirror the Pseudo-Dionysian pattern of ascent into silence. For Pseudo-Dionysius, whose negative theology owes as much to the 'Neoplatonist' philosophy of 'Proclus' as to the teachings of the Gospels or the epistles of St. Paul, the soteriological action of apophasis is conceived, not only semantically, but also through a series of extended, 'hierarchical' metaphors, both 'ecclesiastical' and 'celestial'. Indeed, this process of 'unlike likeness', in which the soul aspires to be uplifted 'beyond unknowing and light', owes much to the Neoplatonic conception of monadic contemplation derived from Plato's *Parmenides* (c.350 BCE). Here the 'One', or the 'Good', is described as 'ineffable in its simplicity', the means of its contemplation a necessary process of abstraction away from the limiting complexities of the senses. Consequently, I saw in the cosmological dynamic the potential of engaging with the concept of negation through abstraction, of elevating the discourse from the psychophysical dimension of the subjective monologues onto the objective plane of the astrophysical.[27]

The means by which I elected to perform the action of this negation was inspired, not directly from the fields of either literature or theology, but rather from the field of the visual arts. Of particular influence was the work of the German sculptor Joseph Beuys. Primarily active throughout the sixties, seventies, and eighties, Beuys' radical sculptural practice, which involved materials as diverse as 'felt', 'fat', 'honey', and even physical performance through 'ritualistic' action, was firmly rooted in the idea of process, and the state of transformation. As Mark Rosenthal observes, 'Beuys [had a] compulsion to explain his work', and indeed the action of explanation, of performed reflexivity, served to heighten what the sculptor saw as art's function to 'induce a state of contemplation, imaginary possibility, or a desire to change the world'. For Beuys, who rejected the notion that art should be concerned only with the fabrication of decorative objects, the creative act and its dynamic influence on its audience was of paramount importance. To be sure, as his career progressed, the more conventional aspects of his work, such as the material physicality of created forms traditionally associated with the field of sculpture, increasingly gave way to a series of 'lectures in which he delineated his…artistic theories by making diagrams on blackboards'. However, these blackboards, despite their physicality, were not considered directly sculptural *in themselves*, but rather as the 'relics' of sculpture, and were often exhibited as such. Whilst this certainly endowed them with something akin to a sculptural identity, Beuys regarded the actual sculpture as being 'social', embodied in the transmission and reception of the idea conveyed through his performance, or 'action', at the time of the blackboards' composition. Thus, works like *The Capital Room* (1970-1977), for example, which comprises numerous blackboards, a film projector, and various other miscellaneous objects, functions more like a form of documentation than as a sculptural presentation in its own right, the real art having taken place in the kinetic artist-audience transference at the time of the blackboards' creation. Consequently, the installation of these objects serves to remind us that this process took place, like the negatives of a photograph or a canister of un-projected film. The art was in the action.[28]

That the concept of 'movement' was fundamental to Beuys' aesthetic thinking may be discerned from his *Theory of Sculpture*. Here the artist, inspired by the writings of Heinrich Wölfflin and Paul Klee, reinterpreted sculptural practice as the exchange between diametric elements or states, between 'chaos' and 'order'; the 'undetermined' and 'determined'; the 'organic' and the 'crystalline'; the 'warm' and the 'cold'; 'expansion' and 'contraction'. As Rosenthal remarks, '[Beuys] wanted to oppose historically obdurate and fixed sculptures with a new type of sculpture that was as mutable as life itself'. This can be seen, both in the materials he chose to work with – materials like fat, honey, and 'dead animals', all of which court 'physical and chemical change' – and in his desire to include his audience in the creative act through the performed transference of information.[29]

This dynamic of elemental movement can be clearly perceived in a piece like *Manresa* (1966). Named after the 'Catalan village in the Pyrenees where Ignatius Loyola, recovering from the war wounds which ended his career as a romantic adventurer, entered a phase of deep meditation and began in 1523 to write his *Ejercicios espirituales*', this action was concerned with the interplay between 'intuitive' and 'rational' modes of thought and what Beuys saw as their 'inherent [role within] creativity'. As Caroline Tisdall observes, '[Beuys'] admiration was for Loyola, not for the institutionalised Jesuit tendency. What inspired him was the example of meditation and the kind of discipline that forces a way through to higher levels in human thought'. Thus, the action can be seen, not only as a metaphorical embodiment of Loyola's own point of transformation from soldier to saint at the village of Manresa (as revealed from the title), but also as a means of bringing that point into the present, of translating it to his audience through his action's symbology. To this end, Beuys created a sculptural dialectic between what he termed 'Element 1' and 'Element 2'. The former comprised a half-cross – a recurrent symbol throughout his oeuvre often representing the need for 'healing' – mounted on the wall, against which rested a copper rod. The latter comprised a box of scientific paraphernalia, including, amongst other things, a battery, lightbulbs, and a piece of chalk. During the course of the action, Beuys took the chalk from the box and completed the cross on the wall. Then he took the copper rod from the cross and used it to complete the electrical circuit in the box, thereby animating the lightbulbs. In so doing, he created something akin to a Heraclitian 'opposing coherence'. Each element acted upon the other, in effect negating their apparent antonymity, and creating what Beuys termed 'Element 3'. Yet Element 3 remained profoundly mysterious, ultimately being beyond the sculptural embodiments of the action, and Beuys ended the performance by asking the question: 'Where is Element 3?' Whether this question was rhetorical or not must remain a point of conjecture, however, in the light of what we know of Beuys' creative practice, the answer was most probably 'the audience'. If one interprets *Manresa* in a quasi-alchemical light, then the transmutation of the sculptural elements also transmutes the audience through their meditation on the action. Consequently, they become the true subject of Beuys' creativity, empowered through their absorption of his aesthetic symbology to re-sculpt themselves *and* the world. All is sculpture; all is movement.[30]

Another influence on my thinking about the means of performing the primary negation was the work of the contemporary American artist, Matthew Barney. Barney's practice owes much to the legacy of Joseph Beuys, his work at once concerned with the concept of transformation and rich with symbolic associations. Of particular interest was Barney's epic masterpiece, *The Cremaster Cycle* (1994-2002). This monumental creation, which has been described by Nancy Spector as 'a polymorphous organism of an artwork, continually shifting guises and following its own eccentric rules', is as bizarre as it is complex, embracing a 'multivalent' iconography whose 'incestuous intermingling of materials...defies any hierarchy of artistic mediums'. The five sequences which make up the cycle, created out of order between 1994 and 2002, exist simultaneously as 'film', 'drawing', 'photography', and 'sculpture'. Indeed, as Spector observes, 'Barney's visual language is protean', with each form informing the others, like facets reflected in a fractured mirror. Equally confusing is Barney's eclectic range of subject matter, which, on a first encounter, appears as perverse as it is random. *Cremaster 1* (1995), for instance, is concerned with a fantasy-like American football stadium, and centres on an usherette called 'Goodyear' whose stiletto-heeled shoes excrete 'grapes'. *Cremaster 2* (1999), by contrast, is 'based loosely on the life of Gary Gilmore', the Utah murderer who advocated his own execution, and includes numerous references to both the escapologist 'Houdini' and to the hive-life of 'bees', whilst *Cremaster 3* (2002) focuses on the erection of the 'Chrysler Building', and features allusions to the sculptural practices of 'Richard Serra' and to the Masonic initiation ritual. Further eccentric diversity is also to be found in the last two instalments. In *Cremaster 4* (1994), 'an impeccably dressed red-haired satyr' called 'the Loughton Candidate' tap-dances his way through the floor 'and finds himself crawling along a strange underground passage' which appears to be '[p]artly intestine, partly womb', whilst '[t]wo futuristic motorcycles battle it out on the roads of the Isle of Man', and in *Cremaster 5* (1997), we encounter 'a tragic love story, a lamentation on separation and loss set in the romantic dreamscape of late- nineteenth-century Budapest' and populated with strange hybrid creatures born from the mind of a character called 'the Queen of Chain'. The viewer, as he or she encounters these filmic sequences, off-set by monumental sculptural installations, and delicately delineated drawings mounted in peculiar 'self-lubricating plastic frames', could be forgiven for feeling completely bewildered. Nevertheless, there *is* a conceptual unity belying *The Cremaster Cycle*'s formalistic and thematic diversities. As Spector explains, '[w]hilst the *Cremaster* cycle expands outwards in time from the period of an individual life to the passage of centuries, it also describes what is by comparison almost a nanomoment: the first six weeks of an embryo's development'. In other words, Barney's visual epic is, in effect, an elaborate creation myth, and when understood in this light the seemingly bizarre interplay of images and forms are transformed into potent 'biological metaphors'. *Cremaster 1*, for example, which has the feel of 'a candy-coated musical revue' relates to the earliest phase of the embryo's progression. Thus, its 'decidedly feminine' quality, embodied in the character of the usherette Goodyear and her all-girl 'chorus', can be seen as being symbolic of the fact that the 'developing embryo is always by default female'. Consequently, the film, sculptures, and drawings of *Cremaster 1* all pertain to a 'tautological state of self-identification' and act as a metaphor for an 'organism [that] feels at one with the world'. Here there is 'no sense of contradiction or conflict'. Rather, we are presented, as Spector points out, '[with] a narcissistic paradise of total undifferentiation'. *Cremaster 5*, by contrast, which relates to the final sexual determination of the embryo, embodies the concepts of 'cellular division, gonadal migration, [and] testicular descension' through the conflict-rich metaphors of the tragic love story and the Queen of Chain's strange mutant fantasies, ultimately presenting the viewer with the creation of a 'male'. When understood in these terms, *The Cremaster Cycle*, whilst still highly unusual, does make sense. There *is* a conceptual unity, and once the viewer is initiated into its rules (think back to the Masonic initiation ritual from *Cremaster 3*) the game is fun to play. One simply needs the key to realise that one is looking at a door.[31]

These ideas of transformation, of transference, process, and embodied metaphor, inherent in the creative practices of Beuys and Barney, presented me with the solution of how I would activate the primary negation – interfacing the cosmology with the personas – and thereby start the Pseudo-Dionysian pattern of ascent through abstraction. In an action apposite to my apophatic inspiration I thought to create a second textual hemisphere, an 'unlike likeness' whose presence, much in the manner of Beuys' elemental *Manresa*, would initiate a conceptual reaction. Thus, in a marked contrast to the self-evidently poetic monologues, my second textual hemisphere would incarnate as a series of critical essays in which the personas would be recreated in an analytical form, at once both emphasising their historicity and cultural significance whilst simultaneously revealing to the reader their hermetic dimension.

Enthused, I began to envision the new dynamic working as follows. On the one hand there would be the monologues, written in the guises of admirable people, whose seemingly random configuration would appear to deny their epic unity. On the other there would be a series of critical reincarnations – one for each persona. These critical reincarnations would have a tripartite structure, with each subsection performing a specific function. Firstly, under the heading 'Cosmological Paradigm' they would introduce, in scientific language, the astrophysical epoch to which the persona corresponds. These sections, as befitting their scientific theme would be completely impersonal, concerned only with imparting the information in as clear and as rational a manner possible. Secondly, under the heading 'Textual Interpretation: Theory', the relevant biographical data would be interrogated and, depending on the persona, the applicable philosophical, theological, literary, or art historical information would also be assessed and interpreted. Like the 'Cosmological Paradigm' sections, these would similarly be written in an academic style, avoiding the use of the personal pronoun.

My reason for wanting to present these subsections in so impersonal a manner had much to do with the issue of gaining the reader's trust. I wanted to prove that my poetic interpretation of these historical/mythological figures was based on sound scholarship; something doubly important when one considers my desired identification of these figures with different elements of Big Bang cosmology. I felt that it would have been wholly unreasonable of me to expect the reader to accept this interpretation on the power of my word alone. By engaging with the critical material in such an objective way, I believed that the strength of my position would be greatly increased. The reader would be able to directly apprehend that my cosmological identification was firmly rooted in academic learning, that my choice of say Nietzsche to represent the Radiation Era was not simply idiosyncratic fancy but rather, when seen in the light of both his life and philosophy, at once reasonable and intelligent.

Additionally, by electing to write these subsections in a formal academic manner, I believed that I would not only be building trust with my readers, but that I would also be able to emulate, in prose, the authorial impersonality of epic poetry. Like the symbiotic relationship between the intuitive and the rational in Beuys' *Manresa* I envisioned the two textual hemispheres occupying a coequal artistic status.

To be sure, there is also a literary precedent for fusing the creative with the critical in both Eliot's notes to *The Waste Land* (1922) and in the extensive footnotes which David Jones weaves into his Modernist epic *The Anathemata* (1952), for here too the critical fuses with the creative; both are part of the art. Thus, when understood in this light, the projected role of the critical reincarnations in performing the primary negation of the apophasis would not reflect any deficiency in the poetry – far from it. Rather, the poetry would only be part of a wider creative dynamic.

The final component of the critical reincarnations would come under the heading 'Textual Interpretation: Practice', and strike a different tone from the two previous subsections. Here the authorial impersonality would recede and my own voice, as epic poet, would articulate the creative processes/decisions involved in the monologues' creation. It is essential to remember that the issue of authorship in the epic tradition is an important one and far from unproblematic. In the ancient world, for example, Homer was believed to be a 'blind poet' from the island of 'Chios', and numerous myths, such as his rivalry with 'Hesiod' and their fabled 'contest', whilst having no basis in historical fact, did much to make him into a cultural hero of epic proportions. Later commentators, by contrast, such as the American scholar Milman Parry, have argued that the Homeric epics represent the condensation of an 'oral' tradition. On this argument, the blind poet of Chios, praised by the likes of Aristotle and Alexander Pope, dissolves into the shared lines of 'his' work. Indeed, in many ways, this anticipates the post-structuralist considerations of Barthes'

'Death of the Author', in which a text is seen as 'a tissue of quotations drawn from the innumerable centres of culture', and where the mythical, omnipotent figure of the author is reduced to the role of a 'mediator' or 'shaman' whose ultimate textual action is the revelation of 'the negative where all identity is lost'. By electing to use the personal pronoun in these final subsections of the critical reincarnations, to in effect create *myself* as a persona through the necessarily reductive action of trying to articulate the inarticulate complexities of the creative act, I thought to utilise the paradox at the heart of the archetypal epic poet, a poet who is simultaneously present and absent, active and passive, as a further gesture of negation.[32]

The 'Textual Interpretation: Practice' subsections would also serve another, even more crucial function. Like the hinges of a diptych, or the copper rod from *Manresa*, they would bring the poetry and the criticality into alignment, revealing how the monologues, despite their apparently arbitrary sequencing, actually pertain to the abstract unity of the Cosmological Paradigm. Thus, as I have said, each hemisphere was to be considered part of the epic, or rather as *giving rise* to the epic, for I came to realise that the fundamental coherence required to give the work a truly epic identity actually existed, like Beuys' Element 3, in the hermeneutic exchange *between* the poetry and the criticality – something which may be termed a conceptual, or disembodied poetics.

It was within this conceptual space, between the poetry and the criticality, that I saw the projected action of the posterior negation, or what I came to think of as the apophasis of the singularity. As we have seen, the primary negation was to be realised through the hermeneutic exchange, the monologues negated through their abstract identification with Big Bang cosmology. However, I saw that within this action there would be a fundamental paradox, for whilst the personas could be seen to correspond with the cosmological paradigm in a *linear* fashion, progressing from the Radiation

Era to the final stages of entropic decline, a profound tension would remain between one persona and the next; the tension of chronology; the tension of *time*. Thus, whilst Nietzsche, for example, might correspond to primordial fire, and Caravaggio to say the early phase of the Matter Era, their relationship with each other would be necessarily problematic, because Caravaggio, who lived nearly three centuries *before* Nietzsche, would be signifying a cosmological period which occurred *after* that represented by the philosopher. In a gesture akin to Derrida's concept of '*différance*', I foresaw that this would lead to a form of conceptual implosion, in effect negating both the primary negation of the cosmology and the kataphatic dimension of the poetry. It was for this reason, and not just out of deference to the epic tradition, that I wanted to use historical figures for the monologues – I specifically wanted the temporal properties of their relative historicities.[33]

During the process of refining my epic conception I had attempted to write the singularity as a sort of proem. Not only did this gesture become superfluous in light of the reconceived dynamic, but it was also, in any case, intellectually flawed. As we have seen, the singularity, because it pertains to infinite values, cannot be expressed in mathematical form. It is, in effect, a hypothetical postulate – a counter-conceptual point of silence. Consequently, trying to give it literary expression was more than a little absurd. It cannot be written, it can only be inferred. Indeed, its essential inexpressibility draws it into a negative affinity with the Pseudo-Dionysian belief in the ineffability of the Godhead; each lies beyond conceptuality and actuality; each is, and is not, silent, and is neither. Thus, I would offer no persona for the singularity. Rather, it would be implied through the action of the posterior negation, unwritten in its mystery, eloquent in its silence. Ultimately, the whole epic undertaking would be a means of counter-expressing the divine singularity which is the singularity of the divine, and it was amusing to observe that at the moment the reader grasped the totality of the epic's unity it would cease to be an epic at all.

For the present the apophasis of the singularity remains far in the future. As my friends have been so fond of reminding me this is very much a life's work, and the text(s) published here is merely the beginning of my voyage across the wine-dark sea. It is important to stress that I regard everything as being in a state of flux. The tailor's tacks are very much in place and, like Pound with his *Cantos*, I consider the monologues and their associate critical reincarnations to be drafts. In other words, I reserve the right to rewrite. I have provisionally entitled the unfolding epic *Silence*, after the linguistic difficulties associated with apophatic theology, and in this volume have separated the two hemispheres. Here the dramatic monologues come first, followed by the critical reincarnations. I have also provisionally subdivided the monologues (and thus by extension the critical reincarnations) into two 'books'. What is here termed 'Book One' concerns the persona of Nietzsche and his associate syphilitic identities, which, through the revelation of the poetry's critical reincarnation, are shown to correspond to the Radiation Era.

'Book Two', by contrast, is more complicated, concerning the early phase of the Matter Era, and involving three distinct personas: Caravaggio, Leonardo da Vinci, and St. Hieronymus. The grouping of these three personas into a single book covering a distinct phase of the Universe's development made it expedient to have only one 'Cosmological Paradigm' for all three voices. However, in accordance with my original design for the critical reincarnations, each persona has its own 'Textual Interpretation: Theory' and 'Textual Interpretation: Practice' subsections.

This explanation out of the way, there remains nothing else to do but commend myself to Calliope. Thus ends my proem.

NOTES

[1] Ian Ridpath, ed., *The Oxford Dictionary of Astronomy* (Oxford: Oxford University Press, 2003), 437, 50; Peter Coles, *Cosmology* (Oxford: Oxford University Press, 2001), 9, 11, 57; Ridpath, 50, 51, 374, 113, 381, 284; Coles, 9; Ridpath, 371, 100, 51.

[2] Thomas Mautner, ed., *The Penguin Dictionary of Philosophy* (London: Penguin Books, 2000), 603, 292, 391.

[3] Mautner, 351.

[4] J. P. Williams, *Denying Divinity: Apophasis in the Patristic Christian and Soto Zen Tradition* (Oxford: Oxford University Press, 2000), 2, 3, 24; E. A. Livingstone, ed., *The Oxford Concise Dictionary of the Christian Church* (Oxford: Oxford University Press, 2000), 169; Williams, 4, 5, 4, 8.

[5] A. C. Spearing, *'The Mystical Theology of St. Denis' in The Cloud of Unknowing and Other Works* (London: Penguin Books, 2001), 1; Raymond Gibbs, *The Poetics of Mind: Figurative Thought, Language and Understanding* (Cambridge: Cambridge University Press, 1994), 6.

[6] Williams, 4, 5, 84.

[7] Aeschylus, 'Prometheus Bound' in Aeschylus: *Prometheus Bound, The Suppliants, Seven Against Thebes, The Persians*, tr. P. Vellacott (London: Penguin Books, 1961), 21, 24, 21; Friedrich Hölderlin, 'Letter to Böhlendorff' in *Hymns and Fragments by Friedrich Hölderlin*, tr. R. Sieburth (Princeton: Princeton University Press, 1984), 5.

[8] Janet Burroway, *Imaginative Writing: The Elements of Craft* (London: Penguin Books, 2007), 215.

[9] Humphrey Carpenter, *A Serious Character: The Life of Ezra Pound* (London: Faber and Faber, 1988), 423.

[10] Aristotle, *Poetics*, tr. M. Heath (London: Penguin Books, 1996), 9, 38, 9, 30, 38, 40; Malcolm Heath, 'Introduction' in Aristotle, *Poetics* (London: Penguin Books, 1996), liv; Aristotle, 38; Heath, liv; Aristotle, 40, 38; Heath, lv, lxi; Aristotle, 40.

[11] E. J. Kenney, 'Introduction' in, Ovid, *Metamorphoses* (Oxford: Oxford University Press, 1986), xvii, xviii, xv; Ovid, *Metamorphoses*, tr. A. D. Melville (Oxford: Oxford University Press, 1986), 1, 374, 359.

[12] Ted Hughes, *Tales from Ovid* (London: Faber and Faber, 1997), iii, 144, 74.

[13] Louis Zukofsky, "A" (London: John Hopkins University Press, 1993), 18; W. B. Yeats, 'A Packet for Ezra Pound' in *Motive and Method in The Cantos of Ezra Pound*, ed. L. Leary (New York: Columbia University Press, 1969), 60.

[14] Ezra Pound, 'Canto IX' in *Selected Poems: 1908-1969* (London: Faber and Faber, 1977), 121.

[15] Pound, 'Canto IX', 125-126.

[16] Ezra Pound, 'Canto II' in *The Cantos of Ezra Pound* (New York: New Directions Publishing Corporation, 1993), 6, 9, 7, 8; Hugh Kenner, 'The Broken Mirrors and Mirrors of Memory' in *Motive and Method in The Cantos of Ezra Pound*, ed. L. Leary (New York: Columbia University Press, 1969), 4; Pound, 'Canto II', 6; Homer, *The Iliad*, tr. R. Fagles (London: Penguin Books, 1991), 77; Kenner, 4; Ezra Pound, 'Make it New' in R. Pope's *Creativity: Theory, History, Practice* (London: Routledge, 2005), 60.

[17] Kenner, 4; Kenney, xxvii; M. C. Howatson and Ian Chilvers, eds., *The Oxford Concise Companion to Classical Literature* (Oxford: Oxford University Press, 1996), 550.

[18] Ezra Pound, 'Piere Vidal Old' in *Personae: Collected Shorter Poems* (London: Faber and Faber, 2001), 29.

[19] B. S. Flowers, *Browning and the Modern Tradition* (London: Macmillan Press, 1976), 96.

[20] Marsilio Ficino, 'On divine frenzy' in *Meditations on the Soul: Selected Letters of Marsilio Ficino*, tr. members of the Language Department of the School of Economic Science, London (Rochester: Inner Traditions International, 1997), 64.

[21] Richard Stamelman, 'The Graven Silence of Writing' in *From the Book to the Book: An Edmond Jabès Reader*, tr. R. Waldrop, P. Joris, A. Rudolf, and K. Waldrop (London: Wesleyan University Press, 1991), ix.

[22] John Keats, 'Letter to Richard Woodhouse, 27 October 1818' in *The Letters of John Keats*, ed. R. Gittings (Oxford: Oxford University Press, 1970), 157.

[23] Peter Wilson, *A Preface to Ezra Pound* (London: Longman, 1997), 82.

[24] Philip Larkin, 'High Windows' in *Collected Poems* (London: Faber and Faber, 2003), 129; Andrew Motion, *Philip Larkin* (London: Methuen, 1982), 31.

[25] Motion, 60, 22.

[26] Plato, *The Republic*, tr. D. Lee (London: Penguin Books, 2003), 241.

[27] Mautner, 452; Williams, 22, 68, 71; Pseudo-Dionysius, 'The Mystical Theology' in *Pseudo-Dionysius: The Complete Works*, tr. by C. Luibheid (New York: Paulist Press, 1987), 135; Williams, 22; Mautner, 431; Williams, 22.

[28] Ian Chilvers, *The Oxford Concise Dictionary of Art and Artists* (Oxford: Oxford University Press, 2003), 61; Caroline Tisdall, *Joseph Beuys* (London: Thames and Hudson, 1979), 94; Mark Rosenthal, 'Joseph Beuys: Staging Sculpture' in *Joseph Beuys: Actions, Vitrines, Environments* , eds. S. Braeuer, C. Elliot, and J. Watkins (London: Tate Modern Publishing, 2005), 48, 26.

[29] Rosenthal, 25; Tisdall, 101; Rosenthal, 25.

[30] Tisdall, 110-113; Rosenthal, 39; Richard Geldard, *Remembering Heraclitus the Philosopher of Riddles* (Edinburgh: Floris Books, 2000), 157; Tisdall, 113, 110.

[31] Nancy Spector, 'Only the Perverse Fantasy Can Still Save Us' in *The Cremaster Cycle*, ed. M. Barney (New York: Guggenheim Museum Publications, 2003), 4, 34-36, 43, 44, 60; Massimiliano Gioni, *Matthew Barney*, tr. N. J.

Ross (Milan: Electra, 2007), 68, 66; Spector, 65; Gioni, 39; Spector, 33, 65, 33-34, 65.

[32] Betty Radice, *Who's Who in the Ancient World* (London: Penguin Books, 1973), 135; Bernard Knox, 'Introduction' in Homer's *The Odyssey* (London: Penguin Books, 1997), 6; Howatson and Chilvers, 267; Knox, 14; Roland Barthes, 'The Death of the Author' in *Image, Music, Text*, tr. S. Heath (London: Fontana Press, 1977), 146, 142.

[33] Mautner, 142.

HEMISPHERE ONE

Poetry

Book One

Why am I a destiny?

Even this mirror marvels
my reflection, touching the
genius of my naked skin…

I know Frau Fino watches me,
oh yes,
watches my dithyrambs lighting
10 **the darkness,**
yes,
watches as I whirl, a stark-sane
maenad in the temple of my
room,
lust splitting her lips
from pout to smile,
as I dance for the gods to come...

The English can't cook,
20 **it's hell on the stomach,**
the stench of the sick-pot full-high
with fever, and the Kaiser's an
arsehole, blind to my glory…

What did Bismarck
say?
Ah yes, the Jews…

Silence

"Es gehört dem Vaterland, die
30 *Juden von unserer*
Lebensweise auszuschließen."

Syphilis spat from Prussia.
I'll write you
like mercury
as though you'd kill me…

The wind shits bedsores
laughing the shutters…
40

My window shatters
Arcadian fantasies…

Let Yahweh shit on him.

I will shit on him.

Shit thunder.
50

(There aren't enough bullets
to realise Hell)

So tomorrow I'll go to the
Piazza Castello,
drink coffee
at the Caffè Romano,
watch life cascade
through this quiet arcade
60 **of memory…**

Here it's a renaissance.
Sunshine blossoms
on the Carignano,
golden petals of the eye
like raindrops
falling,

the
silence
of
Carmen
sung mute
over Italy,
borne over rooftops,
dreaming eternity…

Genoa was Winter.

Turin is Summer.

And if I'm still
I can hear her speaking
longingly reaching
the words of her rivers
to listen
to listen

I follow her rivers
over the city
like music
like Wagner
their breathing is holy
sensual and holy

I see her face
I know it well
but here they love me
truly love me
the waitress smiles
"Good night, Professor."
and morning has no tears…

You see, Köselitz how well I am?
What a city! How right you were,
my dearest Heinrich, to suggest

it, really, I cannot thank you enough,
it's a revelation. Only
yesterday I was walking over
110 **the Po Bridge when it occurred to**
me, in one of those startling moments
of epiphany, that Turin
is superb, no truly, beyond
good and evil (!!). I think it no
exaggeration to say that
***here* is my philosophy, founded**
in the very stones of Guarini.
Consider its aristocratic
tranquillity, its ancient poise,
120 **its European solemnity –**
is this not *Zarathustra*? Or
at least its words, lulled into relief
by rust-reddened brown and the guileless
hue of ochre? Of course one must
accept a certain ennui where most
architecture is concerned (this
is natural in such a *décadent*
age) but *here*, Köselitz a universe
is possible! To this effect
130 **I often find myself in the**
Valentino Park pondering
horticulture, or, if the weather's
fine, taking a stroll past the Ponte
Vittorio, smiling graciously
at those I meet, and thinking of
all the magic still locked inside
my head. I suppose I'm a little
like Odysseus – only he
never wrestled with the serpents
140 **of Bayreuth! But truly, Heine**
don't I look well? Who could resist
these seasons? The air, the unspoken
promise of the sea – it's Alpine!
Sometimes I feel as though the whole
of existence were focused on

a moment – as though time, space, the
very birth-blood of identity
were somehow reborn – as though I'd
overcome myself, and by
50 **overcoming *become* myself –**
and all this in the present tense!
You must surely understand my
enthusiasm? You are, after
all, a composer… And I? Well,
there are melodies and then there
are *melodies!* True, I'd rather
be a Basel professor than
God, but Peter, Peter, Peter,
it's not without sensation. Who
60 **could deny the wonderful treatment**
I receive at my trattoria?
Doesn't the Manager lavish
attention on me as though I were
royalty? Or at the Market?
Clearly the old woman selects
for me only the sweetest grapes!
No, here I'm not Phaeton but the
Sun, and my chariot transfigures
everything, *everything*… Why, just
70 **the other day Herr Fino was**
commenting on the radiance
of my appearance! ("My good, Nietzsche
you look like a god.") Now, granted
I've recently changed my tailor,
but consider, Pierre my profile –
am I not the very image
of Caesar? There's something about
the application of the nose
in such matters (and a Roman
80 **knows more than most) that goes someway**
in distinguishing the tenor
of a soul. As you know from my
books I've an uncanny sense
of smell – one might say 'preternatural'

if one were feeling frivolous! –
and so I pride myself, above
all things, on my ability
to sniff out intellectual
putrefaction. Unfortunately
190 **the nineteenth century's more than**
a little overripe – one gets
a whiff of Schopenhauer even
between the cleanest of sheets – and
so I find myself in a constant
state of excitement! I sneeze, with
un-Germanic ferocity,
one scintillating work after
another. Honestly, nothing's
safe, nothing's beyond the range of
200 **my oh-so-critical nostrils!**
The Kaiser; Bismarck; that bloated
fatality of millennia:
CHRISTIANITY **– all must dance**
the Dionysiac dance of
my pen… Not that the Germans read,
you understand? That would require
a certain *délicatasse*
completely foreign to the Prussian
mind! No, instead they dwell in the
210 **superficial comfort of the**
Ideal – a tearful indulgence
milked from the udders of Hegel,
whose only seduction lies in
its lie of deliverance. And
still **they dream! Even when life**
roars its senseless fury, *still* they
cling to 'reason' (the unholy
ghost of reason) – that festering
pustule of the will to *décadence* –
220 **that turgid expression of the**
slave-monger's soul! Have they not heard?
Has it not been said to them from
the beginning? From the very

foundation of the Earth, no less?
And still – *STILL* – when all's stripped away
the lie remains – beautifully
ugly – humanity's whore –
that final confection: the lie
of perfection – and always *beyond…*
230 But I've come too early. The World's
not ready to understand itself –
it's too young, too serious, too
busy 'living' to have lived – it
does not, cannot, *will not* see
delusion in illusion – *will not*
brace itself for life – embrace itself
as life – reach for that transcendence
overreaching understanding
and *live*, not in some twilight state
240 of angst, but with daimonic frenzy
realise its potential! Rejoice!
Sing unto itself dithyrambs
of eternity! Affirm and
not negate! Drink fire! *LIVE!* Yes, as
I would live – without fear, without
regret! *Yes!* – cry with its entire
being: "I willed it so!" *And mean it.*
This has been my prophecy; yet
who was there to hear it…? But really,
250 though, everything's so cheap in Turin –
a transvaluation of all
values you might say! Just think: a
meal at my trattoria costs
a mere one franc fifteen centimes –
can you imagine? For this I
get a generous portion of
minestra (served either dry, or,
if I prefer, as bouillon),
a pasta dish (*very* tasty,
60 you know?), followed by an excellent
helping of the tenderest meat!
Naturally one gets all the

accoutrements – spinach, rolls, etc –
and, for a few centimes extra,
even a little wine… Until
now I never knew what it meant
to enjoy eating. I used to
retch at the sight of food as
though my body were rejecting the
270 rite of existence, but *here!* Suffice
to say I've a rapacious
appetite – and not only for
food! I rave with a hunger
to know the nature of my
universe *so* passionate, *so*
restlessly intense, that I fear
a complete implosion of the
senses! It's euphoric! A sublime
intoxication of the mind
280 *so* potent, *so* terrible, that
it threatens consummation! I
can't breathe for divinity – she's
here, stifling me with the dark
eruption of her eyes like
Ariadne burning the shore
of Naxos with her tears… I sense
you don't believe me, Heine – you
think I'm lying, perhaps, or worse,
quite mad? But I ask you, what's saner?
290 To believe in a god you've never
seen? Or to *know*, through blood and bone,
the force that moves the World? I think
my Zarathustra puts it best
when he says that

I am solely my body,
nothing beside;
my soul and my body
you cannot divide…

300

You'll no doubt appreciate

the profundity of these lines;
they convey a certain something –
a certain 'gravitas' you might
say – unique to my genius…
And what genius, Heine! Never
has there been an energy like
it – it's dynamite! Why, in a
single quatrain I've achieved the
unthinkable – *yes!* the birth of
the body – the death of the soul!
I've burnt away the centuries
of lies – torn chalice from altar –
revealed blood as wine! Nothing is
beyond me – not even the arching
firmament of stars! My reach is
immortal, Heine – *I'm* immortal –
the only begotten son of
God – *and God is dead…* What? Hadn't
you heard? Yes, I've killed him – *me*, the
blind runt of Röcken – *I* have murdered
God! Huh! You don't believe me – such
lack of faith! Can't you hear the grave-
diggers? Can't you smell the sickening
stench of death? Oh even gods
decompose, Heine – even gods
rot! But no one understands the
enormity of my crime. It's
too fantastic! Too profound! It
asks too much – *demands* too much – and
yet is natural, so natural – oh
so very much like love that I
know I'll be forgiven… But who
needs forgiveness? It's time to grow
up, Heine; time to become the
music. Why should I hide? – cower
behind the weakness I despise
while all around me slumber? What
value are their dreams if dreams alone
are living? What price existence

when it cheapens Life of meaning?
Yes, Life is terrible; but the
fury of that terror is our
own – *why deny it?* No! – one must
be superior: not only
in loftiness of mind, *but in*
***contempt!* Then (and only then) will**
mankind breach its destiny… I
refer, of course, to the coming
350 **of the Superman – that pernicious**
viper whose force of *Will* exalts
creation to sublime disdain!
***He shall be magnificent:* a**
being untouched by the torments of
this world – ripe in his divinity!
Pride, strength, mastery of *Will – these*
shall be his attributes. And what,
you ask, of 'pity'? Ha! – had you
but understood you'd know that pity's
360 **for the damned – a legacy of**
sickness! The Superman shall have
no *pity,* but through his great
volition sweep the *décadent*
aside… I left the house early
this morning. The quiet light was
weeping. And passing through the streets
I felt its grief; felt the weight of
Winter burdening the stones – frost-
bitten cobbles like bodies beneath
370 **me; grey, battered faces lost like**
a crowd… *"Ich bin Gott!"* I cried, "*Ich*
***bin gekommen!"* – But no one**
was listening. I cried again –
louder this time – desperate to
be heard: *"I AM GOD. I AM COME…"*
Then I saw the horse. Its neck was
twisted, taut with pain, and its eyes…
…I *knew* those eyes. I'd seen them in
Genoa, in Sils-Maria,

80 in Venice, Basel, Stresa, Rome –
the parsonage at Röcken had
had those eyes – my mother's eyes. *My*
eyes… – The whip was laughing now, its
lips like blood – I felt…exalted,
yes, as though my world were breaking –
as though the passion of a sun
were ripening my veins – thrashing
me *over, over, over…* – And
the horse was bleeding. And *I* was
90 bleeding. Like mercury. Like fire.
Like the burning sores that cinder
on my skin... – Like a memory
of love distending into darkness –
and *over, over* – lashing through
my tears – through the searing ache of
nothing tearing into nothing –
through the eviscerating moment,
plunging to decay… And I asked
myself: "Have I been understood?"
00 (*as the mocking faces sundered*
on my shore) –
"Have I been understood?"
(as the faceless voices hungered
me for more) –
"Have I been understood?"

Dionysos against the Crucified…

10

*

420

[Scene: The House of Agathon, Athens]

"…yes but, Socrates you've already
said that 'justice' is not *Justice*,
that 'honour' is not *Honour*,
430 **that 'knowledge', far from being *known*, denies**
the knower!
Am I then to hold that all is dark?
That the total of my life
(such as it is)
is less than that which dreaming might
deceive?
Or should I wake?
And if so, to what?
As far as *I* can see you've simply
440 **sought for obfuscation,**
preferring to perplex me
than to tame my heart to
reason…
And now – *now* – like the naughty satyr
that you are,
you say that I should *thank* you!
Yes, *thank you!*
Imagine how that makes
***me* feel –**
450 **poor little Agathon –**
my head a-whirl with wine
and 'wisdom'!
Not that *you* care –
there's too much of the
beast in you…
Oh, but can't you
comprehend

the *horror* of your words?
The harm, Socrates, the harm!
460 If only for a moment you might see
(oh I don't know)
the 'crushing mayhem' you expose? Then you'd
starve your tongue
(or else abide
a sweeter melody)…
But no – *no* – you want to spit,
you want to tear!
Like Sisyphus laughing in the House of Death
you mock at every law –
470 and not content with laughter,
smash!
Oh, *I* have seen your demon
daily dance in the Agora –
I have listened, Socrates,
as every man you meet
swift-falls to chaos!
So tell me, *philosopher:*
why?
Why play the gadfly with this
480 subtle-speak for Sparta?
Why seek to sunder
Athens from her soul?
What? No answer?
Mmmm,
I think Meletus right to call *you*
'corrupter', for corrupt you are!
A podgy old sileni:
ugly, smelly and –"

490 "PISSED!"

<laughter>

"Come on, Socrates –
you've heard what this

Lycian *flute-girl* has to say!
Throw her some balls!"

"Oooh, listen to the General!
500 **Careful, Alcibiades – I'll cry!"**

"Now, gentlemen,
***please* – this is supposed to be**
a symposium! As your symposiarch
I feel it is my duty to – "

"POUR WINE!"

"Tell us, Agathon: why does Eryximachus
510 ***always* host your parties?"**

"Yeah, he's always *SO* serious…"

<murmurs >

"If I'm serious, *Critias*,
it's because Agathon here delights
in inviting bum-fucks like you!"

520 **"Oh go on, be fair, Eryximachus:**

The boys don't like
Critias
'cos he has a
shitty ass!

– and besides, it doesn't do
to upset one of the Thirty
***(if you know what I mean…)*."**
530

"Yeah, well that's typical of you,
Aristophanes – make everything
political, why don't you?

But honestly, who here actually
preferred the corruption
of the Democracy?
No,
what the new Oligarchy offers is – ”

“BOLLOCKS!”

“Mmmm, they’ve got *my* vote!”
“*Firm leadership.*”

“Spartan dictatorship!”

“Oh how I *love* seeing men getting all…*hot.*
More wine, boys?”

“I am a doctor, sir –
yes, a *doctor!*
<groans>
I think *I* ought to know better than *you*
what’s good for the
body politic!”

“Oh spare us the metaphors,
for Melpomene’s sake!
You’re an ass, Eryximachus – ask anyone!
No, no, better –
ask Socrates! *Yes*, he’ll give you a diagnosis –
and faster than any *doctor…*”

“What do you
say to *that*, Socrates?
Is Eryximachus an ass, or what?”

“Well, Socrates?”

“So-cra-tes?”

"He doesn't seem to be doing much, does he?
Just, er, lying on his stomach
and, um, dribbling…"

"The poor dear –
perhaps he needs a drink?"

"I think he's had enough, don't you?
580 **As his doctor –"**

"Socrates? *Smashed?*
I can't believe it!
He could've drunk Antinous
off his couch!
You *were* watering the wine?"

"Of course I was. You *know* I was!"

590 **"Yeah, well, he**
seems sorely sunk to me…"

"Right – like *rat-arsed!*"

"I think he looks rather cute –
sort of like a baby…"

"He's got a beard."

600 **"PPHUTTT!"**

<coughs>

"Aw, by Zeus, he stinks!
Somebody take him home."

"Nah, let him sleep it off."

"Gents, I propose a toast –"

10

"Yeah, to flatulence!"

<laughter>

"I'm serious –"

"Oh, alright then: to Aeolus!"

<laughter>

20

"That's enough of your impiety,
***Critias* –"**

"Just fill our bowls,
***symposiarch!*"**

"Do you two mind?"

"*Quiet!* The General speaks!"

30

"*Thank you.* As you know,
today's Socrates' birthday.
Athens' greatest denizen has
survived another year!
And yet does the
City celebrate?
Are there flowers in the Agora?
Do the citizens embrace this burly
bulge of wisdom?

40

Do they ogle
at the goggle
of his eyes
in loving wonder?
Or dance?
Or sing?
Or anything but *bitch* about the
'foreign' nature of his ways?
I ask you: do bare feet bear the mark

of Spartan subjugation?
650 Do wise words speak some lie?
Or lie upon a civil tongue of truth?
This man – this man
has borne the blood-blow
of our laws;
endured the sweaty grease of
blade and limb.
And even as this world in
queasy motion
made to clash into the
660 shades of hell –
still he stood firm!
I speak of Potidaea.
That iron-maddened throng
where war-lorn Ares stung the screech
of havoc in our ears!
There,
amid that human sea,
I found myself alone –
shield-wrecked
670 upon the bloody rocks
of sheer
abomination.
I could taste
Death.
See
Death.
Be
Death.
– But the fury of the Furies' drum
680 drove on –
Hounding.
Scarring.
Maiming.
Marring.
– Flaying to the steaming brink of bone…
I hardly felt the spear,
but fell –

fell
to scrape the anger of the earth!
690 Fate was breathing now:
iron mask like rust
in the clawing dust;
eyes, moist slits,
mocking at my wound…
I watched its weathered sword
tarnishing the air;
waited for the rhythm
of its blow
to rend my life
700 with thunder!
Thank *Zeus* it never came,
for *Socrates*,
swift as Achilles,
lunged into the fray!
You should've seen him,
he fought like Heracles,
each move a fiery lesion
of the Sun…
And when it was over,
710 when the tinderlust of War
had cindered through the day,
he gave *me* his victory.
Me!
I would've died…
Gentlemen, please, raise your wine –
praise with me
the virtue of a man
whose courage,
Codrus knows,
720 transcends his mortal breadth
of time.
Gentlemen, please, to Socrates."

"To Socrates."

"Socrates."

Silence

"Socrates."

730 **"Socrates."**

"URRRP! – *That*, Alcibiades
(or at least I think one of you's
Alcibiades)
is what I think of *that*…or you…or
whatever it was you
just said…just now? Yes…something
about a goatskin…a
goatskin…winesack?…

740 ***Yes!*…a goatskin winesack,**
stuffed with…with…
wine…yes…wine –
where's my wine?
Eryximachus!
Eh?
What?
Eryximachus!
Wine!
Yes…wine –

750 ***No!***
Give it here! …see? *See? Slurrrrp* – ah!
URRRP! Mmmm…better…
yes…
What are you looking at, huh? *What?*
Have you seen a god?
Is that it?
Hmmm?
Mmmm…more wine…
I can taste a god's blood in

760 **my mouth…yes…**
the black blood
of a god cloying round
my tongue…

Listen!

Listen...shanoohshehim?
Eh?
Shanoohshehim?
...Mmmm...
I can see him...*y'hear?*
...Rain...rain pattering
on Solon's stones...
wine clotting...
words
creeping with
the vine...
Can y'hear 'em?
Eh?
Can y'hear 'em?
...Panpipes...yes...panpipes
fermenshing
Phryishia...
Nysa danshing...
...caves o'themountains
pisshedwivairshong...
Where's Xanthippe? Hmmm?
Where is she?
...Oh, I feel sick...
Agathon!
Agathon...come here...
come here...
...I've got something to tell you...
it's about...
Xanthippe...yes...
about Xanthippe...
come here...listen...
SHE'S A BITCH!
...yes...
...a bitch...
....Mmmm...nagging
and...

...oh...
...there's shoh
many...many of you...
THUAARRK!
Hem, a-hem...
Mmmm,
that's better...
Wine!
...more wine...yes...
810 *Slurrrrp* – ah!
...yes...never get
married...no...you'll
never get married...
there's nothing...
nothing but the screaming...
the screaming
of the screaming...the heady musk
of bodies...yes...
brazening the air...
820 Can y'smell 'em?
Huh?
Can y'smell 'em?
...Oh, I can smell 'em...
They're *Rank!*
...yes...
rank...
bodies stinking...
bodies...yes...
a skin-clad whirl
830 of snake and drum...
Can y'feel it?
Huh?
Can y'feel it?
Cymbals!
Cymbals!
The hunger of *cymbals!*
Agavë bleeding,

foaming,
bleeding…Ino screaming…auloi screaming…
40 **and the drumbeat thrashing,**
and the thyrsoi thrashing,
and the bodies burning,
thrashing,
burning,
and the darkness yearning,
and the darkness burning,
and the hunger
of the hunger
of the hunger
50 **of the hunger**
of limbs
of heads
of breasts
of fire –

”

Διόνϋσοσ
στϱέφω

60

I. Pentheus

Try and see it my way. I mean,
it is *my* kingdom. I mean, don't
tell me you didn't notice. Surely
you must've known? I mean, how stupid
are you? *Hello* – I'm talking to
you. Look at me. *LOOK AT ME!* That's
better. You see? There's no need to
70 **be difficult. We'd get along**
fine if only you'd listen. It's
not too much to ask now, is it?
Not too much for a king to ask;

to ask that a prisoner listen?
Is it? To ask that a prisoner
listen to a king? Well? *IS IT?*
It gets cold. Down here. At night. Very
cold. Can you feel the shadows licking
at the flame? Licking at your skin?
880 Can you feel the darkness, cold against
your skin? Can you? It'll get colder.
Yes. Deeper and colder. And perhaps
you'll cry out. Perhaps you'll scream to
be heard. But no one'll hear you. No
one'll listen because *you* don't
listen. No one'll hear because
I won't let them hear. And you'll wait.
Yes. Wait in your hunger.
They're mad
890 because of you. You know that? – No.
Don't say anything. *Just listen.* –
You've made them mad. Yes. Burnt them with
your madness. My wife. My mother.
Why, even old Teiresias
has put on skirts and staggered to
the hills! Crying like a girl. Mewing
with your madness. I mean, I'm the
only one who's sane, aren't I? I'm
the only one who knows *what* you
900 are.
Look at you. Blonde curls stroking
your foreign skin. Your lips moist. Thick
and moist with your hunger. You disgust
me. This isn't Lydia. It's
Thebes. *My Thebes.* Whose god do you think
you are? The Cymbals. The Thyrsoi.
The Dancing. So what? I know you're
a lie. Oh, you can rape Cithaeron.
You can plead the Mountain's 'blood' courses
910 through your veins. But not my aunt's. Not
Semele's. *That* touches my crown.
And you'll not touch my crown. Not even

if you are Zeus's son! (As if).
I wonder what you're thinking. – No.
Don't tell me. Let me guess. – You hate
me, don't you? Like all of them you
hate me. I'm not Cadmus. I mean,
only Cadmus was truly Thebes.
Only *he* was loved by the gods.
20 But what does that mean? *Loved by the*
gods. Between ourselves, the gods know
nothing of love. Oh, they know how
to take. Yes. How to take. But love?
I don't think so.
And then there's you.
You'd take us all. But you're no god.
I've seen them on the hills. You know
that? The women of Thebes. Half naked.
Bleeding. The mothers of Thebes. Smashing
30 their babies' brains against the rocks.
They laugh. You know that? Laugh for the
joy of their 'god.' Laugh for you. And
it's funny, because I have wept
their tears.

40
II. Ariadne

You were
there too
remember

I can't have
been alone
or held
half-dreaming
50 the likeness

of a dream

I felt your
warmth touch
the darkness

felt your
words against
my skin

960

and *knew*

III. Cosmogony [1]

before eyes
before ears
before nose
970 **before tongue**
before skin
before hair
before heart
before lungs
before veins
before blood
(the spatter of blood)

the void knew the void
980 **the void was one**

And the void said:
I am alone.

And the void said:
I will sunder darkness.

And the void said:

Let light know light.

And an egg
blazed from the darkness.

And the void said:
I behold my son.

And the void said:
He shall be my father.

And the void said:
His will be done.

And the egg
blazed in the darkness.

IV. Hangover

WAIT! By all the gods, Eumaeus –
wait! It is I, Ikarios,
your friend! What's all this talk of poison?
I? Poison *you?* May Hera strike
me if I lie! WHY? Why would I?
But I don't want your farm! No, I'm
not saying it's shitty. It's very
nice. Bit small… ALRIGHT! Alright, I
know you're angry. Yes, I can see
the pitchfork. I'm not blind. *No,* I
don't want to be! Look, why don't
we sit down and talk about this?
Reasonably. I've got a headache
too. Yes, my mouth's like a satyr's
arse. Yes, my gut's the Aegean.
Yes, your voice *is* fucking loud – but
am I threatening you? *We drank*

from the same bowl. Remember? You
saw Erigone filling it!
Would my own daughter try and poison
1030 me? The daughter I've fed and clothed
these eighteen years? Be reasonable,
Eumaeus! Well you weren't doing
much complaining last night, now were
you? "Ambrosia," you said. "More,"
you said – why, we must've got through
three whole skins! What do you mean it's
all a blur? *They're on the ground.* Look.
We danced round them. You *must* remember!
You even said you loved me… Fair
1040 enough if you want to forget
that (to be honest so do I),
but surely you've not forgotten
the dancing? Tell you what. You put
the pitchfork down…and…I won't bear
a grudge – how about that? No. Right.
What d'you say to a couple
of goats? Alright, three goats. Look, this
isn't my fault! *I'm a victim*
too. It was the stranger, wasn't
1050 it? *He* brought the vines. *He* showed me
how to harvest their fruit – how to
make wine. *Blame him!* Eumaeus? PLEASE!

V. Leaving Pallene

Who am I, Pallene?
When you look at me what do you see?
1060 Your husband?
The murderer of your father?
A man?
Can't you see that
this is *so small?*

I can't breathe.
I could scream.
The meanness of my world shrinks imagination.
Like glass
mocking sunlight
70 **I mock another's glory.**
That other is *myself*, Pallene.
All I still might be.

I see the dullness in your eyes.
You don't understand.
You'd keep me like some panther
caged by loving bars.
Quiet.
Domestic.
80 ***Small.***
But I won't be tamed, Pallene.
I won't rest in your womb.
Your skin may be soft,
but softer is your will –
the honey-drug of Circe!
Well, I've drunk enough of your smallness.
Could I really be content with *this?*
To be King of Chalkidike –
as mortal as your father?
90 **When Sithon fell I saw the pity of our lies.**
To die each day; each day to die
and call it living!
Small, Pallene.
So very small.

Tears?
For whom are you crying?
You?
Or *me?*
00 **Your beauty mocks me with the grave.**
Should I stay here?
Watch the hilarity of age
laugh across your skin?

Silence

Marvel as each tender line
is gnarled into my agony?

Some fate fidelity.

You'd keep me from what's mine!
1110 **Faithful in your lap I'd lie in death;**
share in your mortality.
All dreams,
all expectations *gone* –
drowned amid the corpses of the Styx!

I want to *live*, Pallene.
I want to *be* the sun within me,
not some shadow on the funerary ground
of *your* humanity.
1120 **My father is a god.**
The God of gods.
Why then should I not seek
***my* portion of divinity?**
I am the bastard blood of Zeus.
Nature's in my veins.
An intoxicating Life –
all but immortal!
And I will be immortal.

1130 **Laugh, Pallene.**
Laugh alone.

VI. Cosmogony [2]

Who has seen?
Who has heard?
Who has known?
1140

Sing of Eros, first of gods.

Sing of his hatching.
Sing of his Light.
How his wings rayed the black of the Sun.
How his loins bled the body of Night.

Through Night came Gaia:
Mother of Earth.
Through Night, Ouranos:
150 ***Father of Sky.***
Through Night, Ananke:
Brooder of Time.

From Eros bled the Song of Night.

VII. The Wisdom of Silenos

160

Midas m'boy, gimmie some wine!
And may I say, I love what you've
done with the soft-furnishings? Ah,
yes, but it's a funny thing – thank you –
it's a funny thing. Who'd've thought
I'd be back in y'palace, slurpin' y'wine,
so soon, eh? Who'd've thought it? Eh?
Who'd've thought it?
URRRP! **Ah, yes, a**
170 **fine vintage – blackberries, figs, yeeeessss,**
and just a hint of ***ripe Nymph!*** **Eh?**
But where are m'manners? How are
yah? Like the ears by the way. ***Very***
you... **Yes, I heard about that. Well,**
if you will play silly buggers
with the gods what y'expect? Still,
no real harm done. Who knows, it
might even become fashionable...
Me? Oh, I've been ***very*** **busy,**

1180 **yes, *very busy.* There was this**
Dryad, y'see? Or was she a
Naiad? Come t'think of it, she
might've been Nereid? Or
was she an Oread? Oh, bugger
I've forgotten! Anyway, she
was very fit – kept me runnin'
about for months – ah, y'too kind –
yes, feisty little thing, never
did catch her – turned into an ash
1190 **tree. (Mmmm, must've been a**
Meliae). Ah, well, I mean, that's
the trouble with Nymphs, isn't it?
Clothed in dew, very pretty an'
all that, but no spunk for the firm-
n-furry! What?
– Between you an'
me, if y'want a good hard shag,
y'better off with a Centaur!
At least they're good for a gallop!
1200 **('A gallop' – ha!). Y'health, sir! Y'health!**
***SLUUURRRP!* Ah! But it's good t'see yah,**
lad. Good t'see yah – oh, much obliged –
yeeeessss, but I'm sure y'didn't bring
me all the way t'Phrygia,
'cross all the spicy deserts of
Arabia, 'cross oceans of
Sirens, mountains of Giants, the
back of a Harpy and the balls
of a Cyclops, simply t'sample
1210 **y'wine…**
What is it? Tell ole Uncle
Silenos. – Mind you, if it's about
those ears there's nothing I can do…
Apollo's a jealous god, m'boy – always
has been. Y'should've seen him when
he was a tot – oh the temper
tantrums! *"Artemis took my bow!"*
"Artemis broke my arrows!"

"Artemis! Artemis! Artemis!"
On and on and on – and oh gods,
if he hadn't been a god I'd've
strangled the little runt!
– But what
were y'thinkin'? Eh? What were
y'thinkin'? Sayin' Pan's music
was better! I ask yah! I mean,
I'm sure it was. But t'say it?
T' say it! – Zeus!
Ah, well, never
mind – as Teiresias once said:
"What's done is done." And besides – they'll
give yah somethin' t'talk about
at parties...
– More?! No, no, I…oh,
alright, just a little. Anyone'd
think y'were tryin' t'get me pissed!
HEEAAHH! P-potent stuff! Seems, I dunno,
stronger somehow… Ha! Reminds me
of a bloody odd weekend I
once spent on Circe's island. Y'know
the sort o'thing: twenty naked sailors
turnin' int'pigs an' a
hangover t'split the summit
of Olympus! Have t'admit,
I forget the main *thrust* of it,
'though I vaguely remember dancin'
a dithyramb with a lovely
lad called…oh, what was it? Ah, yes,
Perdicas, yeeeessss, Perdicas, that
was it… Nice arse (at least before
he turned int'a pig)… Never
did keep in touch… Ah, well, that's the
trouble when y'bein' held
prisoner by the witch-bitch of
Asphodel – tend to forget who
yah are, let alone who y'with!
Wonder how I escaped?

*Oh...*oh,
I feel strange.
1260 Wh-what was in that
drink?
Midas?
Is that you? No...no
it's a donkey... 'Ello,
donkey...
'ELLO!
Hm-hm-hm.
Yeeeeeeeeeeeeeeessssssssss,

d-**on**-keeeey!
1270 'Ello...
Wh-what're
y'sayin'?
Eh?
What're y'sayin'?
Y'can't speak...
speak...
what're y'sayin'?
HUUUUUNNNHH!
I can't tell y'that!
1280 *You're a donkey!*
No...
I can't tell y'that...
Ok...ok, I'll tell yah...
but y'gotta promise...*promise*...
not t'tell any...
any...
other donkeys...ok?
Ok...ok...I'll tell yah...
but it's between you,
1290 me,
an' y'ears...
ok?
Ok.

Die soon,
’cos it were better yah were never born.

00

VIII. Hera

I see you’ve *another* bastard,
husband. And who’s the mother this
time? A swineherd, perhaps? No? Oh.
Well, that’s something, I suppose. At least
the Queen of Heaven wasn’t shafted
for a pig! Let me guess – a Nymph?
Am I right? No? A princess, then?
10 One of Cadmus’ brood.
– *Oh I see*
everything. Why the thunder-face?
Did you think I didn’t know? No,
really – it’s *pathetic.* Give him
all eternity and a god
is still a man! You’re as subtle
as a bull, my dear. – How thick do
you think I am? No, no, I’d like
to know. Tell me, mighty Zeus: how
20 thick *is* white-armed Hera – Thunder’s
‘bimbo’ wife? So thick she failed to
see him creep across the clouds? So
thick she failed spy him slither
into Thebes? *I saw you!* Each night
I saw you. Yes. Saw how you swapped the
lightning of your beard. Saw how
you took the features of a man,
a mortal man – the better, I
supposed, to ease a mortal girl!
30 And so I followed you. Yes. Put
off these shining clothes, the garland
in my hair, these armlets forged on

Etna's fiery wheel – *put them off* –
and in the raiment of a snake,
worried at your heel…
Have to say,
I thought you'd better taste. Thirteen
years old and breastless like a boy!
But you had her just the same. Oh
1340 yes. Took her tear of blood – laughing
as she squealed. And all the while slimy
in your form: now a lion, now
a bear, now a grunting bull! – Poor
child! Must've thought she was being
ravished by a zoo!
Ah, but
Aphrodite knows, you have a
way with women. I saw bestial
horror smoulder into love. Saw
1350 her eyes maturing to a woman's
gaze. *And I knew she'd have to die.*
You've never understood me. Never.
You think I'm heartless; callous; cool
beyond compare. You think that I
despise the Eros-heart. That I
burn with ice!
– Oh you are a *fool!*
Can't you see? See the murder of
my love? See the beauty that is
1360 yours, in flesh, in me? *Teiresias*
sees better than you! All hail Zeus:
blind King of Heaven! *Zeus* who prefers
shepherd boys and virgin girls. *Zeus*
who'll sleep with any *whore* rather
than his *wife!*
DON'T TOUCH ME! You smell
of her. Still. After all this time.
And you're holding her *thing*. What was
it like, Zeus to bear it in your
1370 thigh? To fashion in your manly
flesh a womb? To hold nine moons of

hairy blood?
– Remember how she
died? Remember how you *made her*
die? Can't you taste her on the breeze?
Taste her memory? Aren't her ashes
in your mouth: words of guilt?
That's right –
hit me. *Go on.* Oh, you've made it
380 cry – *she* was crying – crying *fire* –
fire laughing at her hair, her loins –
her breasts of *fire* – eyes widening
to *fire* – screaming *fire* – *fire* laughing
at her skin – white skin cackling
fire!
Do you feel her heat, Zeus?
Do you feel her burn?
I saw her
burn! Saw as you tore the water
390 from the Sun! Saw as you bleached the
magma of her bones!
– *Oh you were*
magnificent. Yes. A searing
supernova! Naked in your
godhood!
– What was it like to kill
her, Zeus? *What was it like to feel*
her burn?
Hu-hu-hu-hu-hu-hu-
400 hu-hu-hu-hu-hu-hu-hu-hu –
pathetic! The God of gods weeping
for a girl. – What do you care if
one of *them* lives or dies? What do
you care if a mortal woman
dies? They don't matter. *Not to us.*
They're the merest atoms of
a season; the slightest breeze; half-formed
thoughts teeming for a mind. – They're
not *real.* Not like us…
410 I watched

you save it from the flames. Watched you
cup it in your hand: that half-formed,
half-heard thought of humanity.
Such tenderness.
And I smiled, Zeus.
Oh yes. I smiled at love. A love
as perverted as yours. The love
of a god for his mortal child.
Oh yes, I smiled. Because I had
1420 made you feel a mother's pain. Because
I had wept her tears into your
eyes. Because you are a fool.

IX. Theseus

silence
1430 is better
it is
opaque
ambiguous
to give
utterance
is to
define
and to
define
1440 is to
restrict
anything
might be
everything
born in
silence

X. Cosmogony [3]

And Night said:

I am the beauty of the Earth.

And Night said:

I am the beauty of the Sky.

To them I am a river.
To me they are a Sea.

They catch me in my torrent.
They spice me with their salt.

As I am pure so they are vast.
As I am dark so they are deep.

Let gods be born between them.
Let my Universe know Life.

XI. Sea-Change

Why should I tell 'ee ought? 'Tain't as
though ye'd understand – none as
understand tha' didn't see – the
foamin', roamin' thunder o'the
waves – salt-surf-an-spumin' t'the
choppin' thrust o'the tide…
Ye'd not
understand…
But *if* I told 'ee?

What then, eh? Would yer thank me for
m'tale? Would yer? Huh! The words er
dry on m'tongue. Be better yer
1490 leave. 'Tain't nothin' t'be gained by
dredgin' up the drowned – or the *worse*
than drowned…
Huh. Alright. Stay. But don't
as say I didn't warn 'ee. Yer
can buy me a drink an' all. 'Tmight
jus' help t'slick m'mind…

Colours
vivid through m'eyes – like the Sirens'
1500 madness playin' – bold colours o'the Sun
playin' the fevered lights o'dreams –
hot, so hot wi'the pulse o'wine…
An' I can see him. His dark, dark
eyes grape black i'the phantom swirl,
an' his voice –
Huh. But I get ahead.
Yer wanna know how, an' why, an'
when. Yet none as matters when yer've
seen – yer know tha' how, an' why, an'
1510 when er jus' marks i'the sand – jus'
marks, nothin' more…
I were the helmsman
'board a merchant ship. We'd sailed
from Tyrrhenia, land o'horses –
our compass bound for Samos –
Aeolos' wind swellin' our sails.
The gods, we thought, were with us.
But Hades lurked beneath the waves,
plottin' some revenge.
1520 An' the wind
changed…
Have yer ne'er a wondered at
yer fate? Ne'er a wondered at the
turns tha' vein like rivers through a
day? One choice another river

an' eventually the sea…
I've
wondered…
We were blown t'the cape
30 **o'Sounion – 'cross wild waters,**
buffetin' the waves – our boat-wood
blasted by the rage o'Tethys –
our cargo lost for Poseidon's
play…
I remember how the salt
it stung me. How it cut int'
m'eyes, m'cheeks, m'hands – how I
clung ont'the rope, bleedin' wi'the
brine, knowin', *knowin'* tha' the bow'd
40 **break an' every man be gargled**
t'his grave…
An' then the world were
calm…
Can yer imagine the stillness?
The quiet wonder o'the stillness?
How it lay upon our weathered
ship, breathless i'the storm-washed light?
'Twere as though we all'd died…
An'
50 **then… An' then I saw him. He were**
standin' top the juttin' main, his
night-hair dancin' spite no ocean
breeze. From his shoulders poured a purple
cloak – wine pourin' t'the wine-dark
sea – an' his face – his face *shone*.
I tell 'ee, tha' were the moment
when I knew ought'd ne'er a be
the same. Tha' m'world were now a
foreign place – a foreign island,
60 **hauntin' dreams…**
'Twere the Capt'n said
we'd take him – tha' he were the
son o'some king – tha' he'd buy
his weight in ransom – turn our

fate t'gold.
But I as knew this were
an evil thing – knew this man were
not a man – nay nor yet a vision
but the flesh o'holy flesh – 'scended
1570 from Olympos t'thunder in
our midst…
Yet the Capt'n an' all
the other crew bound him wi'their
chains – li'cargo caught an' keeled
they cast him t'the deck, laughin'
as he lay there, docile as a
doe…
Huh. Fools.
I can see their faces
1580 now: smilin' an' grinnin' an' laughin' –
Fools. None as thought he mi'be more
than royal gain – tha' he mi'be
more than eye's dim water sees – a
god brought low by human greed!
Fools.
How they danced an' sang an' jeered
roun' their young 'prince' – danced an' sang an'
jeered as though it were some wild
beast they'd felled…
1590 Huh. Have yer ne'er a
wondered at yer blindness? Ne'er a wondered
why yer canna see? It be *there.*
But yer eyes, an' yer mind, an' yer
heart er jus' too small. Jus' too small…
Somehow he were standin' – I couldn't
tell 'ee how, but he were standin' –
his chains a coilin' t'the deck –
his body glowin' wi'an eerie
fire…
1600 I could feel the ship a shakin'
wi'his power – feel unnatural
forces strainin' i'the hold.
We had new cargo ri'enough –

save i'were the livin' kind!
An'
then the deck burst.
Out o'the deck
burst shoots – vines dancin' – mast-ward windin' –
up, up – leaves unfurlin' – fat grapes
ripenin' t'a melody
o'wine…
We all were starin', 'mazed
by wha' we saw – an' then the stranger
changed –
Huh. Yer think I'm lyin', perhaps?
Think I'm tellin' tales int'm'dregs –
pissed outta m'mind?
Think wha' yer
like.
I saw.
Ye gods, I saw – saw
a god changin' 'fore m'eyes!
First
he were a lion, proud mane lashin' –
then a bear, pawin' at the air –
then a serpent –
then a bull –
a
panther –
a tiger –
a leopard –
I tell 'ee, 'twere the very sight
o'sorcery…only real,
jus' as real as ye er now…
Mayhap yer thinkin' tha' were the
end? Arrrh, 'tis ne'er the end – for they
wha' bound an' mocked him – they wha' dared
i'blindness t'conceive his ransom –
they were unt'his likeness touched,
an' caught amid the catalyst
o'change, changed int'the legless
dancers o'the sea!

Aye – dolphins
t'a man!
Only I were spared
(if yer call *this* spared).
He spoke t'me…
Huh. I can hear his words now,
li'honey pourin' i'm'ear –
1650 **thick wi'mystery – deafenin'**
li'rain…
He spoke t'me…
An' I
drowned for listenin' –
drowned i'the
mystery o'his words, until –

Nah. Ye'd not understand. None as
understand tha' didn't see.
1660 **None**
as haven't drowned…

XII. Semele

…so in you…
love me…
1670 ***love me?***
sense like violets
effacing
appetite of tears

XIII. Bacchantes

Evoë
Evoë
Evoë
Evoë
Evoë
Evoë
Evoë
Evoë
Evoë
Evoë

XIV. Naxos

Silence is better
it's opaque   ambiguous
and the waves
pass the waves
and echo to my sails
        Athens
and my father
        waiting
and the promise

Silence

waiting
home
yes
but wind wills
my sails
and I feel
I've forgotten
1710
me
you've forgotten
me
I'm waiting
by your ocean
waiting
for your love
pregnant with love
and silence is harsh
1720 harsh
lit morning
mourning
your love

and I see her
weeping
the sea is
weeping
her tears become me
1730 silence
becomes me
weeping the ocean
gleaning her
tears
in the promise
of morning
I'd not have
forgotten
not in the morning
1740 the mourning
of love

I think I can
hear him
yes
I can hear him
his voice sings honey
the livening air

50 where are you
calling
whose voice am I
calling
her name hurts my memory
I can't keep her name

So yes I'm coming
I see her
60 weeping
her beauty hurts me
moist with desire
and I feel that I
know her
how can I know her
the memory turning
Nysa turning
Nymphs were dancing
Satyrs dancing
70 the cave so fragrant
the sea is fragrant
I know I know her
have to know her

know I've forgotten
but cannot remember
sand and skin
and softly rolling
80 the moonlight

Silence

rolling
clouds like sea

to see him coming
his night-hair
flowing

home
yes
1790 sailing
home
to see my father
proudly standing
waiting to see me
see me returning

and yes I see him
like Zeus
I see him
1800 a god descending

with waves
descending
music and
laughter
waves like
laughter
and the Maenads
dancing
1810 and the Satyrs
dancing
over
dancing over
sand and waves
waves and laughter

I know he's
falling

320 my father's
falling
I know I've
forgotten
the sails
forgotten
my wife
forgotten
I know he's
falling
330 my father's
falling

like petals
like honey
like wine

descending
with waves descending
our love ascending
340

I know he's
falling

like petals
like honey

like wine

350

XV. Agavë

I'm hungry.

The wine is dizzy
in my brain –

1860

and the lion looks tasty,
so very tasty,
in the light of the flame.

*

The Strings of Orpheus

To Musaeus, my son – greetings.
I give you these teachings,
scarred on gold,
that through reciting
you may
remember.

1

………or the hunger of Thrace.
Man-eaters emerging from the stink
of their caves,
bodies sweaty with man-fat gleaming
hotter than Helios and Iris's wings,
her rainbow reflection
colours my brow
and I pray on my lyre,
play on my lyre for the living,
soothing beast-life…….
……..……………………….music
and the promise of living –
their faces calming to the psalming
of music, the breeze-life of leaves
laughing the trees,
and I know there'll be peace

2

…………so then……
….you…..my father?
You ask of [my] father?
Some speak of Apollo,

the sun god healing.
Others Oeagrus,
half-god of the sea.
I do not speak him

[…]

1910

my mother's the goddess
men call Calliope –
musing golden through the prophet's
dreams

3

1920

Say nothing and you'll hear me:
my music is silence –
like rippling water cocooned by
a tree.
Her shade is flowing,
down with the river,
purpling rocks to gleam with
the sky.

Have I seen you bathing
1930
smooth with the river?
Have I seen the [river]
caress with the sky?

[…]

But the linger of twilight
sings with the moonlight –
the lace-like petal
of the night-moth's wing

1940

4

Apollo rises. I see him like blindness
in the black of my eyes,
teaching ………………………..
……………………my vision…
and the………..half-heard…….
….remembrance……you 950
……………..…or the
promise of vision…………..
…………….the wine god tamed.
***"Dionysos!"*………**
..…..called from the cave…
***"Dionysos!"* ……………….**
………………..glimpsed in water

960

5

I remember Iolcus,
Jason, son of Aeson,
and the greed of Pelias……...
…..the fleece…………
and sailing…..in the eyes
of Medea…………………..
…………sailing to Colchis

970

[…]

the sirens stirred us with
their madness – brain-frying
madness!
I could see the Argonauts
reeling at their oars…………
………moaning…..the pleasure
….madness……………….

1980

and we……….to the rocks
……………the looming rocks
of Colchis…………………
my lyre playing,
drowning their madness…
pull of the oars……..
………..and free

1990

6

Where did I meet her?
…the moment of my birth
……..twined love and distant….
stars over Thessaly…….saw you
………………..knew you…..
the day of our meeting
swans were mourning…….
knew of our parting

2000

…death in [our] parting….
the Styx
dividing………abiding our distance
……………the half-light of
Hades
……never forgotten

2010

7

I'll sing of Apollo's bee-loving son,
Aristaeus…
How he……..the dryads
………..dancing…….poppies….
lusting
like his father….

tender skin
….silk through grass……..
and Eurydice…
……his thigh-loving hunger
……………………………
……………snakebite……
…………………then she…
…or watching out of dreams
the sulphurous earth
erupting………black horsed
chariot of Dis……then downward
they

8

Whose grief will weep the earth?
Whose tears will water life?
Who'll grieve for the griever?
Who'll grieve me when I'm gone?

Nine summers.
Nine winters.
Nine strings on my lyre.

I've waited for Eurydice.
I've waited for death.

[…]

then where the rock-mouth grows,
mocking sun-life with darkness,
be swallowed.
Breathe with darkness and grieve
with the dead.

There you'll find the godless river.
There you'll find the love you seek."

I thanked him. And passing to the

2060

[…]

…of the river………………
……….death giving Acheron
…….Charon scowling………
face rotting…………………..
……………corpseless shades
waiting for the crossing……..
…………….and I…………..

2070 **passing Cerberus**

[…]

"Eurydice, I'm coming…"

[…]

you lingered in the darkness,
knowing I would find you

2080 **……………………………**
………Persephone smiles
at the beauty of my lyre,
its music, our music
filling the deadland,
swelling the deadland
……….I take your hand
…mustn't look back……
……Elizabeth[?]………..
……*must see you*………

2090 **mustn't look back……….**
……Elizabeth[?]………..
must see you

I look at her through my moustache

she looks hairy

Leipzig that summer

Lou and Paul

how long am I here

Eurydice

9

I can't move
can't catch each

Running The grass

thought

how long am I here
how long have I been

Running The grass

here

dried urine

why won't she change the sheets
when I was the Kaiser
I always had clean sheets
I'd ride through Berlin

Running The grass

in my bed

Silence

and the people would admire
my sheets

but Eurydice's gone

and I'm running through the grass
tearing through streams
2140 over rocks
through trees
breathless
hunted
thing

I running

my life

2150

you see Köselitz how well I am
but they've taken my nightcap
locked my piano
I can't move
why won't she let me move

I hate her and her Jew-hating husband
but I can't tell her
can't
2160

over the burntland running
the brazen lands of Greece
running

I know they're after me
they'll tear me to pieces
everything I've done
my head floating
singing
2170 behind me

out to Lesbos
the wine-dark sea

and if I'm still

and if I'm still
I'll hear her speaking
longingly reaching
80 **the words of her rivers**
to listen
to listen

I'll follow her rivers
over the city
like music
like Wagner
their breath will be holy
sensual and holy
90

I'll see her face
know it well
for here they'll love me
truly love me
my girl will smile
"Good night, Professor"

when mourning has no tears

Poetry

Book Two

UNSTILL LIFE

'He painted a Divine Love who subjugated the Profane…'
~ Giovanni Baglione, *Life of Caravaggio*

The City of Valletta, Malta, 1607

At first the light is subtle.
It doesn't cut the skin,
doesn't preach a definition. Rather
it mates with the shadows,
too soft to be holy, smooth
like goats' milk.

And I think, perhaps,
that here is peace.
The peace of not knowing
nor needing to know. The peace
of abstraction you can't understand.

There are no angels here.
No apostles, no priests, no martyrs,
no whores.
This isn't Jerusalem, Emmaus, or Cana –
it's not even Rome.
You can't see Lazarus, Matthew, or Christ.
There is no God.
At first the light is subtle.

Then it cuts the skin.

Its blade is almost tender like a mother's
breast –
it suckles out form.
30 And slowly there emerges,
from the strangeness of this cataract,
a semblance of reality.
A painting of lines,
sinuous, knotting to the features of a man –
a mirror-mask of pain.
You can almost taste the moisture of his
eyes,
those bewildered, frightened, depths of light.
Taste the moisture of his eyes,
40 and know they catch your own.

Half-glimpsed, his veined hand twitches,
fumbles for a hold.
Fabric weaves like brushwork,
flows like velvet down the tautness
of his frame.
Each muscle screeches silence.
And the blood is almost beautiful.

50

"If my Lord would keep still.
The light.
Thank you."

Stupid sod.
Why does he think he's standing there?
Alof de Wignacourt.
Alof the fucking bore.
Still. I like his money.
60 I like his castle more. Nice, thick walls.
A man might almost be safe in here.
Safe.
Is anyone safe from God?
Still.
At least he's not the Pope.

I am tired of running.

Running and running and running,
grinding the pigment of the earth.
70 You'd think I'd scrape some hole,
some deep forgotten nowhere
where life grows thin.
Some grave in which to hide.
As if I could hide.

There're no graves for the living.
No shadows to caress the sunlit
guilt of living.
There's no redemption for the damned.
80 Everything I've done,
everything I am
is breathing,
will go on breathing,
breathing when my skeleton haunts
my skin,
when worms make love to the sockets
of my eyes –
a vain mortality.

90 So much for death.
So much death.

Look at him.
The Grand Master of the Order of St. John.
Bred on worship.
Fat with the poverty of Christ.
Nice, isn't it?

Where were *you*, my Lord
00 when God laughed at Milan?
People stinking in the fever
of their homes,
raw with the weeping sorrows
of their 'sins'.

It's said the city
reeked of prayer. That from San Giovanni
to the Northern Gate

you could smell the pitiful stench of tears.
110 Tears.
Their bodies drowned the river.
Skull-lit faces ghosting her light.
Dead eyes haunted by her waters' sun.

I remember my father

(I'm not sick, Michele)

sick in his eyes. The drawn lines
120 cutting down into his face,
laughing at his skin.

You, my Lord…you stand *rude*
in your health. Flesh
swelling your armour,
the cold comfort of your steel
a less tender kind of skin.

He died.
130

But of course he died.
They all died. *Go on dying.*
And the pity of it is…I didn't cry.
Couldn't cry. Not even when
they took him, shrouded, my father,
bereaved of light. Even when
they took him I couldn't cry.

"Quicker if you're quiet, my Lord."
140

And still. For fuck's sake,
stand still. If the boy can do it,
why can't you?
'Siege science'? God…

That summer… That summer,
when the lime trees sang down from Caravaggio,
their leaves stroking the ache of their fruit.
And the ripening shimmer of your thigh,

150 smooth in the grass,
soft with the dimpled kissing
of the breeze.

Chiara. My gypsy. So far from Giotto.
The dirt of your hands etching your life,
stained fingers staining the motion
of the sky.

I remember the dark smell of your hair,
160 its black touch moistening the virgin earth,
trembling dew,
the warmth of your breath
blushing the sunlight…

So far away.

I wish I could sleep.
Each wakeful night
170 sweats black without the stars.
Faces on faces, dead like moonlight –
unholy ghosts breathing my room's stale air.
They all hate me.
Baglione, Cesari…Tommasoni…yes…
and I know I should be sorry,
and I am sorry.
But it's too late.

Where does it begin?
180 My heart? My mind?
Or in the movement of my hand?
Painting is like touching,
but the touching is *so cold.*
I can see the bodies in the canvas,
they spark and crack like a goldsmith's forge…
But their terrible beauty
melts into nothing –
the unfeeling masks
of Bacchus and Christ.

190

My life's a rotting basket of fruit.
It ripens the eye, but turns the stomach –
each painful stroke
a testament for flies…

God

To think my life has brought me *here.*
To *you*, my Lord
200 and all *like you.* The rich. The vain.
The fat.
Fear, my Lord… It's *fear*, my Lord
that teaches men to crawl,
to barter, to worm,
to bastard their respect –
it's *fear*, my Lord
that whores them to deceive,
each smile, each kiss
the chancre of some dream –
210 it's *fear*, my Lord –

And I am afraid.

Oh God, I am afraid.

My prayers choke through the darkness…
But God doesn't listen. He *knows* what
an evil thing I've done.
There can be no light.
220 I'm like the Baptist, chained in the bowels
of Judea –
my gory head Pope Salome's prize.

Death loves me.
He is my muse.
I paint him and paint him, but he never leaves.
He's been a boy with flowers,
a weeping girl,
Judith, Holophernes, a den of vice…
230 When I see him in my glass

he smiles my name.
He wears my skin and a crown of weeds.
Death loves me.

I must get back to Rome.
I need to breathe the Tiber's rank, brown air.
I need to wash in her filth…yes…
'cleanse' my body of my *immortal* sins.

Even if I *could* go back
there'd be no peace. There's blood,
like memory, in every stone –
in each darkened turning
that lurks from the sun…

I remember Filli and Duto, grinning with wine,
the tang of their laughter
wounding the night.
I remember how
we'd gutter through the streets,
through the drunk illumination
of a painted scream,
like sunken angels,
moist with guilt,
the suck and thrust and stench of guilt –
a fist of hunger –
tears of glass –
Sbirri –
Bravi –

…the tenderness
of flesh and steel…

You.
It's always *you.* My archangel.
My demon.

I can feel your laughter in my ear.
The licking tongues of Medusa's hair,
teasing me

(Look, *look*)

And I know what I'll see,
what I always see
when the light cries out…

Nothing.

280 **Then our faces merged by shadows –**
pushing together,
tearing apart… Our pulse
quickens… And we
turn... A single movement, smooth
yet sharp… Lines kiss…
Agile words stretch into silence…
Judith screams… Magdalene
weeps… Water glimmers
in a dark carafe…
290

The lizard *bites.*

ANATOMY

O investigator of this anatomy of ours, do not be saddened by the fact that your knowledge is bought with someone else's death, but rejoice that our Creator has consecrated your mind on such an excellent instrument…

~ Leonardo, *Fragments of a Spiritual Autobiography*

It might be a dream,
10 but I think I remember
the shadow of wings.

I'm in my cradle
when this shape
glides down, blinding
the sunlight.

And though I don't know
what it is
20 I'm not afraid. I laugh.

And as I laugh
something soft
brushes my mouth…

"Un libro del cazzo!"
"Bastardo!"
"Fatti i cazzi tuoi!"

30

Consider, Salai, *just consider*,
the deformity of their conceit!
I may not be a 'learned' man,
exhuming *(as they can)*
dead words of dead ideas –
I may not have a toga
for a tongue, or like some grotesque
twist my face around the
40 'crystals' of the stars –
but even *I*
might quote what Marius
once said – yes, in Sallust, ha! –
that
"*Those who dress in the efforts of others*
seek to strip ME of my own…"

Don't they understand? Can't they see?
What use, Salai, *what use*,
50 are the feathered scratchings
of flightless minds?
What value are their words?
'Learned' words! Words on words,
inking death!

No…no,
Nature is my mistress.
I'll not rely on ageless dreams
of timeless years,
60 but on experience –
yes, *EXPERIENCE!*

They despise me because *I* can see.
Because *I'm* not afraid!
Oh they're afraid,
yes, afraid of the quenchless
thirsting of the dark –
afraid that the world
is stranger than it seems –
70 that Nature suffers

laws which cleave imagination!

FOOLS!
FOOLS!
FOOLS!

How they love to swagger
in their pious robes –
how they love their 'miracles'…

80

Huh! *Miracles.*
'Miracles' that melt the minds of men –
a senseless alchemy!

I tell you, Salai, they don't even know
the meaning of their skin!
How can they claim to think,
when everything *they are*
remains a mystery?

90 No –
NO! *They are as beasts!*
Mere conduits for filth –
unworthy of humanity!

Salai: *[yawns]* Bad day?

In me la morte, in te la vita mia;
100 tu distingui e concedi e parti el tempo;
quante vuo', breve e lungo è 'l viver mio.
Felice son nella tuo cortesia.
Beata l'alma, ove non corre tempo,
per te s'è fatta a contemplare Dio.

Force is Spirit,
inviolable,
invisible,
110 the gift of violence.

By violence it lives,
and at liberty
dies.

...and as well as a musician, my Lord,
I am also a specialist in the science of war.
I have studied what your 'experts'
recommend, and (in truth) find little
120 to commend them.
Oh they know the *rudiments* of war
(no doubt from many years
of sprawling on the field) but lack...
a maestro's application.

I, on the other hand, through tireless
effort and...ingenuity of mind,
have conceived an *esercito* of machines,
as unique as they are deadly,
130 and offered *only* to you.

If you will look here, my Lord,
you will see how I've designed
a vehicle, covered and with cannon,
which I believe will supersede
the elephant!

Imagine the chaos, my Lord,
you'd be like Hannibal!
140 Hannibal *with guns...*

The design is, in part, inspired
by a tortoise shell, and –

er...yes, my Lord...I am...also a painter.

Verrocchio, my Lord?

Yes, yes, he is...quite good.

150

The copper orb...er...adorning the Duomo

is also from his bottega…

I designed it. Well…I helped…

It's one of the greatest achievements
of Florence, my Lord.
Not that Florence is anything to Milan…
Milan's lovely.

Yes, my Lord…I also do plumbing…

Force is Spirit,
the mover
and remover,
a changer of bodies
so hungry
for death.

Salai: **It's funny. But I never used**
to think of Hell... Godless nights
without the *pleasure* of sin.
Weird shadows of a sickly flame
and the *smell*…

Yeah well…the dead wash less
than the living. Their puckered
flesh reeks on the bone.
A cold life…
rotting like purple flowers…

And I'd like to say it's beautiful.
That *somehow* it's beautiful.
But it's not.

***He* thinks it's beautiful…**
Such…*tenderness*… The way he strokes
her limbs… Peels back her skin...
It's almost… Yeah well, what do
I know?

I wonder who she was?
The Madonna? St. Anne?
...a lifetime of neglect

forgotten in the darkness...
Was she alone when she died?
200 Did she love?

He doesn't care.

Ser Piero, my father.
His dried olive eyes
won't look at my mother.

"That woman –
210 *Caterina –*
bought for 12 soldi
and the lies of sweet wine!"

Veggio co' be' vostr'occhi un dolce lume
che co' mie ciechi già veder non posso;
porto co' vostri piedi un pondo addosso,
che de' mie zoppi non è già costume.

220

And what of the eye?
Men say the eye gives light, Salai!
That it shines onto the world...
But think. How could the eye give
light?
Emanate for many miles,
yet take no time?

Why, to see the sun should
230 waste a month –
but look, it's there, in the sky,
the moment it's desired.

No, the eye *receives…*

Mmm…
typical Verrocchio…

240 Tall, sinewy Jesus Christ
(somewhat flat)…

Tall, sinewy John the Baptist
(somewhat flat)…

A really bad palm tree…
and a truly awful dove…

*Oh the talent…*it's blinding he ever
250 gets commissioned…
Then again, what do *they*
know about art?
Sandro's sucking on Lorenzo's tits,
and he can't paint.
Yes, and Ghirlandaio's no better –
nor Vannucci either.
Thank God he's gone back
to Perugia!
Too much cabbage, too much
260 of the time – *and his work* –
well, let's just say
it smelled.

A painter *(a good painter)*
should focus on two things.

Firstly, he should seek the
semblance of form –
drawing out of sketching
270 the patience of his eye.
This is vital. For if a painter
cannot see, *truly see*,
the patterning of lines,
how they curve and shade

the body into light,
subtly revealing
(yet also concealing) –
if he cannot see,
then what is his appeal?
280

Secondly, he must show
the life within, performing through
the body the gestures
of the mind.
It's simply not enough
to emulate alone –
a painter must know,
truly know,
the subject of his eye.
290 *This too is vital.*

Huh. But look at Verrocchio...
All his people are the same.
They do not breathe through
their 'illusion' –
they do not live.

Take the Baptist, look at his arm.
It's freakishly long.
300 Why, if he dropped it down
it would scrape the ground!
And his skin…
Yes…well…that's tempera for you.
The stale old eggs of a bound
excrescence!

Now the Flemish Masters,
they prefer oil…
The lucent warmth of flesh…
310 Even our own Cennini
wrote about it:

"Grind colour by colour,
as you did for fresco,
save where you worked them

with water
mix them with oil…"

Etcetera, etcetera…

320

Trouble is, the Florentines,
in spite of all their innovation,
are so *painfully* conservative.

Oh they'll build the greatest
Duomo in Christendom,
yes…
They'll carve sculptures
to rival the Ancients,

330

yes…
Some of them might even
master perspective…

But paint an altarpiece with oil?!

Hahahahahahahahahah

Actually, I doubt most of them
would even notice…

340

So. Do I do it?
Well…I suppose I can't make
it look any worse.
And after all,
Verrocchio said he could trust me…

Yes…it's *my* angel.

Why not?

350

The Prior of San Donato:

But when will it be finished,
'Maestro' da Vinci, uh?
Answer me that! The contract

said twenty-four months –
thirty at the most.
And you've taken…
360 **I don't know… What?**
Three years?
Don't think that running
off to Milan gets you out of it –
remember, you owe the commission
to your father…
Personally, *I've* always
preferred Botticelli!

370

29th January 1494

Pink cloth for making hose…….4 lire, 3 soldi.
Lining……………………………………….16s.
Making………………………………………..8s.
For Salai……………………………………..8s.
Jasper Ring…………………………………..13s.
Sparkling stone……………………………...11s.
For Caterina…………………………………10s.
380 **For Caterina…………………………………10s.**

Total: 8 lire, 2 soldi.

(Life is getting expensive.)

The old man told me that he was
***a hundred years old*,**
and that despite a certain weakness
390 **he felt no pain.**

Then, as we were talking, he died
the most *beautiful death*.

And so intrigued, I took him
to the mortuary…

Salai: Welcome to Imola… Why the *fuck*
are we here? …a gut of tangled streets,
all shit and knives… The drunken tang
of sex, pissing into violence,
and the thick breath of soldiers
sweating on our skin…

Which is nice. But even nicer
is the Borgia…

Our Cesare thinks he's Caesar…
Forlì, Pesaro, Rimini, Cesena…
Yeah well…the Romagna fell
to his hungering steel…
And we? *Oh we fell.*

There's something sick about power.
It's like a beautiful disease
…a death's-head between the thighs…
Silk rustles…
And for a moment you believe…

For it is among the horrors
of the dead, Salai,
that we shall find the truth
of the living.

Yet so many are cut
by the sharpness of their fear.

(Here, hold that)

They will not spend
their nights with corpses –
they cannot abide
the vile incision of the smell,
or the sight of quartered flesh,
flayed of immortality.

440 *(Keep the candle steady)*

And even if they were
unafraid,
they may not have the skill
to capture what they see.

But to be a painter, Salai,
you must understand
the brushwork within.

450

(Put your finger there – there)

Interesting…
she was with child…

Leo X: *Necromancy!* They say *Necromancy!*
I warn you, da Vinci – these so-called
460 'experiments'
spit in the face of God!

Leonardo: Holy Father, I –

A riddle, my Lords:

Their food is stolen,
470 *And many are drowned*
By those fearing
The sting of revenge.

The answer?
'Bees'.

And the Great Bird shall rise
Over Monte Cecero.

480 And the Universe shall wonder.
And eternal fame shall alight
On the nest where it was born!

Have made a study of wings.
In *Nature* nothing is wanting,
nothing superfluous.
Can reproduce, yes,
(bird = an instrument operating
according to mathematical laws)
490 with equivalent movements,
but not equivalent strength.

...deficient only in power of sustaining
equilibrium.

Man is not a bird.
But may partake in the life of a bird (?)
Imitation in the life of man...

500 *Think:*
the life residing in the bird's members
operates in accordance with their need.

Operation in relation to the *Impetus*
(power transmitted from mover
to the moveable).

Lines of movement rising in two kinds:
1. Spiral in the manner of a screw.
510 2. Rectilinear and curved.

The bird rises on high via a circular movement
in the pattern of a screw,
making its reflex movement
against the coming and flight of the wind.

NB: bird thus turns upon right
or left side.

520 *Observe:*

the analogy of air and water.
Birds swim in the air…

Motion of flight
= motion of swimming.

Tail of bird/rudder of ship…

Construct apparatus to imitate bird.
530 ***Remember:***
Life of bird's members
balanced to the whole.
Man must observe bird's movements.
Adapt to movements.
Preserve equilibrium.
Substance's resistance to air = air's to substance.
The beating of its wings lifts
the heavy eagle high
(cf. the sails of a ship).
540

A man with large enough wings
might overcome air resistance
(correct attachment, etc).

Must be free from waist upwards.
Balance like in a boat.
Body + machine in counterbalance –
shifting, where necessary, in relation
to changing centre of resistance.
550

Actually, less bird more bat…

Membranous wing structure.
~~**Membranes act as framework**~~
No rather act as method of connecting
framework…
True, feathered wings are more
powerful in structure
(penetrable – feathers are separate –
560 **air passes through them, etc)**
but bat's wings are useful.

Confused revolutions. Angle of resistance.
Varied elevation.
NB: bat's membrane binds whole.
(cf. canvas).

Ought to dissect bat.
Concentrate on this and design
accordingly…

570

Joints to be made of STRONG tanned leather.
Rigging to be made of cords
of VERY STRONG silk.

Important:
in case of accidents, test over water!

580 **Volo con le vostr'ale senza piume;**
col vostro ingegno al ciel sempre son mosso;
dal vostro arbitrio son pallido e rosso,
freddo al sol, caldo alle più fredde brume.

O time,
O jealous age,
you hunger all things
in a lingering death.

590

Even Helen,
for all her violent
beauty,
wept in the dust.

(What have I achieved?)

Corpus Hermeticum: **As I slumbered in my body**
600 **I heard the whisper of a voice**
as loud as infinity:

Silence

"I am Poimandres," it said,
"*Nous* of the Supreme.
I know you, and am with
you in eternity."

"Then teach me," I replied,
"that which is eternal."

610

And everything was Light.

Ginepro/Ginevra
VIRTUTEM FORMA DECORAT

Letter of Authorisation
18th August 1502

620

Know that I, Cesare Borgia, Duke of Valentinois, Lord of the Romagna, do hereby empower the bearer of this document, my most esteemed court architect, Leonardo da Vinci, to make a full and proper survey of the offensive and defensive capacities of my states and, finding anything wanting, to make such alterations as he may deem necessary. He and his entourage, as my agents, are to be received with all due hospitality, and he is to have every facility, be it castle, wall, or trench, open to his inspection for measurement and evaluation. Regarding state works which are already in the course of completion, it is my wish that every engineer be willing to further any undertaking that he may consider more advantageous to the protection and betterment of that state…

630

See? Borges business.
Open up…

Leonardo: **God's sake! How many times, Giacomo?**
You're a devil, boy. A salai!

640

Salai: **But, Maestro the –**

Leonardo: **I don't want to hear it. No more lies.**
Now, come and look at this…

Di Ser Piero
di.s.p.ero
dispero

silk tears the air
the tattered
scream of banners
and blood
nostrils and cannon
flare in the dust
shot and smoke and war-light
the blind eye of the sun
steel wounded like flesh
like tears
like hooves pounding
a *sfumato* of pain

A painter should be solitary,
absorbing everything he sees –
a second Nature,
whose mirroring of beauty
gifts beauty to the eye.

For the eye is justly called
the window of the soul.
It is first among the senses.
It informs and reforms
the patterns of the mind
…the sensus communis…
It is the lord of mathematics.
It has measured out the stars.
It is the father of architecture,
of perspective,
of the painter's hand.
It is…bright darkness,

God's light receiving –
beholding like a vision
a miracle of forms.
Here, in the eye,
690 here is the divine –
the touching of the Universe…

Do not pity the lonely painter.
For by the beauty of his eye,
and the vision of his hand,
he may be truly called
the grandchild of God.

700

Nel voler vostro è sol la voglia mia,
i miei pensier nel vostro cor si fanno,
nel vostro fiato son le mie parole.
Come luna da sé sol par ch'io sia,
ché gli occhi nostri in ciel veder non sanno
se non quel tanto che n'accende il sole.

710 Salai: 'Maestro da Vinci'… What do I first
remember?
A flourish of silk? *Il Moro's* fool?
The dance of planets at the turn
of his hand?
Or his eyes…cold like fire?
"Giacomo."

Nah…that's bollocks. I remember
the gold.
720 Just sitting there on the table…
A florin…*smiling*…
And I took it. My second day,
and I took it.

And it's funny…cos…I don't think
he minded.

"You're a devil, boy. A salai!"
But I don't think he minded...
That strange smile that
730 **wasn't there...**
***"Fuck you,"* it said,**
"You'll never understand."

I never understood him... An endless
apology of dreams...
Wings without birds...
"A bird should be free, Salai –
it should spread its wings."
Yeah well...the stallers thought he was mad...
740 **Good money for nothing... For a dream...**

Buchi della verità

the spit of lies
wine slurs into laughter
into words
angel of Bacchus
St. John of the wilderness
flesh
750 **in the torchlight**
swelling the darkness

Father where are you

A ghost
like an image.

760 **The Madonna**
and St. Anne.

The Child
from the womb.

The act of coitus
is so disgusting that,
770 were there no
pretty faces,
the human race would
surely cease…

Giorgio Vasari: Sometimes Heaven, transcending Nature,
gives forth a prodigy,
780 whose beauty, grace, and skill
so far exceed the mortal gifts of Man
as to echo after God!

Such a man was Leonardo da Vinci,
the son of Ser Piero da Vinci,
a notary of Florence…

790 I thought I was learning
how to live,

but I was learning
how to die.

Verrocchio: Tell me, di Credi,
does that angel look strange to you?

WILDERNESS

Anthony said, 'He who sits alone and is quiet has escaped from three wars: hearing, speaking, seeing: but there is one thing against which he must continually fight: that is, his own heart.'
~ *Sayings of the Desert Fathers*

The Desert of Chalcis, 374 CE

10

Αυτος γάϱ εστιν ή ειϱήυη ήμων ό ποιήσας τα
αμφότεϱα εν και το μεσότοιχον
του φϱαγμου λύσας την εχθϱαν
εν τη σαϱκι αυτου Αυτος γάϱ εστιν ή ειϱήυη ήμων
ό ποιήσας τα
αμφότεϱα εν και το μεσότοιχον
του φϱαγμου λύσας την εχθϱαν
εν τη σαϱκι αυτου **Cum enim ad**
20 **imaginem et similitudinem**
Dei conditi sumus ex vitio nostro
et personas
nobis plurimas superinducimus

plurimas

plurimas

and the wind laughs sand laughs laughs in
30 **the wind Rome seems unreal the**
laughter of a dream dreamt in

sand the promise of a dream dunes
of sunblight the laughter of hunger
wild eyed nowhere oasis dreaming

FOCUS

O Lord, have pity.
I'm blind,
40 **Can't see.**
Sand streams my eyes,
Strains my thoughts to visions.
O Lord, I cannot see.

O Lord, have pity.
My ribs hack through the
Carcass of my chest.
Laughing. Hungry.
Mad demons, Lord,
50 **In the madness of your sun.**

O Lord, have pity.
My skin's a blister,
Charred from bleeding.
Dried like your fig tree,
Withered in summer.
O Lord, Lord

I have lost my body
60 **And become my body.**

I have lost.

כּלה ***[kā/lã]***

רשעה ***[ré/šáʿ]***

שה ***[śeh]***

שבר ***[šé/ber]***

The day you spoke to me
the trees were in flower.

You came into the garden,
your palla, careless, trailing
on the ground, your eyes,
questioning. A smiling word,
silent amid the scent of thyme.

And I think, in that moment,
I knew. Not love, but its likeness,
trapped in water. Sunlight laughing
in the fountain's glass.

And I watched you speaking with Rufinus.
Your words caressing
in the arbour's shade, tender like blossom.
An intimate distance of petals
and hands, fragile like touching.

I hated him then.
The grace of his freedom
caging your smile. Each gesture
lithe with the bliss of desire.
Svelte with your innocence.

כלה

– רשעה

Are you there?

I can't see.

There're snakes here.

Snakes.

I don't like snakes.
110 They writhe out of the ground,
blackened coils of sinuous flesh.
Loathsome. Dancing.
If you watch them they begin to
blur. Shed their skin.
You can see the
tangled birth of limbs,
the writhing,
licking mass of limbs,
the hissing
120 swirl of silk and arms.
They rouse the
heated breath of sand.
Sultry. Yearning.

Haunches flexing
with a thrash
of heels.
You can feel their
voices bite the air.
130 Whoring words
through sunlight
burning.
The soothing touch
of scented hands.
I can feel
their fingers
snake my hair –
their kiss of
moonlight cool
140 ***like water –***
the bliss of
drowning –
angels' wings –
the tenderness
of blossom
falling –
the heady
musk of
lissom skin –

150 ***the tenderness***
of blossom
falling –
licking tongues –
angels' wings –
the agony of
blossom
falling –
blossom falling –
tongues of
160 ***wings –***
licking
tongues of
moonlight
falling –
blossom drowning –
angels' wings –
the agony
of moonlight
falling –
170 ***licking tongues –***
the bliss
of wings –
of tenderness –
of blossom
falling –
of tenderness –
of –

OUT!

180 **Ha-ha-ha-ha-ha-ha-ha-ha-**
ha-ha-ha-ha-ha –
"Hieronymus."
Who are you? Where are you?
"Hieronymus."
Who are you?
What do you want?
"I have watched
you squat amongst the bones,

your eyes longing for the guilt
190 *of the dead.*
How many tombs, Hieronymus?
How many tears until your corpse
is dust?
Did you think I'd hear you, Hieronymus?
Did you think I'd
find your body in
the dust?"
Lord?
Is that you? I can't see. There're
200 shadows in my eyes. Patterns dance like
broken sunlight. But the sun itself
has gone.
"Look at me."
I can't, Lord.
"Look at me."
Cicero?
Marcus Tullius Cicero? Here?
Alive? No. No, you're dead. Dead these
four hundred years. Murdered by
210 Marc Anthony. What are you?
"What are you?"
I, I am a Christian.
"Liar. Ciceronianus es,
non Christianus."
No.
"Yes. You grovel in your cell, your
belly low
to the earth.
You pray upon your knees
220 *and mortify*
your flesh.
But blood and filth
can't wash you clean,
Hieronymus.
You reek of death."
Get away from me.
"I know you, Hieronymus."
I am a Christian.
"Pagan. Idolater.

230 *Nabēlâ'. You lie to God,*
don't lie to me.
I know you. Each painful thought
buried in the sand.
Each sunburnt prayer
left unanswered.
We all want
to be loved, Hieronymus.
We all want to feel His love.
Sometimes it burns, Hieronymus.
240 *Is love a sin?*
Does it make of us
a wilderness?"

Leave me!

"The day she spoke to you
the trees were in flower.
I can feel her
sunlight
laughing off water.
The bitter reflection
250 *of petals*
and hands.
Can you feel it too,
Hieronymus?
Our words caressing
in the arbour's shade,
tender like blossom –
an intimate twining
of petals
and hands?"
260 Please.
"She never
loved you,
Hieronymus.
Never reached
out to touch you.
She never loved you,
Hieronymus.

But she loves me.
What are you, Hieronymus?
270 *Nothing. A corpse burnt by the*
madness of God.
But God doesn't love you,
Hieronymus.
He doesn't hear the
vomit of your heart.
No one loves you,
Hieronymus.
No one but me.
Worship me,
280 *Hieronymus.*
And I will
love you."

Help me.
Lord...help me.

Alone.

290 A breeze strokes
the sand,

and for a moment
it dances.

Who are you?

I know you.

300 And yet...

Yes.

Yes, I'll follow.

Your sunlight laughs
like water in my eyes.

And for a moment
0 **I can see.**

HEMISPHERE TWO

Critical Reincarnations

Book One

Cosmological Paradigm

Radiation Era

Time: 10^{-43} seconds – 30,000 years after singularity.

Temperature: 10^{34} K – 10^{4} K

Owing to the inherent mathematical complexities when attempting to conceive of infinite values our concept of 'time' necessarily begins after the point at which time might be said to have *literally* begun. Thus, because the Universe is speculated to have originated from a point of singularity in which 'temperature and density were infinite', and because mathematics, even within the field of Quantum Mechanics, finds such figures incalculable, time must be said to *meaningfully* begin at the earliest point of feasible, numerical definition. Consolidating the work of German physicist Max Karl Ernst Ludwig Planck, whose conception of quanta in 1900 laid the foundations of Quantum Theory, cosmologists are able to speculatively calculate back to within 'about a millionth of a second after the Big Bang'. This brief, dense and intensely hot period of the Universe's infancy is known as the Planck Era, and is generally thought to have been dominated by the effects of quantum gravitation; a particularly elusive phenomenon, whose prime constituent, the graviton, remains hypothetical. It is believed that during this period (0-10^{-43} seconds after singularity) the temperature of the Universe cooled to 10^{34} K, and is the earliest phase of what cosmologists have termed the 'primordial fireball' or 'Radiation Era'.[1]

Following the Planck Era, the next, and considerably more substantial epoch (10^{-43} seconds – 30,000 years after singularity) of the primordial fireball, comprised the fleeting 'Hadron' and 'Lepton' Eras, in which heavy atomic particles were formed and reacted at an incredibly high speed. The resultant state of combustion saw many of these particles suffer annihilation. Thus, only a relatively limited number of electron-positron pairs endured into the post-lepton phase, which began a mere second after the Big Bang and boasted a temperature of 5×10^{9} K. The remaining millennia of the Radiation Era were marked by a steady expansion of the Universe, concurrent with an increasing drop in its temperature.[2]

Textual Interpretation

Radiation Era:

- Nietzsche in Turin
- Socratic Interlude
- Dionysos Dismembered
- The Strings of Orpheus

Theory

Friedrich Wilhelm Nietzsche (1844-1900) was born the son of a Lutheran pastor from the Saxon village of Röcken and named after the German Kaiser, Friedrich Wilhelm IV. Indeed, viewed retrospectively through the writings of Nietzsche's mature life, both of these facts seem ironically auspicious. His vitriolic attack against Christianity in *The Anti-Christ* (1888), in which he describes the religion of his day as 'depraved', and his repeatedly expressed loathing for all things Germanic, bear witness to this irony as well as to a volatile, sometimes even hysterical, vein in his character. As a child, 'when thwarted in his desires, [he] would roll over on his back and kick his little legs in the air'. In adult life, when similarly provoked, he would lash out with his pen; a prime example of which is to be found in a letter written to his friend Franz Overbeck in 1882. Here the philosopher, recently rejected by the Russian poetess Lou Salomé, explodes his bewildered frustration onto the page:

> I have suffered from the humiliating and tormenting memories of this summer as from a bout of madness… It involves a tension between opposing passions which I cannot cope with… I am now being broken, as no other man could be, on the wheel of my own passions… My lack of confidence is now immense – everything I hear makes me feel that people despise me… My relation to Lou is in the last agonising throes – at least that is what I think today. Later – if there will be any 'later' – I shall say something about that too. Pity, my dear friend, is a kind of hell – whatever the Schopenhauerians may say.
>
> I am not asking you, 'What shall I do?' Several times I thought of renting a room in Basel, of visiting you now and then, and attending lectures. Several times too I thought of the opposite: to press on in my solitude and renunciation, till I reach the point of no return, and – [3]

It is his closeness to the brink of madness, of passion, of hope, and of death, which renders Nietzsche's personality at once so repulsive and alluring. That he was himself keenly aware of his paradox is evident from the numerous self-reflexive references which permeate his work. In one breath he can describe himself as 'dynamite', in the next as a 'buffoon'. The would-be destroyer of decadence is, by his own admission, a '*décadent*'. Yet in the same paragraph, from his eccentric autobiography *Ecce Homo* (1888), he proudly declares himself the *décadent's* 'antithesis'. This playful/terrifying courtship of personal instability is central to the Nietzschean aesthetic; and, as a consequence, it is virtually impossible to formulate a stable definition of the philosopher's 'true' position. Indeed, in his essay *Nietzsche's Voices*, Ronald Hayman argues that, far from possessing a unified philosophical objective, Nietzsche's writings embody 'a variety of voices' whose subjective alterity is counterpoised by a Dionysiac allegiance to 'falsification'. Thus, it is through this restless assumption of masks – from the madman in *The Gay Science* (1882) to the anti-prophet in *Thus Spoke Zarathustra* (1883-5) – that Nietzsche externalises his internal fluidity; a condition perhaps most eloquently expressed through the voice of the philosopher in *Beyond Good and Evil* (1886):

> when I analyse the event expressed in the sentence 'I think', I acquire a series of rash assertions which are difficult, perhaps impossible, to prove – for example, that it is *I* who think, that it has to be something at all which thinks, that thinking is an activity and operation on the part of an entity thought of as a cause, that an 'I' exists, finally that what is designated by 'thinking' has already been determined – that *I know* what thinking is. [...] In place of that 'immediate certainty' in which the people may believe in the present case, the philosopher acquires in this way a series of metaphysical questions, true questions of conscience for the intellect, namely: 'Whence do I take the concept of thinking? Why do I believe in cause and effect? What gives me the right to speak of an "I", and even of an "I" as cause, and finally of an "I" as cause of thought?' Whoever feels able to answer these metaphysical questions straight away with an appeal to a sort of *intuitive* knowledge, as he does who says: 'I think, and know that this at least is true, actual and certain' – will find a philosopher today ready with a smile and two question-marks. 'My dear sir', the philosopher will perhaps give him to

> understand, 'it is improbable you are not mistaken: but why do you want the truth at all?'[4]

By rejecting the Cartesian dictum *cogito, ergo sum*, indeed the very notion of a definite, cognitive identity, Nietzsche's philosopher appears to think himself out of existence. However, the implied maxim *I cannot think I am* is equally unsatisfactory, for even this negation is an act of personal definition. What matters then is not the impossibility of cognitive self-construction, but its *improbability* as an 'objective truth'. That the philosopher is conceiving himself as the cause of his thoughts (and therefore as a valid 'thinker') is obvious; indeed, he does it again and again. What matters, however, is the *subjectivity* of this process, for subjectivity necessarily implies fluidity: the fluidity of a perspective through time. Consequently, when the philosopher denies the proposition of intuitive self-knowledge, he is, in fact, seeking to bring us toward a deeper understanding of the dialectic between *internal* flux and *external* form; a dialectic that criticises the foundations of a stable identity, and thus necessarily draws the nature of selfhood into a dramatic tension.

It is this singular duality of the self, this duality of flux and form, which harmonises the fractured notes of Nietzsche's voices into a discordant melody. This overarching dualism is perhaps given its most explicit argumentation in his first book, *The Birth of Tragedy out of the Spirit of Music* (1872), for it is here that Nietzsche inaugurates his famous Dionysos-Apollo binary. Despite being criticised for its Wagnerian idolatry and Schopenhauerian aestheticism, *The Birth of Tragedy* is in fact seminal for understanding Nietzsche's metaphysical polymorphism. Indeed, this innate instability, at once manipulated and manipulating, manifests the inherent complexities of his plurality. Here Nietzsche the writer and Nietzsche the written merge through what may be termed a negative ontology – a symphonic compression of binaries, whose very construction initiates a deconstructive pattern of negation. Right from the onset the psycho-textual question of identity is paramount, for *The Birth of Tragedy* is arguably not a work of philosophy but an exercise, albeit an eccentric one, in classical philology. At the time of its composition, the twenty-six-year-old Nietzsche held the chair in that field at the University of Basel, and indeed it would not have been unreasonable to expect him to have written in a manner more in keeping with the philological conventions of his day. That he chose to effectively ignore them, and instead write a quasi-metaphysical work, seemingly in praise of Wagner's music, did much to alienate him from his contemporaries. The extent of this alienation is highlighted by Michael Tanner in his introduction to Shaun Whiteside's 1993 translation of the text:

> The impact of its first publication was very considerable, though not, for the most part, in the way that Nietzsche could have hoped. Certainly its dedicatee, Richard Wagner, was thrilled by it... [b]ut academic opinion was outraged, as was only to be expected, though it seems that Nietzsche had not anticipated it. An old enemy from his schooldays, Ulrich von Wilamowitz-Moellendorf, fired an initial salvo in May with the title *Philology of the Future! A Reply to Friedrich Nietzsche's Birth of Tragedy*, a piece of abusive academic polemic remarkable even by the standards that prevail in the world of scholarship. Nietzsche didn't reply himself, but his close friend Erwin Rohde weighed in with a rejoinder in the form of an open letter to Wagner, called *Afterphilologie!*, a difficult word to translate: it means, roughly, 'Pseudo-Philology', but *After* is also the German for 'arse', and there is a long tradition...of using the word in both senses simultaneously. Wagner, too, joined in the fight; and Wilamowitz continued the undignified squabble. Like all such battles, the outcome was indecisive, except that there was no doubt that Nietzsche had done himself a great deal of harm in professional circles, at the same time as he had decisively launched himself on the cultural scene.[5]

The above passage is revealing in a number of ways. Firstly, there is the issue of Nietzsche's apparent naivety; something ostensibly borne out by a letter written to his former teacher, Friedrich Ritschl, shortly after the book's publication. Here Nietzsche expresses his desire 'to win over the younger generation of classical philologists', adding that it would be 'shameful if [he] did not succeed in doing so'. Given what we know of this younger generation's reaction to *The Birth of Tragedy*, and indeed the academic style in which they wrote their own philological works, Nietzsche's hyperbole seems more than a little absurd; so much so, in fact, that one begins to question his sincerity. As a professor working within the field it would have been expected for him to know what the reaction was likely to be. This being the case, he simply cannot have expected his 'manifesto' to have been anything other than a calculated explosion, and thus any pretension to the contrary seems suspiciously affected. Secondly, there is the issue of 'Afterphilologie', or 'Pseudo-Philology' – something that leads us directly into the realm of masks. Although Rohde's *double entendre* was intended as a sting against Wilamowitz it can nevertheless be seen as reflecting back onto *The Birth of Tragedy*. Here we have a text that both is and is not philological. The subject belies the form and the form the subject. As the work of Friedrich Nietzsche, Professor of Classical Philology at the University of Basel, it is indeed 'After' in both senses of the word. However, this may very well be the point, for by constructing so subversive a book, whilst simultaneously making claims on those he was most likely to alienate, Nietzsche succeeds in generating an act of personal displacement.[6]

This act of displacement is mirrored in the central argument of the text, namely that Hellenic culture can be understood as comprising two opposing forces, the Apolline and the Dionysiac, and that these forces achieve a paradoxical unity through the Choral Odes of Attic Tragedy. Here it is worth expatiating on the etymology of these terms in order to understand how Nietzsche is using them to interpret what he sees as the central tenet of Classical aesthetics. 'Apolline' is derived from the Greek god Apollo, the son of Zeus, King of the gods, and Leto, a Titaness. He was the twin-brother of Artemis, goddess of wildlife and women, and his central place of worship was Delphi, the site of his famous 'oracle'. Apollo's epithet 'Phoebus' (Bright One) bears witness to his role as a god of light, manifest in both his literal association with the sun and as a metaphor for his dominion over prophecy, medicine, poetry and music – all of which might be said to illuminate mankind. Paradoxically, he was also the god of plague, and his roles in both *The Iliad* (c.720 BCE) and the *Homeric Hymn to Apollo* (c.800-500 BCE) are characteristically violent. However, for the Greeks of the Classical Age, the period in which Attic Tragedy flourished, Apollo was seen as the epitome of rational order, and it is worth remembering that the dictums 'Know thyself' and 'Nothing to excess', so indicative of the Hellenic aspiration toward a reflexive moderation in all things, adorned the wall of his shrine at Delphi. As the classicist E. R. Dodds remarks in his philosophical study, *The Greeks and the Irrational*:

> The Greeks had always felt the experience of passion as something mysterious and frightening… Aristotle compares the man in a state of passion to men asleep, insane or drunk: his reason, like theirs, is in suspense.[7]

Thus, Apollo was cast as a protector of civic order, a limiter of passion whose light enabled both the individuating benefits of self-knowledge, and from this knowledge, a life of equilibrium.

Whereas the 'Apolline' may be said to embody the spirit of individuating control, the 'Dionysiac', by contrast, determines quite a different character. The cultural origin of the god Dionysos, from which the term 'Dionysiac' derives, is difficult to establish. Unlike Apollo, he is mentioned only once in both *The Iliad* and *The Odyssey* (c.700 BCE), and each incident is of very minor significance, amounting to nothing more than an aside and ascertaining little of the god's nature. We learn of his connection with the island of Dia, with Mount Nysa, Ariadne, Theseus, Artemis, Lycurgus and the sea-nymph Thetis, but not a word is spoken about his provenance or powers. In order for such allusions to have worked it is clear that the Homeric audience of the eighth century BCE would have been familiar with his mythology, and thus that his cult had been established in Greece for some time. However, anything more substantial than this cannot be inferred.

The Homeric Hymns to Dionysos (c.800-500 BCE), by contrast, are more revealing. The first is primarily concerned with the place of his birth, and during the process of rejecting many traditions, reveals the profound complexity of his myth:

> Some say it was at Drakanon,
> some on windy Ikaros,
> some in Naxos,
> divine child,
> bull-god.
>
> Others say it was beside
> the deep whirling waters
> of the river Alpheios
> that Semele gave birth to you,
> pregnant from Zeus who loves thunder.
>
> Others, lord, say you were born at Thebes.
>
> I say they lie...[8]

Clearly the origins of Dionysos were very much a point of conjecture, with many different places claiming a cult status for the god. After boldly giving these rivals the lie, the anonymous poet of the *Hymn* asserts his/her own claim:

> The father of men and gods gave birth to you
> far from human beings,

hiding you from white-armed Hera.

There is a certain Nysa,
a mountain peak flowering with forests,
far off in Phoenicia,
near the streams of Egypt…[9]

For the poet it appears to be Zeus and *not* 'Semele' who is the mother, and the *Hymn* is the earliest extant source (after *The Iliad*) to attribute Dionysos' place of birth as 'Nysa'. What is more, we are also told precisely where Mount Nysa is: 'far off in Phoenicia,/ near the streams of Egypt'. This is important for a very specific reason: it expresses the god's foreignness. Whereas 'Drakanon' was most probably located on the island of 'Kos', and 'Ikaros' and 'Naxos' are both islands in the Aegean, Phoenician 'Nysa' is something manifestly distinct from the Hellenic world. Dionysos, it would seem, is not of Greek origin; and yet there is something in the next stanza which implies that he is not of Phoenician origin either:

No one comes there with his ship,
none of the human beings with the power of
speech.
For it has no harbour,
no place to anchor for the swaying ships,
but sheer cliff circles it, very high
on every side, and it grows
many lovely, desirable things…[10]

The above presents us with a non-place, a fantasy whose fabulous geography takes us beyond the bounds of human experience. It is a pure myth, whose geographical reference, rather than elucidating the issue, actually makes things more confusing. Indeed, in many ways, the above is reminiscent of Said's description of the 'European invention' of the Orient:

a place of romance, exotic beings, haunting memories and landscapes, remarkable experiences.[11]

Thus the 'Nysa' of the *Hymn* can be seen as an Oriental vision in which male gods give birth and to which no human has access, save through the epiphany of poetry. It is clearly 'somewhere else' as it is clearly 'nowhere', and consequently it is tempting to read 'Nysa' as a metaphor for paradise. Certainly there are striking similarities between the *Hymn*'s description of Mount Nysa and that of the Elysian Fields in Book Six of *The Odyssey*:

> But about your own destiny, Menelaus,
> dear to Zeus, it's not for you to die
> and meet your fate in the stallion-land of Argos,
> no, the deathless ones will sweep you off to the
> world's end,
> the Elysian Fields, where gold-haired Rhadamanthys
> waits,
> where life glides on in immortal ease for mortal man;
> no snow, no winter onslaught, never a downpour
> there
> but night and day the Ocean River sends up breezes,
> singing winds of the West refreshing all mankind...[12]

Each describes a tranquil haven sheltered from the harsh realities of nature, and each is inaccessible to the living (i.e. the mortal). Indeed, it is possible that the *Hymn*'s 'divine child', born from his male mother into a paradise, in some way alludes to a god of soteriological significance. Nysa may only be inaccessible to the living, and, like the Elysian Fields, may await the favoured after death. However, at present, this must remain a point of speculation.

Just as we can read 'Phoenicia' as a symbol for the god's foreignness, so the Egyptian 'streams', rather than serving as a literal geographical signifier, may well allude to the cultural influences of Dionysos' cult. Certainly, it is interesting to note that in his *Histories* the Halicarnassian scholar, Herodotus equates Dionysos with the Egyptian god 'Osiris', an identification whose mythologic implications will be discussed presently. For now it is sufficient to observe that if we accept a metaphorical interpretation of the *Hymn*'s geography, then the description of Nysa as a Phoenician mountain 'near the streams of Egypt' need not lead us to conclude that the cult of Dionysos was necessarily of Phoenician origin. What is important is that the *Hymn* focuses our attention on the god's otherness – something manifest in the *Hymn*'s repeated use of rejection. Dionysos is constantly being pushed away. He is *not* from 'Drakanon', 'Ikaros' or 'Naxos', he is *not* from 'Thebes', nor did 'Semele' give birth to him by the 'river Alpheios'; and even when we are given a piece of positive information in the form of the Phoenician connection, this is swiftly contradicted by its geographical inaccessibility. Rather he is a *total* foreigner; a foreign god, whose mountain home, unlike the Olympos of the Old Greek Pantheon, cannot be seen. Dionysos, like Nysa, is something elusive.[13]

The elusive nature of the god is further compounded by the *Hymn*'s closing address. Here the poet states:

> I greet you Dionysos,
> god who appears as a bull,
> you and your mother Semele,
> whom they call Thyone.[14]

By asserting that 'Semele' is Dionysos' mother the *Hymn* directly contradicts itself; a contradiction which may on the surface seem highly problematic. It has been clearly stated that 'The father of men and gods gave birth to you'; that Zeus is the mother and not Semele. By suddenly changing the maternal dynamic the reader might well feel more than a little disconcerted. However, despite its paradoxical appearances, there are two explanations for Dionysos' bizarre parentage, the first being mythological and the second being textual. In his *Histories*, Herodotus states that Dionysos was 'the son of Semele, daughter of Cadmus'. He also goes on to say that

> Dionysus, as soon as he was born, was sewn up in Zeus' thigh and taken to Nysa, which is in Ethiopia above Egypt.[15]

What seems clear from the above is that Dionysos was born twice, once from his female mother Semele, the daughter of Cadmus, King of Thebes, and once from his male mother Zeus, the King of the gods. It seems likely that it is this myth which the author of the *Hymn* had in mind, and, that being the case, the contradiction evaporates. Indeed, the apparent starkness of the 'contradiction' is most probably due to the fragmentary nature of the *Hymn*. The surviving text is manifestly incomplete, abruptly switching as it does from the beautiful description of Nysa to what is clearly the middle of a speech by Zeus:

> There is a certain Nysa,
> a mountain peak flowering with forests,
> far off in Phoenicia,
> near the streams of Egypt.
>
> No one comes there with his ship,
> none of the human beings with the power of
> speech.
> For it has no harbour,
> no place to anchor for the swaying ships,
> but sheer cliff circles it, very high
> on every side, and it grows
> many lovely, desirable things.
>
> 'And they will set up many statues in the temples.
> As these things are three,
> so every three years forever
> shall mortals sacrifice to you
> perfect hecatombs at your festivals'.
>
> The Son of Kronos spoke
> and nodded with his dark brows…[16]

If the text is incomplete, as it certainly appears to be, then it is reasonable to assume that a fuller treatment of the myth would have been contained within the missing stanzas. Indeed, the question of textual corruption is paramount, for the majority of *The Homeric Hymns* can only be traced back to the fifteenth century. Apart from a few scraps of ancient papyri, ninety percent of *The Hymns* are the material product of the Renaissance, with the first printed edition being published in 1488. Edited by the Florentine humanist, Demetrios Chalcondyles, *The Hymns* appeared with *The Iliad* and *The Odyssey* as the collected works of Homer. They were also incomplete, excluding what are now the last twelve lines of the *1st Hymn to Dionysos* and the entire *1st Hymn to Demeter*. These two texts were not discovered until 1777, appearing, of all places, in Moscow. Consequently it is no wonder that the *Hymn* should present such interpretive difficulties, and any conclusions drawn from so uncertain a document must be tempered with caution.

The *2nd Hymn to Dionysos* is more forthcoming. Not only is it complete, but the god also takes an active role in the narrative, thus enabling us to ascertain more of Dionysos' nature. After an invocation, in which Semele is once again described as his mother, we are presented with Dionysos, in the form of a young man, standing on 'a shore of the desolate sea':

> Dionysos
> I will call to mind,
> son of glorious Semele.
>
> How he appeared
> on a shore of the desolate sea,
> there, where the cliffs jut out,
>
> looking like a young man
> in the flower of youth.
>
> Rich dark hair flowed round him,

> a purple robe hung down
> from his strong shoulders...[17]

In the above it is possible to perceive similar themes to those already discussed in relation to the previous *Hymn*. Firstly, there is the issue of the 'Rich dark hair' which 'flowed round him', something that may be symbolic of foreignness. It is true that the 'Bronze Age' Greeks of the Homeric epics are depicted as having long hair; indeed *The Iliad* frequently gives Agamemnon's army the epithet 'long-haired Achaeans'. However, by the time the *Hymn* was written (and certainly if it was composed during the latter century of its timeframe, c.600-500 BCE) the Greeks had come to associate long hair with barbarians. The sixth century philosopher Pythagoras was known as the 'long-haired Samian' because he is said to have worn his hair long as a 'tribute to his Phoenician ancestry'. It was a mark of *otherness*, and whilst it could be argued that the author of the *Hymn* was using the image of long hair as a Homeric device, it could equally signify the foreign nature of the god. Secondly, there is the 'purple robe' which 'hung down from his strong shoulders'. Admittedly, this could be nothing more than a simple signifier of godhood, for as the historian Robin Lane Fox remarks in his study of Alexander the Great, a purple robe was one of the 'usual' trappings of a god (and those who would impersonate them). He cites the story of the Athenian painter Parrhasios who

> had walked in the streets of Athens, dressed in a purple robe, a golden crown, a white ribbon and golden shoes, carrying a golden staff and claiming to be son of Apollo, god of the arts...[18]

and that of the faith healer Menecrates who

> cured various cases of epilepsy of which the doctors had despaired and as epilepsy was known as a sacred disease, its healer, who asked for no pay, could fairly claim to be divinely inspired: Menecrates thus called himself Zeus, dressed in the usual purples and golds

> and surrounded himself with a troupe of former patients, who also attired themselves as gods [19]

As can be seen, both of these men signified their 'divinity' in the culturally accepted manner, and likewise the 'purple robe' of Dionysos undoubtedly carried these connotations. Nevertheless, there remains the fact that up until the end of the sixth century BCE the Phoenicians imported all the purple dyed cloth in Magna Graecia. Famous throughout the Mediterranean world for their sea-faring enterprise, the Phoenicians offered Hellenic civilisation 'Egyptian and Assyrian goods'. By having Dionysos dressed in a 'purple robe' the author of the *Hymn* might well have been making a comment about the imported nature of the god. Certainly it is interesting to note that the *Hymn*'s main narrative concern is with sea faring. After appearing 'on a shore of the desolate sea' Dionysos is kidnapped by Tyrrhenian (Etruscan) pirates and lies bound on the deck of their ship, awaiting ransom. He is for that moment effectively cargo; a product to be shipped somewhere else, and as such ripe with metaphor.[20]

Another important revelation of the *Hymn* is its manifestation of the god's powers. In order to escape from the pirates, Dionysos transforms into a lion:

> ...then the god
> turned into a lion
> inside the ship, terrible,
> on the highest part,
> and roared loudly. [21]

a feat that unsurprisingly terrifies the crew:

> Everyone was terrified,
> they ran to the stern
> in a panic...[22]

He also demonstrates a supernatural power over vegetation:

> Suddenly a vine
> sprang up the sail
> to the top,
> spreading out both ways,
> and grapes hung down
> in clusters
> all over it
> and a dark ivy
> curled
> around the mast
> blossoming with flowers
> and sprouting
> lovely berries…[23]

Here something fundamental about the god is revealed; not only do we become acquainted with his power, but with his *type* of power. His province is manifest through the dance of the vine. He is a vegetation deity, and, more importantly, a vegetation deity deeply associated with intoxication.

The vegetation deities of the ancient world were inextricably entwined with the passage of the seasons and thus with the concept of fertility. They represented, according to James Frazer,

> the yearly decay and revival of life, especially of vegetable life…personified as a god who annually died and rose again from the dead. In name and detail the rites varied from place to place: in substance they were the same.[24]

A similar expression of this parity can be found in Laurence Coupe's study, *Myth.* Here we are presented with the story of Osiris as the archetypal fertility narrative:

> Osiris, god of vegetation, being the object of universal love and admiration, provokes the envy of his brother Set. Set has him buried alive in a coffin, which is then thrown out to sea. Isis, goddess of vegetation, finds his body, washed up at the

> Lebanese port of Byblos and caught in a tree. She hides the corpse, but Set finds it and cuts it into pieces, scattering it over the land of Egypt. Isis recovers all the parts except one, the penis. Even so, having the gift of magic, she is able to make Osiris father a child, Horus. Thereafter, on ceremonial occasions the reigning king of Egypt represents Horus and the deceased king is referred to as Osiris. This story might serve as the paradigm...of fertility myth.[25]

Osiris (Life) in the guise of Summer is killed by Set (Death) in the guise of Autumn. In his coffined state Osiris represents the seed in the field, with his subsequent dismemberment indicative of the harvest. After this act of individuation follows a period of Winter in which Isis, in her role as the mother of Spring, remakes Osiris, thereby regenerating the Earth. The miraculous nature of this event is characterised by the improbable birth of Horus.

Here it is worth recalling Herodotus' claim that 'Osiris [is] the Dionysos of the Greeks'. Indeed, the mythological similarities between Osiris and Dionysos are clearly discernable when one considers that the god was born twice. These similarities deepen further when we examine these lines from the opening speech of Euripides' *Bacchae* (c.406 BCE):

> I am Dionysus, son of Zeus. My mother was
> Semele, Cadmus' daughter. From her womb the fire
> Of a lightning-flash delivered me.
>
> [...]
>
> I see
> Here near the palace my mother's monument, that
> records
> Her death by lightning. Here her house stood; and
> its ruins
> Smoulder with the still living flame of Zeus's fire –

> The immortal cruelty Hera wreaked upon my
> mother.[26]

What these lines reveal is a reason for Dionysos' double birth. It was Zeus' lightning that killed his first mother Semele, thus forcing the King of the gods to take up the maternal mantle. Not only this, but the death was the result of his wife Hera's machinations. Like Osiris' fate at the hands of Set, so Dionysos, as a foetus in Semele's womb, meets his 'demise' as the result of another's jealousy.

This story of divine vengeance and rebirth is fleshed out further in Ovid's *Metamorphoses* (8 CE). On hearing that 'Semele [is] pregnant by great Jove [Zeus]', Juno (Hera) disguises herself as Beroe, Semele's 'Epidaurian nurse', and connives her way into the girl's confidence. It is from this position of trust that she enacts her terrible revenge:

> They talked of many things and then the name
> Of Jove came up. 'I pray it may be Jove',
> She sighed, 'All these things frighten me. So often
> Men, claiming to be gods, have gained the beds
> Of simple girls. But even to be Jove
> Is not enough; he ought to prove his love,
> *If* he is Jove. In all the power and glory
> That's his when heavenly Juno welcomes him,
> Beg him to don his godhood and take you
> In the same power and glory in his arms'.
> So Juno moulded Cadmus' daughter's mind.[27]

That night Semele asks her lover to grant her anything she may ask for. Unwittingly Jove agrees, pledging his word as a god to give Semele whatever she might wish. Thus, when she asks to see him in his divine form, the King of Heaven cannot but obey:

> He would have locked her lips;
> Too late: her words had hastened on their way.
> He groaned: her wish could never be unwished,
> His oath never unsworn. In bitterest grief

> He soared ascending to the ethereal sky,
> And by his nod called up the trailing clouds
> And massed a storm, with lightnings in the squalls,
> And thunder and the bolts that never miss.
> Even so he tried, as far as he had power,
> To curb his might, and would not wield the fire
> With which he'd felled the hundred-handed giant.
> That was too fierce. There is another bolt,
> A lighter one, in which the Cyclops forged
> A flame less savage and a lesser wrath,
> Called by the gods his second armament.
> With this in hand he went to Semele
> In Cadmus' palace. Then her mortal frame
> Could not endure the tumult of the heavens;
> That gift of love consumed her...[28]

The rest is pretty much as Herodotus would have it:

> From her womb
> Her baby, still not fully formed, was snatched,
> And sewn (could one believe the tale) inside
> His father's thigh, and so completed there
> His mother's time. Ino, his mother's sister,
> In secret from the cradle nursed the child
> And brought him up, and then the nymphs of Nysa
> Were given his charge and kept him hidden away
> Within their caves, and nourished him on milk.[29]

Dionysos is born anew from the 'womb' of his father to be suckled in paradise.

There is another version of the Dionysos myth; one that fits even closer with the Osiris paradigm. According to the classicist, Carl Kerényi it originated in ancient Crete, thus predating the Theban narrative of Zeus and Semele:

> The love of Zeus and Semele is radically humanized. In an older version of the story of the birth of Dionysos, Persephone is seduced by her own father. This version appeared until late antiquity in the

> didactic poems of the Orphics, but in the first century B.C. the historian Diodorus Siculus states expressly that this was the Cretan version. The vacillation between Persephone and Demeter, preserved in Diodorus, corresponds to the equally vacillating iconography of the Knossos coins, which show a Demeter-like head of Persephone in connection with the labyrinth. Here we have an allusion to the so-called Orphic story of the god's birth, known to us as the birth of Zagreus. This myth seems to differ from the Theban myth of the god's birth even in the person of the mother.[30]

Apart from a few scattered fragments embedded in the works of grammarians, historians and philosophers, the myth of Zagreus finds its fullest expression in the sixth book of the *Dionysiaca* (c. fifth century CE), a sprawling, baroque epic by the Egyptian poet Nonnos. In characteristically florid style, Nonnos describes the rape of Persephone by her father Zeus and the startling events that ensue:

> Ah, maiden Persephoneia! You could not find how to escape your mating! No, a dragon was your mate, when Zeus changed his face and came, rolling in many a loving coil through the dark to the corner of the maiden's chamber... By this marriage with the heavenly dragon, the womb of Persephone swelled with living fruit, and she bore Zagreus the horned baby, who by himself climbed upon the heavenly throne of Zeus and brandished lightning in his little hand... But he did not hold the throne of Zeus for long. By the fierce resentment of implacable Hera, the Titans cunningly smeared their round faces with disguising chalk, and while he contemplated his changeling countenance reflected in a mirror they destroyed him with an infernal knife...his limbs...cut piecemeal by the Titan steel...[31]

Perversely, having just been brutally dismembered, the infant god springs into life as 'Dionysos' before undergoing a series of fantastic *Metamorphoses* :

> [He] changed into many forms: now young like crafty Cronides…now as ancient Cronos, heavy-kneed, pouring rain. Sometimes he was a curiously formed baby, sometimes like a mad youth… Again, a mimic lion he uttered a horrible roar… Sometimes he poured out a whistling hiss from his mouth, a curling horned serpent covered with scales… Then he left the shape of the restless crawler and became a tiger… [Then] like a bull emitting a counterfeit roar from his mouth he butted the Titans with sharp horn…[32]

Unfortunately, for Dionysos, Hera once again intervenes and the god is dismembered for a second time:

> So he fought for his life, until Hera with jealous throat bellowed harshly through the air – that heavy-resentful step-mother! and the gates of Olympos rattled in echo to her jealous throat from high heaven. Then the bold bull collapsed: the murderers each eager for his turn with the knife chopt piecemeal the bull-shaped Dionysos.[33]

As with the myth of Osiris the fertility subtext is clear. Zagreus/Dionysos (Osiris) personifies Life and the Titans (Set) personify Death. Once again the act of dismemberment can be read as a symbol of the harvest, with the god's rebirth signifying the return of Spring. That the god is dismembered more than once emphasises the cyclical nature of the seasons, and his *Metamorphoses* represent the sheer diversity of existence. Thus Dionysos may be seen as an embodiment of the '*Zoë*' or Life Essence: a fertility god whose association with Persephone – and therefore with the grain goddess Demeter – contextualises him within the mystery cults of ancient Greece.[34]

The term 'mystery cult' carries with it connotations of secrets and shadows, of strange rituals and mystical illuminations. Whilst these connotations are not entirely misplaced, they nevertheless fail to encompass the breadth of complexity surrounding these diverse forms of ancient religious devotion. From the mysteries of Eleusis near Athens to the rites of Magna Mata at Rome, mystery cults embodied a variety of ritualistic practices whose inherent mythologies distinguished them, not only from each other, but also from their associate deity's manifestation within the wider religious community. However, despite the exclusive elements of each cult, there remains enough parity for the classical philologist Walter Burkert to offer the following generic definition:

> Mysteries [were] a form of personal religion, depending on a private decision and aiming at some form of salvation through closeness to the divine.[35]

As 'personal' and 'private' forms of religion they provided a sharp contrast to the official cults of the state, whose focus was the maintenance and welfare of the polis, and in which participation was mandatory. Indeed, the mysteries 'were anything but…unavoidable', being a matter of personal discretion and solely focused upon the spiritual needs of the individual. For example, a person of uncertain health may well have sought admittance into the mysteries of Isis, an Egyptian goddess who was believed to be 'Health deified', and who, by the Hellenistic era, had temples and shrines situated at 'many places' throughout the civilised world. If the correct rituals were observed, and '*iatreia* [healing fees]' paid to the officiating priests, then the supplicant could expect to enjoy the goddess' favour. Likewise, those wishing for 'the promise of…a happy afterlife' could have journeyed to Eleusis, where, according to Herodotus, 'anyone [could] be initiated into the mysteries'. These initiations took place as part of an annual 'autumn festival' called the 'Mysteria' during which a

> procession went from Athens to Eleusis and culminated in a nocturnal celebration in the Hall of Initiations, the Telesterion, capable of holding thousands of initiates, where the hierophant revealed 'the holy things'.[36]

Those who had seen these 'holy things' were considered 'blessed' and could expect divine protection in the Underworld.[37]

The narrative of the Eleusinian mysteries was the myth of Persephone and her mother, and is preserved in the *1st Homeric Hymn to Demeter* (c.800-500 BCE). Here Persephone, whilst gathering 'roses and crocuses' with the 'deep-breasted daughters of Okeanos', happens upon a wondrous 'narcissus' from whose 'root there grew a hundred blooms' and

> which had a scent so sweet that all
> the wide heaven above and all the earth
> and all the salt swelling of the sea
> laughed aloud.[38]

Entranced, she 'reached out both her hands to take/ the lovely toy', but at that moment

> the earth with wide paths
> gaped open in the plain of Nysa,
> and He Who Receives So Many, the lord,
> sprang upon her with his immortal horses,
> the son of Kronos with many names.
>
> He caught hold of her, protesting,
> and he took her away, weeping,
> in his chariot of gold.[39]

Far off, Persephone's mother Demeter hears her daughter's cries and, 'casting a dark-blue cloak over her shoulders', goes 'searching' for her. However, 'neither the gods nor human beings' want to tell her where she is, and

> For nine days [Demeter] roamed over the earth
> with flaming torches in both her hands,
> and she never once tasted ambrosia
> and the sweet drink of nectar,
> nor sprinkled water on her skin,
> so deep in grief was she.[40]

Finally she decides to question Helios, 'he who watches gods and men', and the son of Hyperion informs her that it was Hades who abducted Persephone. Not only this, but that he did so on the instruction of none other than Zeus. 'Outraged/ with the son of Kronos' Demeter

> withdrew from the company of gods
> and from high Olympos, and she went
> to the cities of mortals and their rich fields,
> disguising her form for a long time.
> And no one who saw her knew her,
> no man or deep-breasted woman,
> until she came to the house of wise Keleos,
> the lord of fragrant Eleusis.[41]

Here, in the guise of an 'old woman', she becomes nursemaid to Keleos' newborn son Demophoon, and secretly plans to make the boy immortal. Each day she

> anointed him with ambrosia
> as though he were born from a god,
> breathing on him sweetly as she held him to her
> breast.
> But at night she buried him in the heart of the fire,
> like a torch, without his dear parents knowing.
> And it was a great wonder to them
> how he grew far beyond his years,
> and he was in appearance like a god.[42]

All is going well until one night Demophoon's mother, Metaneira, sees Demeter in the act of burying her son in the fire. Alarmed, she makes to intervene, but by so doing earns the enmity of the goddess:

> Demeter was enraged,
> she snatched the dear child out of the fire
> with her immortal hands…
> and she threw him away from her on to the ground,
> her heart seething with fury.[43]

By interrupting the rites, Metaneira has denied her son his immortality; now 'it is impossible for him/ to escape the fate of death'. However, his proximity to Demeter has earned him 'undying honour', and it is worth noting that it is at this point in the narrative that the goddess prophesies her mysteries:

> 'I am Demeter, the honoured one,
> who for mortals and immortals alike
> has been made the greatest blessing and source of joy.
> But come, let all the people build for me a great temple
> and an altar beneath it, below the steep walls of the city
> above Kallichoron, upon the rising hill.
> And I myself will inaugurate my mysteries,
> so that from now on you may perform them in all purity
> and be reconciled to my heart'.[44]

In this moment of revealing her true identity to the Eleusinians, in this moment of being *seen*, Demeter foretells a system of atonement whereby mortal and immortal will meet, not in the equality of a shared immortality, but through the reconciliation of a ritual purity. Here the character of Demophoon is particularly pertinent, for he is the embodiment of the Divine Child conceived as initiate. As such he represents a new covenant between the human and the divine, a rebirth into a blessedness that was once the reserve of heroes. Indeed, the Eleusinian mysteries seem to embody the spirit of Athenian democracy, allowing 'anyone' to be initiated and thus to be 'blessed'.

The theme of reconciliation is carried on throughout the remainder of the narrative. Having revealed her divine form and prophesied her mysteries, Demeter withdraws to her new temple and broods over the fate of her daughter:

> …golden-haired Demeter sat there,
> far away from all the blessed gods
> she stayed there, wasting with longing
> for her deep-breasted daughter.[45]

Her rage is such that she withholds the harvest, at once depriving the humans of their food and thus the gods of their offerings. Indeed

> she would have destroyed utterly
> the mortal race of human beings, starving them
> to death, and deprived those who live on Olympos
> of the glorious honour of gifts and sacrifices,
> if Zeus had not noticed it and reflected upon it in his
> heart.[46]

Realising that the situation cannot be allowed to continue, Zeus sends first Iris and then 'all the blessed gods' to appease her wrath, each offering 'many beautiful gifts and honours' if she will allow the harvest to return. Demeter refuses; the only thing that will placate her is the release of her daughter. Consequently, Zeus sends Hermes, 'the Slayer of Argos', down into the Underworld in order that he might

> win over Hades with soft words
> and…lead Persephone out of the murky darkness
> into the light among the gods…[47]

This he duly does and Hades releases Persephone from the House of Death. However, before she leaves, Hades tricks her into eating a single pomegranate seed so that she cannot 'stay away forever/ with the venerable Demeter'. Despite this, mother and daughter are happily reunited, and it transpires that Persephone will only have to spend a 'third part/ of the circling year' in the Underworld. For the 'other two parts' she will remain with Demeter 'and the other immortal gods'. Satisfied with this, Demeter agrees to return the harvest and the world is saved.[48]

It is now that the theme of reconciliation reaches its final embodiment. Having 'let the crops/ spring up from the rich fields', Demeter and the Eleusinians inaugurate her 'sacred mysteries'. Naturally enough, the *Hymn* does not reveal the particulars – expressly stating that no one 'may inquire into or speak about' her 'awesome rites'. However, what *is* manifest is their *meaning*. Throughout the *Hymn* a series of allegories; Demeter and Persephone; Demeter and Demophoon; Demeter and the Eleusinians; have promoted the idea of *loss* and *return*. This is essential for an understanding of what the mysteries represent, of what they *mean* to the initiate both in this world and the next. The *Hymn* explicitly informs us that

> Blessed is the one of all the people on the earth
> who has seen these mysteries.[49]

swiftly adding that

> whoever is not initiated into the rites,
> whoever has no part in them,
> that person never shares the same fate when he dies
> and goes down to the gloom and darkness below.[50]

By being reconciled to the goddess, by participating in her rites, the initiate can expect a 'blessed' lot in the life to come. Yet the fullness of this promise may be best understood when one contextualises the soteriological nature of Demeter's mysteries within the wider context of her attributes. Demeter is goddess of the grain, and the poet Hesiod, in his *Theogony* (c.725 BCE), provides her with the epithet '[she] who feeds all'. As such, Demeter may be seen as the personification of the harvest and thus inextricably linked with the passage of the seasons. More than this, she is the source of life, equitable with the *Zoë*. Without her all mortals would die and the gods would be denied their offerings. Thus reconciliation with Demeter is a reconciliation with the pattern of life; a harmonisation with the *Zoë*, whose blessedness extends even through the illusory death of winter. By partaking in the mysteries the initiate does not receive eternal life in the physical world, but rather a heightened understanding of the forces that underpin it. Seen through the filter of the *Zoë*, the initiate realises at once their smallness *and* significance. They can objectively appraise their role within the wider pattern of life; a life in which death is wholly natural and commensurate with birth.[51]

It is little wonder then that we find Herodotus state that 'the *Iacchus* song...is always sung at [Demeter's] festival'. 'Iacchus' was a cult name of Dionysos and his association with the Eleusinian mysteries strengthens the relationship between the goddess and the *Zoë*. Indeed, the Cretan version of Dionysos' myth, in which Persephone sires Zagreus, has much in common with Demeter's nurturing of Demophoon. It is a mortal blessedness in which the Divine Child, although doomed, nevertheless partakes in his mother's divinity. Zagreus is reborn as Dionysos, the metamorphosing embodiment of Life, whilst Demophoon, although denied immortality, becomes emblematic of the mysteries. In each instance a personal transfiguration is undertaken; a transfiguration that is mirrored in both human and divine terms, and which embodies the possibility of mortal reconciliation with the immortal forces of the Universe. In many ways, Demophoon and Zagreus are twins, their associate myths highlighting the parities and diversities between initiates and gods. Thus the mysteries do nothing to challenge the hieratic structure of the Universe but rather seek its clarification. What alters is the initiate's status in relation to other, uninitiated mortals. Those like Demophoon who have seen the goddess (Demeter) have, by extension, seen the god (Dionysos-

Zagreus). They have become enlightened as to the nature of the *Zoë*, both in the Universe *and* in themselves.[52]

As well as associating 'Iacchus' with the Eleusinian cult, Herodotus also discusses 'the Dionysiac mysteries'. Whilst the Mysteria at Eleusis was 'notable for [its] purity', the Dionysiac rites were notorious for their immoderation. In the fourth book of his *Histories*, Herodotus narrates the story of Scylas, a Scythian king who was 'initiated into the mysteries of Dionysus' much to the horror of his people:

> **Now the Greek custom of celebrating Dionysiac rites is, in Scythian eyes, a shameful thing; and no Scythian can see sense in imaging a god who drives people out of their wits. On this occasion, therefore, at the initiation of Scylas, one of the Borysthenites slipped away and told the Scythians, who were waiting outside the town, of what was going on. 'You laugh at us', he said, 'for being possessed by the spirit of Dionysus when we celebrate his rites. Well, this same spirit has now taken hold of your own king; he is under its influence – Dionysus has driven him mad. If you don't believe it, come along and I will let you see for yourselves'. The chief Scythians present accepted the offer, and the man took them secretly to the top of a high building, from which they could get a good view of what was happening in the streets. Presently a party of revellers came by, with Scylas amongst them; and when the Scythians saw their king in the grip of the Bacchic frenzy, they were profoundly disturbed and, returning to the army, let every man know of the disgraceful spectacle they had witnessed.[53]**

The overriding impression from the above is one of self-disintegration. By participating in the rites, Scylas has cast off his persona as the Scythian king and become 'possessed' by the god. Thus the difference between these mysteries and the rites of Demeter at Eleusis is manifest. Rather than receiving blessedness through witnessing the divine,

Dionysos' initiates actually *become* the god, and consequently their experience is charged with the immediacy of a violent metamorphosis. As with the Cretan Dionysos so the initiate becomes the subject of change. Like Scylas, they reject the personality of their mundane lives and engage in acts that transgress the moral strictures of society. By embodying the god they appear to embody madness. Yet this madness, as Plato has Socrates say in the *Phaedrus* (fourth century BCE), 'is a fine thing' because it comes from 'divine dispensation'. It is a realisation of the human participation in the *Zoë* ; an awakening whose intensity, charged with a *this-worldly* vitality, celebrates the principle of a life force that is at once intimate *and* individually transcendent.[54]

Another striking difference between the Eleusinian and Dionysiac mysteries is the nature of their respective geographies. Whereas Demeter's rites were performed 'exclusively at Eleusis' the rites of Dionysos were performed 'everywhere'. Indeed, Burkert points out that, due to Dionysos' association with wine, 'every drinker…could claim to be a servant of [the] god'. However, in terms of a practically organised religious movement (as opposed to the private indulgences of an individual) it was necessary for there to be a series of itinerant charismatics who could bring the god's *telete* [initiation ceremony] to the people. A prime example of this charismatic practice is to be found in Euripides' *Bacchae*. Written toward the end of the poet's life, when he had withdrawn from Athens to the Court of King Archelaus of Macedon, the *Bacchae* offers a fascinating insight into the evolution and practice of the Dionysiac cults in Greece. Having travelled

> …first to the sun-smitten Persian plains,
> The walled cities of Bactria, the harsh Median country,
> Wealthy Arabia, and the whole tract of the Asian coast
> Where mingled swarms of Greeks and Orientals live…[55]

a disguised Dionysos arrives in his mother's city of Thebes and begins to instigate his rites. On hearing of this 'astounding scandal', Semele's nephew Pentheus returns to his kingdom determined to 'put a stop to [the] outrageous Bacchism' of this 'upstart god'. Indeed, much can be gleaned from Pentheus' opening speech. Unable to perceive the god beneath the mask, the King can only see an 'Oriental conjurer' who is busy enticing 'young girls with his Bacchic mysteries'. As far as he is concerned Dionysos is 'dead, burnt to a cinder by lightning/ Along with his mother'. The man now operating in Thebes is a foreign interloper, a golden haired 'magician' who has even succeeded in bewitching the sage Teiresias with his 'bowls full of wine'. Thus for Pentheus it is essential that this 'new god' be eradicated. He is a corrupter of civic and moral order:

> Our women, it seems, have left their homes on some
> pretence
> Of Bacchic worship, and are now gadding about
> On the wooded mountain-slopes, dancing in honour
> of
> This upstart god Dionysus…our women go creeping
> off
> This way and that to lonely places and give
> themselves
> To lecherous men…[56]

of piety:

> *He's* the one – this foreigner –
> Who says Dionysus is a god; who says he was
> Sewn up in Zeus's thigh. The truth about Dionysus
> Is that he's dead, burnt to a cinder by lightning
> Along with his mother, because she said Zeus lay
> with her.
> Whoever the man may be, is not his arrogance
> An outrage?[57]

and of the old:

> Why, look! Another miracle! Here's Teiresias
> The prophet – in a fawnskin; and my mother's
> father –
> A Bacchant with a fennel-wand! Well, there's a sight
> For laughter!
> Sir, I am ashamed to see two men
> Of your age with so little sense of decency...[58]

In addition to these transgressions, the acts of this 'foreigner' threaten to undermine Pentheus' throne on a very personal level. As the son of Semele, Dionysos is Pentheus' cousin and, as a god, his claim to the Theban throne might be deemed the stronger. Indeed, even if Dionysos were dead, and the 'Oriental conjurer' merely a charlatan, the popularity of the 'Bacchic mysteries' among the people could feasibly see Pentheus deposed and the 'magician' crowned in his stead. Thus the King's opposition to the new cult has as much to do with his personal claim to power as it has to do with any of the 'objective' reasons cited above. He is frightened of losing control, not only of his throne, but also of his sense of self. Pentheus' fear is the fear of Apolline rationalism when faced with the strength of primal passion. He rejects Dionysos, not because he is foreign, far from it, but because he is all too familiar. It is here that the metaphor of 'family' may be properly understood; Dionysos is indeed related to Pentheus – he *is* Pentheus. Beneath the Apolline mask of civilisation, of calming, shaping rational order, the primal passion of Life remains. Teiresias in his wisdom knows this:

> It will be said, I lack the dignity of my age,
> To wear this ivy-wreath and set off for the dance.
> Not so; the god draws no distinction between young
> And old, to tell us which should dance and which
> should not.
> He desires equal worship from all men: his claim
> To glory is universal; no one is exempt.[59]

but Pentheus is too frightened to surrender his sense of self. By refusing to join 'the dance', by refusing to recognise his true nature, Pentheus is condemned to die a most unnatural death. Thus, on attempting to infiltrate the 'Bacchic rites', and thereby gather damaging evidence against the cult, Pentheus is seized by the maenads (who include his mother Agauë and his aunts Ino and Autonoë) and is torn to pieces:

> Agauë was foaming at the mouth; her rolling eyes
> Were wild... She grasped
> [Pentheus'] left arm between wrist and elbow, set her foot
> against his ribs, and tore his arm off by the shoulder.
> It was no strength of hers that did it, but the god
> Filled her, and made it easy. On the other side
> Ino was at him, tearing at his flesh; and now
> Autonoë joined them, and the whole maniacal horde.
> A single and continuous yell arose – Pentheus
> Shrieking as long as life was left in him, the women
> Howling in triumph. One of them carried off an arm,
> Another a foot, the boot still laced on it. The ribs
> Were stripped, clawed clean; and women's hands, thick red with blood,
> Were tossing, catching, like a plaything, Pentheus' flesh.[60]

It is interesting to note that Pentheus' death mirrors that of the Cretan Dionysos at the hands of the Titans. By rejecting the personification of Life in the form of the god, Pentheus is dismembered in a manner that mimics the fertility allegory of the Osiris/Dionysos myth. Indeed, it is significant that the chief perpetrator of his murder is Agauë, the woman who gave him birth. Again the image is cyclical; like the seasons his life has come full-circle. However, unlike Dionysos, he has no prospect of rebirth. Pentheus has reacted against nature at the most fundamental level – his own being – and consequently dies at his life's source.

Thus we may discern the nature of Dionysos and consequently the meaning of the term 'Dionysiac'. The god may be seen as an embodiment of the *Zoë* : an irrational, indomitable force of nature that stands in direct opposition to the Apolline idealisation of dispassionate order. Like the Dionysos of *The Homeric Hymns* and the Dionysos of Euripides' *Bacchae*, the *Zoë* is often regarded as something frightening and foreign. It is a subversion of civilisation because it refuses to acknowledge the boundaries that constitute society. This may well be the reason why the *Hymns to Dionysos* seem to be forever pushing the god away. He is a dangerous, uncontrollable power who, for the sake of individuating structure, must be kept at a distance. Yet the irony remains that Dionysos' otherness is a myth for, as the *Zoë*, he is the essence of all things.

Having explored the divine etymology of the terms 'Apolline' and 'Dionysiac', and having found our definitions, we will now examine the influence exerted by these gods over *The Birth of Tragedy*. Indeed, it is amusing to note that in his *Attempt At A Self-Criticism* (1886) Nietzsche dismisses his first work as 'a book for initiates'. Whilst this most probably refers to *The Birth of Tragedy*'s Wagnerian overtones, there is nevertheless something profoundly religious in both its argument and style. It is, as Nietzsche observes, 'so sure of its convictions that it is above any need for proof', and consequently asserts its claims with the authority of the Delphic Oracle. Thus it is no surprise that we find Nietzsche beginning his book with the characteristically bold statement:

> We shall have gained much for the science of aesthetics when we have succeeded in perceiving directly, and not only through logical reasoning, that art derives its continuous development from the duality of the Apolline and the Dionysiac; just as the reproduction of the species depends on the duality of the sexes, with its constant conflicts and only periodically intervening reconciliations.[61]

The metaphysical aspirations of the text are betrayed through Nietzsche's immediate championing of an almost mystically direct, and it appears at least partially illogical, perception. That this 'perception' affords an insight into the Dionysos-Apollo binary, and that this binary is likened to the reproduction of the species, gives it a gravitas that seems to transcend the merely aesthetic. What is apparent is that *The Birth of Tragedy out of the Spirit of Music* is not simply a book about Ancient Greek art. Neither is it a panegyric on the life and works of Richard Wagner. It is, beneath its 'terribly protracted and excitably portentous' passages, a self-insinuating embodiment of Nietzsche's flux and form. That it pretends, albeit feebly, to be otherwise is all part of its self-conscious performance.[62]

Indeed, the notion of performance is central to the text's thematic identity, embodied both in the phenomenon of Attic Tragedy and in its presiding deity, Dionysos. Yet the complexity of this performance is compounded by its syncretic dynamic; namely the psycho-aesthetic fusion of the Apolline with the Dionysiac. That the author sees this fusion as a 'metaphysical miracle' goes someway to illustrate the deep grain of paradox inherent in his argument. From the onset Nietzsche is at pains to show us how logically irreconcilable the Apolline and Dionysiac are; how there exists between them a 'tremendous opposition' that can only be breached by a 'Hellenic' force of 'will'. One is left in no doubt that this coupling should *not* be possible, and yet somehow, miraculously it occurs, birthing a 'work of art that is as Dionysiac as it is Apolline'.[63]

To properly understand the syncretic dynamic of this 'miracle', and indeed the personal, performative implications arising from it, we will begin by looking at the way in which Nietzsche conceives his 'tremendous opposition' through the metaphysical dualism of his binary. For Nietzsche the Apolline pertains to the 'plastic' arts of sculpture, painting, and epic poetry, to an idealisation of individuated surfaces, a 'dream reality' whose aesthetic 'perfection' invariably lulls us into a realm of 'beautiful illusion'. This illusory state, as narcotic as it is 'sun-like', filters and refines our perception, unconsciously shaping the world around us and consequently defining our sense of self. In short it makes life as we understand it both 'possible and worth living', yet Nietzsche is at pains to express the 'pathological' dangers of this deception, for its 'reality' is gained at the expense of the real. Here Nietzsche's debt to Schopenhauer is manifest, and indeed the perceptual dualism of *The World as Will and Idea*, itself highly indebted to both Hindu and Buddhist philosophy, can be clearly discerned at the metaphysical core of *The Birth of Tragedy*. Thus whilst discussing the nature of Apolline dream reality, Nietzsche makes the following, revealing observations:

> Men of philosophy...have a sense that beneath the reality in which we live there is hidden a second, quite different world, and that our own world is therefore an illusion; and Schopenhauer actually says that the gift of being able at times to see men and objects as mere phantoms or dream images is the mark of the philosophical capacity. Thus the man who is responsive to artistic stimuli reacts to the reality of dreams as does the philosopher to the reality of existence; he observes closely, and he enjoys his observation: for it is out of these images that he interprets life, out of these processes that he trains himself for life.[64]

Here, through the direct comparison of artistic and philosophic 'stimuli', a comparison whose reactive parities insinuate an active correspondence, Nietzsche widens the Apolline dynamic from the aesthetic to the universal. Consequently, the dream-like quality, which Nietzsche sees as characteristic of the 'plastic' arts, may be read as pertaining to sensory experience as a whole; an experience whose 'phantoms' and 'images' constitute a mere performance. Thus behind this transitory dance of dreams there lurks the implication of a higher reality unfettered by the falsity of the senses.

In *The World as Will and Idea*, Schopenhauer argues that this 'higher reality' is to be understood as a primal, 'indivisible…will': a 'will' that, in itself, is to be seen as 'entirely free from all forms of the phenomenal'. Yet like the Atman-Brahman correspondence of the *Upanishads* (c.700 BCE-c.200 CE), Schopenhauer's concept of 'will' is inextricably bound up with what he terms the 'pure knowing subject'. For Schopenhauer, this subject is

> the support of the world…the condition (that is universal and always presupposed) of all phenomenon, of all object.[65]

Consequently, '[e]veryone finds himself to be this subject', however,

> only in so far as he knows, not in so far as he is an object of knowing.[66]

To paraphrase, Schopenhauer builds upon Kant's *Critique of Pure Reason*, arguing for a radical reinterpretation of the functions and limitations of *a priori* and *a postitori* knowledge. Kant had argued that the assumptions of traditional metaphysics were fundamentally flawed because they attempted to make substantive claims about the nature of existence independently of experience. For Kant, all such claims were 'synthetical *a priori* judgements' and revealed nothing about the world as it is *in itself*, the world of 'noumena', but were rather the product of our cognitive apparatus and thus limited by our subjective position within 'causality'. True, Kant thought that certain synthetical *a priori* judgements *could* be maintained – such as '[a]rithmetical propositions' – but only on the understanding that they did not pertain to some intrinsic reality independent of ourselves. For Kant, such synthetical *a priori* judgements were only possible because of the spatio-temporal nature of our cognitive processes, and thus could not be meaningfully distinguished from the mechanics of their construction. Any claims made about the world only related to its phenomenal appearance and had nothing to do with the reality of noumena. Indeed, such a reality, insofar as it could be said to exist, existed only as a hypothetical postulate and not as a meaningful metaphysical space which the mind could inhabit. Thus, through what he termed 'the principle of sufficient reason', Kant 'limited' metaphysics to consist on the one hand of a 'transcendental philosophy',

> [a] system of all the concepts and principles belonging to the understanding and the reason, and which relate to objects in general, but not to any particular given objects...[67]

and on the other of a 'physiology of pure reason' that had

> nature for its subject-matter, that is, the sum of given objects – whether given to the senses, or...to some other kind of intuition...[68]

Consequently, metaphysics remained firmly within the bounds of the phenomenal world, its function a self-reflexive process of rationalistic analysis, a process of critique, in which synthetical *a priori* judgements were scrutinised in the light of *a postitori* knowledge. In short, it was a metaphysic of restraint – one that denied cognitive meaning to any notion of a transcendent reality.

Whilst Schopenhauer is prepared to accept Kant's 'principle of sufficient reason' as a means of determining our conscious relationship with *most* objects of phenomena, he is sceptical of Kant's assertion that the world of noumena falls 'absolutely...beyond the limits of experience'. For Schopenhauer, Kant had overlooked a fundamental interrelation between object and subject – an interrelation whose implications necessarily undermine the *Critique of Pure Reason*'s rationalistic dualism. To this effect, Schopenhauer argues that each one of us has access to the world of noumena through nothing less intimate than our own bodies; for it is the body which occupies the uniquely privileged position of being both object and subject *simultaneously.* Indeed, Schopenhauer is at pains to stress that our experience of the world is 'entirely communicated through the medium of the body', that it is the body 'whose affections are...the starting-point' for our 'understanding [of] perception', and consequently the 'support of the whole world as idea'. Therefore, whilst the body remains on the one hand merely

> an idea like every other idea, an object among objects [whose] movements and actions are only familiar...as the changes in all other perceived objects...[69]

it is, conversely, the *means* of that perception. Thus, '[t]he body', Schopenhauer argues,

> is given in two entirely different ways to the subject of knowledge... It is given as an idea in intelligent perception, as an object among objects and beholden to the laws of objects. And it is also given in quite a different way, as that which is immediately known to everyone, and is signified by the word *will.* Every true act of will is also at once and without exception a movement of the body: [one] cannot really will the act without being at the same time aware that it manifests itself as a movement of [the] body. The act of will and the movement of the body are not two different things objectively known, which the bond of causality unites; they do not stand in the relation of cause and effect; but they are one and the same, although given in two entirely different ways – immediately, and again in perception for the understanding. The action of the body is nothing but the act of the will objectified, i.e., passed into perception.[70]

It is this reasoning that enables Schopenhauer to move his thinking from the individual to the universal for, unless one is afflicted with solipsism, one must assume that this 'double knowledge' is the 'key' to understanding 'the character of every phenomenon in nature'. After all,

> [if] we wish to attribute the greatest known reality to the material world which exists immediately only in our idea, we give it the reality which our own body has for each of us; for that is for everyone the most real thing. But if we now analyse the reality of this body and its actions, apart from its being our idea, we find nothing in it but the will; with that even its reality is exhausted. So nowhere can we find another kind of reality to attribute to the material world. Thus if the material world is to be something more than merely our idea, we must say that besides being idea (that is, in itself and according to its inmost nature) it is what we find immediately in ourselves as *will.*[71]

Consequently, through 'the analogy of our own bodies', we are able to apprehend that the 'inner nature' of all phenomenon – when 'set aside [from] their existence as idea of the subject' – must 'be the same as that in us which we call *will*'. This *will*, therefore, does not designate an 'unknown quantity…arrived at only by inference' but the intimately apprehended ground of being, the synthesis of *a priori* and *a postitori* knowledge, whose fundamental character necessarily transcends the plurality of 'idea'. Thus whilst all 'idea…all object' relate to Kant's world of phenomena, the underlying reality of *will*, which is the ground of all existence, is none other than the '*thing-in-itself*,' the world of noumena.[72]

A notorious pessimist, Schopenhauer views his metaphysical principle of *will* in an exclusively negative light. Despite being the *thing-in-itself*, and as such free from all forms of the phenomenal, the *will* does not constitute some tranquil unity. Rather it is to be understood as an 'endless flux', an '[e]ternal becoming' through countless 'manifestations', a 'hungry', self-consuming, process of 'objectification' which Schopenhauer perceives as a causal chain of 'suffering'. Hence

> man needs animals for his sustenance, and the animals, down through their grades, need one another; then they, too, need plants, which in their turn need soil, water, chemical elements and their combinations, the planet, the sun, rotation and orbit round the sun, the angle of the ecliptic and so forth. Fundamentally this is the result of the will's having to consume itself, for besides the will there is nothing else, and it is a hungry will. Hence the chase, the apprehension, the grieving.[73]

Put more succinctly, all 'willing arises from need, therefore from deficiency, and therefore from suffering'. It is an eternal circle, an eternal recurrence of pain borne by an insatiable series of 'desires'. Thus in human terms, no sooner has a desire for a particular object or sensation been 'checked' than it is supplanted by a new craving. 'Every goal attained', observes Schopenhauer, is merely 'the starting-point of a new lap in the race, and so on *ad infinitum*'. We are never content because the *will* in us, being an endless flux, is antithetical to contentment. Thus

> as long as our consciousness is filled by our will, as long as we are given up to the urgent prompting of desires with their constant hopes and fears, as long as we are the subject of willing, we can never have lasting happiness nor peace.[74]

Despite the deep pessimism inherent in Schopenhauer's vision there nonetheless remains the faintest glimmer of hope, for we *can* be free 'from the slavery of the will', if only momentarily. For Schopenhauer, this release occurs

> when some external cause or inward disposition lifts us suddenly out of the endless stream of willing...[75]

and enables us to perceive objects 'without subjectivity', apart 'from their relation to the will'. As such, we forget 'all individuality', thereby

> suspending…that kind of knowledge which follows the principle of sufficient reason, and comprehends only relations; the state by means of which, at once and inseparably, the perceived particular thing is raised to the Idea of its whole species.[76]

Thus we, in turn, are raised 'to the pure subject of will-less knowledge' and for a moment experience a 'painless state' of 'well-being'. It is here that one can most clearly discern the influence of Plato on Schopenhauer's thinking, and indeed the Platonic notion of *Ideal Forms*, expounded in Middle Period Dialogues such as the *Symposium* (fourth century BCE) and the *Phaedrus*, has a deep parity with Schopenhauer's Ideas of 'pure contemplation'. For example, in the *Symposium*, through the persona of the wise-woman Diotima, Plato argues for a personal transcendence through abstraction – in this instance via the contemplation of something 'beautiful':

> When someone goes up by these stages, through loving boys in the correct way, and begins to catch sight of that beauty, he has come close to reaching the goal. This is the right method of approaching the ways of love or being led by someone else: beginning from these beautiful things always to go up with the aim of reaching that beauty. Like someone using a staircase, he should go from one to two and from two to all beautiful bodies, and from beautiful bodies to beautiful practices, and from practices to beautiful forms of learning. From forms of learning, he should end up at that form of learning which is nothing other than *that* beauty itself, so that he can complete the process of learning what beauty really is.[77]

This pattern of ascent is at once a widening of consciousness *and* a stripping away of the phenomenal constituents that define perception. From something as particular as the 'beauty' of a single body the perceiving consciousness expands (or dilutes) to the appreciation of 'all beautiful bodies'. In Schopenhauerian terms, this would be interpreted as the dilution of the subjective, willing, preference for a particular physical configuration and a move towards an Idea of beauty 'in which the will reaches the highest grade of its objectification'. Following Plato's analogy, we can see how this 'objectification', through an ever-greater abstraction, transcends from the physical, causal world of phenomena – from beautiful bodies to the beautiful practices in which these bodies engage and so forth – into a detached, Ideal state; a state which is 'not cluttered up with human flesh and colours and a great mass of mortal rubbish', but is rather 'divine' in its will-less perfection.[78]

An even more penetrating example may be found in the *Phaedrus*. Here, through the persona of Socrates, Plato expounds his theory of the soul and in so doing employs one of the most famous similes in Classical literature. The simile of the 'horses and…their charioteer', found in *Phaedrus* 246b, provides a clear antecedent to Schopenhauer's conception of the 'denial of the will' through pure contemplation:

> Let us…compare the soul to a winged charioteer and his team acting together… First of all we must make it plain that the ruling power in us men drives a pair of horses, and next that one of these horses is fine and good and of noble stock, and the other the opposite in every way. So in our case the task of the charioteer is necessarily a difficult and unpleasant business… Soul taken as a whole is in charge of all that is inanimate… When it is perfect and winged it moves on high…but the soul that has shed its wings falls until it encounters solid matter. There it settles and puts on an earthly body, which appears to be self-moving because of the power of the soul that is

> in it, and this combination of soul and body is given the name of a living being...[79]

Like Schopenhauer's 'hungry will' so Plato's 'vicious horse', possessed by 'wantonness and boastfulness' and 'utterly heedless of...the driver's whip and goad, rushes forward', moved by the 'stings of desire'. As can be seen from the above, it is the wilfulness of this 'lustful horse' which interrupts the 'inanimate' contemplation of the soul and traps it in the causal world of 'solid matter'. It is desire which leads to the 'great discomfiture' of suffering, and it is only through 'the moderating influence of modesty and reason', personified by the 'upright and clean-limbed' horse, that the 'higher elements' of the soul may 'prevail' and find 'peace'. As with the *Symposium*, Plato advocates the chaste contemplation of 'absolute beauty' as a path out of the 'walking sepulchre which we call a body' and towards a 'mystic vision' of 'pure...light'. The soul thus freed regains its wings and ascends to the 'changeless and serene' realm of the *Ideal Forms*, a

> region...without colour or shape, intangible but utterly real, apprehensible only by [the] intellect...[80]

There it

> beholds absolute justice and discipline and knowledge, not the knowledge which is attached to things which come into being, nor the knowledge which varies with the objects which we now call real, but the absolute knowledge which corresponds to what is absolutely real in the fullest sense.[81]

Thus through a pure contemplation of absolute beauty, of Beauty *in-itself*, the soul conceives an objective knowledge of timeless, causeless reality and, as a consequence, is cleansed from the 'pollution' of its mundane, causal existence.[82]

It is little wonder then, given Plato's eloquent promotion of the contemplation of absolute beauty as a means of psychic release, that in book three of *The World as Will and Idea* Schopenhauer favours 'aesthetic' experience as the medium most conducive to the denial of the will. For Schopenhauer, the 'purely objective frame of mind', upon which this transcendence is contingent, is most readily 'facilitated…from without by congenial objects' of 'aesthetic contemplation' – be they objects of 'natural beauty', or '[m]anufactured articles' derived from the 'fine art' fields of 'architecture', 'sculpture', 'painting', 'poetry' and 'music'. Indeed, it is towards these 'inorganic', fine art productions that Schopenhauer steers the greatest weight of his argument, for through them, he argues, it is possible to discern an ever-greater objectification of the *will* – an objectification analogous to the *Symposium*'s refinement of knowledge through the concentration of the mind upon the Idea of beauty. Thus from architecture,

> whose aim is to elucidate the will's objectification at the lowest grade of its visibility[83]

to tragic poetry,

> which presents to us…the highest grade of the will's objectification…[84]

it is possible to discern a pattern of ascent which strongly resembles the beatific system revealed by Plato's Diotima.

However, despite the elevated position which Schopenhauer accords to tragic poetry in his pantheon of the arts, it is music which he sees as occupying the most elevated status of all – a status born out of a fundamental alterity:

> The (Platonic) Ideas are the adequate objectification of will. To stimulate the knowledge of these by depicting particular things (for works of art are themselves always representations of particular things) is the aim of all the other arts (and is possible

> only by a corresponding change in the knowing subject). Thus all these arts objectify the will only indirectly by means of the Ideas; and since our world is nothing but the manifestation of the Ideas in plurality, through their entering into the *principium individuationis* (the form of knowledge possible for the individual as such), music, since it takes no account of the Ideas, is entirely independent also of the phenomenal world, ignores it altogether, could to a certain extent exist if there were no world at all; this cannot be said of the other arts. Music is as *direct* an objectification and copy of the whole *will* as is the world itself, indeed, as are the Ideas whose multiplied manifestation constitutes the world of individual things. So music is by no means (as are the other arts) the copy of the Ideas, but the *copy of the will itself*, whose objectivity the Ideas are. This is why the effect of music is so much more powerful and penetrating than that of the other arts, for they speak only of the shadow while music speaks of the essence.[85]

Thus for Schopenhauer, music and the *will* enjoy a unique relationship, with the former acting as the unmediated, Idealess simulacrum of the *thing-in-itself*. Consequently, by displacing one's willing through the appreciation of music; by objectifying the *will*, not as an Idea manifest as phenomena, but as the reflected essence of the *thing-in-itself*; by experiencing the *will* aesthetically, as art through pure contemplation; the pure knowing subject succeeds in denying itself entirely – indeed, in momentarily attaining a death in life. For it is this correspondence between music and the *will* ; between the 'inexhaustible variety of possible melodies' and 'nature's inexhaustible variety of individuals'; between 'the human heart', music, and 'the true nature of all things'; that enables us to experience, without 'incidentals and so also without...motives', emotions such as 'joy, sorrow, pain, horror, delight, merriment [and] peace of mind'. Thus, whilst the music lasts, we are suspended from causation, held by the paradox of our active-passive contemplation of the *thing-in-itself*.[86]

Nietzsche's relationship with Schopenhauer's metaphysic, like his relationship with the field of Classical philology, is both playful *and* subversive. Superficially, Nietzsche is a Schopenhauerian, just as superficially *The Birth of Tragedy* is a philological study. He repeatedly cites from, or makes reference to, Schopenhauer's work, and appropriates much of Schopenhauer's metaphysical terminology. However, the reality of the situation is far more problematical than a simple case of discipleship, for Nietzsche is *using* Schopenhauer's metaphysic in the wider scheme of his displacement. That the performance is a good one, with the differentiation apparent only at the heart of his textual labyrinth, is consistent with *The Birth of Tragedy*'s thematic and stylistic theatricality. Indeed, the overt displacement, that of the text's philological/philosophical identity, goes some way to mask the layering of *The Birth of Tragedy*'s wilful instability.

Thus, right from the beginning, Nietzsche makes the Schopenhauerian gesture of defining the Apolline as the *principium individuationis* – as that which makes individual existence possible. As we have already seen, Nietzsche regards the Apolline as pertaining to the 'plastic' arts of sculpture, painting and epic poetry, to an idealisation of individuated surfaces that may now be understood as bearing a marked correspondence to Schopenhauer's Ideas of pure contemplation. Consequently, Apolline art objectifies existence through its concentration on 'phenomena' – indeed, through its *construction* of phenomena through the power of its 'illusion'. For this is what the *principium individuationis* does: it maintains the 'cognitive forms of appearance' and, by so doing, emerges 'triumphant over a terrible abyss'. Apolline objectification, Apolline illusion, is the direct condition of 'time, space, and causality', an illusion which we are 'utterly caught up in', indeed which is essential for the maintenance of 'empirical reality'. For Nietzsche, the Apolline is not merely an aesthetic concept in the trivial sense of the term. Rather, like Schopenhauer, Nietzsche has raised the aesthetic to a very high status indeed; to such a high status, in fact, that he feels able to boldly proclaim:

> it is only as an *aesthetic phenomenon* that existence and the world are eternally *justified.*[87]

Thus we *need* Apolline art, not merely as an entertainment, as a 'diversion' in the mundane sense of the word, but rather as a metaphysical justification for our individuality, for our sense of perspective.

Here, once again, Nietzsche displays a Schopenhauerian disposition by conceiving the world in a dualistic light. For if the Apolline pertains to the world of phenomena and acts as the *principium individuationis*, and if this is to be understood as an illusion, then there must be a higher reality behind this 'veil of Maya', this veil of appearances. The name which Nietzsche ascribes to the 'mysterious ground of our being', to that which lies behind the veil of Apolline illusion is, of course, the Dionysiac. As discussed during our etymological excursion, the god Dionysos, from whom the term 'Dionysiac' derives, is equitable with the life-force or *Zoë*. It is thus not difficult to apprehend how Nietzsche came to identify the allegorical properties of this hungry, savage, wine-mad god, with the Schopenhauerian concept of the *will*, for both embody a 'primal Oneness' whose nature is 'suffering'. Therefore, just as the Dionysiac corresponds metaphysically to Schopenhauer's concept of the *will*, so it finds its aesthetic correspondence in nothing less than 'music'.[88]

Thus far *The Birth of Tragedy* may be seen as a 'philological' interpretation of *The World as Will and Idea*. Through his metaphysical-aesthetic correspondences Nietzsche has transposed onto the Classical world the mechanics of Schopenhauer's nineteenth-century German Idealism. Indeed, such an anachronism is in itself an act of displacement, and one that counterpoints the text's philological-philosophical paradox. For Nietzsche is not merely using philosophy in a philological space, he is treating the past as the present, Greece as Germany. Fourteen years later, Nietzsche was to write in his *Attempt At A Self-Criticism*:

> I *spoiled* the grandiose *Greek problem*, as I saw it, by adulterating it with the most modern ideas![89]

In fact, the act of adulteration runs much deeper than a simple fusion of 'Dionysiac intimations with Schopenhauerian formulae', for Nietzsche, not content with simply imposing Schopenhauer's metaphysic on antiquity, seeks to actively displace it. This displacement is most apparent through Nietzsche's widening of the Dionysiac's aesthetic correspondence. Rather than merely pertaining to the *will* as music, to the pure essence of the *thing-in-itself*, the Dionysiac dilates, through its encounter with the Apolline, to embrace *all* the musical arts. For Nietzsche these include 'singing', 'dancing' and 'lyric poetry', thus corrupting the Schopenhauerian divide between arts which correspond directly to Ideas (architecture, painting, sculpture, poetry, etc) and music, which Schopenhauer sees as standing removed from Ideas through its complete objectification of the essence of the *will*. Indeed, by identifying music with the Dionysiac, Nietzsche is also displacing traditional divine appellation for, as we saw earlier, in Ancient Greece this art came under the sole auspices of Apollo. Thus Nietzsche is not only disregarding the central tenet of Schopenhauer's metaphysical aesthetics – whilst at the same time appearing to defer to the authority of his alleged 'master' – he is simultaneously reinterpreting the Hellenic Pantheon in the light of his own argument.[90]

Consequently, the confusion over *The Birth of Tragedy*'s form, the anachronistic transposition of Schopenhauerian metaphysics onto the ancient world, and then the subversion of this metaphysical system through Nietzsche's widening of Schopenhauer's aesthetic conception of music, engenders a symphonic compression of binaries, each intimating, through various degrees of atunement, the grand paradox of Attic Tragedy. A prime example of this binary action is to be found in the figures of Homer and Archilochus, whom Nietzsche characterises as 'Apolline' and 'Dionysiac' respectively, and consequently perceives as leading towards the 'metaphysical miracle' of the tragic stage. For Nietzsche, Homer is the epitome of the 'Apolline...artist', the 'aged, self-absorbed dreamer' whose 'remote', narrative voice, endowed with the 'stern, popular philosophy' of the heroic age, soberly defines its actions and intentions. Thus Homer is an 'objective' artist endowed, through the sculptural distance of his vision, with the 'Apolline impulse to beauty'. Archilochus, by contrast, is everything that Homer is not: a 'subjective' artist, a 'lyric poet' who 'sings...through the full chromatic scale of his passions and desires'. His verse is visceral, charged with 'the cry of his hate and scorn', with 'the drunken outpourings of his desire'. For Nietzsche, it is this welling, bubbling, 'subjective' voice, this screaming 'I' so full of 'craving', which intimates the first artistic stirrings of the primal Oneness of the *will.* Consequently, Nietzsche seeks to identify the lyric processes of Archilochus' Dionysiac poetry with the composition of music, and by so doing makes a very valid point: that of the identification in the ancient world of the 'lyric poet with the musician'. Indeed, the lyric forms in which Archilochus worked, such as the melic and the iambus, were designed for performance at symposiums and were accompanied by a lyre. Thus Nietzsche argues that the identity of lyric poetry is inextricably bound up with the principle of music, birthing out of a 'musical mood' and not out of 'an ordered causality of ideas'. Consequently, the Dionysiac artist begins his creation

> thoroughly united with the primal Oneness, its pain and contradiction, and produces the copy of that primal Oneness as music...[91]

However, Nietzsche is swift to observe that this 'music' does not make a lyric poem, indeed cannot make a lyric poem, for it lacks the causal subject of an Idea. In order to find a form, in order to become intelligible as language, it must to a certain extent surrender to the influence of Apollo. Thus,

> under the Apolline dream influence, this music is revealed to [the lyric poet] as an *allegorical dream-image*. That reflection of primal pain in music, free of images and concepts, redeemed by illusion, now creates a second mirror image as a single allegory or example.[92]

What Nietzsche is conceiving is a process of ideation; a mingling of the Apolline with the Dionysiac; a necessary tempering of the 'primal contradiction and primal suffering' of the *will* with the 'primal delight in illusion'. From this 'allegorical dream-image' emerges a personal expression, still charged with the music of the primal Oneness, but which can now speak out to the world 'from the very depths of being'. Thus, for Nietzsche, the 'subjectivity' of a poet such as Archilochus is not the subjectivity of the Apolline individual. Rather it is the collective subjectivity of the Dionysiac multitude. It touches the Apolline, indeed *needs* the Apolline, but ultimately, through its kinship with primal music, reaches after something new.[93]

It is from this Homer-Archilochus antithesis, from the primal melding of lyric poetry, that Nietzsche lights upon the dithyramb in his 'evolution' towards the apotheosis of Attic Tragedy. The etymology of the word 'dithyramb' is obscure, and it is most probably not of Greek origin. It appears to have originated in 'Corinth' sometime towards the end of the seventh century BCE, and was first introduced to Athens by the lyric poet 'Lasus of Hermione'. In 509 BCE the first dithyrambic competition was held at Athens during the spring festival of Dionysos, 'the Great Dionysia', and subsequent generations of poets, including Simonides, Pindar and Bacchylides, included the dithyramb as part of their repertoire. Surviving examples, such as Bacchylides' *Ode 18*, reveal a strong dramatic element, and indeed Aristotle, in his Poetics, states that 'tragedy…arose from the [choral] leaders of the dithyramb'.[94]

For Nietzsche, the concept of the 'Dionysiac dithyramb' is charged with an intoxicating power. Under its influence, he argues, 'man's symbolic faculties are roused to their supreme intensity'. A 'new world of symbols' is required, a whole

> symbolism of the body, not only the symbolism of the mouth, the eye, the word, but the rhythmic motion of all the limbs of the body in the complete gesture of the dance.[95]

In the dithyramb,

> all the other symbolic forces, the forces of music…rhythm, dynamics and harmony…suddenly find impetuous expression.[96]

It is here that Nietzsche sees the very 'essence of nature' personified, and thus the most profound objectification of the primal Oneness conceivable. The dithyramb puts into artistic form the Dionysiac 'Spirit of revel and rapture', embodying the violence of the maenads that we glimpsed in Euripides' *Bacchae*. However, it is the dithyramb's very intensity, its very 'liberation of all the symbolic forces', its very rape of the Apolline through the savagery of its demands, that necessarily means that the 'dithyrambic votary of Dionysus is…understood only by his fellows'. For Nietzsche, only those who have achieved a 'peak of self-negation', who have, like Archilochus, learnt how to sing from the very depths of being, are able to bear the dithyramb's meaning. Thus for the 'Apolline Greek', whose greatest fear was the irrational, such a raw expression of reality, barely mediated by the soothing light of illusion, would have been met with the utmost 'terror'. This fusion of Archilochian lyric with maenadic frenzy was simply too extreme – revealing, through its piercing contrast to the dreaming, individuated life of Apolline man, 'the horror and absurdity of existence', the endless hunger of the primal *will*. If life was to be redeemed, if mankind was going to bear absolute reality, to see the world as it is *in-itself* – and go on living – then there needed to be a ritual taming of the Dionysiac, an 'artistic release from the repellence of the absurd'.[97]

Thus it is through these abortive fusions, through these terrific couplings and sparking reactions, that Nietzsche brings us onto the tragic stage. Despite occurring at the epicentre of *The Birth of Tragedy*, it is, in effect, Nietzsche's metaphysical *coup de théâtre*, his ultimate displacement through the passionate implosion of Dionysiac flux and Apolline form. In line with Aristotle, Nietzsche transforms the 'ecstatic horde of Dionysiac votaries' into the tragic chorus, and thus moves towards the great catharsis of his Dionysos-Apollo binary. By placing the dithyramb on stage, by objectifying the primal *will* as a chorus of 'satyrs' – thereby symbolising the animal 'archetype of man' beneath the 'mendacious finery...of culture' – Nietzsche engenders the means by which 'the image of Dionysus' may be 'revealed' whilst at the same time remaining paradoxically shielded. The solution, if such it may be called, lies in the architectural context of the Athenian Theatre coupled with the nature of the Apolline characters that populate the stage. Thus for Nietzsche, the tiered terraces of the amphitheatre enabled the spectator 'to *overlook* the whole of the surrounding cultural world', indeed to be suspended from life in a moment of pure contemplation. They could watch the 'sublime chorus of dancing, singing satyrs' below them, see their primal essence reflected in the Dionysiac fire of the chorus, without getting burnt. Their vantage point enabled the necessary objectification, the necessary distance, for the primal reality of the *will* to be mediated without engendering the horror of despair. This objectification was further aided by the purely Apolline elements of the tragic experience, namely the characters and events with which the chorus interacted. The suffering heroes of the tragic stage, such as Aeschylus' Prometheus or Sophocles' Ajax, took upon themselves the full brunt of the Dionysiac frenzy. They *suffered*, and the spectator watched them suffer, indeed gained a cathartic release through the experience. Thus as the chorus enfolded the tragic hero – commenting, questioning, not tied to a single identity or form, but always moving as the action dictated, mimicking 'the constant destruction of phenomena', the 'primal relationship between the thing in itself and the world of appearances' – so the spectator, whose individuality was subsumed into the crowd, became part of the choral process, *became a satyr*, and as such was able to look 'upon the god', not with Apolline terror in the face of the absurd, but with a 'new vision', clarified by the aesthetic heat of the moment. Thus for Nietzsche the experience of Attic Tragedy was a fundamental inversion of the spectator's identity; an 'abandonment of individuality' through the realisation of the true essence of the self, *concurrent* with the maintenance of illusion. Consequently, in Attic Tragedy Nietzsche saw the 'Dionysiac chorus continuously discharging itself in an Apolline world of images', and as such engendering the ultimate *fusion* and *displacement* of life and art; the ultimate paradox of flux and form.[98]

It is a fascinating trait of Nietzsche's biography that art and life cannot be meaningfully extrapolated. The shrapnel-like voices that make up his work, diverse, sharp and invariably contradictory, resonate with the detonation of experience. Even during his adolescence Nietzsche seems to have been concerned with his potential as literature for, as the German scholar Rüdiger Safranski observes in his study, *Nietzsche: A Philosophical Biography*,

> During his high school and college years, from 1858 to 1868, he penned no fewer than nine autobiographical sketches, each following the general theme of 'How I became what I am'.[99]

Twenty years later, when he came to write his eccentric autobiography *Ecce Homo* along remarkably similar thematic lines, Nietzsche stood on the cusp of an experience that would end his literary career and provoke his final living persona. The flux and form which had been the guiding displacement of his life's work, personified so keenly in *The Birth of Tragedy*, was soon to become the grand displacement of his life.

When Nietzsche arrived in Turin in April 1888 his mood was buoyant. The previous months he had spent in Genoa had not been happy ones, and Turin, with its 'aristocratic calm' and 'most beautiful cafés' seemed to be 'a discovery of the first importance'. He found lodgings on the Via Carlo Alberto, renting a room in the third-floor apartment of the news-vender Davide Fino, his wife and two daughters. The apartment was well situated, standing opposite the Palazzo Carignano and affording a pleasant view of the Piazza below. Here Nietzsche worked 'from early in the day until evening', finding time, so he ecstatically wrote to his friend Peter Gast shortly after his arrival, to hear Bizet's *Carmen* performed at the 'Teatro Carignano' and dine out frequently at an 'excellent *trattoria'* he had discovered not far from the Piazza Castello. Indeed all his letters from these early months in Turin speak with a renewed vigour, with a zest for life bordering on the euphoric. 'Really', he wrote to Gast,

> there must be some energising element in the air here – to be at home here will make one a *king* of Italy…[100]

In June, Nietzsche left Turin for Sils-Maria. His reason for departing from a place with which he had so evidently fallen in love was purely pragmatic. All his life Nietzsche had suffered from an extremely sensitive constitution, and by June 'even the fresh air of the Alps could no longer keep the temperature from rising' too high for his fragile health to bear. As the biographer Curtis Cate observes in his study, *Friedrich Nietzsche: A Biography*:

> Nietzsche was almost permanently unwell, suffering not only from acute eye-aches every time he tried to

> read for more than an hour or two, but also from nausea, stomach upsets and even vomiting…[101]

Thus Nietzsche sought refuge in the 'cool highlands of the Engadine' until the summer heat abated and he could safely return to Turin once more.[102]

The journey from Sils-Maria back to Turin in the September of 1888 was to be the last journey of Nietzsche's sane life, for a shroud was soon to descend over his mind, silencing him forever. Yet at the time nothing appeared to be amiss. He resumed his room on the Via Carlo Alberto with Davide Fino and his family, once again took to enjoying the Turin cultural scene, and, most importantly, continued with his writing. Indeed the closing months of 1888 were to be possessed of a startling productivity, with Nietzsche producing no less than three major works: *Twilight of the Idols*, *The Anti-Christ*, and of course *Ecce Homo*. He also maintained a steady stream of correspondences, detailing the minutiae of his daily life as well as his intellectual preoccupations. It is to these last works that we will now turn in order to gain a greater understanding of Nietzsche's negative ontology, its textual expression and its devastating biographical ramifications.

Whereas *The Birth of Tragedy* had seen Nietzsche playfully destabilise both the field of Classical philology and Schopenhauer's metaphysic through his eccentric transposition of nineteenth-century German Idealist philosophy onto Attic Tragedy, *Twilight of the Idols*, by contrast, lashes out with a barely restrained ferocity against the moral figures and influences of Nietzsche's day. Indeed, its subheading, 'How to Philosophise with a Hammer', goes some way towards illustrating the profoundly destructive nature of the work. Thus it is no surprise to find the Nietzschean scholar Michael Tanner remark, in his 1990 introductory essay to R. J. Hollingdale's 1968 translation of the text, that its tone is 'predominantly strident, even shrill'. To be sure, *Twilight of the Idols* sees Nietzsche 'on remarkably negative form'; to such an extent, in fact, that the text even appears to be at war with itself. For example, in the sixth division of the section entitled 'What the Germans Lack', Nietzsche proudly asserts:

> my nature…is *affirmative* and has dealings with contradiction and criticism only indirectly and when compelled…[103]

proceeding to assert with equal conviction two sections later:

> My taste, which may be called the opposite of a tolerant taste…in general…dislikes saying Yes, it would rather say No…[104]

It is perversities such as this that have led some critics to assume that *Twilight of the Idols* bears the hallmarks of Nietzsche's encroaching madness. However, as Nietzsche admits in a discarded draft from section three of *Ecce Homo*: 'My writings are difficult', and indeed the paradoxical sentiments expressed above, far from being out of character, are, in fact, characteristic of Nietzsche's philosophical enterprise – an enterprise that spanned some sixteen years of writing. Throughout that extended period, Nietzsche was to continuously indulge in similarly provocative acts, and it is unwise to interpret the peculiarities of these late works directly in the light of his imminent collapse.[105]

It is here worth bearing in mind these lines from the third part of *Thus Spoke Zarathustra* (1883-85), for they seem to reflect something of the intention and design of Nietzsche's highly unstable work:

> To you, the bold venturers and adventurers and whoever has embarked with cunning sails upon dreadful seas,
> to you who are intoxicated by riddles, who take pleasure in twilight, whose soul is lured with flutes to every treacherous abyss –

> for you who do not desire to feel for a rope with cowardly hand; and where you can *guess* you hate to *calculate* –
>
> to you alone do I tell this riddle that I saw – the vision of the most solitary man.[106]

It is exceedingly tempting, and not at all unprofitable, to read the above as a self-reflexive dialogue, for its seems fitting to perceive Nietzsche as a bold adventurer cunningly sailing upon the 'dreadful seas' of his philosophy. He is indeed 'intoxicated by riddles', and the man who once described himself as a 'nuance' cannot fail to take a certain pleasure in the ambiguous hues of twilight. However, most important of all is 'the vision of the most solitary man', a role which Nietzsche frequently assumes, indeed which seems central to his self-conception.[107]

In a letter written to the musicologist Carl Fuchs, during his stay in Sils-Maria during the summer of 1888, Nietzsche proclaims:

> It is not necessary at all – not even desirable – that you should argue in my favour; on the contrary, a dose of curiosity, as in the presence of a foreign planet, with an ironic resistance, would seem to me an incomparably more intelligent attitude.[108]

Here we can see Nietzsche deliberately courting an image of alterity; and it is a profoundly provocative stance. Despite the innocuous veneer of its tone, what the above makes clear is that this 'foreign planet' called Nietzsche does *not* want allies, does *not* want a relief from his solitude – far from it. Rather he wants an 'ironic resistance', a cerebral war of dissonance, in which the incendiary power of his work will rock the very infrastructure of being – to whit, the minds of his readers. For Nietzsche the solitary man, the perennial outsider, is also 'an inner tension of pathos through signs' – a textual combatant whose necessary battleground is consciousness. Thus when encountering a text like *Twilight of the Idols* – indeed when encountering any of Nietzsche's works – it is important to be mindful that Nietzsche is deliberately seeking a complex process of alienation: the alienation of himself from himself, himself from his readers, and his readers from his work.[109]

Nietzsche's 'ironic resistance', like the Socratic irony of Plato's early dialogues, is profoundly destructive, engendering a complete destabilisation of the status quo. We saw this embryonically in *The Birth of Tragedy*, when Nietzsche exploded his identity both as a philologist and as a Schopenhauerian, and in a mature work, such as *Twilight of the Idols*, it is hardly surprising to find this 'resistance' enacted with an even more 'warlike' intensity. Indeed, what this latter work intimates is a total displacement of the very foundations of society: the wilful opening of a 'treacherous abyss'. By screaming for a 'transvaluation of all values', whilst simultaneously refusing to provide a stable rationale for their replacement, Nietzsche is threatening the ground of identity more aggressively than ever. 'What alone can *our* teaching be?' he asks in the eighth division of the section entitled 'The Four Great Errors', before denying any meaning whatsoever to the nature of our existence:

> What alone can *our* teaching be? – That no one gives a human being his qualities: not God, not society, not his parents or ancestors, not he *himself* (– the nonsensical idea here last rejected was propounded, as 'intelligible freedom' by Kant, and perhaps also by Plato before him). No *one* is accountable for existing at all, or for being constituted as he is, or for living in the circumstances and surroundings in which he lives. The fatality of his nature cannot be disentangled from the fatality of all that which he has been and will be. He is *not* the result of a special design, a will, a purpose; he is *not* the subject of an attempt to attain to an 'ideal of man' or an 'ideal of happiness' or an 'ideal of morality' – it is absurd to want to *hand over* his nature to some purpose or other. *We* invented the concept 'purpose': in reality purpose is *lacking*.[110]

'God', as Nietzsche had first written six years previously in *The Gay Science* 'is dead', likewise all ideals, all principles, all causes. Even Nietzsche's use of the word 'fatality' seems fatal, disenfranchised as it is from any notion of a higher purpose. Most startlingly of all, Nietzsche would even deny Mankind's right to self-creation, dismissing Kant's 'intelligible freedom' as 'nonsensical', and leaving us trapped in a paralytic limbo, stripped of cause and effect. For Nietzsche nature is design-less, will-less, and purposeless, and we, as part of nature, partake of these negativities. Indeed, here Mankind is seen as a purely negative digression of a purely negative 'whole'. Indeed not *even* negative, for Nietzsche would appear to have removed the apparatus necessary in order for the concept 'negative' to have any tangible value. That is if Nietzsche were being consistent with anything other than his consistent inconsistency. For having cast humanity into a treacherous abyss, having forcibly stripped it of everything that makes it what it is – be that the empowerment of faith or the self-creating accountability of action – he has the audacity to call this nihilistic paralysis, this total negation, 'the great liberation', the restoration of 'innocence', as though these terms could, in such a wasteland, have some positivistic value. Having denied all ideals Nietzsche mockingly, almost madly, returns to the Ideal.[111]

It is the concept of return, indeed of *recurrence*, that brings us onto *The Anti-Christ*. No less polemical than *Twilight of the Idols*, this short, sharp laceration of morality sees Nietzsche re-imagine the binary dynamic that we first encountered in *The Birth of Tragedy*. Addressed to the 'very few', this turgid 'thunderstorm' seeks to draw 'back the curtain on the *depravity* of man', to reveal the fundamental antithesis between the true natures of 'good' and 'bad', and by so doing cleanse the world of 'every kind of uncleanness of concept and value'. For Nietzsche, the good is to be identified as all 'that heightens the feeling of power, the will to power, power itself in man', whilst the bad is to be understood as all 'that proceeds from weakness' –

something which Nietzsche sees as finding its most dangerous embodiment in 'Christianity'. Indeed, amid Nietzsche's latest tirade against the 'false idea' of progress, against the 'dreadful spectacle' of '*décadence*' in man, it is possible to perceive the echo of the Dionysos-Apollo binary. The will to power, like the primal Oneness of the Dionysiac, is something raw and terrible: a savage force, whose pleasure is derived, not from 'contentment' but through the ceaseless hunger for 'more power' – not from 'peace' but through 'war'. Likewise, in Nietzsche's concept of Christianity it is possible to perceive the resonance of the Apolline: a 'denial of life' that tempers the will to power through its '[a]ctive sympathy for the ill-constituted and weak'.[112]

Contextually, of course, the differences are numerous. Unlike the Dionysiac Oneness of *The Birth of Tragedy*, the will to power is profoundly individualistic; indeed it actively resists the mentality of the 'herd'. Rather it is

> [r]everence for oneself; love for oneself; unconditional freedom with respect to oneself.[113]

Conversely the 'moralic acid' of Christianity seeks to dissolve the individual's will to power, and as such would seem to be in opposition to the Apolline's role in *The Birth of Tragedy* as the *principium individuationis.* The subject matter is also far removed from the pseudo-philology of Nietzsche's early career. The Attic stage has gone, and the new stage that Nietzsche has set for himself is 'the day after tomorrow'. Nevertheless, it is equally possible to argue, and with conviction, that these differences are, in fact, superficial – that beneath Nietzsche's 'war on [the] theologian instinct' there abides the same set of tensions, the same battle of flux and form that we discerned at the heart of *The Birth of Tragedy*. Indeed, *The Anti-Christ*, like *Twilight of the Idols* before it, is a profoundly unstable work. For all its posturing, for all its hyperbolical cries for a 'revaluation of all values', the text is built upon a fatal opposition. By seeking to displace Christianity with its 'antithesis', by prizing 'contempt' over 'pity', this world over the next, Nietzsche fails to revalue anything, for these antitheses are of course *conditional* upon the very thing they claim to oppose. Ultimately their identity cannot be extrapolated, and Nietzsche's 'day after tomorrow' – itself a non-space, a 'Hyperborean' fantasy – is merely the dreamt inversion of today. Thus in *The Anti-Christ* we once again find a negative ontology, unfounded and foundering, whose nature, like the Dionysos-Apollo binary, the binary of flux and form, exists in a mutual displacement of concurrent definition.[114]

The concept of recurrence is a recurrent theme throughout Nietzsche's work, embodied both in the return of ideas, as evinced by the above, and as a philosophical principle in its own right. Nietzsche's doctrine of the eternal recurrence makes its first appearance in *The Gay Science* where it is offered merely as a hypothetical postulate and *not* as a metaphysical truth. 'What if', asks Nietzsche,

> some day or night a demon were to steal after you into your loneliest loneliness and say to you: 'This life as you now live it and have lived it, you will have to live once more and innumerable times more; and there will be nothing new in it, but every pain and every joy and every thought and sigh and everything unutterably small or great in your life will have to return to you, all in the same succession and sequence…' Would you not throw yourself down and gnash your teeth and curse the demon who spoke thus? Or have you once experienced a tremendous moment when you would have answered him: 'You are a god and never have I heard anything more divine.' If this thought gained possession of you, it would change you as you are or perhaps crush you. The question in each and every thing, 'Do you desire this once more and innumerable times more?' would lie upon your actions as the greatest weight. Or how well disposed you would have to become to yourself

> and life to crave nothing more fervently than this ultimate eternal confirmation and seal?[115]

By posing these questions, by urging us to live our lives *as if* we would have to relive each minute detail again and again, Nietzsche may be seen as seeking to awaken a concern for the qualitative nature of our existence. Thus this early formulation of the eternal recurrence may be seen as a spur to reflexivity, as a spur towards a life of the self-empowered will, a life without regrets, in which each thought, each action, is so well conceived as to be unafraid, indeed intoxicated, at the prospect of its perpetual return.

In the three years between the completion of *The Gay Science* and completion of *Thus Spoke Zarathustra*, Nietzsche's conception of the eternal recurrence had undergone something of a metamorphosis. As this passage from 'The Intoxicated Song' of *Thus Spoke Zarathustra, Book Four* makes clear, the hypothetical 'What if?' has vanished and in its place is to be found what appears to be a powerful, poetic assertion of the eternal recurrence's metaphysical truth:

> What do you think, you Higher Men? Am I a prophet? A dreamer? A drunkard? An interpreter of dreams? A midnight bell?
>
> A drop of dew? An odour and scent of eternity? Do you not hear it? Do you not smell it? My world has just become perfect, midnight is also noonday,
>
> pain is also joy, a curse is also a blessing, the night is also a sun – be gone, or you will learn: a wise man is also a fool.
>
> Did you ever say Yes to one joy? O my friends, then you said Yes to *all* woe as well. All things are chained and entwined together, all things are in love;
>
> if ever you wanted one moment twice, if ever you said: 'You please me, happiness, instant, moment!' then you wanted *everything* to return!

> you wanted everything anew, everything eternal, everything chained, entwined together, everything in love, O that is how you *loved* the world,
>
> you everlasting men, loved it eternally and for all time: and you say even to woe: 'Go, but return!' *For all joy wants – eternity!*[116]

Even more interesting is Nietzsche's marriage of the eternal recurrence to yet another system of binary displacement. Like the pre-Socratic philosopher Heraclitus of Ephesus, who once cryptically observed that 'good and bad are the same', so Nietzsche's Zarathustra, in an intoxicated, Dionysiac state of mind, beholds the 'opposing coherence' of all things. 'Midnight' is 'noonday' and 'pain' is 'joy'. Everything is chained together – 'all things are in love'. Indeed, this latter term is revealing, for Nietzsche was later to state that '[t]hat which is done out of love always takes place beyond good and evil'. In *The Anti-Christ*, the term 'Beyond', through its association with the Christian conception of God, is given to mean 'nothingness', and it is tempting to see a correspondence between these sentiments and the passage from *Thus Spoke Zarathustra* cited above. If 'midnight' *is* 'noonday'; if 'pain' *is* 'joy'; if good and evil are indeed *one and the same*; if 'all things are in love' and 'love always takes place beyond good and evil', then it is possible to discern Nietzsche conceiving an act of displacement on a truly cataclysmic scale for, by this logic, everything is beyond itself, everything *is* nothing. Thus the eternal recurrence – rather than evincing the will to power through an affirmative (but hypothetical) desire to live one's life again – becomes symbolic of this causal displacement, for everything recurs upon itself in a single moment: a single moment that is simultaneously *every* moment and, paradoxically, *no* moment at all.[117]

This cataclysmic displacement of the eternal recurrence, this negative ontology, finds its ultimate literary attunement in *Ecce Homo*. Written 'in just under three weeks', between the 15th October and the 4th November 1888, the text is the culmination of Nietzsche's life's work: a bizarre, volatile fusion/confusion of autobiography, philosophy and sheer buffoonery. Indeed the 'idiosyncratic' nature of Nietzsche's style, with its near perpetual use of hyperbolae and a self-aggrandisement bordering on megalomania, has led critics such as Tanner to label the work as a 'parody'. This reading is useful, up to a point, for *Ecce Homo* can indeed be seen to be wilfully destabilising the expectations of its alleged genre. By inverting the form's traditional 'lack of explicit self-congratulation', by discarding the mask of polite (and evidently false) 'modesty', Nietzsche is indeed subverting convention. However, there is manifestly more to *Ecce Homo* than simply 'mischievous intent' on the behalf of its author, for the text is more than merely an exotic species of autobiography – it is, beneath its giddying froth of absurdity, an 'aggressive pathos', a violent act of suffering that enables Nietzsche, amid the 'terrible noontide abyss' of his life, to 'overcome' himself. In a refraction of Zarathustra's desire to be swallowed by the sun, Nietzsche has transformed into a terminal star around which his memories and works orbit like planets: 'Fräulein Lou von Salomé' and 'Richard Wagner'; 'The Gay Science' and 'Twilight of the Idols'; 'Schopenhauer', 'Bismarck' and 'The Birth of Tragedy'; all bask in the light of Nietzsche's dwindling sun. Each recurs; and in its recurrence is at once transfigured *and* consumed – for Nietzsche the '*décadent*', the *décadent*'s 'antithesis', is in the throws of turning supernova.[118]

In his brief preface to the work, a solitary paragraph of some twelve lines, Nietzsche states:

> On this perfect day, when everything has become ripe and not only the grapes are growing brown, a ray of sunlight has fallen onto my life: I look behind me, I look before me, never have I seen so many and such good things together. Not in vain have I buried my forty-fourth year today, I was entitled to bury it – what there was of life in it is rescued, is immortal. The first book of the *Revaluation of All Values* [viz. *The Anti-Christ*], the *Songs of Zarathustra*, the

> *Twilight of the Idols*, my attempt to philosophise with a hammer – all of them gifts of this year, of its last quarter even! *How should I not be grateful to my whole life?* – And so I tell myself my life.[119]

What is immediately striking about the above is its parity with the passage from 'The Intoxicated Song' that we analysed earlier. Just as Zarathustra hymned: 'My world has just become perfect', before beginning to expound the doctrine of the eternal recurrence, so Nietzsche begins *Ecce Homo* along equally idealistic lines. The day on which Nietzsche chooses to celebrate his life – symbolically given as his birthday – like Zarathustra's great noontide, is described as 'perfect'; and of course it is important to be mindful that that which celebrates remembers, and that which is remembered returns. Thus it is not unreasonable to conjecture that Nietzsche intended *Ecce Homo* to be more than a complicated parody of an autobiography: that it is, in fact, analogous to the eternal recurrence, and that Nietzsche is drawing everything together with the express purpose of cancelling everything out.

Indeed the image of ripeness on which he dwells in the first sentence seems particularly pertinent for 'the grapes are going brown'. Grapes are of course associated with Dionysos, and Dionysos, as we saw earlier, is the embodiment of the life-force or *Zoë*. Yet this ripeness, described as a 'going brown', seems more indicative of decay than maturity; indeed seems to signify the onset of death. Dionysos, as we have seen, has a particular significance in Nietzsche's philosophy, and it is possible that Nietzsche is using the image of decaying grapes as a portent of his own encroaching philosophical silence. Despite his projected magnum opus, the *Revaluation of All Values*, it is feasible, as we shall discuss presently, that Nietzsche knew the dangerous state of his health; that he knew that in all probability *Ecce Homo* would be his last work. That being the case, we can see how the concept of the eternal recurrence becomes the final affirmative denial of a paradoxical life: a final ironic resistance against the inevitable alienation of death.

Unsurprisingly for its 'genre', Nietzsche spends a great amount of energy throughout the book trying to 'bear witness' about himself, trying to say *who* he is. However, intriguingly/worryingly the answer is *not* Friedrich Nietzsche, sometime professor of Classical Philology at the University of Basel, ex-Wagnerian and itinerant philosopher – at some point in his imaginative life Nietzsche appears to have undergone an apotheosis. Indeed the book's very title *Ecce Homo* – 'behold the man' – invoking the words spoken by Pontius Pilate when he brought the tortured Christ before the crowd (John 19:5), indicates the disturbing tempo of Nietzsche's 'witness'. To be sure, despite his virulent abomination of Christianity in *The Anti-Christ* Nietzsche appears to have a certain respect for Jesus, a man who, despite having an 'intrinsic hatred of reality' – hence his recourse to a kingdom *not* of this world (John 18:36) – 'died as he lived, as he *taught*' without any of the hypocrisy that Nietzsche sees as saturating the Christian Church. Thus 'What [Jesus] bequeathed to mankind', writes Nietzsche in *The Anti-Christ*,

> is his *practice*: his bearing before the judges, before the guards, before the accusers and every kind of calumny and mockery – his bearing on the *Cross*. He does not resist, he does not defend his rights, he takes no steps to avert the worst that can happen to him – more, *he provokes it*... And he entreats, he suffers, he loves *with* those, *in* those who are doing evil to him.[120]

Likewise Nietzsche's practice has also been one of suffering, whether that be the endurance of 'an extremity of pain', engendered through a profound 'physiological weakness', or the intellectual burden of being an 'untimely' man. Indeed, in their respective ways, both Christ and Nietzsche can be seen as embodying wilfully antithetical positions within their particular societies. Each is an outsider; and each is deliberately called to account for their 'transgressions' – Christ by provoking his crucifixion and Nietzsche by provoking *his* 'death' through the writing of *Ecce Homo.* Arguably the absurdity of the parallel is as manifest as it is 'blasphemous', and yet it is very much in keeping with the 'laughing seriousness' that characterises the work. For despite the portents, Nietzsche is not *literally* claiming to be Christ, nor even Christ-like, as in the sense understood by Thomas à Kempis, but rather *like* Christ – a man killed by his beliefs. Indeed, by adopting the thorny crown of this 'ironical divinity', this *man of sorrows*, this very inversion of Hellenic godhood, Nietzsche seeks to displace his identity with its antithesis. For by standing before the mirror dressed as Christ, Nietzsche is able to see everything he *is* transposed onto the reflection of everything he is *not.* Ultimately, the similarities exist to elucidate the differences.[121]

Thus, whilst *like* the suffering Christ, it is once more to Dionysos that Nietzsche returns for his supreme transfiguration. Right from the beginning of Nietzsche's philosophical career the figure of Dionysos has haunted his work – explicitly in *The Birth of Tragedy*, and then implicitly through various other incarnations down until *Ecce Homo.* Zarathustra, the Ubermensch (Overman/Superman), the eternal recurrence – all bear the mark of Dionysos, the supreme embodiment of the will to life. Consequently, it comes as no surprise to hear Nietzsche declare in *Ecce Homo*'s Foreword: 'I am a disciple of the philosopher Dionysos'. However, as the unfolding text reveals, this relationship is far from an un-problematical case of discipleship, for it can be no coincidence that Nietzsche has identified Dionysos as a 'philosopher'; the role in life he *himself* has chosen. Even in the Foreword we get an intimation of the lurking, personal complexities entwining Nietzsche with the god. Thus in the opening chapter, modestly entitled 'Why I Am So Wise', Nietzsche begins the process of paring away the layers of his life, of scratching off the dead layers of his factual history in order to reveal the 'divinity' within. The first casualties are his parents. His father, who died at the age of thirty-six when Nietzsche was only five years old, is dismissed as a 'reminder of life, not life itself', whilst his mother, with whom Nietzsche never had an affectionate relationship, is abused as a 'poisonous viper'. A little further on, after having denied his German lineage altogether and claimed, quite erroneously, to be 'a pure-blooded Polish nobleman', Nietzsche remarks offhandedly:

> One is least related to one's parents: it would be the most extreme sign of vulgarity to be related to one's parents.[122]

Having made way for something more appropriate – for he has such a 'sovereign feeling of distinction' that he would not even 'award the young German Kaiser the honour of being [his] coachman' – Nietzsche proudly declares:

> Higher natures have their origins infinitely farther back, and with them much had to be assembled, saved and hoarded. The great individuals are the oldest: I don't understand it, but Julius Caesar could be my father, or Alexander, this Dionysos incarnate...[123]

Here Nietzsche, who clearly considers himself to be one of life's 'great individuals', has not only dislodged himself from the nineteenth century, but hypothesised a pedigree that is at worst heroic and at best divine. A man like Alexander the Great *could* be his father, indeed *should* be his father – a man who is none other than 'Dionysos incarnate'. Not only is Nietzsche Dionysos' disciple, it seems he would be his son as well.

Yet ultimately Nietzsche is not content to be merely *the son* of a god, for that does not reflect the depth of his 'Dionysian endowment'. Indeed, during his commentary on *Thus Spoke Zarathustra*, Nietzsche, praising the brilliance of his work, observes:

> The like of [*Thus Spoke Zarathustra*] has never been written, never felt, never *suffered* : thus does a god suffer, a Dionysos.[124]

The distance between Nietzsche and Dionysos has all but closed, and in the final chapter, hyperbolically entitled 'Why I Am A Destiny', the identification becomes complete. 'I am not a man', he screams, 'I am dynamite', before going on to prophesy: 'I shall one day be pronounced *holy*'. The final 'shattering thunder-clap' occurs when Nietzsche, now reborn as Dionysos, the great '*immoralist*', the 'god of darkness', the Anti-Christ, makes his last tirade against Christianity, spitting phrases such as moral '*vampirism*', and 'will to the lie'. Yet ultimately, as we have seen so often before in Nietzsche's work, it comes down to a focused conflict of antitheses. 'Have I been understood?' he asks, in the solitary line that closes the text, '*Dionysos against the Crucified...*' The question is doubtless rhetorical, and seems to be addressed, not so much to the reader, as to himself. Indeed, as we saw in his brief preface, it was Nietzsche's intention to tell himself his life. *Nietzsche* is his audience, and so *Ecce Homo* – 'behold the man' – is not only autobiographical but also auto-centric in a very particular sense. What we are then witnessing is an intimate psychological process akin to the cathartic displacement of Attic Tragedy. For having displaced the *character* of Friedrich Nietzsche with Dionysos, the author then proceeds to place Dionysos in direct antithetical conflict with Christ, knowing full well that, according to his doctrine of the eternal recurrence, Dionysos and Christ are eternally *one and the same*. Here, at the end of Nietzsche's literary career, life and death, the affirmation and denial of the will, words and silence, all spark and fuse and disappear.[125]

The closing months of 1888 saw Nietzsche experience a seeming improvement in his health. In a letter written to Peter Gast on the 30th October – towards the end of the composition of *Ecce Homo* – he remarks with gusto:

> I have just seen myself in the mirror – never have I looked so well. In exemplary condition, well nourished and ten years younger than I should be[126]

going on to comment that since 'choosing Turin' for his home he has become much 'changed in the honours' that he does himself:

> I rejoice, for example, in an excellent tailor, and set value of being received everywhere as a distinguished foreigner. I have succeeded amazingly well at this. In *my* trattoria I receive without any doubt the best there is[127]

The overwhelming feeling is one of euphoria, of a man ripening into his life. Yet like the browning grapes of *Ecce Homo*, Nietzsche's ripening was indicative of his decay.

The question of precisely when and where Nietzsche contracted syphilis is uncertain. Tanner remarks that upon a visit to Cologne in 1865 Nietzsche had 'been taken to a brothel against his will' but had 'left again at once', apparently highly embarrassed by the whole experience. Nevertheless, despite his initial reluctance, it seems likely that Nietzsche, in keeping with so many university students of 'the 1860s and 1870s', did indeed have an encounter with a prostitute around this time, for in 1867 he was treated by 'two Leipzig doctors for a syphilitic infection'. This treatment would have included a course of 'mercury, arsenic and iodine', and under the 'influence of these strong poisons' the symptoms would have 'abated', to such an extent, in fact, that Nietzsche might have thought himself cured. However, according to William J. Brown, in his clinical study *Syphilis: A Synopsis*, 'All syphilis is latent at some time during its course', and years may elapse before its manifest return. Indeed, Nietzsche's 'euphoria', expressed in letters such as the above, rather than evincing an improvement in his health, in fact reveals the onset of tertiary, or neurosyphilis. As the critical biographer Lesley

Chamberlain, in her study *Nietzsche In Turin: The End of the Future*, remarks,

> As the brain loses mass, the result of tertiary syphilis, the human consciousness seems to effervesce in megalomania.[128]

To be sure, as the weeks wore on, the extravagances of *Ecce Homo* began to break into Nietzsche's life. The Finos, who had always found their lodger somewhat 'eccentric', became disturbed when he took to 'playing the piano alone in the dark'. Indeed, even more disturbing was the fact that he was not playing any recognisable music but simply 'striking cords between long periods of silence'. However, they really started to worry when Nietzsche, in all seriousness,

> asked for his room to be decked out as a temple, with frescoes, so he could receive the King and Queen of Italy.[129]

His behaviour in public was also beginning to take an alarming turn. On two occasions he was seized by an attack of 'uncontrollable grimacing and weeping', and on occasion would 'harangue' people in the street, claiming he was 'God come to earth in human form'. Fortunately, his Italian was not sophisticated enough to cause any serious trouble.[130]

That Nietzsche was tragically aware of his condition is hinted at in a letter written to Peter Gast on the afternoon of his second fit of grimacing (2nd December). He had been hearing a concert at the Teatro Carignano when his face suddenly 'kept making grimaces'. This, Nietzsche tries to maintain, was 'in order to get over a feeling of extreme pleasure' that the concert had aroused. Yet it included a ten-minute long 'grimace of tears', and Nietzsche's cheerful tone is not altogether convincing. When he writes: 'Ah, if you could have been there!', one gets the sense that it is not to hearing the music that he is referring. Indeed, Chamberlain maintains that Nietzsche was fully aware of what was happening to him, and that from 'cheerful' epistles like the above to grand gestures of defiance such as *Ecce Homo*, he was engaging in a practice of '*amor fati* ', trying to transvalue the horror of his 'unavoidable decay' into something life-affirming. To be sure, on this argument – and it *is* in keeping with Nietzsche's theatrical personality – even his haranguing of 'anonymous' members of the Turin public becomes part of a self-conscious performance. For by deliberately cultivating the 'errant behaviour to which his syphilis was driving him', Nietzsche was able to regain some modicum of control, and the man behind the mask, 'the ordinary sick man', was thus able to 'slip away and fade, off-stage, in peace'.[131]

On the 3rd January 1889 Nietzsche saw a 'cart-driver furiously beating his lagging nag' on the Via Po. Overcome, Nietzsche ran forward and threw his arms around the horse's neck, before collapsing, unconscious to the ground. There is some confusion over what happened next, for, as Curtis Cate observes, 'the first printed account of the incident did not appear until thirteen years later in an Italian news paper', however it seems that someone, recognising Nietzsche, went to fetch Davide Fino. Whatever the precise nature of events, Nietzsche was carried home to the Finos' apartment and put to bed. When he awoke his sanity was completely gone. Letters written after the incident of January 3rd reveal the depth of his derangement. For example, he wrote to his friend Jakob Burckhardt, 'I would much rather be a Basel professor than God', and in a gesture emulating the grand displacement of *Ecce Homo*, signed several other equally bizarre epistles variously 'Dionysos' or 'The Crucified'. By now his behaviour was completely unbearable. As well as constantly hammering away at the piano, he would also sing at the top of his voice – and Signora Fino even came across him 'prancing naked round [his] room, enacting solitary Dionysian rites'. Unable to cope, the Finos' contacted Nietzsche's friend, the theologian Franz Overbeck, and the philosopher was removed to the university clinic at Basel, where he was diagnosed with 'paralysis progressiva'.[132]

Nietzsche was to spend the last ten years of his life in a vegetative state, a prisoner of the body that had betrayed him and of a mother and sister whom he hated. It is ironic to think that the man who had so vociferously preached the will to power should have been reduced to such a disempowered condition. Lying there in his sister's house in Weimar, Nietzsche had transcended both life and death, held, like a mockery of his Zarathustra, in a perpetual noontide. Yet the greatest irony of all was to be his funeral, for the man who had spent his life attacking Christianity was, at the behest of his sister, given a formal *Christian* burial in his late father's graveyard at Röcken. So it was in death that Nietzsche's life, like his life's work, recurred.

Practice

Introduction and Radiation Era 1 (Planck Era)

The first book of *Silence* corresponds to the first thirty-thousand-years of the Universe. As we saw in the 'Cosmological Paradigm' this epoch encompasses the Radiation Era and is marked by its density, intense heat, and great volatility. Thus the syphilitic Nietzsche, with his fluid identity, his wild hyperbolae, and explosive philosophy, seemed to me to be the ideal voice to personify this astrophysical phenomenon. I decided early on that whilst Nietzsche would be the voice of the first book, this voice, in keeping with its essential fluidity, would itself inhabit other connected identities. Consequently, after the overtly Nietzschean monologue which opens the book, the voice dilates into an inversion of Plato's *Symposium*. This, in its turn, becomes a variety of dismembered voices concerning the myth of Dionysos, before transforming into a collection of Orphic fragments. These fragments, through the course of their progression, return us to the overtly Nietzschean persona once more. What may be seen from this is not only a marked progression from the Planck Era (Nietzsche) through the Hadron and Lepton Eras (the Symposium) and down through the cooling phases of the

Radiation Era (Dionysos Dismembered) towards the encroaching Matter Era (Strings of Orpheus), but also an essential faithfulness to Nietzsche's philosophy, for the entire book may be seen as evincing the doctrine of the eternal recurrence. It begins and ends with Nietzsche, and even when his voice is not directly speaking his influence remains.

In regards to metre, I decided that the traditional English epic line, the iambic pentameter – to be found in works such as Milton's *Paradise Lost* (1667) and Wordsworth's *The Prelude* (1805) – was too formal, lacking the fluidity needed to correspond to the mercurial nature of the subject matter. Thus, I have adopted a combination of free and octosyllabic verse patterns, allowing for a great variety of cadences and with the intention of mirroring the natural rhythms of speech. Particularly in regards to the more 'formal' octosyllabic sequences, I have taken great care to ensure a near constant use of enjambment in order to disrupt any feeling of contrived regularity. The stresses within these octosyllabic lines also vary with great regularity, corresponding to the tempo of what is being said. Likewise, in the interests of naturalism, I have avoided overt poeticisms, unless I felt that they facilitated some purposeful, dramatic effect.

Thus the opening sequence of the Nietzsche Monologue (lines 1-101), signifying the very earliest moments of the Planck Era, is composed in free verse so as to convey a sense of molten fluidity. Equally the typography, with lines spreading out over the page, echoes this tremendous state of flux, for I intended that there should be a strong aural-optic correspondence running throughout the epic. In addition to this there is naturally a thematic correspondence, with the opening lines of this sequence:

> *Why am I a destiny?*
>
> Even this mirror marvels
> my reflection, touching the

genius of my naked skin...

anthropomorphising the newly born Universe. As may be observed from the above, the line 'Why am I a destiny?' echoes the title of the final chapter of *Ecce Homo*, and indeed throughout the Nietzsche Monologue I have made every effort to root what is being said to direct examples from Nietzsche's life and work. For example, lines 7-17 refer to the biographical account cited earlier of Signora Fino discovering Nietzsche dancing naked in his room, whilst the reference to the horrors of English cooking in line 19 is drawn from *Ecce Homo.* In narrative terms this sequence provides the historical (as opposed to astrophysical) context of the first book. Lines such as:

The wind shits bedsores
laughing the shutters...
My window shatters
Arcadian fantasies...

indicate that the narrative is taking place in the mind of the paralytic Nietzsche during his 'incarceration' at his sister's house in Weimar during the 1890s. The subsequent action, seemingly set in Turin, is in fact taking place within Nietzsche's inactive and diseased body. Not only is this paradox in keeping with Nietzsche's philosophy of opposing coherence but it also has cosmological implications, for by beginning with decay, by making the beginning an end, the poem may be seen as conforming to the Big Bang/Big Crunch theory, in which the Universe, having expanded to its pinnacle, collapses back in on itself, only to explode outwards once more.

At line 104 the free verse subsides and the octosyllabic blank verse begins. Consequently, at this point the tone changes from the fluid and lyrical to the more concrete, as Nietzsche's mind becomes rooted in the fantasy of a particular time and place. In this sequence I have made use of several of Nietzsche's letters, and the 'person' to whom this sequence is addressed, the composer Heinrich Köselitz (who composed under the pseudonym 'Peter Gast'), was a frequent correspondent – indeed the man who recommended Turin to Nietzsche in the first place. Thus compare, for example, lines 104-129:

> You see, Köselitz how well I am?
> What a city! How right you were,
> my dearest Heinrich, to suggest
> it, really, I cannot thank you enough,
> it's a revelation. Only
> yesterday I was walking over
> the Po Bridge when it occurred to
> me, in one of those startling moments
> of epiphany, that Turin
> is superb, no truly, beyond
> good and evil (!!). I think it no
> exaggeration to say that
> *here* is my philosophy, founded
> in the very stones of Guarini.
> Consider its aristocratic
> tranquillity, its ancient poise,
> its European solemnity –
> is this not *Zarathustra*? Or
> at least its words, lulled into relief
> by rust-reddened brown and the guileless
> hue of ochre? Of course one must
> accept a certain ennui where most
> architecture is concerned (this
> is natural in such a *décadent*
> age) but *here*, Köselitz a universe
> is possible!

with this passage from a letter written by Nietzsche to Köselitz on 7th April 1888:

> But Turin! Dear friend, I congratulate you! Your advice met my deepest wishes! This is really the city which I can now use! This is palpably for me, and was so almost from the start… What a dignified and serious city! Not at all a metropolis, not at all

> modern, as I had feared, but a princely residence of the seventeenth century, one that had only a *single* commanding taste in all things – the court and the *noblesse*. Everywhere the aristocratic calm has been kept: there are no petty suburbs; a unity of taste even in matters of colour (the whole city is yellow or reddish-brown)... Incredible – what serious and solemn palaces! And the style of the palaces, without any pretentiousness; the streets clean and serious – and everything far more dignified than I had expected! The most beautiful cafés I have ever seen. These arcades are somewhat necessary when the climate is so changeable, but they are spacious – they do not oppress one. The evening on the Po Bridge – glorious! Beyond good and evil![133]

Hopefully something of Nietzsche's informal manner, something of his enthusiastic, animated style (as well as the particulars of this correspondence) has translated across into the poetry.

Another example of near direct textual adaptation comes at line 319:

> What? Hadn't
> you heard? Yes, I've killed him – *me*, the
> blind runt of Röcken – I have murdered
> God! Huh! You don't believe me – such
> lack of faith! Can't you hear the grave-
> diggers? Can't you smell the sickening
> stench of death? Oh even gods
> decompose, Heine – even gods
> rot!

This corresponds closely to the following passage from *The Gay Science*:

> The madman jumped into their midst and pierced them with his eyes. 'Whither is God?' he cried; 'I will tell you. *We have killed him* – you and I. All of us are

> his murderers [...] Do we hear nothing as yet of the noise of the gravediggers who are burying God? Do we smell nothing as yet of the divine decomposition? Gods, too, decompose...[134]

The only pronounced variation is that in the Nietzsche Monologue Nietzsche has, in the megalomania of his madness, taken sole responsibility for the crime. Indeed, I have conveyed Nietzsche's mental instability throughout the narrative in a variety of ways. The most noticeable is the sharp oscillations in tone which permeate the text. For example, between lines 230 and 249:

> The World's
> not ready to understand itself –
> it's too young, too serious, too
> busy 'living' to have lived – it
> does not, cannot, *will not* see
> delusion in illusion – *will not*
> brace itself for life – embrace itself
> *as* life – reach for that transcendence
> overreaching understanding
> and *live*, not in some twilight state
> of angst, but with daimonic frenzy
> realise its potential! Rejoice!
> Sing unto itself dithyrambs
> of eternity! Affirm and
> not negate! Drink fire! *LIVE!* Yes, as
> *I* would live – without fear, without
> regret! *Yes!* – cry with its entire
> being: 'I willed it so!' *And mean it.*
> *This* has been my prophecy; yet
> who was there to hear it...?

Nietzsche is engaged in a full-scale tirade against the cowardice of the World, but then, halfway through line 249 the tone completely changes:

> But really,
> though, everything's so cheap in Turin –

a transvaluation of all
values you might say! Just think: a
meal at my trattoria costs
a mere one franc fifteen centimes –
can you imagine? For this I
get a generous portion of
minestra (served either dry, or,
if I prefer, as bouillon),
a pasta dish (*very* tasty,
you know?), followed by an excellent
helping of the tenderest meat!
Naturally one gets all the
accoutrements – spinach, rolls, etc –
and, for a few centimes extra,
even a little wine…

Suddenly he is extolling the virtues of Turin's economic living and the merits of his favourite trattoria. This thematic transition also has its metrical correspondence. Whereas the first passage is manic, possessed with a racing pattern of heavy stresses and frequent repetition:

too young, *too* ser*i*ous, *too*
bu*sy* 'liv*ing*' to *have* lived…

the latter passage abruptly slows right down to a meandering, walking pace. The tone is perfectly cheerful, indeed possessed of a totally different character.

Another way in which I have conveyed Nietzsche's instability is through the various appellations he gives his correspondent. Köselitz is variously 'Heinrich' (line 106), 'Peter' (line 158), 'Pierre' (line 175), and most frequently 'Heine' (line 140, 287, 306, etc), and whilst the first three might be legitimately attributed to Köselitz (after all his Christian name was 'Heinrich' and his pseudonym was 'Peter/Pierre Gast') by calling him 'Heine', Nietzsche is confusing him with a different Heinrich altogether. Heinrich Heine was one of Nietzsche's favourite poets, and as Walter Kaufmann points out in his commentary on *The*

Gay Science, it was a passage from Heine's posthumously published *Letzte Gedichte und Gedanken* (1869), that inspired Nietzsche's first ruminations on the doctrine of the eternal recurrence. Thus Nietzsche's confusion over the person to whom he thinks he is speaking, coupled with the importance of Heine on Nietzsche's intellectual development, not only engenders a sense of mental instability but also elucidates the thematic drive of the narrative.

Just as the Nietzsche Monologue begins with a reference to the closing chapter of *Ecce Homo*, likewise, in a gesture towards the doctrine of the eternal recurrence, it ends with a reference as well. Having prophesied the coming of the Superman, Nietzsche casts his mind back to the incident of his collapse on 3rd January 1889. As he imagines himself lying sprawled on the Via Po he asks, just as he does in the closing line of *Ecce Homo* :

> 'Have I been understood?'
>
> *Dionysos against the Crucified…*

Radiation Era 2 (Hadron and Lepton Eras)

As we discussed in the 'Cosmological Paradigm' the fleeting Hadron and Lepton Eras saw the formation and high-speed reaction/annihilation of heavy atomic particles. I have decided to personify this in the first book of *Silence* by an inversion of Plato's *Symposium*, in which the company chose to abstain from heavy drinking and devote their conversation to philosophy. The reasoning behind this decision is twofold: firstly, there is the fact that this reaction can be effectively conveyed through the drunken behaviour of the guests – for drunkenness, both physically and socially, engenders instability and reactivity; and secondly, Nietzsche had a particular dislike for Plato's Socrates, whom he classed as a '*décadent* ', and whose morality he saw as responsible for destroying the Dionysiac spirit of the

Ancient Greeks. Thus, in keeping with the Nietzschean arc of Book One, I have made Socrates become a Dionysiac satyr and, in direct contradiction to the tradition that however much Socrates drank he never got 'drunk', I have depicted him as being thoroughly inebriated.[135]

In imitation of their drunkenness the typography sways across the page, and to add to the sense of inebriated disorientation I have decided to avoid tabulating the various speakers. Rather, I want the reader to be left, slurring between the different voices, uncertain precisely who is speaking. To emphasise words that are shouted, such as Socrates' cheerful interjection 'BOLLOCKS!' at line 540, I have put them in a bold, uppercase font. Likewise, to intimate slurred speech, I have created neologisms such as 'shanoohshehim' (line 765) (*can you see him*). Indeed, I intended the overall tone of this sequence to be playful, and thus something of a relief after the darker, heavier character of the Nietzsche Monologue.

Radiation Era 3

Following the Dionysiac Socrates comes Dionysos himself, the ultimate embodiment of primal life. In an attempt to emulate both the Cretan and Theban variants of his mythology, as well as intimate the expanding nature of the early Universe, I have made this sequence comprise thirteen separate voices. Thus, whilst the narratives mirror the Theban version of Dionysos' myth, the structure of the sequence mimics the Cretan dismemberment of the infant Zagreus at the hands of the Titans. In line with the concept of metamorphosis the poetic style, tone, and gender/species of the speaker varies between each monologue, and, in keeping with his elusive nature, Dionysos himself speaks directly, as an individuated voice, only once (see: fifth segment *Leaving Pallene*). For example, in the first monologue (*Pentheus*), written in the octosyllabic metre outlined earlier, we find Pentheus, the unfortunate king of Thebes, berating the imprisoned

Dionysos in his dungeon, whilst in the second in a lyrical free verse form we hear Ariadne lamenting her abandonment by Theseus (*Ariadne*). Yet again, the eleventh segment Sea-Change tells the story from the *2nd Homeric Hymn to Dionysos* through the eyes of the sailor who survived, and is written in a colloquial dialect, whilst the segment entitled *Naxos* is a lyrical three voice medley, in which the personas of Theseus, Ariadne and Dionysos mingle through a euphonic exchange. By contrast, in *The Wisdom of Silenos* we find the drunken leader of the satyrs (and Dionysos' old mentor) being 'entertained' by King Midas. This story, inspired by Ovid's version in the *Metamorphoses*, sees Midas getting Silenos drunk in order to find out the secret of his wisdom. The answer, given in *Silence* as: 'Die soon,/ 'cos it were better yah were never born' (lines 1295-1296) is disturbing, and features in *The Birth of Tragedy*, where Nietzsche uses it as evidence of the absurd horror of life beneath the calming light of Apolline illusion. This sequence also boasts an Orphic cosmogony, which, in keeping with the sequence's governing dynamic, is itself dismembered (see segments III, VI and X). The reason why I included it is twofold: firstly, because I saw it as reflecting back onto the epic's wider astrophysical concerns, offering a mythological alternative to scientific theory; and secondly, because, as we shall see presently, the Orphic and the Dionysiac are very much connected.

Radiation Era 4

Following the pattern of Nietzschean antitheses we see the Apolline follow swiftly in the wake of the Dionysiac, for *The Strings of Orpheus* act as an Apolline 'antidote' to the preceding Dionysiac violence. According to legend Orpheus was the 'son of the Thracian King Oeagrus and the Muse Calliope' – a servant of 'Apollo' whose gift with the lyre was unprecedented. Not only could he tame 'wild beasts', but he could also inspire 'trees and rocks' to move at the sound of his music. He travelled with the Argonauts on their quest to find the Golden Fleece and, probably most famously of all, went down into the underworld in search of his lost love Eurydice. However, in his study *The Greek Myths*, Robert Graves furnishes this further piece of information:

> When Dionysus invaded Thrace, Orpheus neglected to honour him, but taught other sacred mysteries and preached the evil of sacrificial murder to the men of Thrace, who listened reverently. Every morning he would rise to greet the dawn on the summit of Mount Pangaeum, preaching that Helius, whom he named Apollo, was the greatest of all gods...[136]

Thus Orpheus is the perfect Apolline hero, seemingly embodying all the attributes needed to (de)stabilise the Dionysiac. This Apolline sensibility is carried further by the sequence having nine poems in imitation of the nine strings of the lyre, and in astrophysical terms *The Strings of Orpheus* can be read as prophesying the encroaching structure of the Matter Era, which, as we saw in the 'Cosmological Paradigm' began 30,000 years after the Big Bang.

Nevertheless, there remains a final Nietzschean twist, for as Graves continues:

> In vexation, Dionysus set the Maenads upon him at Deium in Macedonia. First waiting until their husbands had entered Apollo's temple, where Orpheus served as priest, they seized the weapons stacked outside, burst in, murdered their husbands, and tore Orpheus limb from limb. His head they threw into the river Hebrus, but it floated, still singing, down to the sea, and was carried off to the island of Lesbos.[137]

Thus, in emulation of the above, I have made the structure of *The Strings of Orpheus* fragmentary, and yet, paradoxically possessed of a lyric coherence. For, whilst the syntax is incomplete, the words and phrases that remain, like Orpheus' singing head, retain a certain harmony. There is thus a sense here of Nietzsche's opposing coherence and, in keeping with his doctrine of the eternal recurrence, the narrative ends with Nietzsche once more a paralytic in his sister's house in Weimar.

NOTES

[1] Ian Ridpath, ed., *The Oxford Dictionary of Astronomy* (Oxford: Oxford University Press, 2003), 50, 363, 374.

[2] Ridpath, 196, 258.

[3] Friedrich Nietzsche, 'The Anti-Christ' in *Twilight of the Idols and The Anti-Christ*, tr. R. J., Hollingdale (London: Penguin Books Ltd, 2003), 129; Curtis Cate, *Friedrich Nietzsche: A Biography* (London: Pimlico, 2002), 6; Friedrich Nietzsche, 'Letter to Franz Overbeck: Postmarked Rapallo, December 25, 1882' in *Selected Letters of Friedrich Nietzsche*, ed. and tr. C. Middleton (Cambridge: Hackett Publishing Company, Inc., 1969), 199.

[4] Friedrich Nietzsche, *Ecce Homo*, tr. R. J. Hollingdale (London: Penguin Books Ltd, 1992), 96, 10; Ronald Hayman, *Nietzsche's Voices* (London: Phoenix, 2003), 37, 36; Friedrich Nietzsche, *Beyond Good and Evil*, tr. R. J. Hollingdale (London: Penguin Books Ltd, 2003), 46.

[5] Michael Tanner, 'Introduction' in F. Nietzsche, *The Birth of Tragedy out of the Spirit of Music*, tr. S. Whiteside (London: Penguin Books Ltd, 1993), vii-viii.

[6] Friedrich Nietzsche, 'Letter to Friedrich Ritschl (Basel, January 30, 1872)' in *Selected Letters of Friedrich Nietzsche*, ed. and tr. C. Middleton (Cambridge: Hackett Publishing Company, Inc., 1969), 93.

[7] M. C. Howatson and Ian Chilvers, eds., *The Oxford Concise Companion to Classical Literature* (Oxford: Oxford University Press, 1996), 45; Jules Cashford, tr., 'Hymn to Apollo' in *The Homeric Hymns* (London: Penguin Books

Ltd, 2003), 28; Friedrich Nietzsche, *The Birth of Tragedy out of the Spirit of Music*, tr. S. Whiteside (London: Penguin Books Ltd, 1993), 26; E. R. Dodds, *The Greeks and the Irrational* (Los Angeles: University of California Press, 1997), 185.

[8] Jules Cashford, tr., '1st Hymn to Dionysos' in *The Homeric Hymns* (London: Penguin Books Ltd, 2003), 3.

[9] Cashford, '1st Hymn to Dionysos', 3.

[10] Jules Cashford, 'Note to The 1st Hymn to Dionysos' in *The Homeric Hymns* (London: Penguin Books Ltd, 2003), 149; Cashford, '1st Hymn to Dionysos', 3-4.

[11] Edward Said, *Orientalism* (London: Penguin Books Ltd, 2003), 1.

[12] Homer, *The Odyssey*, tr. R. Fagles (London: Penguin Books Ltd, 2004), 142.

[13] Herodotus, *The Histories*, tr. A. de Sélincourt (London: Penguin Books Ltd, 2003), 154.

[14] Cashford, '1st Hymn to Dionysos', 4.

[15] Herodotus, 155.

[16] Cashford, '1st Hymn to Dionysos', 3-4.

[17] Jules Cashford, tr., '2nd Hymn to Dionysos' in *The Homeric Hymns* (London: Penguin Books Ltd, 2003), 100.

[18] Homer, *The Iliad*, tr. R. Fagles (London: Penguin Books Ltd, 1990), 99; John Strohmeier and Peter Westbrook, *Divine Harmony: The Life and Teachings of Pythagoras* (California: Berkeley Hills Books, 1999), 25; Robin Lane Fox, *Alexander the Great* (London: Penguin Books Ltd, 1986), 445.

[19] Lane Fox, 445.

[20] Herodotus, 3.

[21] Cashford, '2nd Hymn to Dionysos', 103-104.

[22] Cashford, '2nd Hymn to Dionysos', 104.

[23] Cashford, '2nd Hymn to Dionysos', 103.

[24] James Frazer, *The Golden Bough* (Oxford: Oxford University Press, 1998), 302.

[25] Laurence Coupe, *Myth* (London: Routledge, 1997), 1.

[26] Herodotus, 154-155; Euripides, *The Bacchae*, tr. P. Vellacott (London: Penguin Books Ltd, 1973), 191.

[27] Ovid, *Metamorphoses*, tr. A. D. Melville (Oxford: Oxford University Press, 1986), 58, 59.

[28] Ovid, 59-60.

[29] Ovid, 60.

[30] Carl Kerényi, *Dionysos: Archetypal Image of Indestructible Life*, tr. R. Manheim (Princeton: Princeton University Press, 1976), 110.

[31] Nonnos, *Dionysiaca*, tr. W. H. D. Rouse (Cambridge, Massachusetts: Harvard University Press, 1995), 225-227.

[32] Nonnos, 227, 227-229.

[33] Nonnos, 229.

[34] Kerényi, 7.

[35] Walter Burkert, *Ancient Mystery Cults* (Cambridge, Massachusetts: Harvard University Press, 1987), 12.

[36] Burkert, 10, 15, 6, 5; Herodotus, 521.

[37] Burkert, 93.

[38] Jules Cashford, tr., '1st Hymn to Demeter' in *The Homeric Hymns* (London: Penguin Books Ltd, 2003), 5.

[39] Cashford, '1st Hymn to Demeter', 6.

[40] Cashford, '1st Hymn to Demeter', 7.

[41] Cashford, '1st Hymn to Demeter', 8, 9.

[42] Cashford, '1st Hymn to Demeter', 9, 15.

[43] Cashford, '1st Hymn to Demeter', 16.

[44] Cashford, '1st Hymn to Demeter', 16.

[45] Cashford, '1st Hymn to Demeter', 18.

[46] Cashford, '1st Hymn to Demeter', 18.

[47] Cashford, '1st Hymn to Demeter', 19.

[48] Cashford, '1st Hymn to Demeter', 21, 25.

[49] Cashford, '1st Hymn to Demeter', 25.

[50] Cashford, '1st Hymn to Demeter', 25-26.

[51] Hesiod, 'Theogony' in *Hesiod and Theognis*, tr. D. Wender (London: Penguin Books Ltd, 1973), 53.

[52] Herodotus, 521.

[53] Herodotus, 521, 266, 267; Burkert, 106.

[54] Plato, 'Phaedrus' in *Phaedrus and Letters VII and VIII*, tr. W. Hamilton (London: Penguin Books Ltd, 1973), 47.

[55] Burkert, 5, 33; Euripides, 192.
[56] Euripides, 198, 199, 200.
[57] Euripides, 199.
[58] Euripides, 199.
[59] Euripides, 198.
[60] Euripides, 202, 232.
[61] Friedrich Nietzsche, 'An Attempt At A Self-Criticism' in *The Birth of Tragedy out of the Spirit of Music*, tr. S. Whiteside (London: Penguin Books Ltd, 1993), 5; Nietzsche, *The Birth of Tragedy out of the Spirit of Music*, 14.
[62] Nietzsche, 'An Attempt At A Self-Criticism', 5.
[63] Nietzsche, *The Birth of Tragedy out of the Spirit of Music*, 14.
[64] Nietzsche, *The Birth of Tragedy out of the Spirit of Music*, 16, 15, 14.
[65] Arthur Schopenhauer, *The World as Will and Idea*, tr. J. Berman (London: Everyman, 1995), 59, 44, 32, 5.
[66] Schopenhauer, 5.
[67] Immanuel Kant, *Critique of Pure Reason*, a revised and expanded translation based on Meiklejohn edited by V. Politis (London: Everyman, 2002), 39, 211, 94, 38, 507, 539.
[68] Kant, 539.
[69] Schopenhauer, 4; Kant, 212; Schopenhauer, 32.
[70] Schopenhauer, 32, 32-33.
[71] Schopenhauer, 37, 38.
[72] Schopenhauer, 37, 43, 42.
[73] Schopenhauer, 85, 80, 119.
[74] Schopenhauer, 119, 85, 119-120.
[75] Schopenhauer, 120.
[76] Schopenhauer, 120.
[77] Schopenhauer, 120; Plato, *The Symposium*, tr. C. Gill (London: Penguin Books Ltd, 2003), 48, 49.
[78] Schopenhauer, 141; Plato, *The Symposium*, 49.
[79] Plato, 'Phaedrus', 61; Schopenhauer, 186; Plato, 'Phaedrus', 50-51.
[80] Plato, 'Phaedrus', 61, 62, 64-65, 65, 57, 52.
[81] Plato, 'Phaedrus', 53.
[82] Plato, 'Phaedrus', 57.

[83] Schopenhauer, 121, 133, 135, 141, 155, 162.
[84] Schopenhauer, 162.
[85] Schopenhauer, 164.
[86] Schopenhauer, 168, 169.
[87] Nietzsche, *The Birth of Tragedy out of the Spirit of Music*, 16, 24, 25, 32.
[88] Nietzsche, *The Birth of Tragedy out of the Spirit of Music*, 16, 25, 21.
[89] Nietzsche, 'An Attempt At A Self-Criticism', 10.
[90] Nietzsche, 'An Attempt At A Self-Criticism', 10; Nietzsche, *The Birth of Tragedy out of the Spirit of Music*, 17, 29.
[91] Nietzsche, *The Birth of Tragedy out of the Spirit of Music*, 28, 29, 27.
[92] Nietzsche, *The Birth of Tragedy out of the Spirit of Music*, 29.
[93] Nietzsche, *The Birth of Tragedy out of the Spirit of Music*, 29.
[94] Nietzsche, *The Birth of Tragedy out of the Spirit of Music*, 29; Howatson and Chilvers, 186; Aristotle, *Poetics*, tr. M. Heath (London: Penguin Books Ltd, 1996), 8.
[95] Nietzsche, *The Birth of Tragedy out of the Spirit of Music*, 21.
[96] Nietzsche, *The Birth of Tragedy out of the Spirit of Music*, 21.
[97] Nietzsche, *The Birth of Tragedy out of the Spirit of Music*, 21; Euripides, 194; Nietzsche, *The Birth of Tragedy out of the Spirit of Music*, 21, 40.
[98] Nietzsche, *The Birth of Tragedy out of the Spirit of Music*, 41, 42, 43.
[99] Rudiger Safranski, *Nietzsche: A Philosophical Biography*, tr. S. Frisch (London: Granta Books, 2002), 25.
[100] Friedrich Nietzsche, 'Letter to Peter Gast: Turin April 7, 1888, Saturday' in *Selected Letters of Friedrich Nietzsche*, ed. and tr. C. Middleton (Cambridge: Hackett Publishing Company, Inc., 1969), 291; Friedrich Nietzsche, 'Letter to Peter Gast: Turin Friday [April 20, 1888]' in *Selected Letters of Friedrich Nietzsche*, ed. and tr. C.

Middleton (Cambridge: Hackett Publishing Company, Inc., 1969), 295, 296.

[101] Cate, 517, 184.

[102] Cate, 517.

[103] Michael Tanner, 'Introduction' in *Twilight of the Idols and The Anti-Christ*, tr. R. J. Hollingdale (London: Penguin Books Ltd, 2003), 7, 8; Friedrich Nietzsche, 'Twilight of the Idols' in *Twilight of the Idols and The Anti-Christ*, tr. R. J. Hollingdale (London: Penguin Books Ltd, 2003), 76.

[104] Friedrich Nietzsche, 'Twilight of the Idols', 116.

[105] Friedrich Nietzsche, 'Appendix: Variants from Nietzsche's Drafts' in *Basic Writings of Nietzsche*, tr. W. Kaufmann (New York: Random House, 2000), 796.

[106] Friedrich Nietzsche, *Thus Spoke Zarathustra*, tr. R. J. Hollingdale (London: Penguin Books Ltd, 2003), 176.

[107] Friedrich Nietzsche, *Ecce Homo*, tr. R. J. Hollingdale (London: Penguin Books Ltd, 1992), 94.

[108] Friedrich Nietzsche, 'Letter to Carl Fuchs: Sils, Sunday, July 29, 1888' in *Selected Letters of Friedrich Nietzsche*, ed. and tr. C. Middleton (Cambridge: Hackett Publishing Company, Inc., 1969), 305.

[109] Nietzsche, *Ecce Homo*, 44.

[110] Nietzsche, *Ecce Homo*, 16; Friedrich Nietzsche, 'Letter to Paul Deussen: Sils Maria, September 14, 1888' in *Selected Letters of Friedrich Nietzsche*, ed. and tr. C. Middleton (Cambridge: Hackett Publishing Company, Inc., 1969), 311; Nietzsche, 'Twilight of the Idols', 65.

[111] Friedrich Nietzsche, *The Gay Science*, tr. W. Kaufmann (New York: Vintage Books, 1974), 181; Nietzsche, 'Twilight of the Idols', 65.

[112] Nietzsche, 'The Anti-Christ' in *Twilight of the Idols and The Anti-Christ*, tr. R. J. Hollingdale (London: Penguin Books Ltd, 2003), 125, 127, 129, 198, 128, 130.

[113] Nietzsche, 'The Anti-Christ', 128, 125.

[114] Nietzsche, 'The Anti-Christ', 128, 125, 132, 135, 131, 130, 127.

[115] Nietzsche, *The Gay Science*, 273, 273-274.

[116] Nietzsche, *Thus Spoke Zarathustra*, 332.

[117] Heraclitus, 'Fragment 20' in Geldard, R., *Remembering Heraclitus: The Philosopher of Riddles* (Edinburgh: Floris Books, 2000), 158; Heraclitus, 'Fragment 16' in Geldard, R., *Remembering Heraclitus: The Philosopher of Riddles* (Edinburgh: Floris Books, 2000), 157; Nietzsche, *Beyond Good and Evil*, 103; Nietzsche, 'The Anti-Christ', p. 130.

[118] R. J. Hollingdale, 'Note on the Text' in Nietzsche, F., *Ecce Homo*, translated by R. J. Hollingdale with an introduction and notes by M. Tanner (London: Penguin Books Ltd, 1992), xviii; Michael Tanner, 'Introduction' in *Ecce Homo*, translated by R. J. Hollingdale with an introduction by M. Tanner (London: Penguin Books Ltd, 1992), viii; Nietzsche, *Ecce Homo*, 17; Nietzsche, *Thus Spoke Zarathustra*, 289; Nietzsche, *Ecce Homo*, 76, 70, 12, 68, 86, 54, 48, 10.

[119] Nietzsche, *Ecce Homo*, 7.

[120] Nietzsche, *Ecce Homo*, 3; Nietzsche, 'The Anti-Christ', 153, 159, 159-160.

[121] Nietzsche, *Ecce Homo*, 9, 54; Michael Tanner, 'Introduction' in *Ecce Homo*, vii, ix; Nietzsche, 'The Anti-Christ',160.

[122] Nietzsche, *Ecce Homo*, 3, 11, 8, 12.

[123] Nietzsche, *Ecce Homo*, 12.

[124] Nietzsche, *Ecce Homo*, 45, 80.

[125] Nietzsche, *Ecce Homo*, 96, 95, 101, 84, 103, 102, 104.

[126] Friedrich Nietzsche, 'Letter to Peter Gast: Turin Tuesday, October 30, 1888' in *Selected Letters of Friedrich Nietzsche*, ed. and tr. C. Middleton (Cambridge: Hackett Publishing Company, Inc., 1969), 318.

[127] Nietzsche, 'Letter to Peter Gast: Turin Tuesday, October 30, 1888', 318.

[128] Michael Tanner, 'Chronology of Nietzsche's Life' in F. Nietzsche, *Ecce Homo*, tr. R. J. Hollingdale (London: Penguin Books Ltd, 1992), xxi; Ian Kelly, *Beau Brummell: The Ultimate Dandy* (London: Hodder and Stoughton, 2005), 297; William Brown, *Syphilis: A Synopsis* (Honolulu, Hawaii: University Press of the Pacific, 2001), 74; Lesley

Chamberlain *Nietzsche in Turin: The End of the Future* (London: Quartet Books, 1996), 201.

[129] Chamberlain 166, 167, 206.

[130] Chamberlain 205, 206.

[131] Friedrich Nietzsche, 'Letter to Peter Gast: Turin December 2, 1888' in *Selected Letters of Friedrich Nietzsche*, ed. and tr. C. Middleton (Cambridge: Hackett Publishing Company, Inc., 1969), 327; Chamberlain 205, 206, 207.

[132] Cate, 550; Friedrich Nietzsche, 'Letter to Jakob Burckhardt: Turin January 5, 1889' in *Selected Letters of Friedrich Nietzsche*, ed. and tr. C. Middleton (Cambridge: Hackett Publishing Company, Inc., 1969), 346; Friedrich Nietzsche, 'Letter to Franz Overbeck: Received January 7, 1889' in *Selected Letters of Friedrich Nietzsche*, ed. and tr. C. Middleton (Cambridge: Hackett Publishing Company, Inc., 1969), 346; Friedrich Nietzsche, 'Letter to Peter Gast: Postmarked Turin January 4, 1889' in *Selected Letters of Friedrich Nietzsche*, ed. and tr. C. Middleton (Cambridge: Hackett Publishing Company, Inc., 1969), 345; Chamberlain 216; Tanner, 'Chronology of Nietzsche's Life', xxix.

[133] Nietzsche, 'Letter to Peter Gast: Turin April 7, 1888, Saturday', 291.

[134] Nietzsche, *The Gay Science*, 181.

[135] Nietzsche, *Ecce Homo*, 49; Plato, *The Symposium*, 52.

[136] Robert Graves, *The Greek Myths: Volume 1* (London: Penguin Books Ltd, 1960), 111, 112.

[137] Graves, 112.

Critical Reincarnations

Book Two

Cosmological Paradigm

Early Matter Era

Time: 30,000 years after singularity to the present.

Temperature: 10^4 – 3K

After the initial phase of 'quantum gravitation', during which the early Universe is believed to have been dominated by the effects of the hypothetical graviton, and the subsequent era of 'thermal equilibrium', characterised by its plasmatic opacity to 'radiation', the progressive reduction of cosmic temperature precipitated what cosmologists have termed the 'Matter Era'. Thus, whereas the early Universe's expansion 'was dominated by the gravitational effect of radiation pressure', whose intensely 'high energy' caused matter itself to behave like 'electromagnetic radiation', at around 30,000 years after the Big Bang the Universe had cooled sufficiently for 'the gravitational effect of matter' to supersede its radioactive counterpart. This usurpation engendered what cosmologists have termed 'decoupling', so called because, as the 'particles of matter ceased to interact with radiation', matter and radiation began to act independently of each other. Nevertheless, this process remained gradual. After the frenetic atomic exchange which had characterised both the fleeting Hadron and Lepton Eras, the rate at which the newly formed stable atomic nuclei decoupled from the radiation of the Universe varied considerably. For example, whereas neutrinos decoupled 'at a temperature of about 10^{10} K (about 1 second after the Big Bang)…ordinary matter decoupled at a temperature of a few

thousand degrees K (after about 300,000 years)'. Importantly, this prolonged exchange saw the Universe's radiation become transparent to light, thus allowing 'electromagnetic radiation' particles known as 'photons' to propagate freely. The prolonged nature of the decoupling, coupled with the diverse nature of the atomic nuclei concerned, resulted in the formation of regions of varying density. Those with a greater density, and thus a greater gravitational force, attracted the propagating photons, ultimately causing them to lose some energy and thus be at a lower temperature. During the course of millennia, these photonic areas of material density went on to evolve into the stars and galaxies observable today.[1]

Textual Interpretation

Early Matter Era:

- *Unstill Life* (Caravaggio)
- *Anatomy* (Leonardo da Vinci)
- *Wilderness* (Eusebius Hieronymus)

1. Caravaggio: Unstill Life

Theory

The life of Michelangelo Merisi (1571-1610), better known as 'Caravaggio' after the northern Italian town in which he grew up, has been variously described as 'mysterious' and 'bizarre'. One problem of interpretation lies in the fact that Caravaggio left no writings behind him. Unlike Leonardo da Vinci or Michelangelo Buonarroti, who produced assorted notebooks, letters and sonnets, Caravaggio exists entirely in paint – paint and, far more dangerous where reputation is concerned, the reminiscences of others. Three biographies come down to us from the seventeenth century, each very different in style and tone, and each written after the painter's death. The first is by Giulio Mancini, a 'Sienese doctor' who was also a 'writer on art…connoisseur, collector and dealer'. Mancini knew Caravaggio personally, their association taking place during the late 1590s when the painter was resident in the Roman palace of Cardinal del Monte, and his biography is predominantly sympathetic. In the opening paragraph of his work he writes: 'Our times owe much to Michelangelo da Caravaggio for the method of painting he introduced, which is now quite widely followed'. Mancini informs us that Caravaggio was born of 'honourable citizens', and that his father, whose name remains unspecified, held the position of 'majordomo and architect to the Marchese of Caravaggio', who, throughout the early years of the painter's life, was one Francesco I Sforza. Other than this, Mancini tells us little of Caravaggio's childhood, save that he was an apprenticed painter in 'Milan' for some 'four to six years' and that he 'studied diligently'. More revealingly we are told that because of Caravaggio's 'hot nature and high spirits' he would occasionally do 'outrageous' things. Sadly, Mancini neglects to tell us what these 'outrageous' things were.[2]

The narrative now shifts to Caravaggio's arrival in Rome. Mancini places the painter at 'about twenty', which would make the year of his descent upon the City of Light around 1591. Like so many artists of the time, Caravaggio was most likely attracted to Rome by the regenerative vision of Pope Sixtus V who, during his five years as Pontiff, had aspired to transform the crumbling medieval city into a 'most grandiose temple, embellished with the utmost splendour'. Indeed, the sixteenth century had not been kind to the Seat of the Catholic world. The Lutheran schism in Northern Europe, with its strong, faith-based 'Christocentric theology', had posed a serious challenge to the primacy of the Vatican; and, in some ways even more disturbing, Rome herself had been sacked in 1527 by the army of the Catholic

Holy Roman Emperor, Charles V. After the invasion the population had 'dwindled' and the once proud city is said to have had the air of a 'cattle market'. Nevertheless, Rome was to prove far from 'dead', and in 1560, during the pontificate of Pius IV, a second Council convened at Trent to renew Catholicism's stand against the advances of Protestantism, and thereby instigate a 'Counter-Reformation'. One of the most important decisions reached at this Council was to be the new, heightened role of art within the Catholic world. Art would 'inspire intense piety' among the faithful and reveal the 'glory' of Christ's true Church on Earth. It would also, more importantly, emphasise the impoverishment of Protestantism, whose complete renunciation of religious iconography, rather than revealing a strict adherence to Scripture, would instead be seen as symptomatic of its heretical abandonment of God's light.[3]

As we have seen above, this championing of the arts reached its zenith during the pontificate of Sixtus V. This new Rome, this *Roma Sancta*, as a living celebration of a 'renewed Christianity' boasted a 'wealth of new buildings, palaces [and] churches' all lavishly decorated in line with the principles of the Counter-Reformation. To achieve this creative miracle, Sixtus had 'called on all the artists of the peninsula – architects, painters, sculptors, engravers and goldsmiths – to come to Rome' and it seems likely that Caravaggio, as an ambitious young artist from the provinces, responded to this call. Unfortunately, by the time he arrived Sixtus was dead and, like many other artists who had come to Rome to make their fortune, was unable to secure employment. Thus Mancini informs us that upon his arrival in the Eternal City Caravaggio 'had no money'. For precisely how long the painter remained in penury is uncertain; Mancini simply states that Caravaggio came to live with a certain 'Pandolfo Pucci', without offering any further explanation save that Pucci came from 'Recanti' and was 'a beneficiary of St. Peter's'. Yet this information is revealing when one understands the connection. In her study of Caravaggio and his world, art historian Helen Langdon points out that 'Monsignor Pandolfo Pucci...was steward, or Maestro di Casa, to Camilla Peretti, the sister of [the late] Pope Sixtus V Peretti, and [that] the Peretti family had close ties with the Colonna'. Now the Colonna were related by marriage to the Sforza of Caravaggio, and as the painter's father had been in the Marchese of Caravaggio's service, it seems likely that the forces of feudal patronage were at work.[4]

Sadly, this cohabitation proved far from satisfactory, for having taken the young painter into his household, it appears that Monsignor Pucci determined to spend only the bare minimum on his upkeep. Mancini informs us that Caravaggio was given nothing to eat 'but salad...which served as appetizer, entrée and dessert'. Thus it is little wonder that the thrifty churchman earned the appellation 'Monsignor Salad', or that Caravaggio remained in his household for only 'a few months'. Nevertheless, his time with Pucci was not a total failure, for despite having to engage in the 'unpleasant' task of slavishly copying 'devotional images' – perhaps in lieu of rent – he also painted his earliest masterpieces. The first mentioned by Mancini is that of 'a boy who cries out because he has been bitten by a lizard'. Now in the National Gallery in London, *Boy Bitten by a Lizard* (c.1593) is a striking example of Caravaggio's intense theatrical realism. The boy, who occupies the centre of the picture, is 'effeminate', and the art historian Gilles Lambert proposes that the flower behind his right ear and his bare right shoulder 'identify him as a prostitute'. On the table before him there is displayed an assortment of cherries, and in the lower-right foreground a beautifully realised carafe containing a single rose. Yet what seizes the eye is Caravaggio's phenomenal treatment of light. The carafe, filled three quarters to capacity with water, appears *totally* real. Not only does the light play through it, but the water also reflects the image of a window, which, were the painting wider, would be located some distance to the left of the boy. Through such a remarkable effect,

Caravaggio is challenging the boundary of the frame and, by extension, inviting the viewer to become an active participant in the life of the painting. However, arguably even more impressive is the way in which Caravaggio has managed to create a vitality of movement in what is, by definition, a static space. In the single captured moment of the painting we are somehow given an extra-temporal sense of the events preceding and succeeding the lizard's attack. We can envision the boy idly reaching down to take one of the cherries, and, after he is bitten, sulkily placing his bleeding finger in his mouth. By portraying the boy's reflex reaction to a sudden, sharp moment of pain in so tremendously *real* a manner, Caravaggio effectively creates a cinematic sequence in the viewer's imagination. Yet this is not to imply that the viewer is a passive witness to events, for the pain is so intensely realised that *we* feel it too. As the art historian Timothy Wilson-Smith observes, 'the boy's foreshortened shoulder, the contrasting gestures of his hands, and the leftward sloping light' all contribute to the painting's 'dramatic' impact. However, perhaps the most resonant point of viewer-subject identification lies in the boy's beautifully captured expression, the tension around his eyebrows and his tight, slightly open mouth, conveying an emotion somewhere between surprise and indignation. Looking into his dark, tense eyes our empathy is supreme.[5]

In addition to *Boy Bitten by a Lizard*, Mancini informs us that, whilst a resident of the Pucci household, Caravaggio also painted a 'boy who is peeling a pear with a knife'. Although the original is lost, several un-attributed copies of *Boy Peeling Fruit* (c.1593) exist in private collections, and thus it is possible to get some idea of what the original most probably looked like. Superficially the contrast between the two pictures could not be more extreme. Whereas the former offers a virtuoso display of action the latter is quiet and domestic in tone, appearing wholly unassuming in the simplicity of its intent. The boy sits at a rough wooden table, engrossed in the act of peeling a piece of fruit with a small-bladed knife. He cannot be much more than twelve years

old, and his innocence is emphasised by his beautifully laundered, virginal white shirt, which shines brilliantly in the strong, leftward slanting light. However, what captivates the eye is not so much the boy as the exquisitely realised fruit on the table before him, in particular the two soft, ripe peaches that nestle close to the boy's left hand. In the strength of the illusion they appear invitingly tactile and one is almost drawn to touch them until a disturbing association enters the viewer's mind. Rather than peaches it feels more and more likely that we are looking at the boy's genitals, a sense which is enhanced by the gesture and proximity of the boy's left hand. Ostensibly holding a piece of fruit, the cupped positioning of the fingers is strongly reminiscent of the posture of the hand during masturbation. Suddenly we see the picture again as if for the first time. The boy is depicted as being alone in a room rich with shadows, and his shirt, far from being remarkable for its virginal whiteness, is most conspicuous for being alluringly unbuttoned to the waist. This is not a quiet, domestic study of rustic innocence, but rather a tribute to sexual awakening. Indeed, when read in this light, *Boy Peeling Fruit* and *Boy Bitten by a Lizard* have a lot in common, in fact may even be in dialogue. In regard to the latter, Wilson-Smith observes that 'the cherries…and the lizard probably have sexual significance', the lizard's bite symbolising 'the pains of physical love'. Looking once again at *Boy Peeling Fruit* it is possible to discern a physiognomical resemblance between the two sitters. To be sure, they could be the *same* boy depicted at different stages of development, with the former on the cusp of adolescence and the latter in full adolescent bloom. Thus it is possible to argue that with these two paintings Caravaggio is performing a secular diptych that juxtaposes a blossoming sexual awareness with the sharp physicality of sexual experience. If this is the case then *Boy Peeling Fruit* sheds much of its near static reverie, partaking instead in the instantaneous vitality of its twin.[6]

Mancini tells us that both of these pictures were 'painted for sale', however it remains extremely unlikely that Caravaggio

would have been paid much for either of them. As Langdon points out, their 'humble subjects' fell far 'beneath the dignity' of the style of painting then in vogue. Indeed, their very *technique* set them at odds with the prevailing tradition of the day. When Caravaggio came to Rome a movement, latterly known as 'Mannerism', was at its height. Exemplified by artists such as Federico Zuccaro and Jacopo Tintoretto, the Mannerists aspired on the one hand to imitate Raphael's phenomenal skill in arranging numerous and diverse figures into 'grandly harmonious compositions', and on the other, overwhelmed by the achievements of the Buonarrotti generation, to react violently against it. Thus rather than equalling the serene congregations characteristic of the *Vatican Stanzas* (1508-1514), Mannerist painting frequently deviated into a compositional style characterised by either a life-less 'artificiality' or an indulgently 'bizarre' inclination toward figurative distortion. Here Tintoretto's *Last Supper* (1592-94) may serve as a case in point. Although generally revered as one of Tintoretto's 'greatest masterpieces', this 'scene of incandescent spirituality' embodies many of Mannerism's most disquieting tendencies. Unlike Leonardo da Vinci's comparatively restrained fresco of the same name, Tintoretto's rendering of the scene positively bristles with bodies. Rather than a quiet celebration of the Passover in an upstairs room, *this* Last Supper takes place in what appears to be the front room of a tavern. Thus, in addition to Christ and his disciples, we have a cast of waiting staff, washerwomen, and even a playful dog. The frenetic nature of the scene is heightened by Tintoretto's challenging use of perspective. The table, at which the solar-haloed Christ and his disciples engage in uproarious discourse, slants diagonally right into the background, and seems, as a consequence, impossibly long. Indeed, the exaggerated sense of depth produces in the viewer a sensation akin to the strained clarity of drunkenness. To make matters worse, the entire ceiling is a vortex of gushing spirits. Indeed, the painting is as much a testament to excess as an evocation of Scripture.[7]

Another example of Mannerist excess, although arguably of a more successful kind, is El Greco's *Burial of Count Orgaz* (1586). Praised by the art historian Michael Levey for its 'fiery individuality' the painting distorts the human body into the semblance of a weightless 'flame'. Indeed, such is El Greco's technique, that the numerous bodies that make up the painting, both temporal and spiritual, arguably form a single tongue of fire. Occupying the centre-left of the foreground is the dead, blue-faced Count. He wears an elaborate suit of armour and is borne by the supernatural figures of 'St. Augustine' and 'St. Stephen', both of whom are dressed in ornate golden robes. This chromatic brilliance is counterpoised by the shroud of black-clad mourners who occupy the centre of the painting. Yet their density is somewhat disembodying, and so rather than perceiving individual figures what we see is a collection of strangely elongated heads bobbing on a spume of white ruffs. Indeed, the way in which El Greco rakes these mourners 'elongates' the viewer's gaze towards the top portion of the painting. Here the eye swims and flexes as it tries to focus the distortion. What we are looking at are the Heavenly Hosts, the Virgin Mary, John the Baptist, and Christ enthroned in His Glory. However, the manner of their depiction could not be further from the proportioned serenity of Raphael's *Disputa* (1508-09). Instead, their bodies stretch and curve on an elastic mystery of angels and clouds. Face upon face upon face melts into the distance; the whole scene is reminiscent of liquid candle wax. At the zenith of this spiritual plasticity sits the Son of God, Himself a slender wisp of the human form. Indeed, Christ's stretched frailty is only matched by the radiance of His light; and it is *here* that the painting's identification with fire is supreme. Everything in this painting; the Count; the saints; the mourners; the Heavenly Host; feeds Christ's halo – indeed, entreats the eye to partake in the dancing motion of its light. Through his complex manipulation of the body, El Greco powerfully conveys the drama of death and resurrection – of the dependence of all things, temporal and spiritual, on the Light of God.[8]

Yet there is little in the *Burial of Count Orgaz*, or indeed Tintoretto's *Last Supper*, which is subordinate to nature, and nothing which may be termed comparable to the aesthetic dynamics of either *Boy Bitten by a Lizard* or *Boy Peeling Fruit*. As Lambert observes, Caravaggio's work of the early 1590s represents a 'revolution' in pictorial sensibility, and yet it must be recognised that the young painter's style did not originate out of nothing. Firstly, it is important to understand the prevailing artistic tradition of 'Lombardy', the region of Italy where Caravaggio was trained. Stereotyped as 'simple and unlearned' by the Mannerist painters of the south, the Lombards, who were in part influenced by the recent developments in Flemish painting, favoured a more 'naturalistic' sort of art, encompassing forms such as 'landscape and still life'. Regarding the latter genre, it is worth drawing a comparison between the still life *Vase of Flowers* (c.1595) by Jan Brueghel, a Flemish painter and draughtsman active in Italy between 1590 and 1596, and Caravaggio's still life, *Basket of Fruit* (c.1598-99), in order to understand the extent to which Caravaggio's oeuvre may, in part, be seen as evolving out of established aesthetic parameters.[9]

Brueghel's painting is an opulent display of mimetic dexterity. The jewel encrusted vase, which rests on an unspecified surface in the centre of the foreground, gives rise to a flamboyant ovation of tulips, peonies, roses and chrysanthemums. The flowers' vibrant colours are strangely hypnotic, and Brueghel's stylistic softening of their borders endows the painting with the hazy ambience of summer. However, this is not to say that *Vase of Flowers* lacks a certain animation, for Brueghel defies complete inertia, firstly by including some charmingly rendered bees, which busily set about the act of pollination, and secondly, by littering the foreground with fallen petals. Thus the painting skilfully pays deference to the passage of time; ingeniously referencing a subject so closely entwined with the human condition, yet without making reference to the human form.

Caravaggio's *Basket of Fruit* is equally dexterous; however, whilst there is a thematic correspondence between the two paintings, their methods, and thus their impact, remain quite distinct. Here we are treated to yet another example of Caravaggio's near photographic realism. Indeed, as Langdon observes, 'the entire project is controlled by extreme intellectual rigour', forming what is, in essence, 'a statement about the nature of art'. The basket rests to the centre-left of the foreground, and is piled high with apples, lemons, pears, peaches, and grapes – the latter cascading, with an almost sensuous vitality, over the basket's rim. However, one of the most astonishing elements of this composition is the way in which the basket of fruit appears to be tottering precariously over the 'lip' of the canvas. This remarkable effect is achieved in two ways. Firstly, Caravaggio depicts the table on which the basket rests as a simple horizontal line running the entire width of the foreground, and secondly, beneath the basket's 'protruding' base he paints a deep shadow. Consequently, the viewer almost feels compelled to offer a steadying hand in order to divert the seemingly incipient disaster. Another astounding feature of this painting is Caravaggio's treatment of the nature of time. Whilst some of the fruit are indeed wholesome and appetising, a closer inspection reveals a disturbing amount of decay. The apple's red-blushed skin boasts a deep, maggoty hole, the pear is pockmarked, and the numerous leaves, which Caravaggio has interspersed amongst the fruit, are dry and withered. In stark contrast to Brueghel's playful bees and weary petals, Caravaggio paints life in the throes of plunging into death. It is little wonder that Cardinal del Monte, who was Caravaggio's patron during the period in which this painting was executed, is said to have turned away from the picture with 'tears in his eyes'. Here mortality is depicted without sentiment or compromise; as it is in nature; as it is in art; the intimate reality of life.[10]

Besides interpreting Caravaggio's stylistic innovations in the light of his Lombardy training, it is also important to contextualise his work within the broader trajectory of Western art. Whilst Caravaggio's paintings are manifestly anti-Mannerist, both in their style and intent, they are nevertheless conditional upon the technical developments in painting that occurred during the century-and-a-half separating Giotto and Raphael. This period is generally referred to as the 'Renaissance', a word derived from the Italian '*rinascita*', and meaning 'rebirth', so-called because it witnessed 'a revival of the values of the classical world'. In the fourteenth century, writers such as Dante, Petrarch and Boccaccio began to write poetry and prose inspired by ancient authors such as Pliny the Elder, Cicero and Virgil. This classicising literary trend matured into the fifteenth century, perhaps finding its most refined expression in Lorenzo de' Medici's 'Platonic Academy' at Florence; an intellectual coterie which included the renowned poet, musician and theologian Marsilio Ficino, whose *De Christiana Religione* attempted to synthesise Christian and Platonic beliefs. In the visual arts of painting and sculpture the Ancient World exerted an equally powerful influence. It is important to remember that Italy, where the rebirth of classical appreciation may be argued to have originated, was rich with the remains of its Roman past and thus, as the art historian Peter Murray observes, 'the classical tradition had never entirely died out'. It lingered in the ruins of ancient buildings, in stelae, triumphal arches, sarcophagi, and statuary; it was, one might say, carved into the collective memory of the Italian people. Consequently, when a taste for antiquity returned, it is little wonder that it was sculpture, and not painting, which was first to undergo a rebirth, with sculptors such as Giovanni Pisano, and Arnolfo di Cambio, pioneering the new fashion for cleanly defined, antique forms. These sculptural developments were, in turn, to have a profound effect upon the character of painting, providing an alternative paradigm to the rigid Byzantinism which had predominated in the West since the sacking of Constantinople in 1204, and perhaps nowhere can this vicariously classicising transformation be seen more clearly than in the work of the Florentine painter Giotto. Indeed, the 'dramatic' expressiveness of Giotto's style, evinced by works such as his *Arena Chapel Frescos* in Padua (c.1305) infused painting with both 'new ideals of naturalism' *and* a greater 'sense of pictorial space'. Giotto gave his compositions a sculptural solidity coupled with an acute 'psychological insight', and thus his figures, when compared to 'the rigid formality' and 'stereotyped formulas' of Byzantine influenced compositions, appear to breathe. Therefore, it is unsurprising that his contemporaries considered him 'first among Florentine artists' and, as the art historian Ian Chilvers points out, 'to succeeding generations it was clear that a new artistic era began with him'.[11]

Whilst Giotto may be seen as the pioneer of Renaissance painting, it was during the opening decades of the fifteenth century that the medium can truly be said to have cast off the formal vestiges of its medieval past. From these formative years three names stand out as being of special significance, Filippo Brunelleschi, Donatello, and Masaccio, and it is interesting to note that of the three only the latter was a painter. However, as we saw in the case of Giotto, early Renaissance painting was heavily influenced by the developments in other artistic media, and thus it should come as no surprise that Masaccio, regarded by many art historians as a 'founding [father] of the Renaissance' and the man who 'brought about a revolution in painting', was heavily indebted to the architectural and sculptural works of his friends. Indeed, it was the *architect* Brunelleschi who created one of the early fifteenth century's most important pictorial developments: 'linear perspective'. Whereas the Giotto generation had relied on the imprecise technique of 'empirical perspective' to create a fledgling articulation of pictorial depth – something that succeeded in creating a certain amount of 'perspective illusion' but which ultimately left their compositions without a 'coherent spatial logic' – the development of *linear perspective* afforded painters like Masaccio the means of realising 'a completely coherent and consistent sense of three dimensions on a two-dimensional surface'. This optical effect, which is designed to guide the eye to 'a single vanishing point' through the recession of 'orthogonals', or sightlines, is dependent upon a clearly defined 'geometric' environment. Consequently, Classically inspired architecture, which is governed by 'subtle systems of proportion', plays a dominant role in the paintings of this period.[12]

A prime example of this architectural influence can be seen in Masaccio's *Trinity* (c.1427). Here the painter creates an astounding *'trompe-l'oeil'* effect through an impressive display of 'Brunelleschian architecture'. Indeed, the 'coffered barrel vault', which sweeps high over the Trinitarian figures of God the Father, Christ Crucified, and the Holy Spirit (personified in the guise of a dove), facilitates the required geometrical environment for the deployment of Brunelleschi's revolutionary perspective technique, with the orthogonals converging at the base of the Cross. The painting also reveals a strong 'visual dialogue with Donatello'. Even more so than his classicising predecessors, Pisano and di Cambio, Donatello sought to forge a 'heroic style' which combined both 'Christian pathos and classical Roman forms' and in so doing created sculptures endowed with a profound 'emotional force'. In fact, the 'enormous impact' of Donatello's work upon his contemporaries has led Chilvers to describe him as the 'most influential Italian artist of his time in any medium', and looking at the 'monumental scale' of the figures in Masaccio's *Trinity*, with the 'sculptural clarity of their contours', it is easy to discern the sculptor's influence. Looking at the pale fragility of Christ's wounded body we are inescapably reminded of Donatello's own *Crucifix* (1412-13), carved in wood some fourteen years earlier. To be sure, the lifeless angle of the head; the slender, sinuous torso; the loose folds of the loincloth; and the sharp precision of the nails which pierce Christ's hands and feet, all bear witness to Masaccio's 'debt to Donatello'. Equally Donatellan is the figure of God the Father, whose lined countenance and physical 'robustness', is reminiscent of the sculptor's *St.*

John the Evangelist (1410-11). Despite the fact that the figure is fully clothed one senses a solid, proportioned body beneath the superbly realised folds of cloth. Here the Father is portrayed as a *physical* presence and not merely as a *metaphysical* idea.[13]

The implications of Masaccio's artistic synthesis in the *Trinity* were to have a profound effect upon the development of painting for, as we have seen, the fresco's intelligent treatment of Brunelleschian architecture and Donatellan sculpture facilitated, for the first time, a completely coherent and consistent sense of three dimensions on a two-dimensional surface, allowing bodies that appear endowed with the robust solidity of flesh, muscle, and bone to almost move around within their beautifully realised environment. Unlike the works of Giotto, in which his figures exist nearly independently of their scenic context, here the architecture gives coherence to the figures just as the figures give meaning to the space. This heightened spatio-figural awareness is further enhanced through Masaccio's radical treatment of light. Whilst the effect of light in frescos had previously been conditional upon the physical surroundings of the church or cathedral which housed them, in the *Trinity* Masaccio has created a 'fictive realm' of pictorial luminosity. In other words, '[l]ight and shadow *within* the *Trinity* seem unrelated to the ambient lighting of the church, but rather are governed by a hidden light source (or sources) existing only within the sacred realm of the picture space'. Consequently, the 'spatial illusionism' of the composition is greatly enhanced, for the internal interplay of light and shadow upon the figures and the architecture deepens their claim to an autonomous reality. Indeed, the newfound mimetic power of Masaccio's *Trinity* puts one in mind of the legendary story of Zeuxis and Parrhasios, as recounted by Pliny the Elder in his *Natural History*. To see which was the greater painter both entered into a contest, and when Zeuxis drew back the curtain from his painting there was depicted a bunch of grapes so lifelike that 'birds flew down' to peck at them.

Then Zeuxis, 'glorying in the judgement of the birds', asked Parrhasios to draw back the curtain from *his* painting. However, such was Parrhasios' mimetic skill that the curtain, far from being made of cloth, was in fact the subject of his picture. Realising his mistake, Zeuxis 'conceded the prize with honest shame, saying that he had tricked the birds, but Parrhasios had tricked him'. For the Ancients it was the duty of art to imitate life so meticulously as to pass for life itself, and with the advent of Masaccio's *Trinity* we can see the first true intimation of this Classical ideal being tentatively realised within a Renaissance context. As we shall go on to see, Masaccio's mimetic efforts were to be superseded by the likes of Leonardo, Michelangelo, and Raphael. However, the compositional achievement of the *Trinity* is nevertheless highly significant for it communicates, in embryo, what was to become the guiding precept of Renaissance painting: that the imitation of 'Nature' is the root of 'beautiful art'.[14]

The question of what imitating Nature meant in a Renaissance context is a complex one. As early as 1400, the artist and writer Cennino Cennini had, in his *Libro dell'arte*, promoted 'the convincing imitation of nature as the embodiment of artistic value'. However, as the art historian Moshe Barasch points out:

> Cennini also orthodoxly believed in the system of exempla, the well-known method of training artists and guiding them in the production of works of art in the medieval workshop. Cennini used established medieval techniques of copying; he indicated precisely the specific spots in the face where the artist should apply shadows; and he described how his master, Agnolo Gaddi, used to apply a pink touch to the cheeks of his figures and recommended it as a model for imitation. In general, the education of an artist is for him a process of imitating the works of fine artists and of absorbing their style.[15]

It is easy, with hindsight, to discern a profound 'crack' in Cennini's thinking; on the one hand he is endorsing the diligent adherence to a given 'master's manner', and on the other, advising the artist to turn to 'nature' for their models. Nevertheless, it is important to remember that Cennini was writing on the cusp of transition, and thus it would be unreasonable of us to expect the *Libro dell'arte* to articulate a stable aesthetic position. He may be writing *after* Giotto, but he is writing *before* Brunelleschi's development of linear perspective and the composition of Masaccio's *Trinity*; Cennini's aesthetic understanding in 1400 was necessarily limited to the technical faculties of his time. Additionally, it is important to remember how far removed the fifteenth century's understanding of natural imitation is from our own conception. Masaccio's *naturalism*, which allows for the depiction of tangible bodies within an equally cogent environment, is patently not derived from the *direct* imitation of natural forms. Rather he is using synthetic models, which are, in turn, derived from antique paradigms, and thus, whilst the result is mimetically convincing, it has as much to do with mathematics and received archetypes of bodily representation as it has with observing life *in the flesh*. It is *ideal* as much as it is *real*.[16]

To gain a further appreciation of this position we must now consider the writings of Leon Battista Alberti. An intimate friend of both Brunelleschi and Donatello, and an admirer of the works of Masaccio, Alberti is generally considered to be 'the most important art theorist of the Renaissance'. A true polymath, whose interests included literature, sculpture, architecture, and painting, Alberti was to write the first sincerely 'intellectual' treatise on the painter's art, modelled upon antique works such as Vitruvius' *De Architectura*. Originally written in Latin in 1435, *On Painting* was translated into the vernacular the following year; a gesture which reveals that the treatise's intellectualism was not meant to preclude the working artist. Nevertheless, the difference between Alberti's treatise and Cennini's *Libro dell'arte* could not be more pronounced. Whereas Cennini's treatise was still very much part of the 'medieval technical tradition', with its focus on the strictly practical elements of artistic production, such as the mixing of pigments, Alberti's *On Painting* is of a markedly more philosophical character. In part, this is symptomatic of the changing perception of painting during the Renaissance from a mere craft to one of the 'liberal arts', something matched by the increasingly aspirational lifestyles of artists, yet we must not forget that the treatise also contains much which *is* practical, not least its detailed discussion of Brunelleschi's perspective techniques in Book One. It is also highly revealing in its treatment of Nature, its imitation, and purpose. For Alberti, all that is worthy in Nature is 'beauty', and thus the artist must learn beauty from Nature. Here it is possible to detect strong Platonic overtones. Like the *Phaedrus* (fourth century BCE) and the *Symposium* (fourth century BCE), in which the concept of beauty in Nature is seen as a means of transcending the mundane realm of the senses and contemplating the divine 'Forms' of the absolute, so Alberti deems it the artist's responsibility to *select* that which is most 'beautiful' from Nature and not merely to slavishly *imitate* the natural world. To emphasise his point he recites the story of '[t]he early painter Demetrius [who] failed to obtain the highest praise because he was more devoted to representing the likeness of things than to beauty'. Exceeding the legend of Zeuxis and Parrhasios, Alberti makes it clear that mimesis alone is not enough. Rather the painter must create works of art which imitate the truth of beauty *within* Nature, its divine 'symmetry', and not simply mirror the flawed expressions of its outward manifestations.[17]

The aesthetic implications of Alberti's theoretical position are given particularly acute realisation in the works of the three Titans of the 'High Renaissance', Leonardo, Michelangelo, and Raphael. The High Renaissance was a period of intense formal development, in which bodily representation and the architectonics of pictorial space reached new heights of technical 'perfection'. Works like

Leonardo's *Mona Lisa* (c.1503-6) embraced the Albertian notion of Nature, combining a beautifully idealised landscape background with what appears to be an idealised image of maternal anticipation. The painting is also a technical departure from the harsh geometrical dynamics of the early Renaissance. Instead of deploying linear perspective – a technique better suited to the precise lines of artificial constructions – Leonardo gives a sense of recession through his skilful deployment of 'aerial perspective', a system of his own devising which emulates 'the effect of atmosphere whereby objects look paler and bluer the further away they are from the viewer'. An additional sense of mimesis is created through Leonardo's use of 'oil paint'. Whilst he was not the first Italian painter to employ this medium, he nevertheless made it his own, and Chilvers has described his work as marking 'the greatest advance in naturalism in [Renaissance] painting since Masaccio'. Whereas Masaccio worked in either 'fresco' or 'tempera', and thus endowed his figures with the coolness of Donatello's marble, Leonardo's Lisa radiates the almost buttery warmth of flesh, something which is directly conditional upon his decision to work in oil. Were we to reach out and touch her we might expect to sense the blood beneath her skin.[18]

Another important development of this period was artists' increasingly sophisticated knowledge of human anatomy. At the vanguard of this advancement were Leonardo and Michelangelo, both of whom conducted detailed anatomical investigations, the results of which greatly enhanced the mimetic power of their art; and perhaps nowhere can this heightened anatomical awareness be seen more clearly than in Michelangelo's muscular nudes which adorn the ceiling of the Sistine Chapel in Rome (painted 1508-1512). Described by the art historian Gilles Néret as 'veritable temples of flesh', these 'colossal' forms demonstrate the artist's keen understanding of the human body, heeding Alberti's advice that the painter must fully comprehend the structures beneath the skin. Unlike earlier artists such as

Antonio Pollaiuolo, whose *Battle of Nude Men* (c.1460) presents a somewhat anatomically awry representation of the naked male form, the precision of Michelangelo's scalpel enabled him to correctly portray 'at least eight hundred different anatomical structures'. Yet the artist's sophisticated knowledge of the human body did not mean that he was simply copying what he saw *directly* before him. His powerful, Herculean super-beings are palpably *not* literal imitations of Nature, but rather idealised bodies of archetypal beauty. True, they are conditional upon a detailed study of Nature for their existence, but they are not straightforwardly representational; they are not simple mimesis. Once again we are witnessing the Albertian ideal of revealing the truth of beauty *within* Nature and not purely mirroring the flawed expressions of its outward manifestations.[19]

Despite the astonishing achievements of Leonardo and Michelangelo, it is with the mature works of Raphael that we encounter 'the artist who most completely expresses the ideals of the High Renaissance'. Raphael combined Leonardo's grace with Michelangelo's strength to create sophisticated compositions which are remarkable for the balanced elegance of their poise. Indeed, perhaps the greatest example of the painter's 'prodigious ability' to harmoniously orchestrate vast scenes of 'idealised humanity' can be seen in his 'celebrated' *School of Athens* (1510). Arguably the most famous fresco from the Stanza della Segnatura sequence in the Vatican Palace, this painting is a visual embodiment of the Renaissance's love for antique learning, depicting 'the great thinkers of the ancient world, led by Plato and Aristotle, arranged in a majestic architectural setting'. Here everything is possessed of a lucid clarity that is at once luminal, figural and spatial. The 'three barrel vaults' which rise high over the figures, and which bear a marked resemblance to the architect Bramante's design for the 'interior of St. Peter's', create an environment which, due to the clear vision of the sky at the centre of the composition, is 'neither indoors nor outside'.

Rather, as the art historian Marcia Hall points out, it forms 'an appropriate substitute for the grove of Plato's Academy' and, compared to the comparatively claustrophobic architecture of Masaccio's *Trinity*, seems to personify the airy space of rational thought; to speak for the triumph of reason over emotion. This is mirrored in the figures themselves, who combine anatomical precision with urbane plasticity. Curiously, each figure is an *individual*, embodying varied and physiognomically distinct philosophers, including 'Pythagoras', 'Euclid', and 'Socrates', but no figure *individuates*. Instead they are held in a rhythmical 'ebb and flow across the wall, drawing the spectator's eye from one…to another, all expertly integrated within a brilliantly realised imaginary space'. As a consequence, 'no single figure dominates'; rather they are subsumed into 'unified groups that interlock into the design of the whole'. Equally harmonic is Raphael's treatment of light. It is the pure light of the sun, which enters the fictive architectural environment like a heavenly visitant – a visual metaphor for the 'divine' lucidity of the philosophical systems which are embodied in the characters of the fresco. Invariably it shines brightest on the philosophers, diminishing through gentle shadows onto the bodies of their 'disciples'. The effect of this action on the one hand performs in visual language the transference of knowledge from teacher to pupil (and from painting to viewer), and on the other, presents a further means of creating compositional unity. As Hall observes:

> Portions of each disciple receive light, but it may only be an arm, a shoulder, or half a face. The distribution of values, lowest at the core of the group and highest near the periphery, defines the contours of the unit and dictates that we read it as a whole.[20]

The implied hierarchy is therefore subsumed into the luminous dynamic of the fresco: teacher and disciples become one, just as one intellectual group flows, photo-rhythmically into the next. Indeed, this would appear to be the argument of the painting, that 'cosmic harmony is the subject of all philosophical investigation, that it has been investigated by philosophers using various tools and methods, and that, despite the diversity of their languages, their findings can be brought into harmony with one another'. Put succinctly, Raphael's *School of Athens* is a hymn to 'ideal beauty' – to the artist's power to transfigure the forms of Nature into a sublime expression of the mind.[21]

The relationship of Caravaggio's work with the art of the High Renaissance is a tortuous one, simultaneously personifying a wilful reaction against its aesthetic expectations *and* a skilful evolution of its technical achievements. Certainly, to the artist's contemporaries, for whom the intellectual values of Renaissance artistic practice were still dominant, the uncompromising, seemingly unmannered realism of his paintings was by turns both seductive and shocking. His second biographer, Giovanni Baglione, who had known Caravaggio personally and had been his competitor on the Roman art scene, sums up the complex nature of the painter's reception when he writes in his *Life of Michelangelo da Caravaggio* that whilst 'many young artists followed his example…some people thought that he had destroyed the art of painting'. To emphasise his point, Baglione recounts the Mannerist painter Federico Zuccaro's reaction to the three paintings by Caravaggio in the Church of San Luigi dei Francesi in Rome (painted 1599-1602):

> When Federico Zuccaro came to see [the paintings], while I was there, he exclaimed: 'What is all the fuss about?' …and, sneering, astonished by such commotion, he turned his back and left…[22]

This was the commission which 'made Caravaggio famous' and, as the above makes clear, 'aroused a certain envy on the part of his [traditionalist] colleagues'. To be sure, Baglione himself does not seem un-tinged by jealousy,

dismissing the furore surrounding Caravaggio's work as 'propaganda' allegedly orchestrated by 'evil people'.[23]

If Baglione's tone seems inflammatory, then it must be remembered that he harboured a deep personal animosity towards his subject. As Langdon observes, 'Baglione was the first to imitate Caravaggio's style, and Caravaggio, notoriously jealous, [is alleged to have] attacked him in a series of outrageously scurrilous verses, provoking his competitor into suing him for libel'. In fact, his biography, when seen in this context, 'deserves credit for [its] objectivity' and, as Langdon testifies, 'his account has not been proved inaccurate'. True, it is 'mean-spirited', and Baglione 'seizes any opportunity to disparage the artist', but the negative instances which occur throughout the *Life* seem grounded in fact, and should not be dismissed on account of Baglione's personal history or occasionally hyperbolical turn of phrase. Indeed, Caravaggio's rival was perfectly placed to assess the impact of his work, for circumstances led him to occupy both critical camps. As both an *admirer* and a *despiser* of the Caravaggio phenomenon, Baglione was deeply sympathetic to the high feelings which Caravaggio and his work induced in the public.[24]

Equally inflammatory, although less directly personal, is *On Michelangelo da Caravaggio* by the artist's third biographer, Giovanni Pietro Bellori. An 'antiquarian and [art] theorist', Bellori was born after Caravaggio's death and his biography is largely based on the earlier *Lives* by Mancini and Baglione. However, what Bellori's account substantially adds to these previous works is an intensely art historical dimension. For Bellori, who was both a devotee of 'Raphael' and a promoter of the Albertian belief 'that the artist should select the most beautiful parts of nature to create an "idea" of perfect beauty', Caravaggio's compositional style was tantamount to heresy. What shocked Bellori, just as what seems to have shocked the artist's classically influenced contemporaries some seventy years earlier, was

Caravaggio's apparent disregard for the established 'science of painting'. His works, which treated even lofty religious themes 'as though they were everyday events', with their seemingly casual arrangement of figures dressed in the contemporary clothes of the street, unashamedly repudiated the High Renaissance principles of '*invenzione*, decorum, [and] *disegno*'. Bellori makes much of Caravaggio's reputed infatuation with painting *directly* from the 'model', claiming that 'he made no attempt to improve on the creations of Nature'. In one particularly indignant passage he writes:

> Caravaggio suppressed the dignity of art...did as he pleased, and what followed was contempt for beautiful things, the authority of antiquity and Raphael destroyed... Now began the imitation of common and vulgar things, seeking out filth and deformity...[25]

Certainly, Caravaggio is a very *different* artist from Raphael, but the extent to which his works embody an *artless* 'imitation of common and vulgar things' is open to debate. Let us take by way of example *The Calling of St. Matthew* (1599-1600), one of the three paintings from the San Luigi dei Francesi commission. What immediately impresses itself upon the viewer is the tense claustrophobia of the pictorial environment. Unlike the airy expanse of the *School of Athens*, where the architecture of a basilica expands into the sky, here the world contracts into the stifling dimensions of a darkened room. To the left of the canvas are depicted a group of figures in contemporary dress, seated around a rough wooden table on which rest a pile of coins and an inkwell. The only other discernable feature of the room is a dirty window located off centre to the right. It is closed, and whilst not shuttered, appears to admit no light. Rather the scene is lit by an unseen source, in all probability intended to signify daylight coming in off the street. Such a reading would appear to have merit, for standing to the right of the picture, half-outside of the shaft of light which cuts across the canvas, illuminating the table, are two mysterious, shadowy figures who give every impression of having suddenly intruded upon the scene. One is barefoot and grey-haired, his back to the viewer. The other is younger, probably about thirty, his delicately bearded face shown in profile. He is staring fixedly at the figures seated around the table, or rather at one in particular, a middle-aged man with a long beard and a floppy velvet hat. The stranger's right arm is outstretched, his hand pointing almost languidly at the object of his scrutiny, who, seemingly uncomfortable at the attention, gestures to himself as if to query the imposition.[26]

Superficially, the composition appears to have nothing *overtly* biblical about it, and one could be forgiven for supposing that it was a secular work, depicting, as Lambert suggests, either a 'tavern or a gambling den'. Yet this is Caravaggio's genius as a religious painter, his phenomenal ability to transfigure the sacred into the profane, and thereby endow episodes of Scriptural narrative with both immediacy *and* uncertainty. As with earlier secular pieces, such as *Boy Bitten by a Lizard* and *Basket of Fruit*, *The Calling of St. Matthew* possesses a disquieting illusion of time, and although we know that Matthew did indeed obey Christ's summons, the dramatic immediacy of the episode's representation allows us to truly live the moment as if it were unfolding spontaneously before us. Unlike Raphael's timeless figures in the *School of Athens*, whose refined plasticity exudes an untroubled certainty about the divine harmony of the Universe, Caravaggio's bodies exude the uncertainty of mortality. Yet this is not to deny the latter's sincere religiosity, far from it, for the apparent mortality of Caravaggio's figures *heightens* their need for salvation. Thus whereas Raphael's art is an intellectual celebration *of the eternal*, embodied in harmoniously realised antique forms, Caravaggio's art is an emotional striving *for the eternal*, performed through the sinuous incarnations of a troubled reality.[27]

This fundamental difference between the artists' approaches is perhaps most clearly apparent in their differing treatments of light. As we have seen, Raphael's photo-rhythmical approach in the *School of Athens* allowed the painter to orchestrate numerous and diverse figures into a seamless unity. Nevertheless, this use of light, like the composition as a whole, is narratalogically *passive*, subordinate to the painting's almost abstract, intellectual rationale. In *The Calling of St. Matthew*, by contrast, the light is very much an *active* participant; for whilst it increases the mimetic power of the composition, solidifying the figures and defining their environment, it also disrupts the compositional space, just as Christ and his accompanying disciple are disrupting the mundane familiarity of Matthew's world. Indeed, the shaft of light can be interpreted as a luminal embodiment of Christ's divinity, an extension of his gesturing arm, and a much clearer signifier of his status than 'the glimmer of [his] thin gold halo' which is nearly lost amid the interplay of light and shadow. Thus, for Caravaggio, it is light which both *creates* time and *defies* time, allowing the viewer to simultaneously experience the fear of mortality *and* the hope of resurrection.[28]

What the above reading makes clear is that Caravaggio's work is not, as Bellori would have it, simply an artless 'imitation of common and vulgar things', but rather an ingenious, and in many ways highly 'original', means of conveying a 'divine and eternal message [to] the contemporary [seventeenth-century] viewer'. True, Caravaggio is *not* Raphael, but then nor is he trying to be. His work manifestly embodies a very different intellectual position from that of the High Renaissance, and thus it is little wonder that modern art historians invariably regard Caravaggio's pictures as marking 'the beginning of a new age in painting' – the end of Renaissance values, of the search for ideal beauty, and the advent of the powerfully dramatic 'Baroque'. Nevertheless, it is important to remember that, whilst the artist may have rejected the aesthetic ideology of the High Renaissance, he is still very much indebted to its technical advances. For example, whilst Caravaggio's treatment of light and shadow, a technique known as 'chiaroscuro', is in many ways unprecedented, it does have affinities with certain works by Leonardo, most notably da Vinci's enigmatic painting of *St. John the Baptist* (c.1513-1516) in which the luminous body of the saint appears to be emerging out of the swathing darkness of the background. Likewise, Caravaggio is indebted to the High Renaissance's development of correct anatomical representation for the mimetic conviction of his figures. Without the macabre undertakings of artists like Leonardo and Michelangelo, the profound illusionism of Caravaggio's compositional style would not have been possible. Indeed, *The Calling of St. Matthew* exhibits a playful deference to Michelangelo's figurative achievements by imitating 'the pointing gesture...of the hand of Michelangelo's Adam on the ceiling of the Sistine Chapel'. In a further example of the artfulness of Caravaggio's technique, the artist reverses the gesture, thereby making a comment on the incarnation; Christ points in the manner of Adam, but in the direction of God from his forebear's famous fresco. Through this subtle piece of intertextuality, and one which escaped comment by both Baglione and Bellori, Caravaggio testifies that Christ is God become man. Lastly, it is also important to remember that Caravaggio is indebted to the Renaissance's pioneering development of oil paint; a medium that he made very much his own, taking it to new heights of technical proficiency. Exceeding the buttery warmth of Leonardo's Lisa, Caravaggio's figures perform the blood beneath the skin in a truly startling way, leaving the viewer in no doubt that they are modelled from a studied attention to life, and not from the cool indifference of antique marble.[29]

As the above makes clear, the dynamic of Caravaggio's relationship with the tradition of the Renaissance is a complex one, embodying at once an emotional rejection of its aesthetic ideology *and* a technical evolution of its creative forms. To elucidate the issue further it is worth drawing an analogy with certain arguments from T. S. Eliot's essay, 'Tradition and the Individual Talent'. Here Eliot proposes that a successful/mature poet or artist cannot merely content themselves with simply 'following the ways of the immediate generation before [them] in a blind or timid adherence to its successes'. Rather, for Eliot, 'Tradition is a matter of much wider significance. It cannot be inherited, and if [a poet or artist wants it they] must obtain it by great labour'. In other words, the successful/mature artist is the artist who combines a keen 'historical sense' of what has gone before with an evolutionary spirit. They can 'neither take the past as a lump…nor…form [themselves] wholly upon one preferred period'. Instead, they must simultaneously assimilate that which has gone before *and* make something new; make something which is neither a complete break with the past or its slavish imitation. In many ways this mirrors Caravaggio's relationship with both the Mannerists and the classicising attitudes of critics like Bellori. Whereas the latter either fetishise Renaissance tradition through vapid regurgitation or enshrine its aesthetic ideology in hallowed academies of thought – thereby becoming *traditionalists* – Caravaggio's work represents a clear and purposeful evolution of Renaissance artistic practice, becoming, in its turn, an artistic practice which embraces its forebears' achievements without ceasing to be 'individual'. By rejecting the Renaissance's aesthetic ideology, Caravaggio is able to evolve the technical potential of its forms. Consequently, whilst he is emphatically *not* a traditionalist, his work is still very much part of the Renaissance tradition, by virtue of appearing to be something entirely new.[30]

After leaving the household of Pandolfo Pucci, Mancini informs us that Caravaggio 'was struck by sickness and, being without money, was obliged to enter the hospital of the Consolazione'. The precise nature of his malady is uncertain, but as Langdon observes, the charitable foundation of the Consolazione, which was administered by a 'Prior' and staffed by monks, specialised in caring not only 'for those suffering from fever [but also] for the victims of street fights'. As we shall go on to see, Caravaggio possessed both a 'belligerent nature and [a] love of sword fighting', and so the possibility that his hospitalisation was the result of an unfortunate brawl is not to be discounted. If this was the case, then Mancini's use of the word 'sickness' is perhaps euphemistic. Alternatively, Caravaggio may have contracted a fever as the result of some sustained wound. Whatever the truth, he appears to have made good use of his convalescence, for Mancini relates how 'he [painted] many pictures for the prior'. Sadly, Mancini neglects to tell us the subject of these works, however modern scholarship tends to date one particularly interesting composition to this period, the *Self-Portrait as Bacchus* (c.1593-94). Also known as the *Ill Bacchus* this work presents not only, as Wilson-Smith argues, an 'attempt to undermine the lofty pretensions of [the] Renaissance' but also reveals the peculiarly autobiographical quality of Caravaggio's art. Some thirty years before Rembrandt began his famous pictorial exploration of his own personality, Caravaggio offers us a pertinent insight into his temperament, both as an artist and as a man.[31]

Of course it can be dangerous in an age in which art was still largely produced on a 'bespoke basis' to read a painting as in any way autobiographical. Nevertheless, certain factors mitigate in favour of this interpretation. Firstly, it is a self-portrait, and thus the artist, whilst dressed-up, is very much the *substance* of the painting. Secondly, in Caravaggio's case, we know that he produced work 'according to his own inclinations', going against the prevailing fashions of his day. Thus, in contrast to the mainstream Mannerist artists of the time, Caravaggio's work presents a highly *subjective* response to the world around him, and even when he began to be awarded prestigious commissions during the height of his Roman period (1599-1606), the perceived eccentricities of the works led to numerous patrons rejecting them. To be sure, the *personal quality* of Caravaggio's art is one of the numerous objections raised by Bellori, who even goes so far as to attribute the 'dark style' of the painter's mature work to his 'dark complexion and dark eyes', additionally claiming that this pronounced use of shadow was 'connected to his disturbed and contentious temperament'.[32]

In the case of the *Self-Portrait as Bacchus* the interpretive implications are twofold. Firstly, following Wilson-Smith's line, we can read the painting as a potent aesthetic statement. Unlike Titian's radiant representation of the god in his *Bacchus and Ariadne* (1520-23), here Caravaggio strips him of his 'mythological dignity', presenting him as 'just a sickly young man who may be suffering from the after-effects of a hangover', and by so doing, mocks at the Mannerists' tendency to fetishise the antique. Yet the figure is not just Bacchus; it is also Caravaggio. As we saw in our exploration of the Nietzschean voices of Book One, Bacchus, or Dionysos to give him his original Greek name, was the god of wine, embodying its potential to unleash a violent, destructive frenzy. He was the god who made men mad. Consequently, by portraying himself as a *sick* Bacchus, with 'puffy flesh, livid complexion, and…rings around the eyes', Caravaggio appears to be commenting on his own self-destructive violence. Indeed, if this reading were correct, then it would support the theory that his convalescence in the Hospital of the Consolazione was the result, not of a simple fever, but of his Dionysiac temperament.[33]

On leaving hospital, Mancini tells us that Caravaggio 'stayed with Cavaliere Giuseppe'. The Cavaliere Giuseppe Cesari d'Arpino, to give him his full title, was a 'Mannerist painter' who enjoyed 'an enormous reputation' during his lifetime, but whose work is generally regarded by modern art historians as being both 'repetitious and vacuous'. A former 'boy-prodigy', he 'moved in the circles of the papal court…[and] belonged to one of the most active artistic fraternities of Rome, the Accademia degl'Insensati, so

named because they promoted the divine over the evidence of the senses'. As we have seen, such aesthetic values were far removed from Caravaggio's own creative principles, and so it seems unlikely that he learned much from his successful contemporary. Nevertheless, his time in Giuseppe's studio, where he worked as the master's 'assistant', was not entirely wasted. As Lambert points out, '[t]he studio was an excellent place to meet the richest Roman art-lovers: cardinals, ambassadors, and artists of high repute', and it was here, Baglione informs us, that Caravaggio met one 'Maestro Valentino'. Something of 'a dealer in paintings', Valentino appears to have been impressed by Caravaggio's work, and Baglione has to grudgingly concede that he even 'managed to sell a few [of his pictures]'. Indeed, Valentino's efforts on the artist's behalf were to prove extremely providential, for it was through Valentino that Caravaggio was to meet the most auspicious patron of his Roman period, Cardinal del Monte – a man who seems to have 'immediately perceived' that Caravaggio's work embodied a completely 'new way of painting'. Now the artist's life began to take a dramatically upward turn. Not only did he move into the Cardinal's palace, a residence much more congenial than Giuseppe's studio, but also 'it was through Del Monte that he was to win a wider fame and to obtain the most prestigious Roman commissions'.[34]

By all accounts, Caravaggio 'responded badly' to his 'sudden stardom'. As Langdon observes, '[h]e became vain and proud, increasingly involved in street violence, and so famed for his belligerence that news of it circulated through Europe'. Indeed, the more attention he got, the more outrageous his behaviour became. Mancini relates how when Caravaggio's brother, 'a priest, a man of letters and of high morals' came to visit him at the Cardinal's palace, the painter 'declared that he did not know him and that he was not his brother'. 'Thus,' concludes Mancini, 'one cannot deny that Caravaggio was a very odd person'. Additionally, in Bellori's biography, we hear how Caravaggio reacted to

his newly elevated status by wearing only 'the finest materials and princely velvets'. However, Bellori then goes on to tell us that once the painter had 'put on a suit of clothes he changed only when it had fallen into rags', adding, somewhat condescendingly, that Caravaggio 'was very negligent in washing himself'. Whilst these 'eccentricities' were harmless enough (if rather hurtful to his brother and his neighbours' sense of smell), it was not long before his actions escalated, first into a libel case, and then into murder.[35]

The libel case, which took place in the summer of 1603, concerned, as we have previously mentioned, a series of scurrilous verses allegedly written by Caravaggio defaming his rival Baglione. Whether they were indeed written by the artist, or by some associate, remains uncertain, and it is a testament to Baglione's restraint that he does not mention the incident in his biography. Certainly, Caravaggio enjoyed a reputation for being both 'aggressive and insecure', and, as Langdon points out, he 'bitterly resented any artist who came too close to his style'. Considering that Baglione was one of the first to imitate Caravaggio, it is not improbable that the pugnacious painter was somehow involved in trying to besmirch his rival's reputation. Whatever the reality of the situation, the judge was not persuaded by Caravaggio's protestations of innocence – court records reveal that the artist's testimony was both confused and self-contradictory – and when the defendant became abusive he was sent briefly to 'prison'. Although 'the trial seems to have petered out, without reaching a conclusion', Caravaggio spent the winter out of Rome, staying in the Marches town of 'Tolentino', most probably to avoid further accusations by Baglione.[36]

This was not Caravaggio's only encounter with the law during the opening years of the seventeenth century; far from it. Caravaggio was repeatedly 'arrested for carrying weapons without a licence', on each occasion erroneously claiming that his status in the Cardinal's retinue entitled him 'to wear a sword', and on each occasion relying on his patron to get him out of trouble. Indeed, Caravaggio appears to have been fixated by blades and swordsmanship, and it is astonishing how many of his paintings depict the active use of weaponry. Bellori even suggests that Caravaggio preferred the life of a 'bravo' to that of a painter, relating how '[a]fter having painted for a few hours in the day he used to go out on the town with his sword at his side like a professional swordsman, seeming to do anything but paint'. It was on just such an occasion in the spring of 1606 that things finally got completely out of control. The circumstances surrounding the murder of Ranuccio Tommasoni de Terni remain somewhat mysterious, with Caravaggio's seventeenth-century biographers only revealing tantalisingly brief pieces of information. Mancini, for example, simply states that 'as a result of certain events he [Caravaggio] almost lost his life, and in defending himself…killed his foe with the help of his friend Onorio Longhi and was forced to leave Rome'. Here Tommasoni is not named and the reason for their quarrel undisclosed. Baglione, by contrast, seems to be more forthcoming; at least on the surface. He informs us that Caravaggio 'confronted Ranuccio Tommasoni, a very polite young man, over some disagreement about a tennis match. They argued and ended up fighting. Ranuccio fell to the ground after Michelangelo [Caravaggio] had wounded him in the thigh and then killed him'. Whilst Baglione's account is not *wholly* inaccurate it *is* liberal with the facts, not least in his representation of Tommasoni as 'a very polite young man'. The Tommasoni family 'boasted a long tradition of military service' and Ranuccio appears to have been no stranger to the art of the sword. As Langdon observes, 'Tommasoni's name appears constantly in the criminal records [of the time]'. It seems that he was forever 'at the centre of brawls and riots', involved in 'disputes over gambling [and] women' and, like Caravaggio, arrested for illegally 'bearing arms'. Indeed, Tommasoni thrived in precisely the same environment of 'urban thuggery' as his murderer, and Baglione's spin on the events leading up to Tommasoni's death seems a rather obvious attempt to show Caravaggio in the worst possible light. Even Baglione's statement that the fight was over a 'tennis match' is open to question, and may simply be a supposition based on nothing more than the fact that the fight appears to have taken place 'near the tennis courts on the Via della Scrofa'. Tommasoni, as we have seen, was known to fight over women – and both he and Caravaggio had a woman in common, one Fillide Melandroni, a rising *'cortigiana'* (courtesan), who was known to have been simultaneously Tommasoni's lover *and* Caravaggio's 'model', posing for works such as *St. Catherine of Alexandria* (1598). Could their quarrel have been a rivals' duel? Or was it rather a sordid vendetta over a prostitute's fee? This is certainly possible, for there is some evidence to suggest that Tommasoni, who organised a 'crew of tarts', may have acted as Fillide's pimp, but ultimately it must remain a point of conjecture. Equally plausible is that Caravaggio's fatal confrontation with Tommasoni was just another casual street fight that ended badly, for both men were of a pugnacious disposition and both men liked playing with swords. Whatever the case, and Bellori's account furnishes us with no further information save that Caravaggio was also 'wounded' in the fight, on 29th May 1606 the artist found himself a murderer and on the run.[37]

The aftermath of the fateful duel was to change Caravaggio's life forever. He had been at the height of his powers and 'one of the most famous painters in Rome', courted by Ambassadors and Cardinals. Now he was an 'outlaw' running for his life. Whilst it is in many ways understandable that the artist, with his extensive criminal record, should have decided to run, it meant that he suffered the full severity of the law. The Tommasoni family were well connected, and the case had come under 'papal jurisdiction'. When Caravaggio failed to appear before the bar on 28th June he was found in 'contempt of court' and the Pope passed 'a truly terrible sentence' known as the *'pena capitale'* – which translates, quite literally, as 'a price on his

head'. In effect, this meant that 'anyone, in any place, could carry [the sentence] out'; could decapitate the artist and return his severed head to the Pope for a reward. A hunted fugitive, Caravaggio would never see Rome again.[38]

There is some confusion as to where the painter went after fleeing the Eternal City. Baglione says that Caravaggio went to 'Palestrina', whereas Mancini informs us that the painter initially sought refuge in 'Zagarolo where he was secretly housed by the prince'. This version of events certainly sounds plausible, for Bellori, in agreement with Mancini, gives the name of the prince as one 'Duke Marzio Colonna'. Given the connection between the Merisi and the Colonna families, it is not unreasonable to assume that Duke Marzio would have afforded the painter his 'protection'. What all three biographers *do* agree on is that Caravaggio continued to paint. In the light of his predicament this can be seen as revealing both a strong degree of psychological resilience *and* the continued demand for his work amongst discerning patrons. Nevertheless, it must be observed that the canvases produced in the immediate wake of his exile demonstrate, not only a muted compositional dynamic, but also a marked chromatic depression. By way of example, let us compare the two versions Caravaggio painted of *The Supper at Emmaus*. The first, created in 1601, some five years before Caravaggio's exile, is a flamboyant display of theatrical illusionism. As the art historian Francesca Marini observes, '[t]he painting depicts the moment in which the [two] disciples recognize the arisen Christ in their table companion while Christ blesses the bread' and is a fine illustration of the artist's 'customary fidelity to reality'. The disciples, like the innkeeper standing behind Christ's right shoulder, who is 'oblivious' to the spiritual significance of the gesture, wear 'modern clothes' and the measured use of chiaroscuro heightens the scene's naturalistic atmosphere. Equally impressive are the beautifully realised objects spread across the table, including a 'basket of fruit tilting towards us' which is strongly reminiscent of the artist's earlier still-life on the same subject. Yet perhaps the most

striking feature of the composition is the way the gestures of the figures challenge the confines of the pictorial space. Christ's outstretched arm, like the arms of his disciples, which are thrown back in the surprise of recognition, appears to reach out of the picture towards the viewer. This spellbinding illusion of physical communion is further enhanced by the chromatic warmth of Caravaggio's palette. Deep reds and russet browns predominate; colours which seem to draw the viewer into the compositional environment. In short, this version of *The Supper at Emmaus* is a tissue of painterly virtuosity, performing the self-assured swagger of an artist who seems confident of his own genius.[39]

The second version, created shortly after Caravaggio fled Rome in 1606, paints a very different picture. In marked contrast to the above, the painter sets the scene 'the moment after the religious act, when the bread has already been broken and the gesture of blessing signifies an ending'. As Marini observes, '[t]his Christ seems older than the young beardless Christ of the [1601] *Emmaus*'. His face is strangely careworn, and would have been more appropriate in a rendition of Gethsemane. Indeed, everything about this composition signifies both tension and distance. The food spread upon the table is meagre, consisting of only a few unappetising dishes. Likewise the use of chiaroscuro is more pronounced, shrinking the pictorial environment around the tense huddle of bodies. These bodies, in their turn, lack the theatrical flamboyance of their 'forebears'; even the gesture of Christ's hand is muted, hardly reaching across the table, let alone out towards the viewer. Chromatically, too, the composition feels withdrawn. Here washed-out greys and icy blues replace the deep reds and russet browns of the 1601 version, and these cold colours, swathed amid so much darkness, seem to almost push the viewer away. Far from being the pictorial embodiment of a self-assured genius, this work appears to transcend its subject to become a meditation on fear, on the alienation of the exile. To be sure, it is difficult not to read the dramatic shift in style as pertaining to the artist's strained circumstances. As we have previously remarked, Caravaggio's aggression was matched by his insecurity (if not, in part, caused by it), and the nature of the death sentence looming over him, which left him prey to every 'bounty hunter' who cared to try their hand, as well as to 'the long arm of the Roman law', can have done nothing to soothe his already prickly psyche. It is also important to remember that as a 'Catholic' (for despite his violent disposition there is no reason to doubt the sincerity of his belief) the mortal sin of murder would have weighed heavily upon him. Certainly, the accounts of his years in exile suggest that 'he lived in extreme fear, haunted by tumultuous anxieties', and thus it would be extremely odd if these tensions were not somehow reflected in his art. Like the *Ill Bacchus*, the 1606 version of *The Supper at Emmaus* seems to be very much a self-portrait.[40]

After spending some four months in either Palestrina or Zagarolo, Caravaggio decided to move on to 'Naples'. The precise reason for this move is uncertain, and the artist's three seventeenth-century biographers offer no concrete explanation. However, it is possible that Caravaggio had been waiting, somewhat optimistically, for 'a papal pardon' and, when none was forthcoming, 'thought it wise to put a little more distance between himself and the [papal authorities] before the end of the year'. The decision is also likely to have been based on financial considerations. As Lambert observes, 'Naples [was] full of new artistic trends and ideas' and thus was likely to be receptive to Caravaggio's revolutionary art. If this was the painter's thinking then it proved to be correct for, as Bellori recounts, 'he immediately found employment, since his style and reputation were already well known there'. Indeed, the eight months that Caravaggio spent in Naples were to prove highly productive, with Bellori listing no less than four major commissions completed during this time.[41]

Yet despite becoming 'the most famous and productive painter in Naples' the artist does not seem to have been able to settle, and 'by the 26th July [1607] he was established on the small Mediterranean island of Malta'. This restlessness was doubtless, in part, related to the continued threat of apprehension, but Mancini, Baglione, and Bellori all agree that Caravaggio's main reason for going to Malta was to join 'the Knights of the Order of St. John'. Sworn to the 'monastic vows of poverty, chastity and obedience [the Knights] dedicated themselves to the defence of the Catholic faith against the infidel and to the protection of the ill and weak'. To be sure, during the opening decades of the seventeenth century 'the Knights were at the peak of their fame', and, as Langdon observes, '[t]he dream of becoming a Knight of Malta obsessed many young noblemen'. Of course Caravaggio was *not* a nobleman but he was, as we have seen, both 'obsessed with status [and] quick to feel slighted'. Thus, by joining the Knights, Caravaggio would have put himself on the same social footing as his former master, the Caveliere d'Arpino, and *above* many of his other rivals. In addition, by joining the Order, Caravaggio would have been legally entitled 'to wear a sword' – something that was manifestly close to his heart. However, given the nature of his circumstances, other motivations seem more likely. Firstly, it is important to remember that it was a *religious* Order, and thus Caravaggio's desire to join may have been an act of contrition; a means of trying to reconcile himself with God. Secondly, by becoming a member of such a respected community of Knights, the artist may have hoped to 'assist his claim to a pardon'. Certainly, in the short term, the Knights' impressive fortress in the Maltese capital of 'Valletta' would have afforded him protection from both bounty hunters and the law.[42]

Whether the Knights knew that Caravaggio was a wanted fugitive remains uncertain, but as it seems likely that his introduction to the Order's Grand Master, Alof de Wignacourt, came from a member of the Colonna family, then it is entirely possible that the impressive combination of his aristocratic recommendation coupled with his artistic reputation meant that his criminality was overlooked. Certainly, from the moment of his arrival, he seems to have 'moved in the innermost court circles', and, as Langdon points out, 'the early biographies strongly imply that his first Maltese works were portraits of Wignacourt'. Of these portraits one is known to have survived, the famous *Portrait of Alof de Wignacourt* (c.1607-8) which is now housed in the Louvre. Here Caravaggio defines himself as a confident portraitist, presenting his subject as 'consciously dignified, relaxed and authoritative' – quite an achievement when one considers that Wignacourt is depicted wearing nearly a full suit of armour. Only his helmet is absent, being held by an attentive squire who stands dutifully by his master's side. Indeed, 'the splendid black and gold Milanese armour' is an impressive mimetic achievement in its own right, and the artist demonstrates his mastery over light by having it glint beautifully off the polished metal surfaces. Yet the real genius is in the painter's treatment of his subject's face, which radiates humanity without stooping to flattery. Unlike Titian or Van Dyck, Caravaggio does not shy away from the honesty of a receding hairline or a furrowed brow. Rather, with characteristic precision, he presents Wignacourt as a temporal being suspended in a moment in time. Indeed, the Grand Master seems to have been impressed by the portrait, for Baglione recounts how, 'as a sign of gratitude, [Wignacourt] presented him with the Mantle of St. John and made him a Cavaliere di Grazia'. However, here Baglione would appear to have succumbed to an uncharacteristic moment of *favourable* hyperbole for, as Langdon observes, 'he was [in fact] received into the Order on 14th July 1608' – around a year after his arrival and probably several months after finishing the portrait.[43]

The question of time aside, the fact remains that Caravaggio's prestigious skill with the brush, if not his charming personality, seems to have sufficiently impressed the Grand Master, and his acceptance into this illustrious company of Knights meant that he now had the status and protection he desired. To be sure, the pride/gratitude he must have felt at receiving this honour appears to be reflected in a composition he painted around the time of his investiture. The biblical theme of The *Beheading of St. John the Baptist* (1608) was of special relevance to the Knights of Malta, for the Baptist was their 'patron saint', and the painting was commissioned by the Order for the Oratory of the Co-Cathedral of St. John in Valletta. Yet the work also seems profoundly self-reflexive. The scene takes place in an ill-lit dungeon and is striking for its brutality. In the centre of the foreground is the Baptist, lying prostrate on the floor, his nakedness covered by a drape of red cloth – the symbolic colour of the 'martyr' and a signifier that puts us in mind of the mockery of Christ (Matthew 27:27-31). As Wilson-Smith remarks, '[we know that he] is already dead, for the sword with which he has been killed lies abandoned on the ground'. Over the corpse looms the executioner, and in a chilling anticipation of action we can see that he is about to 'prize off' the Baptist's head 'with a knife clutched behind his back'. However, what is arguably most morbid is the trickle of blood which oozes from the gash in St. John's neck. True, Caravaggio had portrayed bloody decapitation before, most notably in his *Judith and Holophernes* (1599), but *here* the trickle of blood spreads out from the neck to form the painter's name. 'In this macabre way,' writes Wilson-Smith, '[Caravaggio] has identified himself with the action', and it is highly tempting to read this identification as pertaining to his *pena capitale* status. Yet if the blood signature can be interpreted as pertaining to his death sentence, then it can also be seen as relating to his redemption. It is important to note that the signature reads 'Fra Michelangelo' and *not* 'Caravaggio' – it is as a Knight of Malta that he identifies himself. Thus we may interpret the blood signature in a soteriological light, for through the martyrdom of the Baptist (or rather through the Order that bears his name), Caravaggio becomes Fra Michelangelo and is redeemed.[44]

After months of running, the artist's life had finally regained some stability. Caravaggio had status, the protection of his brothers, and an audience which appreciated his art. If the painter had been another man then this might have been a profoundly happy conclusion to a brief, unhappy episode; but this man was Michelangelo Merisi da Caravaggio, and once again his world was about to descend into chaos. As in Rome, it appears that his violent temper overcame him. According to both Baglione and Bellori, he got into 'an ill-considered quarrel' with another member of the Order and as a result 'was jailed and reduced to a state of misery and fear'. The right to bear arms was, in this instance, not the right to use them, for by fighting with a fellow brother Caravaggio had contravened one of the cardinal statutes of the Order and, as well as suffering imprisonment, he was also 'deprived of his habit'. The deprivation formally took place on the 1st December 1608 and, as Langdon observes, '[w]ith truly tragic irony, Caravaggio's habit would have been ceremoniously removed from a stool before his own *Beheading of St. John*'. The artist had been a Knight for a mere 'four months'.[45]

In a further dramatic turn, Bellori describes how Caravaggio 'managed to scale the prison walls at night and to flee unrecognised to Sicily'. This was certainly no mean feat, for the painter had been 'cast into the underground cell at the Castel Sant'Angelo [the Order's fortress], a deep, bell-shaped hole, eleven feet deep, and hewn out of solid rock'. As Langdon remarks, '[i]t is...almost inconceivable that Caravaggio could have escaped, unaided from the Castel Sant'Angelo, or so easily found a boat and safe conduct to take him to Sicily'. Perhaps help came from a fellow brother, or from the member of the Colonna family who almost certainly introduced the artist to the Grand Master. Alternatively, it may have been Wignacourt himself, a man renowned for his forgiving nature, who came to Caravaggio's aid, for even if he could not contravene the Order's Rule and save the painter's title, he could well have facilitated his clandestine departure from the island.

Whatever the case, Caravaggio was once more a fugitive, only now he lived in fear of both Rome *and* the Knights of Malta.[46]

The artist remained in Sicily for 'only a year', yet it was to be another period of intense creative activity. Indeed, it is a testament to Caravaggio's character that, despite all his ordeals, he 'neither lost his will to live nor his desire to paint', and Bellori lists the numerous, prestigious commissions completed by the painter during his months on the island, such as 'the altarpiece for the church of Santa Lucia in the port outside [Syracuse]' and 'the Nativity [painted] for the Capuchin Fathers [of Messina]'. Nevertheless, the strain of being Caravaggio seemed to be adversely affecting him. As Langdon observes, '[h]is exile, and the sudden reversal of his fortunes in Malta, may have disturbed his psychological balance', and reports from the time suggest that the Sicilians came to fear him 'as a man deranged'. Finally, convinced that his pursuers were close upon him, and 'no longer [feeling] safe in Sicily…he departed the island and sailed back to Naples'.[47]

It is ironic to note that it was in Naples that events 'finally caught up with him'. One night, outside of the Osteria del Cerriglio – the city's 'most famous tavern' – Caravaggio 'was surrounded by armed men who attacked him and wounded him in the face'. Indeed, according to Baglione, the slashes were so 'severe…that he was almost unrecognisable' and it is probable that his attackers left him for dead. Thus, whilst their identities remain uncertain, it is unlikely that they were bounty hunters, for they would have needed Caravaggio's head to claim their reward. Perhaps they were representatives from Malta, enraged that the artist had escaped from the Castel Sant'Angelo, yet it must be remembered that over a year had passed since his daring night flight to Sicily. Alternatively, given Caravaggio's aggressive disposition, they may have been simply fellow drinkers that the artist had managed to upset – for Naples, like Rome, enjoyed a reputation for quick-tempered violence. What is most *unlikely* is that they were representatives of the papal authorities, for shortly after the assault the artist received word that the Pope, under pressure from Caravaggio's Roman patrons, had finally relented and lifted the death sentence. 'Thus,' writes Bellori, 'as soon as possible, although suffering the fiercest pain, he boarded a felucca and headed for Rome'.[48]

For someone else this could well have been the prelude to a happy ending, but for Caravaggio it was to prove just another twist in the tragedy of his life. When the felucca docked at Porte Ercole – 'a port occupied by the Spanish, not far from the mouth of the Tiber... [and] only a day's ride from Rome' – Caravaggio, in an ironic turn of events, was mistaken for another man and placed under arrest. As Lambert observes, '[w]e do not know how he regained his freedom', but by the time he was released the felucca had sailed away with all his possessions. It is Baglione who, with more than a little relish, paints the most tragic and dramatic version of events:

> In desperation [Caravaggio] started out along the beach under the heat of the July sun, trying to catch sight of the vessel that had his belongings. Finally, he came to a place where he was put to bed with a raging fever; and so without the aid of God or man, he died, as miserably as he had lived.[49]

The year was 1610, and Caravaggio was thirty-eight years old.

Whilst the identity of the artist's last painting remains uncertain, there is one late work that, of all his oeuvre, seems to speak most eloquently for the life and tragedy of Michelangelo da Caravaggio. Looking at *David with the Head of Goliath* (c.1610) one is immediately struck by the quantity of darkness. Two thirds of the canvas is completely smothered in thick black paint; it is unremittingly oppressive. Indeed, one almost feels this darkness to be the subject of the painting, for it is *so* dense it almost has a form. Then the eye comes to rest on the figure of a young man. Emerging from the shadows, his pale, half-naked torso appears to have been cast by the light of an unseen moon, seemingly fragile amid the choking weight of the background. Yet in his outstretched arm he holds the large severed head of a man; and from the tip of a sword, which pierces out from the darkness in the bottom-left foreground, we know that *he*, although a mere boy, is the killer. The youth's face is cold, hard and resolute; he stares down at his victim's head with an expression of righteous contempt. His victim, by contrast, bearded and heavy-eyed, seems wearier than death, his parted lips and knotted brow betraying a consuming, posthumous exhaustion. The image is grimly disturbing, for the light cast on the figures is only another kind of darkness, the darkness of human tragedy. Yet the image is even more disturbing when we realise that the severed head is the artist's self-portrait. To be sure, as Langdon observes, it is likely that Goliath's 'ravaged and scarred face was inspired [by the artist's] attack in Naples', and by depicting himself in such a manner Caravaggio seems to be commenting on the inevitability of his defeat. However, this defeat was not achieved by either the Pope or the Knights of Malta; no, rather it was achieved by Caravaggio himself. Indeed, we can read the painting as a double self-portrait, for here David is no hero but instead an embodiment of Caravaggio's violence – a violence which he could not control and which arguably not only shortened his life but also prematurely extinguished his art. These destructive tensions find a further mirroring in the compositional dynamics of the painting. Like other works produced in the final years of Caravaggio's exile, *David with the Head of Goliath* employs what the art historian Stefano Bottari has termed 'luminalism'. Whilst Caravaggio's use of light had always been ingenious, here it seems to have gained a life of its own, emanating from 'an external source [with the result that it] does not seem an essential part of the forms themselves'. Certainly, by denying the painting a scenic context, and thus a rational source of light,

Caravaggio has essentially invested the composition with three disconnected elements: light, darkness, and bodies. Thus, just as David separated Goliath's head from his body, and just as Caravaggio's violent temperament separated him from any kind of peace, so the very fabric of the composition performs an act of separation – a formalistic act of violence which embodies the dislocated tragedy of the exile.[50]

Practice

As we previously discussed in the 'Cosmological Paradigm', after the initial phases of quantum gravitation and thermal equilibrium, during which the early Universe was dense, hot and volatile, the progressive reduction of cosmic temperature precipitated what cosmologists have termed the Matter Era. Rather than being dominated by the gravitational effect of radiation pressure, whose intensely high energy caused matter itself to behave like electromagnetic radiation, the cooling Universe had by now reached the point where the gravitational effect of matter began to supersede its radioactive counterpart. This usurpation engendered what cosmologists have termed decoupling, so called because it was at this point – approximately 30,000 years after the Big Bang – that matter and radiation began to act independently of each other. This process was gradual – full decoupling did not occur until 300,000 years after the Big Bang – and saw the Universe's radiation become transparent to light, thus allowing photons to propagate freely.

To follow the syphilitic bacchanalia of Nietzsche's primordial fire and personify the early stages of decoupling I decided to use the persona of Caravaggio. Whilst this might, on the surface, seem an illogical decision to make given that the artist predates the philosopher by some two hundred and fifty years and plays no part in his philosophical world, it is important to remember that the

structural dynamic of *Silence* is designed to juxtapose a *rational* correspondence between the personas and the cosmological paradigm and an *irrational*, destabilising frisson between one persona and the next, thereby generating a singularity. Thus, whilst Caravaggio cannot be said to follow the Nietzschean personas of Book One in any rational, chronological sense, the specifics of Caravaggio's life and work *do* relate rationally to the cosmological paradigm. To be sure, it was the dual value of Caravaggio's personal and aesthetic associations which made him the ideal choice to represent this phase of the Universe's development. In the artist's fiery, Dionysiac temperament I saw the means to facilitate a link with the paradigm of primordial fire in Book One, and thus create a sense of progressive, conceptual unity, while in his art I saw the potential to signify the process of cooling and separation inherent in the early Matter Era, with the bodies signifying matter, the darkness radiation, and the luminalist treatment of light the free propagation of photons. It was for this reason that I chose Caravaggio, and not say Rembrandt, Frans Hals, or even Diego Velasquez, for whilst the latter artists at various stages of their careers employed a luminalist technique analogous to that used by Caravaggio during his years in exile, none of them seemed to possess the *personal* sense of conceptual continuity which Caravaggio appeared to afford.

However, despite knowing that I wanted to use the artist for the reasons cited above the question of *how* to embody Caravaggio and his work in poetic form proved to be initially problematical. Firstly, there was the issue of integration. As I have demonstrated, Caravaggio's art is in many ways self-reflexive, yet it exists in a *visual* space, separate from any directly *verbal* articulation of the artist's personality. One possible solution was to make the paintings 'speak', to personify the work rather than the man and thereby reflect the artist *circuitously*. Nevertheless, this seemed unsatisfactory, for whilst it would have performed decoupling through a poetic interpretation of Caravaggio's

artistic vocabulary it would also have mitigated the full-force of the painter's Dionysiac temperament and thus lessened the cosmological continuity from Book One. A better solution seemed to be to locate the act of painting *within* the narrative – to have Caravaggio's monologue take place *during* the creative act and thus integrate the work and the man into a single vehicle of expression. I also decided that a further sense of integration could be achieved through the studied use of metaphors/allusions which pertain to the artist's oeuvre and so, in effect, fuse Caravaggio's personal and artistic vocabularies (lines 191, 224-233, 280-291, etc).

Given that it is Caravaggio's exile work which most strongly embodies the dynamics of decoupling it naturally made sense to set the poem *after* the murder of Ranuccio Tommasoni. Indeed, it was after making this decision that I began to see both the murder and the artist's ensuing exile as being further embodiments of the theme of separation; the separation, in a religious context, of Tommasoni's soul from his body; of Caravaggio from the Grace of God; and, in a secular context, of the artist from his community and the protection of the law. Additionally, this theme of separation, both personal and aesthetic, can also be seen as pertaining to the cosmological process of cooling. By externalising his violent inner turmoil into a static visual space I saw Caravaggio as enacting a plasticising form of catharsis akin to a metaphorical drop in temperature. Also, by deciding to set the poem during the exiled painter's brief respite in Malta, I would be able to give the concept of cooling another point of emphasis, for it was in Malta that the volatile and hunted artist had the chance, however briefly, to 'cool off'.

Having made these decisions further important choices/problems presented themselves. Firstly, I needed to decide on which painting from his Maltese period Caravaggio would be working, and secondly, and perhaps even more importantly, on how the artist would speak. The

painter has received numerous creative treatments, including Derek Jarman's film *Caravaggio* (1986), Peter Robb's quasi-fictional biography *M* (2000), and Christopher Peachment's novel, also called *Caravaggio* (2002). What is most revealing is that each writer creates a very different picture of the artist based, to a greater or lesser extent, on the extant information about his life and character. As we have seen, the biographical data which comes down to us from the seventeenth century is relatively sparse, leaving much room for creative interpretation. Nevertheless, whilst I found none of the above treatments wholly satisfactory, certain characterisations proved more persuasive than others and helped to guide me towards finding *my own* Caravaggio.

Peachment's novel, written in the first person and in the voice of the painter, seemed to me to be almost completely wrong. The narrative begins while Caravaggio is recuperating after his attack in Naples, and Peachment has the artist talk directly to the reader as he recounts the lurid escapades of his life:

> When I was younger my rage would have me in its grip and nothing, *nothing* but hate would govern me. It made me arch my back like a cat, and my very head would smoke with the passion of it. Oh, the things it made me do. Things that would turn your stomach, things that would frighten you to an early death, things that made me feel like a god. And now I can barely raise an arm. That it should come to this![51]

Caravaggio's chatty, engaging tone appeared to be completely at odds with the image of the strange, antisocial man which I had gleaned from Mancini, Baglione, and Bellori. Indeed, the artist's seventeenth-century biographers present, as Langdon observes, 'an oddly isolated figure', yet Peachment's interpretation seemed to me to belie that isolation. Even allowing that the artist's weakened condition may have engendered a temporary aberration from his usual disposition, I was still not convinced by the tone of Caravaggio's voice, his willingness to tell someone else his life-story, or by the way that Peachment seemed to have consigned the painter's uncontrollable rage to his youth, especially when one considers that just such a rageful incident had necessitated his flight from Malta only a couple of years before and cost him his much coveted knighthood. The only aspect which I *did* like was the vein of self-pity running through the narrative, for this appeared to reflect what I saw as Caravaggio's essentially inward looking nature.[52]

Whilst Robb's *M* was an engaging read, with its flights of speculation and its vaguely sensationalist tone, it did not offer a direct performance of the artist's voice, and so was of limited use, although it did impress upon me his restless, almost ravenous energy. For Robb, Caravaggio, or 'M' as he will insist on calling him, was a man who was unwilling, either to control his violence, or to mitigate the radical vision of his art. Far more helpful was Jarman's filmic interpretation of the artist's life and work. What particularly impressed me about the film, aside from the ingenious way in which Jarman reflects Caravaggio's aesthetic modernity by presenting Cardinals with calculators and models on motorbikes, was the artist's essential *quietness.* Jarman's Caravaggio is a man of few words and his violence is strangely, but compellingly, cold. Indeed, I responded very strongly to this pronounced sense of *internality* for it accorded with the oddly isolated figure presented by the artist's early biographers. The majority of Caravaggio's lines take place inside his head as a voiceover and are of a markedly poetic character:

> Bubbles rise around me and burst in the silence – the sea laps in my ears with the song of a summer shell – I sink down slowly and touch the sandy bottom, my body leaves the mark of a corpse on the sea bed – I float upwards in the dust cloud and break the

> surface. 'There he is!' – rough hands tear me from the water. Now I am counting the sheep on the hillside above our house, Pasqualone sometimes counts them with me. His hand parting my hair like the ripples at the bottom of the ocean. Pasqualone! Pasqualone! The mountains echo – then the darkness comes.[53]

The above, which is indicative of the artist's internal narrative, provides an almost abstract counterpoise to the representational strength of both Jarman's visuals and tightly written dialogue, providing a sense of the artist's emotional dislocation from the world around him; a dislocation which he could only bridge with either his art or his violence.

Whilst I was impressed by the internality of Jarman's characterisation of the artist and knew that this was the direction in which I wanted to take *my* Caravaggio, I also knew that the abstract extremity of Jarman's characterisation could not be translated effectively into an *exclusively* poetic narrative space. Indeed, the abstract quality of Caravaggio's internal voice is only so effective because of its filmic context. In other words, it is only fully intelligible because of the other creative components operating around it. The lines cited above bear little literal relation to what is going on in the scene, with the artist lying 'silent' in bed and the characters of Jerusaleme and the two old ladies watching over him. In *Caravaggio* meaning is derived from the subtle correspondence of the *whole* and not from the predominance of any *single* element. By contrast, my interpretation needed to function in a purely textual environment and could obviously not defer narrative particulars to either visuals or extensive episodes of dialogue without seriously problematising its identity as a dramatic monologue.

The solution appeared to be to adopt what may be termed an intermediate internality. In other words, to construct an *internal* voice which also creates its *external* environment. I decided that we would hear Caravaggio's thoughts while he paints and, given that the artist was famed for working directly from the model, these thoughts would create a verbal interpretation of the sitter, something akin to a literary painting. It would also reflect the cosmological paradigm's progression into the Matter Era for, unlike Nietzsche in Book One – who, in his syphilitic madness, addresses the *imagined* person of Heine – Caravaggio's monologue would operate in relation to a specific moment in time concentrated through the act of putting paint onto canvas.

Through considering the above, I suddenly knew which painting I would have Caravaggio working on: the *Portrait of Alof de Wignacourt*. To me, Wignacourt represented the quintessence of Caravaggio's Maltese period, a symbol both of protection and authority, and thus someone that Caravaggio knew he desperately needed but was also, because of his temperament, predisposed to resist. Through using Wignacourt I felt that I would not only be able to signify the cosmological process of cooling through the act of artistic creation, but also provide a further metaphor of separation by having the artist think antagonistic thoughts towards his sitter, thereby marking him out as *the other*. Indeed, in this relationship I perceived the potential to create a full microcosm of early decoupling, analogous to the dynamic of the artist's late luminalist paintings, with Caravaggio, because of his violent disposition, representing radiation, and Wignacourt, as both the sitter *and* Caravaggio's antithesis, representing matter. With this in mind, I saw that the free propagation of photons could be signified through the oscillation between the *literal* treatment of light in relation to the physical properties of the ensuing pictorial composition and what I interpreted as the artist's self-perception as an exile from the divine light of God. In addition, the poem's relationship with the *early* phase of decoupling would also be exemplified by its form, for whilst the theme of separation would be embodied in the specifics of the text, the poem would nevertheless remain a monologue. It would be the function of the next poem, *Anatomy*, using the persona of Leonardo da Vinci, to personify the high phase of decoupling through a radically different architectonic design.

Despite having a clear idea of what I wanted to achieve with Caravaggio, the process of actually writing the poem proved to be far from straightforward. This was due, in no small part, to the artist himself, and whilst I do not subscribe to any mystical notions of spiritual channelling, I nevertheless got the distinct impression that he did not like me, or rather that he did not like being dictated to. There were certain directions in which I could not take his voice, certain words or phrases which sounded hollow on his palette, and whilst I believe that the resultant text *does* successfully perform the early phase of decoupling, I feel it is also important to remember that the Caravaggio of my poem is not merely a cipher for an abstract idea. Indeed, the process of research and writing was highly osmotic – a transformative act of absorption and concentration. Much of what came out through the writing took me by surprise, and not all of it can be clearly accounted for. Caravaggio's troubled relationship with his father (lines 115-121, 129-137), for example, or his memory of the gypsy-girl Chiara (lines 146-165), transcend what we know from the historical records of the artist's life. Yet irrational though it sounds, it was through struggling to write Caravaggio that I felt I got to know Caravaggio, to appreciate his complexities and understand his eccentricities. I found a man fluctuating between guilt and rage; a man who both loved and hated his own violence as he both loved and hated humanity; a man who needed to be touched but also wanted solitude; a man who was taciturn yet eloquent; hot yet cold; a man divided. Ironically, by letting Caravaggio take the lead, he ultimately took me in the direction I wanted to go.

To be sure, the artist's independence of spirit set the tone for Book Two. Not only does each of the three poems have a separate title, but they also enjoy a greater metrical freedom than was present in the predominantly octosyllabic sequences of Book One. Given the strong personalities involved, it seemed important to let each persona 'breathe'; to not dictate form to voice, but to allow voice to dictate form. Thus the rhythms of the lines move in accordance with the nature of the character and the particulars of what is being said. The result is a variety of *vers libre* – hopefully of the intelligent, purposeful kind promoted by Ezra Pound in his essay 'A Retrospect':

> I think one should write vers libre only when one 'must', that is to say, only when the 'thing' builds up a rhythm more beautiful than that of set metres, or more real, more part of the emotion of the 'thing', more germane, intimate, interpretative than the measure of regular accentual verse…[54]

It was precisely a desire to create something more 'real', more 'intimate' and more 'interpretative' that gave rise to the change of metrical character in Book Two. In addition, this progression towards greater metrical freedom is also consistent with the cosmological paradigm which, through the Matter Era, is moving towards ever-greater structural diversity.

NOTES

[1] Ian Ridpath, ed., *The Oxford Dictionary of Astronomy* (Oxford: Oxford University Press, 2003), 371, 51, 284, 284-285, 285, 113, 349.

[2] Giles Lambert, *Caravaggio*, tr. C. Miller (London: Taschen, 2004), 19; Helen Langdon, 'Introduction' in, *Lives of Caravaggio*, ed. and tr. H. Hibbard (London: Pallas Athene, 2005), 8; Helen Langdon, *Caravaggio: A Life* (London: Pimlico, 1999), 4; Giulio Mancini, 'On Michelangelo Merisi da Caravaggio' in, *Lives of Caravaggio*, ed. and tr. H. Hibbard (London: Pallas Athene, 2005), 27.

[3] Mancini, 27; Langdon, *Caravaggio: A Life*, 34; Lavinia Cohn-Sherbok, ed., *Who's Who in Christianity* (London: Routledge, 1998), 190; Langdon, *Caravaggio: A Life*, 33, 34, 7, 23, 35.

[4] Langdon, *Caravaggio: A Life*, 34; Lambert, 23; Mancini, 27; Langdon, *Caravaggio: A Life*, 56.

[5] Mancini, 27, 28; Michelangelo Caravaggio, *Boy Bitten by a Lizard* (c.1593), painted with oil on canvas, and measuring 65.8x39.5cm, it is housed in the National Gallery in London; Timothy Wilson-Smith, *Caravaggio* (New York: Phaidon, 1998), 34; Lambert, 32; Wilson-Smith, 34.

[6] Mancini, 28; Michelangelo Caravaggio, *Boy Peeling Fruit* (c.1593), painted with oil on canvas, and measuring 75.5x64.4cm, one is housed in a private collection in Rome; Wilson-Smith, 34.

[7] Mancini, 28; Langdon, *Caravaggio: A Life*, 57; Ian Chilvers, *The Oxford Concise Dictionary of Art and Artists* (Oxford: Oxford University Press, 2003), 363, 485; Jacopo

Tintoretto, *Last Supper* (1592-94), painted with oil on canvas, and measuring 366x569cm, it is housed in the Church of San Giorgio Maggiore in Venice; Chilvers, 591.

[8] El Greco, *Burial of Count Orgaz* (1586), painted with oil on canvas, and measuring 480x360cm, it is housed in the Santa Tomé in Toledo; Michael Levey, *From Giotto to Cézanne: A Concise History of Painting* (London: Thames and Hudson, 1997), 148; Peter Murray, ed., *The Oxford Dictionary of Christian Art* (Oxford: Oxford University Press, 2004), 236; Raphael Sanzio, *Disputa* (1508-09), a fresco and 10.75m wide, it adorns the wall of the Stanza della Segnatura in the Palazzo Vaticano, Rome.

[9] Lambert, 32; Langdon, *Caravaggio: A Life*, 4, 67, 66; Jan Brueghel, *Vase of Flowers* (c.1595), painted with oil on canvas, and measuring 40x30cm, it is housed in a private collection in Rome; Michelangelo Caravaggio, *Basket of Fruit* (c.1598-99), painted with oil on canvas, and measuring 31x47cm, it is housed in the Pinacoteca Ambrosiana in Milan.

[10] Langdon, *Caravaggio: A Life*, 119.

[11] Murray, 466; Chilvers, 493; Ilan Rachum, *The Renaissance: An Illustrated Encyclopedia* (London: Octopus Books Ltd, 1979), 182; Murray, 466, 214; Chilvers, 241.

[12] Chilvers, 371, 449; Nadeije Laneyrie-Dagen, *How to Read Paintings*, tr. R. Elliott (Edinburgh: Chambers Harrap Publishers, 2004), 79; Chilvers, 371; Laneyrie-Dagen, 81; Chilvers, 449; James Stevens Curl, *The Oxford Dictionary of Architecture and Landscape Architecture* (Oxford: Oxford University Press, 2006), 329.

[13] Masaccio, *Trinity* (c.1427), painted with tempera on plaster this fresco, measuring 677x317cm, is located in the Santa Maria Novella in Florence; Chilvers, 599; J. V. Field, 'Masaccio and Perspective in Italy in the Fifteenth Century' in, Diane Cole Ahl, ed., *The Cambridge Companion to Masaccio* (Cambridge: Cambridge University Press, 2002), 189; G. M. Radke, 'Masaccio's City: Urbanism, Architecture, and sculpture in Early Fifteenth-Century Florence' in, Diane Cole Ahl, ed., *The Cambridge Companion to Masaccio*

(Cambridge: Cambridge University Press, 2002), 51; Field, 191; Murray, 152, 151; Chilvers, 177; Rona Goffen, 'Introduction' in, Rona Goffen, ed., *Masaccio's Trinity* (Cambridge: Cambridge University Press, 1998), 19; Donatello, *Crucifix* (1412-13), carved in wood, and measuring 168x173cm, it is housed in the Santa Croce in Florence; Dillian Gordon, 'The Altarpieces of Masaccio' in, Diane Cole Ahl, ed., *The Cambridge Companion to Masaccio* (Cambridge: Cambridge University Press, 2002), 125; Field, 191; Donatello, *St. John the Evangelist* (1410-11), carved in marble, and measuring a height of 210cm, it is housed in the Duomo in Florence.

[14] Rona Goffen, 'Masaccio's *Trinity* and the *Letter to the Hebrews*' in, Rona Goffen, ed., *Masaccio's Trinity* (Cambridge: Cambridge University Press, 1998), 56, 57, 55; Robin Osborne, *Archaic and Classical Greek Art* (Oxford: Oxford University Press, 1998),. 209; Leon Battista Alberti, *On Painting*, tr. C. Grayson (London: Penguin Books Ltd, 2004), 35.

[15] Moshe Barasch, *Theories of Art 1: From Plato to Winckelmann* (London: Routledge, 2000), 120, 117.

[16] Barasch, 120, 117, 119.

[17] Chilvers, 10; Martin Kemp, 'Introduction' in, Leon Battista Alberti, *On Painting*, tr. C. Grayson (London: Penguin Books Ltd, 2004), 2; Barasch, 117, 122; Alberti, 90; Thomas Mautner, ed., *The Penguin Dictionary of Philosophy* (London: Penguin Books Ltd, 2000), 426; Alberti, 90.

[18] Chilvers, 494; Leonardo da Vinci, *Mona Lisa* (c.1503-6), painted with oil on panel, and measuring 77x53cm, it is housed in the Louvre in Paris; Chilvers, 8, 427, 338, 220, 583.

[19] Gilles Néret, *Michelangelo*, tr. P. Snowdon (London: Taschen, 2000), 26; Luciano Bellosi, *Michelangelo: Painting*, tr. G. Webb (London: Thames and Hudson, 1970), 14; Ross King, *Michelangelo and the Pope's Ceiling* (London: Pimlico, 2003), 148.

[20] Chilvers, 484, 485; Heinrich Wölfflin, 'The School of Athens' in, Marcia Hall, ed., *Raphael's School of Athens*

(Cambridge: Cambridge University Press, 1997), 57; Chilvers, 485; Raphael Sanzio, *School of Athens* (1510), painted with fresco, and 10.55m wide, it adorns the Stanza della Segnatura in the Vatican Palace in Rome; Chilvers, 485; Marcia Hall, 'Introduction' in, Marcia Hall, ed., *Raphael's School of Athens* (Cambridge: Cambridge University Press, 1997), 17; King, 170; Hall, 'Introduction', 17; Ingrid D. Rowland, 'The Intellectual Background of The School of Athens' in, Marcia Hall, ed., *Raphael's School of Athens* (Cambridge: Cambridge University Press, 1997), 156, 157; King, 175; Hall, 'Introduction', 41, 40, 37, 26.

[21] Hall, 'Introduction', 37; Janis Bell, 'Color and Chiaroscuro' in, Marcia Hall, ed., *Raphael's School of Athens* (Cambridge: Cambridge University Press, 1997), 86.

[22] Giovanni Baglione, 'The Life of Michelangelo da Caravaggio' in, *Lives of Caravaggio*, ed. and tr. H. Hibbard (London: Pallas Athene, 2005), 49, 43-45.

[23] Baglione, 43, 45.

[24] Langdon, 'Introduction', p. 9.

[25] Langdon, 'Introduction', p. 9; Giovanni Pietro Bellori, 'On Michelangelo da Caravaggio' in, *Lives of Caravaggio*, ed. and tr. H. Hibbard, (London: Pallas Athene, 2005), 89; Lambert, 54-55; Bellori, 89, 57, 58, 89-90.

[26] Michelangelo Caravaggio, *The Calling of St. Matthew* (1599-1600), painted with oil on canvas, and measuring 322x340cm, it is housed in the church of San Luigi dei Francesi in Rome.

[27] Lambert, 63.

[28] Francesca Marini, *Caravaggio*, tr. M. Hurley (New York: Rizzoli, 2006), 108.

[29] Chilvers, 105; Wilson-Smith, 64; Lambert, 63; Chilvers, 106, 122, Leonardo da Vinci, *St. John the Baptist* (c.1513-1516), painted with oil on wood, and measuring 69x57cm, it is housed in the Louvre in Paris; Wilson-Smith, 64.

[30] T. S. Eliot, 'Tradition and the Individual Talent' in, T. S. Eliot, *Selected Essays* (London: Faber and Faber, 1999), 14, 16, 15.

[31] Mancini, 28; Langdon, *Caravaggio: A Life*, 68, 67-68; Langdon, 'Introduction', 8; Mancini, 28, Michelangelo Caravaggio, *Self-Portrait as Bacchus* (c.1593-94), painted with oil on canvas, and measuring 66x52cm, it is housed in the Galleria Borghese in Rome; Lambert, 39; Wilson-Smith, 32.

[32] Michael Baxandall, *Painting and Experience in Fifteenth-Century Italy* (Oxford: Oxford University Press, 1988), 1; Bellori, 59, 92.

[33] Tiziano Vecelli, *Bacchus and Ariadne* (1520-23), painted with oil on canvas, and measuring 176.5x191cm, it is housed in the National Gallery in London; Wilson-Smith, 32; Lambert, 39.

[34] Mancini, 28; Chilvers, 116; Lambert, 39, 41; Langdon, *Caravaggio: A Life*, 68; Lambert, 41; Baglione, 42; Lambert, 47; Langdon, *Caravaggio: A Life*, 78.

[35] Langdon, *Caravaggio: A Life*, 253; Mancini, 32, 33; Bellori, 92; Mancini, 33.

[36] Langdon, *Caravaggio: A Life*, 152, 254, 272, 273.

[37] Langdon, *Caravaggio: A Life*, 138, 91; Bellori, 76, Mancini, 29-31; Baglione, 52; Langdon, *Caravaggio: A Life*, 137; Simon Schama, *Simon Schama's Power of Art* (London: BBC Books, 2006), 63; Langdon, *Caravaggio: A Life*, 136, 145; Schama, 63; Bellori, 76.

[38] Lambert, 81, 7; Langdon, *Caravaggio: A Life*, 310, 314; Schama, 63; Langdon, *Caravaggio: A Life*, 314.

[39] Baglione, 52; Mancini, 31; Bellori, 76; Michelangelo Caravaggio, *The Supper at Emmaus* (1601), painted with oil on canvas, and measuring 141x196.2cm, it is housed in the National Gallery in London; Marini, 118; Wilson-Smith, 70; Marini, 118.

[40] Michelangelo Caravaggio, *The Supper at Emmaus* (1606), painted with oil on canvas, and measuring 141x175cm, it is housed in the Pinacoteca di Brera in Milan; Marini, 148; Schama, 63; Langdon, *Caravaggio: A Life*, 365, 316.

[41] Lambert, 81; Bellori, 77.

[42] Lambert, 82; Langdon, *Caravaggio: A Life*, 340, 341, 341-342, 342; Lambert, 82; Langdon, *Caravaggio: A Life*, 342.

[43] Langdon, *Caravaggio: A Life*, 347-348, 348; Michelangelo Caravaggio, *Portrait of Alof de Wignacourt* (c.1607-8), painted with oil on canvas, and measuring 195x134cm, it is housed in the Louvre in Paris; Wilson-Smith, 108; Baglione, 52; Langdon, *Caravaggio: A Life*, 355.

[44] Michelangelo Caravaggio, *The Beheading of St. John the Baptist* (1608), painted with oil on canvas, and measuring 361x520cm, it is housed in the Co-Cathedral of St. John in Valletta; Langdon, *Caravaggio: A Life*, 357; Wilson-Smith, 110; Michelangelo Caravaggio, *Judith and Holophernes* (1599), painted with oil on canvas, and measuring 145x195cm, it is housed in the Galleria Nazionale d'Arte in the Palazzo Barberini in Rome; Wilson-Smith, 110.

[45] Bellori, 80; Langdon, *Caravaggio: A Life*, 361, 362, 363.

[46] Bellori, 80; Langdon, *Caravaggio: A Life*, 361, 363.

[47] Lambert, 86; Bellori, 81; Langdon, *Caravaggio: A Life*, 365; Bellori, 84.

[48] Baglione, 53, Langdon, *Caravaggio: A Life*, 382; Bellori, 84-85; Baglione, 53; Bellori, 85.

[49] Lambert, 89; Baglione, 53.

[50] Michelangelo Caravaggio, *David with the Head of Goliath* (c.1610), painted with oil on canvas, and measuring 125x100cm, it is housed in the Galleria Borghese in Rome; Langdon, 'Introduction', 19; Stefano Bottari, *Caravaggio*, tr. D. Goldrei (London: Thames and Hudson, 1971), 4.

[51] Christopher Peachment, *Caravaggio: A Novel* (London: Picador, 2002), 4.

[52] Langdon, *Caravaggio: A Life*, 152.

[53] Derek Jarman, *Derek Jarman's Caravaggio: The Complete Film Script and Commentaries by Derek Jarman and Photographs by Gerald Incandela* (London: Thames and Hudson, 1986), 17.

[54] Ezra Pound, 'A Retrospect' in, Ira B. Nadel, ed., *Ezra Pound: Early Writings, Poetry and Prose* (London: Penguin Books Ltd, 2005), 263.

2. Leonardo da Vinci: Anatomy

Theory

Leonardo da Vinci (1452-1519) is an almost mythological figure. An early chronicler of his life, known as the 'Anonimo Gaddiano,' was to write in the *Codex Magliabecchiano* that:

> [Leonardo] was so rare and universal a man that one could say he was a product of both nature and miracle – not only because of his physical beauty, which was well-acknowledged, but also by virtue of the many rare talents of which he was master.[1]

Likewise, the famous biographer of artists, Giorgio Vasari was to remark in his *Life of Leonardo da Vinci* that:

> In the normal course of events many men and women are born with various remarkable qualities and talents; but occasionally, in a way that transcends nature, a single person is marvellously endowed by heaven with beauty, grace, and talent in such abundance that he leaves other men far behind, all his actions seem inspired, and indeed everything he does clearly comes from God rather than from human art.[2]

Within a decade of his death he had become a demigod, a fusion of the natural and the miraculous. Within thirty years of his death he had become a direct manifestation of the will of God, his every action divine. To a certain extent such aggressive hagiography is understandable, for Leonardo's 'rare talents' transcended painting, the profession in which he was trained, to include 'music', 'sculpture', 'architecture', 'city planning', 'military engineering', and 'theatrical design'. He was also an avid natural scientist, fascinated by 'light' and 'optics', the power of 'water', 'geology', 'flight' and the inner mysteries of the 'human body'. He invented such marvels as 'diving equipment', 'the parachute', numerous 'flying machines', and even a 'mechanical lion' for the entertainment of his future patron, Francis I. Thus, it is little wonder that his early biographers should have idealised him as 'so rare and universal a man', or that the contemporary art historian Ian Chilvers should proclaim him 'the most versatile genius of the Italian Renaissance'. Yet it would be a mistake to equate versatility with accomplishment, for whilst Leonardo's interests were extremely broad, his material achievements were incredibly slight. Even Vasari, who is at pains to idolise the artist, is compelled to lament his lack of productivity. 'Leonardo', he writes, 'started so many things without finishing them', attributing da Vinci's habit of leaving commissions '*non finito*' to his 'volatile and unstable' character. Paintings such as *St. Hieronymus* (c.1480-82) and *The Adoration of the Magi* (c.1481-82) remain in a haunting stage of transition, with bodies like ghosts, or the negatives of undeveloped photographs. Likewise the majority of his inventions, such as his 'armoured car' or his 'helicopter' never went beyond the pages of his notebooks, and in the case of his 'parachute', it is in fact little more than a quaint piece of marginalia, an aside to his investigations into the mechanics of flight. Neither were his notebooks designed for publication, they lack the formal clarity of a treatise, rapidly moving from one topic to the next, and even including

> jokes, doodles, snatches of poetry, drafts of letters, household accounts, recipes, shopping-lists, cast-lists, bank statements, names and addresses of models, and so on...[3]

True, Leonardo does allude to treatises that he was *planning* to write, such as '*On the Human Body*' and the 'book on water', however, the only 'coherent' treatise to emerge was the '*Trattato della pittura*', the *Treatise on Painting*, and this was compiled by his pupil Francesco Melzi *after* Leonardo's death. Thus it is fair to say that da Vinci's genius is fragmentary, largely the product of endless, beautiful beginnings whose varied potentialities spiral outwards into an intriguing, or perhaps frustrating, silence.[4]

Sometimes this silence, as in the case of his flying machines, was inevitable. As the Leonardo scholar, Michael White, observes:

> [Da Vinci's flying machine designs] are based upon sound aerodynamic principles. Yet none of them could have come close to flying, simply because the human occupant could never have generated enough power to propel the machine fast enough to gain the lift it required. Leonardo lived during an age in which sufficient energy to power a flying machine was simply not available, and...he was thwarted by the absence of any form of infrastructure upon which he could build.[5]

Nevertheless, there is no contemporary documentary evidence that da Vinci ever tried to get one of his designs off the ground in order to discover its limitations. Like his unfinished paintings, his 'inventions' remained predominantly embryonic.

The reason behind this 'unstable' character trait has been the subject of much scholarly conjecture. Sigmund Freud, for example, postulated that da Vinci's 'notorious inability to finish his works' stemmed from his 'illegitimacy'. In his case study, *Leonardo da Vinci: A Memory of His Childhood*, Freud forwards the argument that the absence of Leonardo's father, Ser Piero, during the early years of his childhood, and the dominating influence of his 'poor forsaken mother' Caterina who, because of her lowly status, had been prevented from marrying her lover, 'robbed him of part of his masculinity', in effect turning him 'homosexual'. Freud further argues that because of Leonardo's 'neurotic' temperament, his already displaced 'sexual instinctual forces' became sublimated into an obsessive quest for knowledge. This, in its turn, was detrimental to his creative productivity, for the same 'mental activity' which enabled him to examine the multifarious complexities of 'nature', necessarily problematised his understanding of the creative object. He was unable

> to limit his demands, to see the work of art in isolation and to tear it from the wide context to which he knew it belonged. After the most exhausting efforts to bring to expression in it everything which was connected with it in his thoughts, he was forced to abandon it in an unfinished state or to declare that it was incomplete.[6]

As seductive (or not) as Freud's theory may be, it must be remembered that he knew less about Leonardo's childhood than we do today. Ser Piero was not entirely absent for the first 'three [to] five' years of da Vinci's life as Freud is keen to maintain, nor is it likely that Caterina raised him past the age of suckling, for eighteen months after his birth she was married off to Accattabriga di Piero del Vacca, a 'lime-burner' from the nearby village of 'Campo Zeppi'. The young Leonardo remained part of his father's household, a fact which somewhat undermines Freud's hypothesis.[7]

However, where Freud's analysis of Leonardo seems most flawed, is not so much in his heavy-handed attempts at psycho-sexualising his subject, but in his belief that da Vinci's scientific researches were the result of a neurotic aberration which ultimately proved detrimental to his art. Like so many of Leonardo's contemporaries and early biographers, who did not have the opportunity of digesting the full range of da Vinci's thinking, Freud's equation of an arrested productivity with some kind of failure had led to a fundamental misapprehension about the artist's scientific-aesthetic intentions. For da Vinci, art and science were not diametrically opposed, rather they shared a coherent identity through the 'holistic' patterning of Nature. As the Leonardo scholar Martin Kemp observes, 'the *Mona Lisa* and the flying machine were, for Leonardo, the same kind of thing'. Both attempt to

> remake the world…on nature's own terms, fully obedient to natural causes and effects. One is an artificial 'bird'; the other is an artificial remaking of the visual experience of a person's physical presence.[8]

This holistic understanding of Nature, and its potential for scientific and artistic remodelling in the light of its own laws, is perhaps most clearly apparent in Leonardo's investigations into human anatomy. Such investigations clearly had great artistic value for, by understanding the structures of muscles and bones beneath the skin, his ability to replicate these structures realistically in his pictorial work was greatly increased. The exercise was also of great scientific interest, challenging the boundaries set by the ancient medical theorists 'Galen and Pliny', who were still regarded reverently at the turn of the sixteenth century. If Leonardo had ever formally written up and published his treatise on anatomy, the development of medical science would have looked very different. However, between these facets, holding them in tension, resides the governing dynamic of da Vinci's thinking; the relationship between the 'macrocosm' and the 'microcosm'. For Leonardo, 'the body of the human being was a microcosm, mirroring in its whole and parts the macrocosm, or greater world'. In one of his notebooks, now known as the *Codex Leicester*, he writes:

> The earth has a vegetative spirit in that its flesh is the soil, its bones are the configurations of the interlinked rocks of which the mountains are composed, its tendons are the tufa, and its blood is the water in the veins; the lake of blood that lies within the heart is the oceanic sea, and its breathing is the increase and decrease of blood during its pulsing, just as in the sea is the flux and reflux of the

> water; and the heart of the spirit of the world is the fire that is infused throughout the earth, and the seat of the vegetative spirit is in the fires, which in various locations in the world spouts forth in mines of sulphur and in volcanoes.[9]

By deploying a process of 'analogy', in this instance the language of the human body, da Vinci was able to fit the systems of the wider natural world into an intelligible frame of reference – to contain the seemingly infinite within a finite whole.[10]

Given the pioneering character of so many of Leonardo's investigations, it is interesting to note that this 'governing dynamic' is, in many ways, highly conservative. The concept of the microcosm 'was common philosophical property in ancient and medieval thought'. Plato, for example, in his *Timaeus* (c.360 BCE) offers an analogous model for understanding the interrelation between 'Being and Becoming', and Dante Alighieri, in his *Quaestio de aqua et terra* (1320), makes play on 'the role of water in the body of the earth'. What distinguishes da Vinci's appropriation of this well-worn apparatus, however, is the 'fresh urgency and conviction' with which he applies it to the *practical* elements of *material* thought. Ideas for da Vinci invariably contain the embryonic seed of action, be it artistic or scientific. Pure abstract thinking for its own sake held little interest for him, something borne out by his relationship with conventional philosophy and mathematics. As Kemp observes:

> He had no taste for the abstractions of pure philosophy, which he scathingly characterised as a kind of pseudo-knowledge 'that begins and ends in the mind'...[11]

and despite writing next to one of his anatomical drawings 'let no one who is not a mathematician read by principles', his 'arithmetic was erratic verging on poor'. For da Vinci, the only mathematics 'worth doing' was that which had a direct bearing on the visual, such as 'three-dimensional geometry'. If it did not pertain to experiential reality he simply was not interested.[12]

Indeed, the primacy which da Vinci accords the visual, whilst hardly surprising for a man trained as a representational painter, cannot be overstressed. 'He was a supreme visualiser,' writes Kemp,

> a master manipulator of mental 'sculpture', and almost everything he wrote was ultimately based on acts of observation and cerebral picturing.[13]

It is the eye, regarded by Leonardo as the 'chief organ' of the body, which occupies the centre of his thinking. He regarded it as 'the window of the soul', as the prime means 'whereby the understanding may most fully and abundantly appreciate the infinite works of nature'. In effect the eye is the nucleus where the microcosm and macrocosm converge. 'Here the forms,' he writes, 'here the colours, here all the images of every part of the universe are contracted to a point'. Da Vinci understood that this convergence of the visible Universe within the human body was conditional upon something very important to a painter: 'light'. His study of optics had revealed that, contrary to the popular 'Platonic' misconception, the eye did not *emit* 'visual rays', but rather *received* images due to the external action of light reflecting off 'non-transparent bodies'. It is light, therefore, through a process of reflection converging in the eye, which brings the macrocosm *into* the microcosm.[14]

This concept of 'light reflection' is crucial to our understanding of Leonardo's approach to art, science, and the natural world. As we have remarked, the *Mona Lisa* and the flying machine are effectively the same thing, for both attempt to replicate, or *reflect*, the world in accordance with the laws of Nature. By observing the flight of birds, by taking this image into his eye via the reflection of light,

Leonardo was able, in turn, to reflect the physics of this image in his design. Likewise, by observing the physical image of Lisa del Giocondo, by taking it into his eye, he was able to reflect this image onto the painted surface of his panel. As Leonardo was to write in what was posthumously to form part of the *Treatise on Painting*:

> The painter...should act as a mirror which transmutes itself into as many colours as are those of the objects that are placed before it. Thus he will seem to be a second nature.[15]

Consequently, the products of the macrocosmic universe of Nature find their microcosmic duplication through the reflective interpretation of the human body; the painter *receives* the image in his eye and *mirrors* it with his hand, in effect becoming a second Nature.

It is here that we can now see the full significance of da Vinci's microcosm. Far from simply being an analogous way of interpreting the systems of the wider natural world, it is a transformative process, whereby the artist, metamorphosed into a '*Uomo Universale*', a *Universal Man*, reflects through his body the holistic patterning of Nature; indeed becomes his *own* Nature through the deft manipulation of natural laws. Of course, once seen in this way, the scope of da Vinci's work, and his tendency to leave that work *non finito*, takes on a heightened meaning. From a single body, from *his* body, the *Universal Man* gives rise to a multiplicity of forms, both artistic and scientific, which are held in tension by the reflective affinity of light. That these works should often remain unfinished is hardly surprising, for Nature, like Man, is so often in 'flux'.[16]

Practice

Having outlined the dynamic of Leonardo's thinking we will now explore how this dynamic relates to the textual specifics of *Anatomy*. As we have seen, the Caravaggio persona in *Unstill Life* corresponds to the early phase of decoupling. In architectonic terms this is reflected in the narrative's identity as a monologue, with the 'performance' of separation embodied in the thematic and imagistic qualities of the text. *Anatomy*, by contrast, offers a different form of embodiment – one that overtly performs the act of separation through its architectonic design, thereby corresponding to the high phase of decoupling which occurred 300,000 years after the Big Bang. Monologue has 'decoupled' into polylogue.

Central to this polylogue is, of course, the persona of Leonardo. As the title of this sequence makes clear, the concept of anatomisation is intrinsic to the text's identity, and is present both as a literal, physical process (i.e. the act of anatomisation as one of the sequence's prime narrative subjects) and, more significantly, as a conceptual paradigm, reflecting the idea of holistic Nature performed through the microcosm of da Vinci as *Universal Man*. Thus Leonardo the *anatomist* is also the *anatomised*, with facets of his personality, and the objects of his artistic and scientific preoccupations, reflected in various fragmented forms. This conceptual paradigm is, in its turn, reflected onto the cosmological paradigm. Consequently, given the embodied nature of da Vinci's thinking, with his emphasis on material 'experience' over abstract learning, those fragments in which Leonardo speaks represent matter (lines 9-24, 32-96, etc). The sequence also contains a number of counter voices, the most prominent being that of Salai, the young thief whom da Vinci adopted into his entourage during his first Milanese period (lines 172-202, 399-419, etc). These voices invariably act in opposition to the opinions expressed by da Vinci and are thus given to represent matter's antithesis, radiation.[17]

The action of light, so fundamental to both the dynamic of Leonardo's thinking *and* to the process of decoupling, is represented in two ways. Firstly, it appears as a narrative subject, as part of Leonardo's reflections upon its role within the eye and its application in the fields of art and science (lines 221-234). Secondly, and more subtly, it may be discerned in the 'reflective affinities' shared by the fragments. In other words, the ideas raised in one 'material' fragment will be reflected in another, thus allowing light to propagate freely throughout the text. 'Radioactive' fragments, by contrast, pertain to photonic transparency through their *negative* reflection of the da Vinci persona; their counter-physical stance allowing 'light' to pass through them.

In regards to the contents of the fragments the process has been one of considered selection. To incorporate *every* incident of Leonardo's life and make reference to *all* his artistic and scientific activities would have proved unwieldy, and may even have given rise to an epic in itself. Consequently, the selection has been designed to both maximise the impression of Leonardo's personality *and* to convey, as succinctly as possible, what is believed to be the essential dynamic of his thinking. Additionally, the absence of certain well-known particulars, such as his painting of the *Last Supper* or his clay model of the *Sforza Horse*, gives the sequence a characteristically *non finito* quality. Thus, just as the microcosm of Leonardo mirrors the macrocosm of Nature, so the microcosm of *Anatomy* mirrors the macrocosm of decoupling – something which is part of a wider cosmological process and not, in itself, a neatly resolved conclusion.

Fragments Analysis

Due to the complex structure of the *Anatomy* sequence, I will now undertake an analysis of its thirty-seven fragments. The thematic and stylistic character of each fragment will be discussed, and those which relate to matter – i.e. those in which da Vinci is the prime speaker – will be followed by a list of their *reflective affinities* (other 'material' fragments which reflect their thematic focus) and *negative reflections* ('radioactive' fragments which take an opposing thematic focus).

1. 'It might be a dream…' [lines 9-24]

This fragment pertains to a passage from one of da Vinci's notebooks, now known as the *Codex Atlanticus*, in which he describes an early childhood memory:

> Writing about the kite seems to be my destiny since among the first recollections of my infancy it seemed to me that as I was in my cradle a kite came to me and opened my mouth with its tail and struck me several times with its tail inside my lips.[18]

In the light of Leonardo's subsequent preoccupation with the natural world, and with flight in particular, it is hardly surprising that he should have looked back on this early incident and interpreted it as a sign of his 'destiny'. To be sure, the nucleic quality of this almost primal image, with the baby da Vinci intimately touched by Nature, made it an ideal way to start the *Anatomy* sequence. Nevertheless, my treatment differs from the above in a number of respects. Firstly, I have stripped it from its immediate context. Da Vinci is no longer directly linking this memory with the action of writing about 'the kite', but is rather recalling it for its own sake, thus making the image the central point of focus. Secondly, I have transformed 'the kite' into an indistinct 'shadow of wings'. One of the reasons behind this decision was that I wanted to emphasise the artist's courage in the face of the unknown. Thus rather than being afraid by what is a potentially menacing 'shape…blinding the sunlight', he laughs. By making the kite into a shadow of wings I have also made the theme of light an active participant in the fragment. Similarly, the theme of flight and wings will be cast like a shadow over the rest of the *Anatomy* sequence, recurring in various guises throughout the text.

To further emphasise the 'unknown quality' of the experience I have started the fragment with the line 'It might be a dream'. Da Vinci's attitude towards dreams is ambivalent. In one of his notebooks, now known as the *Codex Urbinas*, he writes: 'Experience does not feed investigators on dreams, but always proceeds from accurately determined first principles'. As a scientist Leonardo was keen to dissociate himself from those 'foolish…believers in necromancy [and] alchemy', for whom dreams and the stars played a significant role. Conversely, he recognised the allegorical potential of dreams as a means of representing the nuances of human nature. In one of his *prophesises* – a form of riddle designed for the entertainment of the Milanese Court – Leonardo proclaims:

> O marvel of mankind! What frenzy has thus impelled you! You will speak with animals of every species and they with you in human speech. You shall behold yourselves falling from great heights without suffering any injury; torrents will accompany you, and will mingle in their rapid course.[19]

In dreams, as in paintings, images from the natural world are empowered as metaphors. They also have a strange relationship to time at once drawing on lived experience and, as the above makes clear, rendering it fantastical. In regards to da Vinci's 'recollection' of the kite, Nicholl has observed that the bird's action of opening Leonardo's mouth with its tail is unlikely to have happened, for such an action is outside its usual behavioural patterns. Thus whilst the memory of the kite gliding down may have been genuine, certain particulars of the 'memory' can be interpreted as 'an adult fantasy which has been "projected" back onto [da Vinci's] childhood'.[20]

Thus in this opening fragment the concept of the 'dream' transforms the memory into a metaphor, something that exists outside of a given historical context, and speaks for Leonardo in the full perspective of his life and activities.

The extemporal nature of this recollection is mirrored by the shift in tense between the first and second line:

> It might be a dream,
> but I think I remember…

Caught between the present and the past, the concept thereby gains an archetypal quality.

In terms of metre the fragment maintains a relaxed 'walking pace' throughout. I wanted the *Anatomy* sequence to begin quietly; to start in the intimate space of da Vinci's 'memories'. Indeed, throughout the sequence changes in tone and pace between the fragments act as a further means of performing separation – something that will become immediately apparent when we come to examine the second fragment. The relaxed treatment of the theme is also mirrored in this fragment's stanzaic configurations, for whilst the tercet predominates, the use of a quatrain for the second stanza resists any rigid uniformity. I have allowed the stanzas to 'flow' with the sense of the fragment rather than imposing a fixed rule at the onset of the writing process. In fact, this is highly appropriate when one considers the persona, and speaks for the sequence as a whole and not just for this particular fragment. Just as da Vinci resists comfortable categorisation, so the *Anatomy* sequence, with its changes in tone and pace, and its interruption of stanzaic regularity, is equally mercurial.

Key themes: Birds (flight and in particular wings); light and optics; courage in the face of the unknown; memory; dreams; childhood.

Reflective affinities:

- **'Consider, Salai…' [lines 32-96]**
- **'Force is Spirit…' [lines 107-113]**
- **'…and as well as a musician…' [lines 116-161]**
- **'Force is Spirit…' [lines 164-169]**
- **'Ser Piero, my father…' [lines 205-212]**
- **'And what of the eye?' [lines 221-234]**
- **'Mmm…typical Verrocchio…' [lines 237-349]**
- **'29th January 1494…' [lines 371-384]**
- **'For it is among the horrors…' [lines 423-454]**
- **'A riddle, my Lords…' [lines 467-475]**
- **'And the Great Bird shall rise…' [lines 478-576]**
- **'God's sake!' [lines 638-644]**
- **'Di Ser Piero…' [lines 648-650]**
- **'silk tears the air…' [lines 654-665]**
- **'A painter should be solitary…' [lines 668-697]**
- **'Buchi della verità…' [lines 743-754]**
- **'A ghost…' [lines 757-764]**
- **'The act of coitus…' [lines 768-773]**
- **'I thought I was learning…' [lines 790-794]**

Negative reflections:

- **'Un libro del cazzo!' [lines 27-29]**
- **'In me la morte…' [lines 99-104]**
- **'It's funny…' [lines 172-202]**
- **'Veggio co' be' vostr'occhi un dolce lume…' [lines 215-218]**
- **'But when will it be finished…' [lines 352-367]**
- **'Welcome to Imola…' [lines 399-419]**
- **'Volo con le vostr'ale senza piume…' [lines 580-583]**
- **'As I slumbered in my body…' [lines 599-611]**
- **'Nel voler vostro è sol la voglia mia…' [lines 701-706]**
- **'"Maestro da Vinci"…' [lines 710-740]**

- 'Sometimes Heaven…' [lines 778-786]
- 'Tell me, di Credi…' [lines 798-799]

2. 'Un libro del cazzo!' [lines 27-29]

This is the first of the 'radioactive' fragments, and I wanted the impact to be dramatic. The decision to use extracts from the Italian sonnets of Michelangelo – Leonardo's arch-nemesis – had been decided before I began writing, for the idea of juxtaposing English and Italian seemed an effective way of emphasising the difference between matter and radiation. Of course, not all of the 'radioactive' fragments are in Italian – such a device, if over used, would become tiresome, especially if one does not speak the language. Rather it has been restricted to five of the shortest 'radioactive' fragments. Nor are all of the Italian fragments by Michelangelo. This particular fragment is of my own devising, and reads in translation:

'A shitty book!'
'Bastard!'
'Mind your own fucking business!'

Here the effect of negative reflection works both stylistically *and* thematically. As we have already observed, the pace of the opening fragment is relaxed and the imagery is dream-like. Thus the violence of the above exchange, in a foreign language and in italics (which in this instance is intended to give the impression of shouting), provides an alarming contrast with da Vinci's childhood recollections. The juxtaposition is also ironic, for the first fragment ends with the lines:

something soft
brushes my mouth…

Thematically the sequence plays off the image of childhood from the previous fragment, emphasising Leonardo's illegitimacy. Whilst I do not endorse Freud's elaborate reading of the circumstances of da Vinci's birth, the idea of domestic separation appealed as a further metaphor for decoupling, and recurs throughout the *Anatomy* sequence. As we shall go on to see, Leonardo's illegitimacy *did* have a material effect upon his education and upbringing, and thus is undeniably an important aspect of the da Vinci persona.

The references to 'A shitty book' and minding one's own 'fucking business' pertain to themes raised in the following fragment in which da Vinci lashes out at those who would condemn his lack of formal book learning. Unlike most of the 'radioactive' fragments which, with the exception of the Michelangelo citations, invariably have attributive tabulations, the identities of these speakers remain deliberately uncertain. In many ways they are the direct inversion of Leonardo himself, part of what Jung would have called his 'Ego-Shadow'. [21]

3. 'Consider, Salai…' [lines 32-96]

This fragment was once again inspired by Leonardo's notebooks and reveals a formative influence on his character: his lack of a formal 'education'. Whilst his half-siblings were schooled in Florence, Leonardo had to make do with gaining the rudiments of literacy 'from his family', something which explains why 'Leonardo's natural left-handedness was never corrected'. The reason he was denied a formal education stems from the complex situation surrounding his illegitimacy. It is ironic to note that

> In fifteenth-century Tuscany, young men conceived out of wedlock were untouched by social restrictions so long as they were born into either the nobility or the peasant class.[22]

However, Leonardo, as the son of a notary, had the misfortune of being born into the middle classes where 'illegitimacy was despised'. As White observes, 'the children of these unions were effectively ostracised'. Consequently, Leonardo

> was barred from attending university and could not hope to enter any of the respected professions, such as medicine or the law, because it was strictly against the rules of the professional guilds to accept anyone with his background.[23]

The result, whilst undeniably traumatic for someone of da Vinci's keen intelligence, was in many ways highly beneficial for his artistic and intellectual development. By entering into the lowly profession of an artisan, Leonardo's natural gift for drawing developed into one of the greatest creative talents of the Renaissance. Likewise his intellectual precocity remained un-stifled by the received wisdom of a university syllabus. Rather than learning the doctrines of Aristotle and Plato by rote, Leonardo was able to freely apply his mind to the observable workings of Nature. His prizing of 'experience' over the wisdom of the 'ancients' was to become the defining feature of his scientific-aesthetic endeavours, and the true mark of his extraordinary originality.[24]

Yet for all the intellectual freedom his lack of formal schooling afforded him, one gets the distinct impression that Leonardo's illegitimacy, and the social stigmatisation it brought him, 'pained him greatly'. Indeed, the passage from his notebooks, which I have used as the inspiration for this current fragment, reveals a barely checked bitterness towards those more 'fortunate' than himself:

> I am fully aware that the fact of my not being a man of letters may cause certain presumptuous persons to think that they may with reason blame me, alleging that I am a man without learning. Foolish folk! Do they not know that I might retort by saying, as did Marius to the Roman Patricians: 'They who adorn themselves in the labours of others will not permit

> me my own.' They will say that because I have no book learning, I cannot properly express what I desire to treat of – but they do not know that my subjects require for their exposition experience rather than the words of others…[25]

Who these 'foolish folk' were remains uncertain. However, I have the distinct impression that they do not constitute any actual persons but are rather a projection of Leonardo's own sense of inadequacy, something borne out by his attempts to learn Latin during his first Milanese period. Certainly, it is interesting to note that this 'unlettered man' should take great trouble to quote a classical source to bolster his argument, something that is a recurrent trend throughout his notebooks. It is important to remember that these notebooks were not published during his lifetime, nor, as we have seen, did he make any effort to publish them. Thus one may conclude that these classical references are self-referential, a means of reassuring himself as to the validity of his unorthodox pursuits.

Indeed, the above passage reveals a very different da Vinci from the 'lovable' man who 'commanded everyone's affection' as promoted by Vasari. Here we see da Vinci the misanthrope, the prickly outsider who 'harboured a suppressed hatred for humanity'. To be sure, certain passages from his notebooks are shocking in their severity. The following may serve as a case in point. 'How many people there are,' he writes

> who could be described as mere channels for food, producers of excrement, fillers of latrines, for they have no other purpose in this world; they practise no virtue whatsoever; all that remains after them is a full latrine.[26]

The man whose illegitimacy was judged by his family's society was highly judgemental in his turn.

In this fragment I have endeavoured to capture both Leonardo's independence of mind *and* his misanthropic rage. Thus the fragment has the character of a rant, with da Vinci pouring out his frustration to his servant Salai. Unlike Leonardo's voice in the first fragment, where the metre was relaxed, here tension is conveyed by the heavy accenting of the stresses and the use of alliteration, repetition, and occasional rhyme. Let us take by way of example the opening fifteen lines:

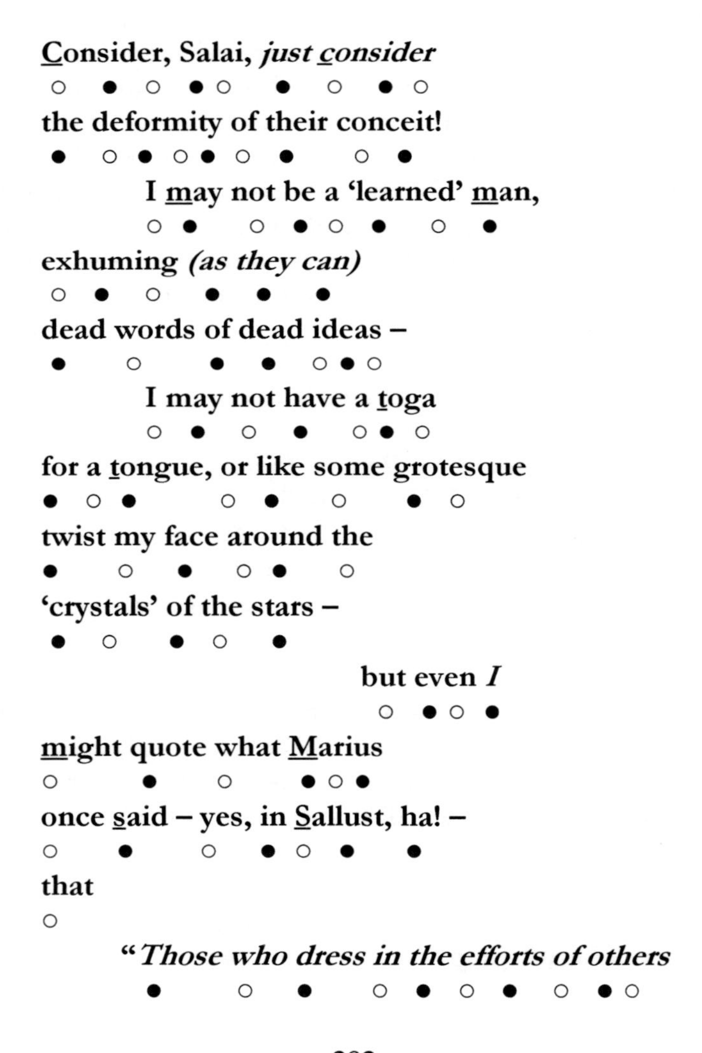

seek to strip ME of my own..."

● ○ ● ● ○ ● ○

In imagistic terms I have endeavoured to load the fragment with ugly or ludicrous imagery. Da Vinci was a champion of the beautiful in both art and Nature, and so it seemed fitting that he should speak of the 'deformity' of his detractors' conceit. Likewise the act of conventional scholarship is derided through the metaphor of grave robbing; they exhume 'dead words of dead ideas' – something which plays off da Vinci's own scientific investigations amongst the dead in order to discover the 'truth of the living' (see fragment: 'For it is among the horrors...' [lines 423-454]). Similarly, their love of the Latin language is likened to having 'a toga/ for a tongue', and the phrase 'or like some grotesque/ twist my face around the/ 'crystals' of the stars' relates to both Leonardo's passion for drawing 'grotesques' and contemporary misconceptions about the nature of the 'heavenly bodies'. The fragment ends at line 96 with Salai yawning and asking mischievously 'Bad day?', because I imagine such outbursts to have been a common occurrence in da Vinci's household. It also provides a tang of 'radiation' in what is otherwise a 'material' fragment.[27]

Key themes: Experience of Nature over book learning; seeing; misanthropy; rage; fear of inadequacy.

Reflective affinities:

- 'It might be a dream...' [lines 9-24]
- 'Force is Spirit...' [lines 107-113]
- 'Force is Spirit...' [lines 164-169]
- 'Ser Piero, my father...' [lines 205-212]
- 'And what of the eye?' [lines 221-234]
- 'Mmm...typical Verrocchio...' [lines 237-349]
- '29th January 1494...' [lines 371-384]

- 'The old man told me…' [lines 387-396]
- 'For it is among the horrors…' [lines 423-454]
- 'And the Great Bird shall rise…' [lines 478-576]
- 'Ginepro/Ginevra…' [lines 615-616]
- 'God's sake!' [lines 638-644]
- 'Di Ser Piero…' [lines 648-650]
- 'silk tears the air…' [lines 654-665]
- 'A painter should be solitary…' [lines 668-697]
- 'Buchi della verità…' [lines 743-754]
- 'A ghost…' [lines 757-764]
- 'The act of coitus…' [lines 768-773]
- 'I thought I was learning…' [lines 790-794]

Negative reflections:

- 'Un libro del cazzo!' [lines 27-29]
- 'In me la morte…' [lines 99-104]
- 'It's funny…' [lines 172-202]
- 'Veggio co' be' vostr'occhi un dolce lume…' [lines 215-218]
- 'Welcome to Imola…' [lines 399-419]
- 'Necromancy!' [lines 458-464]
- 'As I slumbered in my body…' [lines 599-611]
- 'Nel voler vostro è sol la voglia mia…' [lines 701-706]
- '"Maestro da Vinci"…' [lines 710-740]
- 'Sometimes Heaven…' [lines 778-786]
- 'Tell me, di Credi…' [lines 798-799]

4. 'In me la morte…' [lines 99-104]

This fragment is the first of the Michelangelo citations and is a 'partial sonnet' written by the artist during the 1520s. In translation it reads:

> **In me is death, in you my life; you determine, allot and parcel out time; as you wish, my life is short or long.**
> **I am happy according as you are kind. Blessed is the soul, where time does not run; through you it is formed to contemplate God.[28]**

As we have seen, my reason for choosing to incorporate the Michelangelo material was determined by two factors. Firstly, there was the alien quality of the language itself, the physical presence of the Italian within the text creating a profound sense of 'radioactive' otherness. Secondly, and arguably more importantly, there was the personality of Michelangelo and his profoundly antagonistic relationship with da Vinci. Indeed, the two artists could not have been more different. Whereas Leonardo was described by his contemporaries as possessing great 'physical beauty' Michelangelo, by contrast, was regarded as 'ugly'. This physical difference was carried over into their manner of dressing. The Anonimo Gaddiano informs us that Leonardo wore 'a pink, knee-length robe', marking him out as something of a 'dandy'. Michelangelo, on the other hand, was invariably 'shabbily dressed', 'slept on his studio floor', and had a fundamental aversion to washing. Likewise, their manners were at odds, for whilst Leonardo was often perceived as a 'courteous' man, Michelangelo was infamous for his 'sharp temper' and his 'sarcastic tongue'. [29]

Creatively too both men were diametrically opposed. Whilst Leonardo had the tendency to leave his commissions *non finito*, Michelangelo was an artistic zealot who 'worked twenty hours a day' and dominated the fields of sculpture (the *David*, the *Moses*), painting (the *Sistine frescoes*) and architecture (the *Biblioteca Laurenziana*, the *Dome of St. Peter's*). Both men undertook anatomical studies, but whereas Leonardo had scientific as well as aesthetic motivations, Michelangelo was solely interested in developing his art. Neither did Michelangelo have any interest in the wider natural world; he even believed that

'landscape painting should be forbidden' on the grounds that it was only fit 'for children and uneducated men'. For Michelangelo art was the expression of the Sublime Idea, the belief that Man is made in the image of God (Genesis 1:27). As a consequence Michelangelo limited the focus of his painting and sculpture 'almost entirely to the heroic male figure', invariably presenting these muscular forms completely 'nude'. Leonardo, by contrast, largely painted refined, *clothed* women, often including beautifully realised landscapes in the background. They even differed in matters of religion. Michelangelo was a deeply religious man, obsessed with 'morality, purity and the glory of the Roman Catholic Church'. Leonardo, on the other hand, was not a religious man, but was instead drawn by his scientific investigations into a quasi-pantheistic understanding of Man and Nature.[30]

With this in mind, it is little wonder that these two 'giants of the Renaissance' hated each other. Indeed, their relationship was so bad that, during Leonardo's second Florentine period, the two artists could scarcely pass each other in the street without insulting each other. One famous incident, recorded by the Anonimo Gaddiano, shows the level of their animosity:

> Leonardo was walking with P. da Gavine through [Piazza] Santa Trinità, and they passed the Pancaccia degli Spini where there was a gathering of citizens arguing over a passage of Dante; and they called out to the said Leonardo, asking him to explain the passage. At that point, by chance, Michelangelo was passing by, and Leonardo answered their request by saying, 'There's Michelangelo, he'll explain it for you.' Upon which Michelangelo, thinking he had said this to insult him, retorted angrily, 'Explain it yourself – you who designed a horse to cast in bronze, and couldn't cast it, and abandoned it out of shame.' And so saying he turned his back on them and walked off. And

> Leonardo was left there, his face red because of these words.[31]

In fairness to Leonardo the aggression seems to have been all on Michelangelo's side. The latter was a well-known admirer of Dante, and Leonardo's deferral can be interpreted as a sign of his courtesy. Yet in Michelangelo's violent response we can see the fundamentally irreconcilable tension between the two artists, between the cool, rational observer of Nature, and the fiery zealot who believed art to be a 'divine' calling, and who thus could not forgive Leonardo for his seemingly 'dilettante' approach to his work. If Leonardo embodies 'matter' then Michelangelo most certainly embodies 'radiation'.[32]

The choice of Michelangelo's poetry was designed to provide the sharpest possible contrast to the opinions of Leonardo expressed throughout the *Anatomy* sequence. None of the work which I have selected was written during Leonardo's lifetime. However, I consider this temporal disruption a further mark of separation. The current fragment, which is translated above, treats themes of death, time, the soul and God from a markedly Christian perspective, and thereby provides a strong counter-voice to Leonardo's predominantly materialistic interpretation of the workings of Nature.

5. 'Force is Spirit…' [lines 107-113]

This fragment was once again inspired by da Vinci's notebooks, and seeks to encapsulate his thinking about the nature of force and its effect on the material world. In the *Codex Atlanticus* he writes:

> Force is a spiritual energy, an invisible power which is imparted by violence from without to all bodies that are without their natural balance.
>
> Force is nothing but a spiritual energy, an invisible power which is created and imparted,

> through violence from without, by animated bodies to inanimate bodies, giving to these the similarity of life, and this life works in a marvellous way, constraining and transforming in place and shape all created things. It speeds in fury to its undoing and continues to modify according to the occasion.
>
> Retardation strengthens, and speed weakens it.
>
> It lives by violence and dies from liberty.
>
> It transmutes and compels all bodies to a change of place and form.
>
> Great power gives it a great desire of death...[33]

As Kemp observes, 'the framework within which he characterised force was entirely traditional', building on the 'Aristotelian theories' that remained prevalent 'until the reforms wrought by Galileo and Newton in succeeding centuries'. It is important to remember that Leonardo, for all his originality, was still a product of his times, and thus to find him referring to force as 'spiritual energy' is not in the least bit out of character. Rather it represents an attempt to reconcile his experience of bodies in motion with an available vernacular. Consequently, it must be remembered that Leonardo's innovation in the field of mechanics derives, not from his theoretical understanding of force, but from its practical application in his mechanical designs. As White remarks, da Vinci's 'practical mastery was not matched by his understanding of the theoretical principles of the subject'. It is typical of Leonardo that he should start from practical experience and then work backwards to a theoretical position. That this theoretical position should prove derivative (and by later scientific developments wrong) is a pertinent reminder of da Vinci's intellectual limitations. It is also comforting, as it makes him seem more human.[34]

The two fragments which begin 'Force is Spirit' were originally intended as a single unit, and thus present a cohesive tonality. Da Vinci's ruminations on force extend beyond the passage cited above and tend, like so much of his writing, to fall into repetition. Thus it was my intention to present what I saw as the quintessence of his theoretical position. In terms of structure, I wanted to convey the sense of motion both through the typographical arrangement of the lines and by the repetition of sound:

Force is Spirit,
inviolable,
invisible,
the gift of violence.
By violence it lives,
and at liberty
dies.

Force is Spirit,
the mover,
and remover,
a changer of bodies
so hungry
for death.

During the writing process I decided to split this fragment into two. The reason behind this was that I wanted to frame the sixth fragment, which concerns Leonardo's military designs, with his theoretical perspective on force, thereby both increasing the effect of separation *and* heightening the effect of thematic reflection.

Key themes: Motion; bodies; metamorphosis; death.

Reflective affinities:

- 'It might be a dream…' [lines 9-24]
- '…and as well as a musician…' [lines 116-161]
- 'Force is Spirit…' [lines 164-169]
- 'The old man told me…' [lines 387-396]
- 'For it is among the horrors…' [lines 423-454]
- 'And the Great Bird shall rise…' [lines 478-576]

- 'O time…' [lines 586-596]
- 'Letter of Authorisation…' [lines 618-634]
- 'silk tears the air…' [lines 654-665]
- 'The act of coitus…' [lines 768-773]
- 'I thought I was learning…' [lines 790-794]

Negative reflections:

- 'In me la morte…' [lines 99-104]
- 'It's funny…' [lines 172-202]
- 'Veggio co' be' vostr'occhi un dolce lume…' [lines 215-218]
- 'Welcome to Imola…' [lines 399-419]
- 'Volo con le vostr'ale senza piume…' [lines 580-583]
- 'As I slumbered in my body…' [lines 599-611]
- 'Nel voler vostro è sol la voglia mia…' [lines 701-706]
- '"Maestro da Vinci"…' [lines 710-740]
- 'Sometimes Heaven…' [lines 778-786]
- 'Tell me, di Credi…' [lines 798-799]

6. '…and as well as a musician…' [lines 116-161]

This fragment is primarily concerned with Leonardo's ideas as a military engineer. It is interesting to observe that the man who wrote in his notebooks that war is 'the most brutal kind of madness' should have expended so much energy on designing weapons of mass destruction. Indeed, the reason for this apparent hypocrisy is difficult to account for and seems, on the surface, to represent another example of Leonardo's 'fractured personality'. However, one explanation may be derived from the biographical context of these designs. Leonardo seems to have first turned his mind to military engineering shortly after his arrival in Milan in 1481. His reasons for quitting Florence for Milan are uncertain, especially when one considers that he was working on two commissions at the time, but the most likely is that he felt unappreciated. His contemporaries from

Verrocchio's workshop, Domenico Ghirlandaio, Sandro Botticelli, and Pietro Perugino had all been selected by Lorenzo de' Medici to go to Rome in order to paint frescoes for Pope Sixtus IV in the newly constructed Sistine Chapel. This was an important diplomatic event for Florence, marking the end of hostilities between the Republic and the Vatican. The Pope had instructed Lorenzo to send Florence's 'best artists' and, given the latter's 'famed knowledge and patronage of the arts', he doubtless wanted to impress the Pontiff with his city's finest talents. Considering the quality of the work which Leonardo was producing during the 1470s it is strange that he was not included. Indeed, as White observes, 'Leonardo was conspicuously ignored'. Once again the reason is difficult to ascertain, but may, as White suggests, have been the result of an 'ideological clash'. Lorenzo's court was steeped in 'traditional learning and the Classical tradition'. Leonardo, as we have seen, favoured experience over received wisdom. Even when he had struggled to learn Latin a decade later and begun to clumsily graft antiquarian ideas onto his empirical observations – such as his appropriation of the Aristotelian conception of force – he still never had any time for those he scornfully referred to as 'the reciters and trumpeters of the works of others'. Leonardo 'loathed' what he regarded as 'intellectual pretension' and, as White points out, 'openly mocked the social graces and falsities of the courtier'. Although it must remain a point of conjecture, it is 'possible that Leonardo's views had reached Medici ears'. Whatever the case, da Vinci abandoned Florence in the autumn of 1481 and moved to Milan.[35]

Milan was a very different city from Florence and had a very different ruler. Whilst the Medici had gained their ascendancy through commerce, the Sforzas had gained theirs by the sword. The incumbent duke, Ludovico Sforza, called '*il Moro*' because of his swarthy complexion, was the grandson of 'a much honoured *condottiere*'. He was '[r]elatively well educated' but, although he 'placed great value upon using culture as a political tool', he 'never really developed any real aesthetic sense'. It is here that a possible explanation for Leonardo's transition from struggling artist to would-be military engineer may be found. If he wanted to impress Sforza and gain his illustrious patronage then it made good sense to appeal to his military instincts. Certainly, the draft of an introductory letter to *il Moro* found among da Vinci's notes makes it clear that warfare is his speciality. It begins:

> Most Illustrious Lord, having by now sufficiently considered the experience of those men who claim to be skilled inventors of machines of war, and having realised that the said machines in no way differ from those commonly employed, I shall endeavour, without prejudice to anyone else, to reveal my secrets to Your Excellency, for whom I offer to execute, at your convenience, all the items briefly noted below...[36]

The following items include 'mortars', 'flame-throwing engines', 'mangonels', 'covered vehicles...with artillery', and 'sea...vessels that will resist even the heaviest cannon fire'. It is only as an after-thought that he mentions he is also a painter. White interprets Leonardo's change of direction as purely pragmatic. 'To gain a foothold in the Milanese court,' he writes, '[Leonardo knew that] he would have to prostitute his talents, at least until he could impress the Moor with his other skills'. However this really does not seem explanation enough, and is certainly not an ethical justification for a man who claimed to despise war. It must be remembered that Leonardo could have promoted himself exclusively as an artist, or approached a less warlike patron. Another explanation, and perhaps more in keeping with Leonardo's character, is that he was genuinely interested in war machines, not as instruments of conflict, but rather as ways of investigating the manipulation of force through mechanical design. As Kemp observes, part of Leonardo's programme for becoming a 'second Nature' involved him making 'new things on the basis of the inner workings of

nature rather than simply imitating what nature [had] already done'. The war machines provided him with precisely this opportunity, for here, through his keen understanding of 'natural law', he could 'amplify human power a thousandfold'. Like many scientists, I suspect that da Vinci was able to dissociate his work from ethical considerations. He may have genuinely despised war, and it must be observed that he never became a *condottiere*, but in order to get funding to build his machines he knew that he had to endow them with a practical purpose. Whatever the case the war machines remained unrealised. Ironically, Ludovico appears to have been more interested in Leonardo's artistic talents, amongst other things commissioning him to paint a portrait of his mistress, Cecilia Gallerani. In engineering terms, rather than constructing catapults or armoured cars, da Vinci was set to work on the Castello Sforzesco's plumbing.[37]

It is around these circumstances that I have worked this fragment. The precise conditions of Leonardo's first meeting with Ludovico Sforza are unrecorded. Certainly he does not seem to have entered *il Moro*'s service immediately after his arrival in Milan, for he went into business with the de Predis brothers and began work on the first version of the *Virgin of the Rocks* (begun 1483). Thus my treatment is somewhat fanciful, and is strongly based on both the draft of Leonardo's introductory letter and what we know of the artist's subsequent activities in Ludovico's service.

The opening line, '…and as well as a musician, my Lord' refers to a myth, begun by the Anonimo Gaddiano, that Leonardo was sent to Milan by Lorenzo de' Medici to play the lyre for *il Moro*. Considering Lorenzo's apparent coolness towards Leonardo, coupled with the fact that, 'as far as we are aware', he did not receive Medici patronage until the following century, there seems to be no substance to this story. Nevertheless, Leonardo *was* fond of music, and it seemed a playful way to begin the fragment. Indeed, the tone of the fragment is light (which is ironic when one

considers what Leonardo is proposing), and is arguably one of the most humorous in the *Anatomy* sequence. The reason for this 'irony' was that I wanted to juxtapose theme and content as a means of further emphasising the complexity of da Vinci's nature. I also wanted to emphasise the reality of Leonardo's position within the world of Renaissance patronage. Consequently the fragment may be divided into two unequal sections.[38]

For the first twenty-four lines Leonardo is in his element, boasting of his 'tireless effort' and 'ingenuity of mind', and proudly offering the Duke an '*esercito* [army] of machines/ as unique as they are deadly'. The confidence of this expansive language, peppered with 'exotic' words such as '*esercito*' and allusions to Hannibal, is mirrored by the closed nature of the stanzas. Leonardo is in control. Then, at the twenty-fifth line, the tone changes. Ludovico has clearly become bored with da Vinci's progressive ideas about armoured cars inspired by tortoises and, although we do not hear his voice, we know that he has interrupted. The lines as well as the stanzas become fragmented as Leonardo is put on the defensive. In many ways the Duke is anatomising him, teasing out the sinews of truth beneath the bravado. For all his professed interest in military engineering, Leonardo's professional grounding was as a painter. As White observes, 'painters were considered to be on the lowest rung of the artistic and cultural ladder'. The Duke of course knows this and puts Leonardo in his place. For all da Vinci's brilliance, it is Ludovico and not Leonardo who is in control. Ludovico is the greater force; we do not even need to hear his voice to feel his presence. This power is reflected in the line ratio of the two halves, for whilst Leonardo's engineering bravado takes up over half the fragment, Ludovico is able to assert his superior authority in less than half the space. It is perhaps one of the greatest ironies of da Vinci's career that the man who had mocked at the Medici's courtiers became a courtier in his turn.[39]

Key themes: Force; military engineering; death; power; patronage.

Reflective affinities:

- **'Consider, Salai…' [lines 32-96]**
- **'Force is Spirit…' [lines 107-113]**
- **'Force is Spirit…' [lines 164-169]**
- **'Mmm…typical Verrocchio…' [lines 237-349]**
- **'The old man told me…' [lines 387-396]**
- **'For it is among the horrors…' [lines 423-454]**
- **'O time…' [lines 586-596]**
- **'Letter of Authorisation…' [lines 618-634]**
- **'silk tears the air…' [lines 654-665]**
- **'The act of coitus…' [lines 768-773]**
- **'I thought I was learning…' [lines 790-794]**

Negative reflections:

- **'Un libro del cazzo!' [lines 27-29]**
- **'In me la morte…' [lines 99-104]**
- **'It's funny…' [lines 172-202]**
- **'But when will it be finished…' [lines 352-367]**
- **'Welcome to Imola…' [lines 399-419]**
- **'Necromancy!' [lines 458-464]**
- **'"Maestro da Vinci"…' [lines 710-740]**
- **'Sometimes Heaven…' [lines 778-786]**
- **'Tell me, di Credi…' [lines 798-799]**

7. 'Force is Spirit…' [lines 164-169]

See analysis of Fragment 5 ('Force is Spirit…' [lines 107-113]).

8. 'It's funny…' [lines 172-202]

This is the first of the 'radioactive' fragments written in English, and is spoken by Leonardo's servant, Salai. Unlike Michelangelo, who hated da Vinci, Salai's relationship with the artist is more complicated. His real name was Gian Giacomo Caprotti di Oreno and he entered Leonardo's service on the 22nd July 1490 at the age of ten years old. The name 'Salai', by which he is generally known, means 'little devil' or 'imp' and was given to him by da Vinci on account of his mischievous disposition. On only his second day in Leonardo's household he stole some of his master's 'money' and on his third, while a guest in the home of da Vinci's friend Giacomo Andrea, Leonardo records that he 'ate supper for two and did mischief for four', apparently breaking 'three flagons' and spilling 'the wine'. Six weeks later he was still creating mischief, stealing a 'stile worth 22 soldi' from one of da Vinci's assistants called 'Marco'. In short, Salai was trouble. However, one gets the distinct impression that Leonardo was somewhat amused by his exploits. Da Vinci's recordings of the boy's misdemeanours contain what Nicholl has termed 'a curiously personal colouration', transcending a mere itemisation of the 'expenses arising from the boy's misdeeds'. Indeed, their tone is one of 'exasperated fondness', and whilst Leonardo was to write in the margin the words, '*ladro*, *bugiardo*, *ostinato*, *ghiotto* – thief, liar, obstinate, greedy', one senses that he had an almost perverse admiration for such bad behaviour. Certainly, Leonardo was a rebel, at least intellectually, and perhaps he saw something similar in Salai? Alternatively it might well have been an attraction of opposites; perhaps Salai, the liar, the thief, the reprobate, endeared himself to the artist precisely because he was so different? Whatever the case, Salai was to remain in da Vinci's service for the rest of the artist's life, acting as a 'front man' to Leonardo's entourage. He was also, along with Francesco Melzi, the prime beneficiary of the artist's will, inheriting the bulk of Leonardo's artistic legacy. Given what we know of his character, it is unsurprising to learn

that he died in violent circumstances, 'from an arrow wound', in 1524 – only five years after da Vinci's death.[40]

My reason for using Salai as a 'radioactive' counter-voice is based on two factors. Firstly, there is what I interpret as his temperamental otherness to da Vinci, for whilst Leonardo may have found Salai's reprehensible and rebellious antics amusing, Salai's rebelliousness was ultimately of a markedly different character to his master's. It was destructive *not* constructive. Secondly, there is his unique proximity to the activities of the artist. It must be remembered that he was in da Vinci's service for the best part of thirty years (1490-1519), the period during which Leonardo's activities were at their most diverse, and so was in an excellent position to form a strong opinion of his master's personality and work. My interpretation of Salai is that he is essentially loyal to da Vinci, perhaps even fond of him, but that he does not *understand* him. Thus he is a subtler counter-voice than Michelangelo; his 'radioactive' otherness based on *misunderstanding* rather than *hatred*. This crucial difference in Salai's relationship with Leonardo is textually realised through his direct presence as a persona rather than as a citation. Salai engages with da Vinci, whereas Michelangelo, through the interpolated passages of his poetry, merely expresses an opposing point of view.

I have the distinct impression that Salai (along with many of da Vinci's contemporaries) would have found some of his master's preoccupations at best eccentric and at worst repellent. A prime example of such an eccentric/repellent preoccupation is da Vinci's meticulous study of anatomy – something which forms the subject of this fragment. It is important to remember that the study of anatomy was a contentious activity during the late fifteenth and early sixteenth centuries, and was heavily regulated by the Church. Thus, whilst 'dissections of human bodies for the purpose of medical learning' were occasionally permitted within the environs of a licensed 'university', they were subject to heavy restrictions. Firstly, the bodies used had to

be those of executed criminals, and secondly, the dissections had to be carried out in accordance with the theories of the ancient anatomist Galen. Consequently, these dissections were not particularly informative. As White observes,

> the doctor/professor [conducting the dissection] invariably ignored what was displayed and simply trotted out what he and his teachers had been taught.[41]

By purely repeating ancient wisdom, and ignoring the material evidence, the activity was, in effect, rendered 'absolutely pointless'. This was especially true if one happened to be an artist and wanted to really see what was beneath the skin. Antonio Pollaiuolo and Michelangelo, for example, both dissected corpses to 'improve [their] depiction of the human body'. Thus their quest for knowledge necessarily led them into the hospitals and outside of the law.[42]

Leonardo, with his duel interest in the body both as an artistic *and* scientific object, was likewise led into the clandestine world of illegal dissections; and such a world could be dangerous. During his Roman period Leonardo's nocturnal company led to charges of 'necromancy' – a charge which, without his Medici patronage, could well have proved fatal. Not only were the risks of being caught great, but the conditions were vile. In addition to overcoming the psychological 'taboos' of his time, Leonardo also had to endure 'the stressful and repulsive procedures' of conducting a post-mortem examination 'in pre-refrigeration circumstances'. As White points out,

> [Leonardo] had to work fast and in extremely uncomfortable conditions. He had to use…tools he had designed and fashioned himself…and he faced the constant danger of infection from the rotting corpses he studied…[43]

Given the horror and pressures of the environment it is astonishing that he should have produced such beautiful and detailed drawings of his findings.

Whether Salai assisted da Vinci in his anatomical investigations is uncertain, but it is certainly not improbable. Given the complexities of the work an extra pair of hands would have been useful, if only to hold the instruments. That person would have needed to be someone that da Vinci could trust and, as we have seen, despite Salai's juvenile antics there is no reason to doubt his loyalty to his master. Thus this fragment finds Salai watching da Vinci cutting up the corpse of a young woman. I have endeavoured to distinguish Salai's voice from Leonardo's by the use of certain linguistic particulars. For example, unlike da Vinci he is given to using casual, demotic turns of phrase such as the recurring 'Yeah well'. He also indulges in the occasional use of profanities (although not in this particular fragment). This decision was based, in part, on their relative social standing. Whilst da Vinci was the son of a notary (albeit an illegitimate son) and grew up in a comfortable 'middleclass' home, Salai's provenance was, in all likelihood, somewhat different. As Nicholl observes, '[Salai's father] was certainly not well-off, and we know of no connection with a trade'. However, whether he was a 'humble peasant', as he is usually depicted, is less certain. In a legal document dating from this period he is described as '*filius quondam domini Joannis* – the son of Master Giovanni'. Whilst 'the honorific "*dominus*" is loose', it 'suggests that Salai's grandfather Giovanni, after whom he was named, owned some land and had some status'. Nevertheless, it is important to remember that Salai entered da Vinci's household as a '*famiglio*', a term which can be translated as 'servant', 'errand-boy', or 'dogsbody'. Whatever land and status Salai's grandfather may or may not have had, his father seems to have been without, and whilst Salai may not quite have been the '*enfant savage*' of popular legend, the Caprotti family, if not working/peasant class, was certainly lower down the social ladder than the da Vincis – hence Salai's rougher manner of speech.[44]

Another distinguishing feature of Salai's voice, and in tension with his 'rough manner', is his lyricism. During his time with da Vinci he learned to become a painter, and thus it seemed appropriate that this should be translated linguistically as a highly visual means of expression. Unlike Leonardo, who was both an artist and a scientist, the focus of Salai's energies was purely aesthetic. Consequently, I have made his voice more consciously 'poetic'. In so saying, I do not mean that he indulges in archaic poeticisms, or that he has the persona of an aesthete. Rather, I mean that the texture of his voice is imagistic as opposed to intellectual. Salai *responds* with verbal paintings, he does not *interrogate* with verbal diagrams. Thus, he speaks of the 'weird shadows of a sickly flame' (line 175), likens rotting corpses to 'purple flowers' (line 182), and when wondering about the young woman's identity and former lifestyle, juxtaposes her with the Madonna and St. Anne – both popular iconic images (line 195).

This aesthetic proclivity necessarily affects his perception of da Vinci's activities. Try as he might he simply cannot find the physical horrors of dissection in any way beautiful; and he *does* try. What I perceive as the tragedy of Salai's relationship with Leonardo is his failed attempts to see life from da Vinci's point of view; to reconcile da Vinci's activities with his own understanding of the world. 'And I'd like to say it's beautiful', he says in the third stanza, 'That *somehow* it's beautiful', before sadly concluding, 'But it's not'. He wants to see the world through da Vinci's eyes but he cannot. Unlike Leonardo he is unable to transcend the social taboos surrounding the unsanctioned dissection of corpses ('I never used/ to think of Hell' [lines 172 and 173]). Neither is he able to dissociate the corpse from its former life. Indeed, one of the most disquieting elements of da Vinci's character was the coldness with which he was able to examine the dead. One famous incident, and the subject of a later fragment, concerns his dissection of the 'centenarian' whom he met in the Hospital of Santa Maria Nuova, Florence, in late 1507. In the *Codex Leicester* he writes:

> The old man, a few hours before his death, told me that he had lived a hundred years, and that he had felt nothing wrong with his body other than weakness. And thus while sitting upon a bed in the hospital of Santa Maria Nuova in Florence, without any movement or other sign of any mishap, he passed out of this life. And I made an anatomy of him in order to see the cause of so sweet a death...[45]

What is so disquieting is the way in which da Vinci calmly relates how he spoke with the old man and then, without the slightest change of tone, says how he 'made an anatomy of him'. There is no emotional reflection of any kind. In the current fragment, by contrast, Salai cannot help but get emotionally involved. 'I wonder who she was?' he asks in the fifth stanza, adding 'Was she alone when she died?/ Did she love?' (lines 199 and 200). Salai is deeply disturbed by da Vinci's indifference and, emphasising the differences between them (their radioactive/material divide), the fragment concludes with the line, '*He* doesn't care'.

9. 'Ser Piero, my father...' [lines 205-212]

This fragment is concerned with domestic separation – a further metaphor for decoupling, and one which recurs throughout the *Anatomy* sequence. As we have previously discussed, the circumstances of Leonardo's birth had a material effect upon his education and upbringing, and consequently had a decisive impact on his character. Indeed, da Vinci's relationship with his parents was a troubled one. His father, Ser Piero, was something of a 'playboy', a 'hard-working, hard-playing' womaniser who married four times and fathered at least two illegitimate children. He appears to have been 'a self-obsessed man [who had] little regard for family life', and whilst da Vinci refers to him respectfully in his notebooks as 'Ser Piero, my father', one senses that there was a certain coldness between them, and on Leonardo's side, even resentment. Indeed, one entry in his notebooks, and the subject of a later fragment, has Leonardo rearranging the letters of his father's name to make the word '*dispero*', which may be translated as, 'I despair'. It is certainly possible that da Vinci resented his father for not marrying his mother and thereby depriving him of a respectable education and career. It must be remembered that Leonardo abandoned the two 'important' commissions secured for him by Ser Piero towards the end of his first Florentine period and, whilst there is no supporting evidence, it is tempting to interpret this as an attempt to embarrass his father and thereby get some modicum of revenge.[46]

It appears that his relationship with his mother, Caterina, was equally problematic. As we have seen, she was married off to Accattabriga di Piero del Vacca eighteen months after Leonardo's birth and moved to the nearby village of Campo Zeppi. The geographical proximity of Vinci and Campo Zeppi meant that 'mother and child inevitably met on feast days and special occasions'. Yet such encounters were unlikely to have been happy ones for, as White points out,

> by the time Leonardo was old enough to understand that Caterina was his mother he would have seen her with other slightly younger children at her apron and perhaps a baby in her arms. It is not difficult to imagine how the boy must have felt, witnessing the affection his half-siblings received from her, while he was ignored.[47]

Indeed, da Vinci's solitary nature, his reluctance to form close personal relationships, may well stem from the painful reality of his childhood. Both of his parents remarried and both had legitimate children. In such a claustrophobic environment Leonardo's sense of otherness, even alienation, must have been acute. Without conceding to Freud, it should be observed that Leonardo's art is populated with surrogate mother figures, from the *Virgin and Child with St. Anne* (c.1502-1516) – an image containing two avatars of maternity – to the *Mona Lisa* (1503-1506), whose sitter, Lisa del Giocondo, had herself borne three children by the time of the painting's execution. Even more revealing is the fact that Leonardo 'could not bring himself to call Caterina his mother'. In the notebooks and surviving letters she is known simply as 'la Caterina', and such apparent coldness has led White to conclude that da Vinci blamed her, more than his father, for the stigma of his illegitimacy. Their relationship is further complicated by the fact that Caterina may well have lived with the artist in Milan during the last two years of her life. In one of his notebooks, now known as the *Codex Forster*, Leonardo writes succinctly: 'Caterina came, 16th July 1493'. However, there is some confusion as to whether this 'Caterina' was indeed his mother, or simply a servant with the same name; a confusion exacerbated by Leonardo's habit of referring to his mother by her forename. If this *was* a late reconciliation, then it must be observed that when this 'Caterina' died in 1495, Leonardo recorded the 'modest' expenses of her funeral without the slightest trace of emotion.[48]

The theme of separation is mirrored in the structure of the fragment which may be divided into two unequal sections. The first stanza is concerned with Ser Piero and, to reflect his social standing as a successful notary, is arranged as a neat tercet. Whilst it opens with the respectful line 'Ser Piero, my father' the tone of the stanza is negative with da Vinci referring to his 'dried olive eyes' (line 207) which 'won't look at my mother' (line 208). As we have previously discussed, Leonardo often referred to the eye as the window of the soul, and so by describing his father's eyes as dried olives he is making a very damning criticism. I have taken an aesthetic liberty by having Leonardo refer to his 'mother'. My reason for doing so was that I wanted to play off the word 'father' in the opening line.

The second stanza focuses on Caterina. In marked contrast to the first stanza, it is a quatrain – the length reflecting the quantity of blame – and is performed in a different 'voice', although still spoken through the mouth of da Vinci. I wanted to give the impression of the malicious gossip which in all probability surrounded Leonardo's birth, may well have wounded him as a child, and, if so, probably preyed on his mind as an adult. Caterina is referred to as 'that woman' and is likened to both a prostitute ('bought for 12 soldi' [line 211]) and a simpleton ('and the lies of sweet wine' [line 212]).

Key themes: Father; mother; separation; bitterness; illegitimacy; the eye; money; wine.

Reflective affinities:

- 'It might be a dream…' [lines 9-24]
- 'Consider, Salai…' [lines 32-96]
- '…and as well as a musician…' [lines 116-161]
- 'And what of the eye?' [lines 221-234]
- 'Mmm…typical Verrocchio…' [lines 237-349]
- '29th January 1494…' [lines 371-384]
- 'God's sake!' [lines 638-644]
- 'Di Ser Piero…' [lines 648-650]
- 'silk tears the air…' [lines 654-665]
- 'A painter should be solitary…' [lines 668-697]
- 'Buchi della verità…' [lines 743-754]
- 'A ghost…' [lines 757-764]
- 'The act of coitus…' [lines 768-773]

Negative reflections:

- 'Un libro del cazzo!' [lines 27-29]
- 'Veggio co' be' vostr'occhi un dolce lume…' [lines 215-218]

- 'But when will it be finished…' [lines 352-367]
- 'Necromancy!' [lines 458-464]
- 'As I slumbered in my body…' [lines 599-611]
- 'Nel voler vostro è sol la voglia mia…' [lines 701-706]
- '"Maestro da Vinci"…' [lines 710-740]
- 'Sometimes Heaven…' [lines 778-786]

10. 'Veggio co' be' vostr'occhi un dolce lume…' [lines 215-218]

This fragment is the second of the Michelangelo citations and is the first four lines of a sonnet written by the artist in 1534. It may be translated as:

> With your beautiful eyes I see a sweet light which with my blind eyes I certainly cannot see; with your feet I carry on my back a weight which my lame feet certainly could not bear.[49]

The passage is significant in a number of ways. Firstly, on a structural level, it represents a form of counter-anatomy, for the rest of the sonnet may be found dissected at various intervals throughout the remainder of the polylogue. Secondly, its thematic identity as a love sonnet provides a strong contrast with the da Vinci persona. Michelangelo's sexual preference for men is well documented, and indeed this sonnet was written for 'the handsome and refined Tommaso dei Cavalieri, whom he had met in 1532'. As a devout Christian, Michelangelo was tormented by the guilt of 'sin', and as a Dante scholar he knew all too well the popular conception of the fate of sodomites. The relationship was in all probability unconsummated, and the sonnets which Michelangelo wrote to Cavalieri can be seen as a form of sexual catharsis. The question of Leonardo's sexual preferences is more problematical. Whilst Freud and others have assumed he was homosexual, an assumption largely based on his being anonymously denounced for 'sodomy' in 1476 (a denunciation, it must be remembered, that was never substantiated in court), one must be mindful of how anachronistic terms such as 'homosexual' and 'heterosexual' are in a Renaissance context. As theorists of historical sexuality, like Michel Foucault, have argued, prior to the clinical definitions of sexuality in the nineteenth century sexual identity was more fluid. Indeed, as the sexual historian Jonathan Goldberg asserts, 'the Renaissance comes before the regimes of sexuality, and to speak of sexuality in this period is a misnomer'. Neither Michelangelo or Leonardo would have, *or could have*, thought of themselves as being homosexual as the term and its associate lifestyles are understood today, and in the case of da Vinci the question of sexual preference is further problematised by the absence of any directly self-reflexive comment on the matter in his notebooks. True, he expressed a certain distaste for male-female coitus when he wrote in one of his notebooks, now known as *Manuscript A*,

> [that the] act of coupling and the members engaged in it are so ugly that if it were not for the faces and adornments of the actors, and the impulses sustained, the human race would die out.[50]

However, it must be noted that he did not write any love poetry to handsome young men either. Da Vinci does not seem to have been a romantic man of any definable persuasion, and so the presence of a love poem in the *Anatomy* sequence is a further mark of 'radioactive' otherness. In the immediate context of the fragment the reference to 'beautiful eyes' juxtaposes both with the 'dried olive eyes' of the previous fragment, and the rational, scientific approach to the eye expressed in the subsequent fragment.

11. 'And what of the eye?' [lines 221-234]

This fragment relates to da Vinci's scientific investigations into the workings of the eye. As we have previously discussed, Leonardo's optical investigations revealed that, contrary to the popular Platonic misconception, the eye did not *emit* 'visual rays', but rather *received* images due to the external action of light reflecting off non-transparent bodies. One of the ways in which da Vinci came to this conclusion was simple logic. As he writes in one of his notebooks, now known as *Manuscript B*,

> It is impossible that the eye should project from itself, by visual rays, the visual power, since as soon as it opens, the front portion (of the eye) which would give rise to this emanation would have to go forth to the object, and it could not do this without time. And this being so, it could not travel so high as the sun when the eye wants to see it.[51]

I have based the current fragment on the above, but have made certain changes. For example, to emphasise the photonic dimension I have substituted 'visual rays' with 'light'. Neither have I used da Vinci's equation of the visual rays with the front portion of the eye, which, in the above, is described as physically travelling to the object, as this seemed cumbersome to the movement of the fragment. To simplify matters, here light simply travels from the eye to the object. I have also translated the fragment into the present tense by having Leonardo addressing Salai, my reason being that it makes the fragment more dramatically engaging. Thus the fragment brings the eye and the action of light to the fore and once again emphasises Leonardo's favouring of experience over received wisdom.

Key themes: The eye; light; experience over received wisdom.

Reflective affinities:

- 'It might be a dream…' [lines 9-24]
- 'Consider, Salai…' [lines 32-96]
- 'Mmm…typical Verrocchio…' [lines 237-349]

- 'For it is among the horrors…' [lines 423-454]
- 'silk tears the air…' [lines 654-665]
- 'A painter should be solitary…' [lines 668-697]
- 'Buchi della verità…' [lines 743-754]
- 'A ghost…' [lines 757-764]
- 'The act of coitus…' [lines 768-773]

Negative reflections:

- 'Veggio co' be' vostr'occhi un dolce lume…' [lines 215-218]
- 'Necromancy!' [lines 458-464]
- 'As I slumbered in my body…' [lines 599-611]
- 'Nel voler vostro è sol la voglia mia…' [lines 701-706]
- '"Maestro da Vinci"…' [lines 710-740]
- 'Sometimes Heaven…' [lines 778-786]

12. 'Mmm…typical Verrocchio…' [lines 237-349]

This fragment is primarily concerned with Leonardo's activities as a painter and is set during the mid-1470s when he was still an associate of the Florentine artist Andrea del Verrocchio. Leonardo was apprenticed to Verrocchio sometime around the year 1469. The nature of artistic apprenticeship during the Quattrocento meant that the young da Vinci would have lived in Verrocchio's '*bottega*', or workshop, with the other apprentices. As White observes:

> The workshops [of the Quattrocento] bore little relation to the artists' studios of modern myth. They did not presage Monet's sun-splashed retreat or Picasso's Paris garret… Children and animals ran in and out unrestrained, and just beyond the front door the artist's work was displayed for passers-by to peruse and perhaps purchase. Those who worked there – the master, his close assistants and a small

> cadre of young apprentices – also lived on the premises, in cramped, often unhygienic conditions.[52]

It was in such an environment that Leonardo learnt to become a painter. Given Verrocchio's other talents as a 'sculptor' and 'metalworker' it is also likely that da Vinci would have learnt these arts as well, something which probably stood him in good stead when he came to design the *Sforza Horse* during his first Milanese period.[53]

Verrocchio's workshop was one of the largest and most successful in Florence during the middle decades of the fifteenth century and was awarded the 'prestigious' honour of making the 'copper orb' which still adorns the cupola of the Duomo. Thus by apprenticing his son to such a renowned maestro, Ser Piero was arguably giving Leonardo the best start in life that he could. As we have seen, da Vinci's illegitimacy precluded him from entering either the legal or medical professions; to be an artisan was the best to which he could hope to aspire. On a darker note, by apprenticing his illegitimate son, Ser Piero effectively had him put out of the way for, as the above makes clear, apprentices worked and slept in the *bottega*. Whilst Ser Piero's motivations may well have been honourable, and without further evidence it must remain a point of conjecture, this event can also be seen as an attempt to erase the social embarrassment of having his bastard living with his wife and legitimate children. Whatever the case, for those formative years while da Vinci remained with Verrocchio, the maestro became, in effect, his surrogate father.[54]

Leonardo's personal opinion of Verrocchio is uncertain. On the one hand it must be remembered that he spent the best part of a decade living with the artist, and even when he left Verrocchio's workshop in 1477, '[to] set up his own', it is likely that he 'met up with Verrocchio frequently'. As White points out, 'they lived and worked within a few hundred metres of each other' and, without definite evidence to the contrary, there is no reason to doubt that they 'remained friends'. That said, it must also be remembered that Leonardo makes no reference to Verrocchio in his notebooks. As Nicholl observes, '[this] lofty silence [implies a lack] of gratitude to the artist from whom…Leonardo first learnt his craft'. Indeed, as we have seen, Leonardo had a distinct problem with authority figures throughout his life, whether they be Plato, the Pope, Lorenzo de' Medici, or Ser Piero da Vinci. His natural precocity was fused with a tendency to rebel, and nowhere is this more apparent than in the independent spirit of his art. One striking feature of his painting style is its marked divergence from Verrocchio's rather stiff, mannered representation of form. The 'poetic tone' of Leonardo's work is often regarded as 'something entirely new', and nowhere is this stylistic tension between master and pupil more clearly defined than in *The Baptism of Christ* (c.1472-1475/6), a painting on which both artists collaborated.[55]

Collaboration was a common occurrence in Renaissance artistic practice, with the maestro invariably painting the most important figures and his apprentices and assistants painting minor figures and the background. That da Vinci should have had a hand in this composition, painting one of the angels kneeling to the right of Christ, is thus, *in itself*, unsurprising. However, this particular collaboration forms a definitive aspect of the Leonardo legend. As Vasari writes in his biography of da Vinci:

> Verrocchio was working on a panel picture showing the Baptism of Christ by St. John, for which Leonardo painted an angel who was holding some garments; and despite his youth, he executed it in such a manner that his angel was far better than the figures painted by Andrea. This was the reason why Andrea would never touch colours again, he was so ashamed that a boy understood their use better than he did.[56]

The above is clearly an example of what Nicholl has termed 'Leonardolatry' and 'should not be taken at face value'. Leonardo was about 'twenty-one' when the painting was executed; hardly a 'boy'. Nor do we need to believe that Verrocchio abandoned painting, shamed by his apprentice's superior talent, for his *bottega* continued to operate until his death in 1488, and it is reasonable to assume that the maestro had a guiding hand in the works produced. Nevertheless, Vasari's anecdote, and more importantly the painting itself, does throw the relative merits of the two artists into sharp relief. Compared to Verrocchio's elongated, over-sinuous figures of Christ and the Baptist, whose inaccurate anatomy has led to bizarre proportional distortions (such as the Baptist's overlong right arm), Leonardo's 'exquisite' angel seems to belong, not just to a different painting, but also to a different century. The reason for this is due to a softer handling of line, a consistent handling of proportion, and Leonardo's decision to paint the angel with oil rather than tempera.[57]

Oil paint had been known in Italy from as early as the 1390s. It is mentioned in Cennino Cennini's *Il libro dell'arte*, a text with which Leonardo was familiar, and was employed by artists such as Piero della Francesca and Antonello da Messina. Nevertheless its use was limited, often acting as merely a 'finish, modifying the opaque tempera layer with a rich transparent film or glaze', and in Quattrocento painting is more often associated with the Flemish rather than the Italian masters. Thus, by painting his angel with oil, Leonardo was on the 'technical cusp' of his times, prefiguring the standardisation of the medium in the sixteenth century. He was also being highly rebellious, and perhaps even a little disrespectful to his master, for the effect of oil paint is very different from that of tempera, providing a warmer, more resonant tonality, and by deciding to use oil in what was otherwise a tempera work, Leonardo rendered *The Baptism of Christ* a very uneven composition. The desire to be original, to push the boundaries even at this young age, seems to have led da

Vinci to disregard his responsibility as an apprentice/assistant to follow Verrocchio's lead. Thus the little angel is, in effect, not only a microcosm of Leonardo's future achievements as a painter, but also of his temperament as a man. As he was to later write in his notebooks: 'He is a poor pupil who does not go beyond his master'. In all things Leonardo sought to carve out his own path, even, it would seem, at the expense of artistic tact.[58]

The 'action' of the current fragment takes place in da Vinci's mind as he is weighing up whether or not to paint his angel with oil. This is one of the longest fragments in the *Anatomy* sequence and can be divided into four movements. The first (lines 237-250) begins with Leonardo rather dismissively examining his master's work. In light of the above I decided that, whilst da Vinci may have got on with Verrocchio on a personal level, he had little regard for his faculty as a painter. Fragment six has already seen da Vinci damning his teacher with faint praise ('Yes, yes, he is…quite good'[line 149]). Here, in the privacy of his own head, he is less restrained, referring to the figures of Christ and the Baptist as 'somewhat flat'(lines 241 and 244) and rather sarcastically musing 'Oh the talent' (line 249). To introduce the internal nature of this fragment, I have been generous with the typographical arrangement of this opening movement, allowing lines of thought to group into singlets and couplets. To emphasise the considered nature of his thinking I have also employed ellipses which I intend to signify pauses.

The second movement (lines 251-262) sees da Vinci turning his artistic scorn onto his contemporaries in Verrocchio's workshop, Sandro Botticelli, Domenico Ghirlandaio, and Pietro Vannucci – better known as Perugino after his native Perugia. This is a further example of Leonardo's misanthropy and what I consider to be his essential arrogance. It must be remembered that this is a man who is prepared to experiment with his master's painting, and who would later try to pass himself off as an expert military engineer, despite having received no formal training; arrogant indeed. That da Vinci considered himself a superior painter is apparent from his notebooks, where, amongst other things, he chastises Botticelli for his poor handling of perspective. Of course, his reasons for being so critical may well have had as much to do with his feelings of frustration as of superiority. Slightly older and more 'experienced', Verrocchio's assistants, Botticelli and Ghirlandaio both enjoyed Medici patronage. Likewise, Perugino, Leonardo's direct contemporary as one of Verrocchio's apprentices, was later to be among the coterie of artists despatched to Rome to paint the Sistine frescoes, despite being much less talented. To emphasise Leonardo's defensive disdain I have tried to make the other artists sound as ridiculous as possible. For example, Botticelli is described as 'sucking on Lorenzo's tits' (line 253), a reference to the fact that he was Lorenzo de' Medici's favourite painter and is reputed to have dined at his patron's table. The idea of dining and artistic impoverishment is then given a further acid twist when he refers to Perugino's habit of eating too much cabbage – the resulting flatulence from this excess of greens manifesting as his work (lines 259-262). Whether the real Perugino liked cabbage is uncertain, and I must confess that the anecdotal reference is of my own devising. Of course it must be observed that this movement is somewhat anachronistic, for Botticelli and Ghirlandaio did not reach the pinnacle of their success as Medici artists until the 1480s when they came to run highly successful, independent workshops of their own. Neither was Perugino shown any special favours until he was dispatched to Rome, something which occurred after the painting of the *Baptism of Christ.* Nor had he 'gone back/ to Perugia' (lines 257-258) to establish his own *bottega.* Nevertheless, I feel that such temporal liberties are aesthetically justified as they have enabled me to paint a more rounded picture of da Vinci's character and artistic views.

The abuse of Verrocchio and his contemporaries in the first and second movements prepares the way for the subject of the third (lines 264-290). Here Leonardo articulates what he thinks a good painter should focus on in order to create an appealing composition. He is, in effect, psyching himself up; preparing himself to make a break with the stylistic conventions of Verrocchio and the past, and define his own compositional style in the figure of the angel. Indeed, I imagine da Vinci beginning to draw his angel as he 'speaks'. The ideas expressed in this movement are drawn from Leonardo's theories of painting from what later became the *Trattato della pittura*. As Leonardo did not begin to keep his notebooks until his first Milanese period the inclusion of these ideas are once again somewhat anachronistic, although, as with the above, aesthetically justified. That said, while Leonardo may not have begun to write down his ideas until the 1480s, I rather suspect they began growing in his mind during his years in Verrocchio's workshop for, as we have seen, experience was always da Vinci's starting point.

In his *Treatise on Painting* Leonardo places great emphasis on the need for a painter to develop his faculty of seeing and then the skill to translate what he sees into sound draughtsmanship. 'Many are very desirous of learning to draw', he writes,

> and are very fond of it, who are, not withstanding, void of a proper disposition for it. This may be known by their want of perseverance; like boys who draw everything in a hurry, never finishing or shadowing.[59]

This process is gradual and demands great patience, but is vital in order to truly understand 'the lines which distinguish the forms of bodies and their component parts', thus ensuring that 'the proportion of the members…correspond to the whole'. Something which Verrocchio's disproportionate figures clearly lack.[60]

Another recurrent theme throughout the *Treatise* is Leonardo's insistence that a painter should reveal his subject's inner life. According to da Vinci, a good painter should show the 'expressive motion of what passes in the mind of a living figure', thereby avoiding the stale repetition of creating figures that are 'all cast in one and the same mould', something which da Vinci regarded as being 'highly reprehensible', and which can be seen as characterising Verrocchio's style. Looking at the figures of Jesus and the Baptist in *The Baptism of Christ*, one cannot help but feel that Verrocchio has employed the same model.[61]

It is these ideas which I have endeavoured to convey in this movement. In order to reflect the concentration of da Vinci's thoughts, his mental excitation if you will, the tone of this movement is more hieratic than the preceding passages where the voice is markedly demotic. Indeed, there is a rhetorical quality to the lines, as though Leonardo – ever the autodidact – were lecturing himself. This rhetorical quality is conveyed by both the formalistic opening of the stanzas ('Firstly/Secondly') and by the use of repetition:

  A painter *(a good painter)*
should focus on two things.

  Firstly, he should seek the
semblance of form –
drawing out of sketching
  the patience of his eye.
This is vital. For if a painter
cannot see, *truly see*,
  the patterning of lines,
how they curve and shade
the body into light,
  subtly revealing
(yet also concealing) –

if he cannot see,
then what is his appeal?

Secondly, he must show
the life within, performing through
the body the gestures
of the mind.
It's simply not enough
to emulate alone –
a painter must know,
truly know,
the subject of his eye.
This too is vital.

This movement is also of significance to the wider dynamic of the *Anatomy* sequence, for here we see the themes of 'the eye', 'light', and 'the body' reflected in an aesthetic context. Additionally, this movement, with its imagery of the emerging body, also finds reflection in the Caravaggio monologue, thereby providing a photonic link between the two sequences.

Having outlined his aesthetic position, the fourth movement (lines 292-349) sees Leonardo return to both the subject of Verrocchio's artistic limitations and the demotic tone which characterises the majority of the fragment. He criticises both his master's tendency to use stock figures (lines 292-296) and his handling of proportion (lines 298-301), before turning his scorn to the dull effects of tempera (302-305) – the use of eggs in the binding process giving rise to the lines, 'The stale old eggs of a bound/ excrescence' (lines 304-305). It is now that Leonardo begins to muse on the idea of using oil paint, emphasising its popularity with 'the Flemish Masters' (line 307) and the 'lucent warmth' of its effect (line 309), before quoting the passage from Cennini's *Il libro dell'arte* (lines 313-317) where the artist describes the method of preparation.

With this medium in mind, Da Vinci now widens his attack to include Florentines in general, accusing them of being 'so *painfully* conservative' (line 323) that they would never countenance an altarpiece painted with oil (line 334). This is, of course, quite untrue, and as the list of their innovative achievements makes clear (lines 325-332), Leonardo knows this. Florence was one of the great centres of Renaissance culture and, as we have seen, whilst oil painting was uncommon in southern Europe during the fifteenth century it was not unheard of. Indeed, the real focus of his attack is not the Florentines *per se*, but rather Lorenzo de' Medici, the first Citizen of the Republic, and his father, a successful notary of the city; both men whom Leonardo had reason to feel undervalued his genius. Thus once again da Vinci is lashing out at paternal authority figures, his desire to innovate fused with a desire to shock – even though he knows that it is most probably futile (lines 338-339). Nevertheless, the fragment ends on a defiant note. Leonardo *will* use oil, and thereby attempt to assert his independence from Verrocchio, Lorenzo, and his father; from convention, authority, and the past. '[I]t's my angel,' he says, 'Why not?' (lines 347-349).

Key themes: Rebellion; innovation; fragility; the eye; light; the body.

Reflective affinities:

- **'Consider, Salai…' [lines 32-96]**
- **'Force is Spirit…' [lines 107-113]**
- **'…and as well as a musician…' [lines 116-161]**
- **'Force is Spirit…' [lines 164-169]**
- **'Ser Piero, my father…' [lines 205-212]**
- **'And what of the eye?' [lines 221-234]**
- **'For it is among the horrors…' [lines 423-454]**
- **'Ginepro/Ginevra…' [lines 615-616]**
- **'A painter should be solitary…' [lines 668-697]**

- 'Buchi della verità…' [lines 743-754]
- 'A ghost…' [lines 757-764]
- 'The act of coitus…' [lines 768-773]

Negative reflections:

- 'Un libro del cazzo!' [lines 27-29]
- 'It's funny…' [lines 172-202]
- 'Veggio co' be' vostr'occhi un dolce lume…' [lines 215-218]
- 'But when will it be finished…' [lines 352-367]
- 'Welcome to Imola…' [lines 399-419]
- 'As I slumbered in my body…' [lines 599-611]
- 'Nel voler vostro è sol la voglia mia…' [lines 701-706]
- '"Maestro da Vinci"…' [lines 710-740]
- 'Sometimes Heaven…' [lines 778-786]

13. 'But when will it be finished…' [lines 352-367]

This 'radioactive' fragment is spoken through the voice of the Prior of San Donato, and concerns da Vinci's frustrating habit of leaving his commissions *non finito.* The commission in question was for an altarpiece depicting the *Adoration of the Magi* (1481), and the unfinished panel is now regarded as one of da Vinci's masterpieces, although it is likely that the Brothers of San Donato felt somewhat differently at the time.

The Augustan monastery was located at 'Scopeto', a village outside the walls of Florence 'not far from the Prato Gate'. As Nicholl observes, 'it was a rich monastery' and had bought works by the rising star of the art world 'Botticelli'. It was also associated with Ser Piero da Vinci, who had handled the monastery's business affairs since 1479. Indeed, it is highly likely that it was Ser Piero who secured the commission for his son. Since leaving Verrocchio's workshop in 1477 Leonardo had been struggling to establish himself as an independent artist. As White points out,

> Leonardo was many things but efficient businessman he certainly was not, and he had only a sketchy sense of how to provide for himself in a world governed by commercial forces. He heeded little the value of money and let slip offers and commissions as though they meant almost nothing. Yet at the same time, he had no other means of supporting himself.[62]

In light of the above, it seems probable that Ser Piero used his influence with the Brothers of San Donato to get his struggling son the commission. This would certainly account for the strange nature of the contract which was highly prejudicial in the monastery's favour. After all, if the Brothers were going to commission a 'lesser' artist like da Vinci, they would want to get a favourable deal.

'[The contract] stipulated', writes Nicholl,

> that Leonardo should deliver the painting 'within twenty-four months, or at the most within thirty; and in the case of not finishing it he forfeits whatever he has done of it, and it is our right to do whatever we want with it.'[63]

all of which suggests 'that Leonardo already had a reputation for unreliability'. However, one of the strangest elements of the contract was the fact that 'no money was to change hands', rather Leonardo was to be paid in kind. The Brothers of San Donato

> had inherited some land from a financially embarrassed merchant whose will had contained the condition that the monastery could take possession of the land so long as they provided the dowry for his daughter, Lisabetta. Leonardo was offered one-third

> of this estate, but only if he met three conditions: he had to complete the painting within twenty-four [or thirty] months of the commission, Lisabetta's dowry was to become his responsibility, and he had to supply all materials from his own pocket.[64]

That Leonardo agreed to such terms is perhaps indicative of his desperate situation, and if Ser Piero *was* responsible for organising the commission, it cannot have done much for Leonardo's pride to have still been dependent on his father's 'charity'. The only boon was that da Vinci managed to get the 'contract altered after two months so that the monks supplied his materials'.[65]

Leonardo's reason for abandoning the commission in the autumn of 1481 cannot be ascertained with any certainty, however, there are at least two factors which probably contributed to his decision. Firstly, it appears that he found working for the Brothers uncongenial. As Nicholl observes, '[b]y June, three months after the initial agreement, the difficulties of the situation [became] apparent'. He had to ask the monastery to provide Lisabetta's dowry, because he did 'not have the means to pay it', and in order to get enough food to eat and logs for his fire he was compelled to do odd jobs around the monastery, such as 'decorating the monastery clock'; all of which was a far cry from the glamorous career of Sandro Botticelli, who dined with Lorenzo the Magnificent. Secondly, it was around this time that Lorenzo selected his coterie of artists to go to Rome; a coterie which did not include Leonardo (something which, as we have already seen, may have encouraged the artist to quit Florence). Whatever the case, Leonardo abandoned the work in the autumn of 1481 and left for Milan to what must have been the irritation of the Brothers and most probably the embarrassment of his father.[66]

Such is the historical background to this fragment. Although unlikely, given that Leonardo's actions had voided the contract, one might imagine that the disgruntled Prior has followed Leonardo to Milan and is giving him a piece of his mind, reminding him that he owes the commission to his father (lines 364-365) and that he prefers Botticelli (line 367). Another reading, and one less fanciful, is that the Prior is inside Leonardo's head, a manifestation of what may have been his guilt at having abandoned the project and/or his frustration at having only got the commission because of his father. In either case, the fragment serves to emphasise both Leonardo's tendency to leave his works *non finito* and the precarious state of his career towards the end of his first Florentine period.

14. '29th January 1494…' [lines 371-384]

This fragment is almost a direct quotation from the notebooks, and offers an insight into Leonardo's expenditure. As we have seen, da Vinci had little business sense and only a slight regard for the value of money. Nevertheless, as the Anonimo Gaddiano makes clear, he also liked to wear fine clothes and have his hair well groomed. This tendency to live beyond his means is also given comment by Vasari, who remarks in his *Life of Leonardo* that the artist 'owned, one might say, nothing and he worked very little, yet he always kept servants as well as horses'. How he afforded such things is uncertain. Even when he was working for the Duke of Milan during his first Milanese period, Leonardo had to send frequent reminders to his patron to make sure that his modest salary was paid. One possible explanation is that da Vinci lived on credit – something which may throw a different light on his frequently peripatetic lifestyle. True financial security only arrived during his final years at Amboise when he received a generous pension from his patron Francis I.[67]

My reason for including this account list is twofold. Firstly, it draws Leonardo's somewhat extravagant lifestyle into focus; he is buying new clothes, rings and precious stones, as well as supporting both Salai and the woman Caterina (who may, or may not, have been his mother). Secondly, the account list represents a form of self-anatomisation, for here the inner workings of Leonardo's domestic life are laid bare. The additions which I have made to the original are very slight. I have added the word 'pink' to the first entry in order to emphasise (in accordance with the Anonimo Gaddiano) Leonardo's somewhat dandified manner of dressing. Likewise, the melancholic 'Life is getting expensive' (line 384) is also of my own devising, and corresponds to both the pleas for money which Leonardo was making to *il Moro* during this period *and* to the subsequent melancholic utterances in the *Anatomy* sequence.

Key themes: Lifestyle; money; melancholy; anatomy.

Reflective affinities:

- 'Ser Piero, my father…' [lines 205-212]
- 'For it is among the horrors…' [lines 423-454]
- 'And the Great Bird shall rise…' [lines 478-576]
- 'O time…' [lines 586-596]
- 'Letter of Authorisation…' [lines 618-634]
- 'God's sake!' [lines 638-644]
- 'A ghost…' [lines 757-764]
- 'I thought I was learning…' [lines 790-794]

Negative reflections:

- 'Un libro del cazzo!' [lines 27-29]
- 'It's funny…' [lines 172-202]
- 'But when will it be finished…' [lines 352-367]
- 'Welcome to Imola…' [lines 399-419]
- 'As I slumbered in my body…' [lines 599-611]
- '"Maestro da Vinci"…' [lines 710-740]
- 'Sometimes Heaven…' [lines 778-786]

15. 'The old man told me…' [lines 387-396]

This fragment concerns Leonardo's dissection of the centenarian at the Florentine Hospital of Santa Maria Nuova in late 1507, and reflects his emotional detachment in handling the bodies of the dead. Consequently, I have given this fragment the same matter-of-fact tone which da Vinci accords the incident in his notebooks. (See analysis of Fragment 8).

Key themes: Anatomy; emotional detachment; old age.

Reflective affinities:

- **'Consider, Salai…' [lines 32-96]**
- **'Force is Spirit…' [lines 107-113]**
- **'Force is Spirit…' [lines 164-169]**
- **'For it is among the horrors…' [lines 423-454]**
- **'And the Great Bird shall rise…' [lines 478-576]**
- **'O time…' [lines 586-596]**
- **'Letter of Authorisation…' [lines 618-634]**
- **'The act of coitus…' [lines 768-773]**
- **'I thought I was learning…' [lines 790-794]**

Negative reflections:

- **'In me la morte…' [lines 99-104]**
- **'It's funny…' [lines 172-202]**
- **'Welcome to Imola…' [lines 399-419]**
- **'Necromancy!' [lines 458-464]**
- **'As I slumbered in my body…' [lines 599-611]**
- **'Tell me, di Credi…' [lines 798-799]**

16. 'Welcome to Imola…' [lines 399-419]

This is the second of the 'radioactive' fragments to be spoken through the voice of Salai, and concerns the winter he spent with his master at Imola, stronghold of the

notorious Cesare Borgia. The illegitimate son of Pope Alexander VI and his mistress Vanozza Cattanei, Cesare had resigned his cardinalate in 1498, following the death of his younger brother Giovanni the previous year, to become 'Captain of the Church' and reclaim the Papal States of the Romagna. A political marriage to Charlotte d'Albret, the cousin of King Louis XII of France, in 1499 (from whence he gained the title 'Duke of Valentinois' and the Italian name '*il Valentino*') had enabled him to raise a sufficient military force for his campaign. By the 'end of 1500 he was the master of Imola, Forlì, Pesaro, Rimini and Cesena', and when 'Faenza fell to him in [the] spring [of] 1501' he assumed the title, 'Duke of the Romagna'.[68]

Cesare, whose motto, 'recalling his imperial namesake', proclaimed 'Caesar or nothing', was a profoundly dangerous man. 'Totally amoral, vengeful, treacherous and deceitful', *il Valentino* had the unpleasant habit of garrotting those of his circle whom he suspected of betrayal. He was also believed to have poisoned his brother-in-law and to have committed incest with his equally notorious sister, Lucrezia. With this in mind, it is hardly surprising that he should have been the inspiration behind Niccolò Machiavelli's infamous treatise, *The Prince*. What *is* perhaps surprising, given Cesare's lethal reputation, is that Leonardo da Vinci should have found himself working for him in the summer of 1502. The precise nature of their first meeting is uncertain. Leonardo may have met Borgia when he rode into Milan with Louis XII and the French army in 1499, thereby putting an end to Sforza's rule and instigating the most peripatetic phase of da Vinci's career. More likely, however, given the three-year delay before Leonardo entered his service, it may have been Machiavelli, Florentine envoy to Cesare's court and da Vinci's friend who introduced them. Whatever the case, on the 18th August 1502 'an impressively florid document was drawn up', which empowered Leonardo as Borgia's 'architect and general engineer' to conduct a military survey of his states:

> Caesar Borgia of France, by the grace of God Duke of Romagna and Valence, Prince of the Adriatic, Lord of Piombino etc., also Gonfalonier and Captain General of the Holy Roman Church: to all our lieutenants, castellans, captains, *condottieri*, officials, soldiers and subjects to whom this notice is presented. We order and command that the bearer hereof, our most excellent and well-beloved architect and general engineer Leonardo da Vinci, who by our commission is to survey the places and fortresses of our states, should be provided with all such assistance as the occasion demands and his judgement deems fit.[69]

Thus Leonardo, most likely with Salai in tow, set off on tour, and his notebooks become filled with jottings concerning the creation of maps of Cesare's territory, the strength of his fortresses, and improved designs for the bastions of city walls. He also made a characteristically misanthropic statement about the Romagna, calling it 'the realm of all the dullards'. To an extent, da Vinci had achieved under Borgia what he had been denied under *il Moro* – he had transcended being a painter and become a 'military engineer', and this may account for why he was prepared to work for such a dangerous man. That said, the self-proclaimed pacifist, for all his surveying, still did not see any of his war machines realised.[70]

By the Autumn of 1502 things had begun to go wrong for Borgia. A group of 'malcontent captains' amongst his ranks, led by Vitellozzo Vitelli, had begun to ferment an 'armed rebellion', and he found himself 'holed up' in the fortress town of Imola with those soldiers who had remained loyal. Machiavelli was also there, and so was Leonardo. As Nicholl observes, the atmosphere must have been one of 'nervy suspicion', and it is little wonder that Machiavelli made frequent pleas to the *Signoria* of Florence to be recalled, all of which were denied. Leonardo, by contrast, seems to have been remarkably unconcerned by the situation and, whilst his friend was fretting, he was busy making his famous map of Imola, which, by early sixteenth-century standards, is a cartographical wonder.[71]

In this fragment I have placed Salai firmly in the Machiavelli camp, which, given the conditions, seems the much more sympathetic position. 'Welcome to Imola', he says sarcastically, before adding 'Why the *fuck/* are we here?' (lines 399-400). Indeed, the language of the opening stanza is visceral, and is intended to offer a grim alternative to da Vinci's 'beautiful' map. He speaks of 'a gut of tangled streets,/ all shit and knives…' (lines 400-401) and of 'the thick breath of soldiers/ sweating on our skin' (lines 403-404). In light of the extreme distaste which Salai expressed for the act of dissection in his previous fragment, it seemed appropriate that his rather negative description of Imola should have a strongly anatomical flavour. Having expressed his negative view of Imola, Salai then turns his attention to Borgia and his 'Caesarean' exploits (lines 409-413), listing himself and Leonardo among the conquests (line 413). The final stanza sees Salai meditating on the 'sick' nature of power, likening it, and by extension Borgia, to a form of venereal disease with which both he and his master have become infected. This is, in effect, a criticism of Leonardo's seemingly immoral fascination with force, and his willingness to 'prostitute' himself to anyone who will support his dreams. Yet Salai also includes himself in the criticism; he too is to blame, for he evidently cannot bring himself to abandon his master, however much he may disapprove of his lifestyle.[72]

17. 'For it is among the horrors…' [lines 423-454]

This fragment provides the direct 'material' counterpart to Salai's previous ruminations on anatomy, viewing the dissection from da Vinci's perspective. A large proportion of this fragment is based on one of Leonardo's notebooks, now known as the *Windsor Manuscript*, in which the artist explains how many people are deterred from seeking the

truth of the human body, either because they 'fear…passing the night hours in the company of corpses' whose flesh is 'quartered and flayed and horrible to behold', or because they 'lack the skill in drawing', something which is 'essential' if one is going to achieve an accurate 'representation' of what one sees. I imagine da Vinci, so absorbed in what he is doing, to be completely oblivious to Salai's distaste, and in between the stanzas of his 'lecture' I have placed practical interjections, which, by implication, seem to be asking Salai to do something unpleasant, such as hold back a piece of flesh, or one of Leonardo's bloodied instruments. This fragment also answers Salai's questions, 'Was she alone when she died?/ Did she love?' (see Fragment 8, lines 199 and 200), by revealing that the woman was with child (line 454). Additionally, this information also links the fragment with Leonardo's recorded study of a human embryo. True to form, da Vinci is dispassionate in his approach, simply stating that the discovery of her pregnancy is 'Interesting' (line 453).[73]

Key themes: Anatomy; courage in the face of the unknown; artistic skill; motherhood.

Reflective affinities:

- **'It might be a dream…' [lines 9-24]**
- **'Consider, Salai…' [lines 32-96]**
- **'Force is Spirit…' [lines 107-113]**
- **'Force is Spirit' [lines 164-169]**
- **'Mmm…typical Verrocchio…' [lines 237-349]**
- **'29th January 1494…' [lines 371-384]**
- **'The old man told me…' [lines 387-396]**
- **'A riddle, my Lords…' [lines 467-475]**
- **'And the Great Bird shall rise…' [lines 478-576]**
- **'O time…' [lines 586-596]**
- **'Letter of Authorisation…' [lines 618-634]**
- **'A ghost…' [lines 757-764]**

- 'The act of coitus…' [lines 768-773]
- 'I thought I was learning…' [lines 790-794]

Negative reflections:

- 'Un libro del cazzo!' [lines 27-29]
- 'In me la morte…' [lines 99-104]
- 'It's funny…' [lines 172-202]
- 'Welcome to Imola…' [lines 399-419]
- 'Necromancy!' [lines 458-464]
- 'As I slumbered in my body…' [lines 599-611]

18. 'Necromancy!' [lines 458-464]

This 'radioactive' fragment concerns the time during Leonardo's Roman period when his 'nocturnal anatomical researches' led to accusations of necromancy. Summoned before Pope Leo X, Leonardo was 'banned' from practising dissections on unlicensed cadavers. As we have previously observed, it was probably only his Medici patronage which saved his life, for Leo X, whose name before becoming Pope had been Giovanni de' Medici, was the brother of his patron, Giuliano, Duke of Nemours. The current fragment takes the form of a brief dialogue in which da Vinci cannot get a word in edgeways; thus, although Leonardo speaks, the superior power of the Pope renders the fragment 'radioactive', and once again shows da Vinci at the mercy of powerful father figures.[74]

19. 'A riddle, my Lords…' [lines 467-475]

This fragment is based on one of Leonardo's riddles, or '*profezie*', which he wrote during his time at the court of Ludovico Sforza, and which reveals another aspect of the artist's complex, often contradictory character: Leonardo the entertainer. My choice of this particular *profezie* was founded on what I saw as its potential for multiple significations. As Nicholl observes, '[o]ne of the fascinations of [Leonardo's riddles] is their tendency to communicate unexpected meanings beyond the answer'. In light of this, I interpret the image of bees having their honey stolen, and being drowned by those fearing their revenge, in a number of ways. Firstly, we can see reflected the idea of Leonardo's broken home, signified by the implied invasion of the hive by those stealing the honey. Secondly, the implied image of the ransacked hive, itself a highly organised, organic structure, can be interpreted as signifying the dissection of the human body. Thirdly, the image of drowning can be seen as reflecting both Leonardo's fascination with water and with his misanthropy, for not only does mankind steal from nature, but it also destroys what it fears and/or does not understand. Fourthly, we have through the image of bees the idea of flight, something which, as we have seen, preoccupied Leonardo throughout his life and consequently recurs in various guises throughout the *Anatomy* sequence.[75]

It must be observed that I have made certain changes/additions to da Vinci's original *profezie*:

> And many will be robbed of their stores and their food, and will be cruelly submerged and drowned by folks devoid of reason. O justice of God! Why dost thou not awake to behold thy creatures thus abused?[76]

One of the most significant changes is that I have abandoned the pseudo-prophetic structure and made it a straightforward riddle. My reason for doing this was that I did not want to confuse the reader into thinking that Leonardo was some sort of Italian Nostradamus. I have also removed the rather theatrical plea to God in the interests of concentration. By transforming the *profezie* into a riddle it seemed necessary to keep the language tight and avoid florid hyperbole. I have also provided those 'folk devoid of reason' with a reason for their murderous actions – namely a desire to avoid being stung. This in no way diminishes what Leonardo sees as the criminality of their action, for they justly fear revenge for what they have done. On a technical level, it facilitates a smoother passage of verse and has enabled me to employ a little piece of word play ('The sting of revenge' [line 472]), something which I feel Leonardo, himself fond of the occasional linguistic game, would have appreciated.

Key themes: Courtliness; domestic separation; anatomy; water; misanthropy; fear; vengeance; flight.

Reflective affinities:

- 'It might be a dream…' [lines 9-24]
- 'Consider, Salai…' [lines 32-96]
- 'Force is Spirit…' [lines 107-113]
- '…and as well as a musician…' [lines 116-161]
- 'Force is Spirit' [lines 164-169]
- 'Mmm…typical Verrocchio…' [lines 237-349]
- '29th January 1494…' [lines 371-384]
- 'The old man told me…' [lines 387-396]
- 'And the Great Bird shall rise…' [lines 478-576]
- 'O time…' [lines 586-596]
- 'Letter of Authorisation…' [lines 618-634]
- 'A ghost…' [lines 757-764]
- 'I thought I was learning…' [lines 790-794]

Negative reflections:

- 'Un libro del cazzo!' [lines 27-29]
- 'In me la morte…' [lines 99-104]
- 'It's funny…' [lines 172-202]
- 'Welcome to Imola…' [lines 399-419]
- 'Necromancy!' [lines 458-464]

- 'Volo con le vostr'ale senza piume…' [lines 580-583]
- 'As I slumbered in my body…' [lines 599-611]
- '"Maestro da Vinci"…' [lines 710-740]
- 'Tell me, di Credi…' [lines 798-799]

20. 'And the Great Bird shall rise…' [lines 478-576]

This fragment is concerned with Leonardo's investigations into the mechanics of flight and his design for an 'ornithopter' – a flying machine modelled on the paradigm of a bird. As we have seen, the concept of flight was very important to Leonardo and preoccupied him throughout his life. Indeed, da Vinci's obsession with birds and the action of flight is an intriguing one and has yielded many divergent readings. White, for example, proposes that 'the reason Leonardo expended so much energy in attempting to fly came from some convoluted wish to escape'. He literally wanted to fly away from his problems; something which would fit with both his tendency to leave his commissions *non finito* and the peripatetic nature of his life.[77]

Kemp, by contrast, sees Leonardo's apparent wish to take to the skies as part of his desire to 'become a "second nature"'; to create, through a meticulous understanding of Nature's laws, his own bird and thus transcend the myth of 'Daedalus'. Certainly, the notebooks reveal an almost mythological conception of his vision, as this passage from the *Turin Codex* makes clear:

> The big bird will take its first flight above the back of the Great Cecero, filling the universe with amazement, filling all the chronicles with its fame, and bringing eternal glory to the nest where it was born.[78]

Once again Leonardo wants to shock the world; he wants 'to work miracles'; he wants *fame*. This may seem strange in the light of Leonardo's apparent failure to get any of his flying machines off the ground, but as we previously observed, this had as much to do with the technological limitations of his times as with the integrity of his endeavours. To be sure, the above passage from the *Turin Codex* may even be a veiled reference to a proposed test flight. As Nicholl observes,

> The 'big bird' is certainly Leonardo's flying-machine [and] the announcement seems to mean that he was planning a trial flight of the machine from the summit of Monte Ceceri, near Fiesole, just north of Florence. He spells it 'Cecero', which is an old Florentine word for swan – a conjunction of meanings that would be congenial to Leonardo: a good omen, an emblematic connection. A jotting dated 14th March 1505 finds him sky-gazing on the road to Fiesole: 'the *cortone*, a bird of prey which I saw going to Fiesole, above the place of the Barbiga'. This adds a touch of specificity to the possible flight of the 'big bird', but it is curious that there is no independent record of his momentous event, no letter-writer or diarist who mentions it: either it is a well-kept secret or it never happened.[79]

Certainly, without firmer evidence, whether da Vinci ever attempted to test his ornithopter must remain a point of conjecture.

What is certain, however, is that Leonardo based his design upon close empirical observation. His notebooks reveal the studied attention he paid to the action of birds in the air, observing the manner in which they use their wings to gain lift, how 'the lines of movements made by birds as they rise are of two kinds' (either 'spiral' or 'rectilinear and curved'), and how 'the speed of the bird is checked by the opening and spreading out of its tail'. Here we also see the theory of holistic Nature in practice, for Leonardo's radical understanding of the air resistance encountered by a bird derived from his knowledge of the effect of water on a

swimmer. Thus, by a process of analogy, Leonardo came to understand that '[s]wimming illustrates the method of flying and shows that the largest weight finds most resistance in the air'. In addition to external observation and analogy, Leonardo also dissected birds in order to better understand their design, all of which led him to conclude that:

> **A bird is an instrument working according to mathematical law, which instrument it is the capacity of man to reproduce with all its movements but not with as much strength, though it is deficient only in power of maintaining equilibrium. We may therefore say that such an instrument constructed by man is lacking in nothing except the life of the bird, and this life must needs be imitated by the life of man. The life which resides in the bird's members will without doubt better obey their needs than will that of man which is separated from them and especially in the almost imperceptible movements which preserve equilibrium. But since we see that the bird is equipped for many sensitive varieties of movement, we are able from this experience to deduce that the most obvious of these movements will be capable of being comprehended by man's understanding, and that he will to a great extent be able to provide against the destruction of that instrument of which he has made himself life and guide.**[80]

By careful observation and anatomically correct imitation Leonardo believed it was possible for a man to partake in the life of a bird and fly. Indeed, the seriousness of his intentions can be seen from the level of thought which da Vinci put into his ornithopter's design. For example, in order to reduce the problem of equilibrium and provide a strong surface of resistance, Leonardo proposed that feathers should be rejected in favour of a membranous covering (probably to be made out of canvas) inspired by

the wings of a bat. Once again we can see da Vinci taking a holistic approach, and the 'big bird' could equally have become the 'big bat'. Yet for all the effort that went into its conception, the tragedy of the ornithopter is that even if Leonardo had tested his design, he would never have got it off the ground. As we have previously discussed, the human occupant could never have generated enough power to propel the machine fast enough to gain the lift it required, and whilst Leonardo's empirical methods are laudable in the context of early-sixteenth-century thought, literal imitation would simply not have been enough. For Leonardo, flight was to remain a childhood dream; a symbol of destiny and *not* a scientific reality.

In this fragment I have reflected Leonardo's investigations into flight from both a symbolic and scientific perspective. The opening five lines are inspired by his visionary utterances from the *Turin Codex*, however, as with the riddle, I have made certain changes. Rather than using the term 'big bird' – something which has unfortunate connotations with *Sesame Street* – I have instead opted for 'Great Bird', as this carries the same associations of size, does not signify a children's television character, and also adds to the overall impression of grandeur. In order to underline the geographical context of this passage, I have referred to 'Monte' rather than 'Great Cecero' (line 479). My reason for retaining 'Cecero' rather than using the more accurate 'Ceceri' being that I wanted to preserve Leonardo's original wordplay. To emphasise the grand eloquence of this passage I have used uppercase line starts, and the heavy repetition of the words 'and' and 'shall' endows the movement with a decidedly rhetorical quality:

> <u>And</u> the Great Bird <u>shall</u> rise
> Over Monte Cecero.
> <u>And</u> the Universe <u>shall</u> wonder.
> <u>And</u> eternal fame <u>shall</u> alight
> On the nest where it was born!

In anticipation of what he dreams will be his great triumph, Leonardo is trying to sound impressive.

The remainder of the fragment is designed to sharply juxtapose, both structurally and tonally, with the passage above. Having given forth in so 'poetic' a manner, da Vinci now begins to dissect this position by engaging with the scientific realities underpinning his dream. Here I have been selective. It would have been unfeasible to cover *every* aspect of da Vinci's thinking on birds and his design for the ornithopter. Rather I have endeavoured to give the *impression* of his thinking, focusing on key elements, such as the bird's lines of movement in the air (lines 508-510), man's apparent deficiency in sustaining equilibrium (lines 493-494), and the holistic parallel between swimming and flying (lines 521-522). In terms of structure and tone I have endeavoured to make the poetry feel 'scientific', incorporating abbreviations ('cf.', 'NB', 'etc'), injunctions ('*Think*', '*Observe*'), equations ('Motion of flight/ = motion of swimming' [lines 524-525]), and even a crossing out (line 554). This is designed, not only to juxtapose with the 'visionary' sequence which precedes it, but also to imitate something of the linguistic texture of the notebooks, for here, as we have seen, ideas form in quick succession, are frequently repeated, and are occasionally fragmentary. Indeed, here we see the mind of da Vinci in motion, with thoughts forming, metamorphosing, and falling away. The jerky nature of the lines, compared with the smooth flow of the 'Great Bird' passage, is also intended to imitate the artificial movement of the ornithopter's wings.

Key themes: Dreams; fame; flight; anatomy; holistic methodology; becoming a second Nature.

Reflective affinities:

- **'It might be a dream…' [lines 9-24]**
- **'Consider, Salai…' [lines 32-96]**

- 'Force is Spirit…' [lines 107-113]
- 'Force is Spirit…' [lines 164-169]
- 'Mmm…typical Verrocchio…' [lines 237-349]
- '29th January 1494…' [lines 371-384]
- 'The old man told me…' [lines 387-396]
- 'For it is among the horrors…' [lines 423-454]
- 'A riddle, my Lords…' [lines 467-475]
- 'O time…' [lines 586-596]
- 'I thought I was learning…' [lines 790-794]

Negative reflections:

- 'In me la morte…' [lines 99-104]
- 'It's funny…' [lines 172-202]
- 'Welcome to Imola…' [lines 399-419]
- 'Necromancy!' [lines 458-464]
- 'Volo con le vostr'ale senza piume…' [lines 580-583]
- 'As I slumbered in my body…' [lines 599-611]
- '"Maestro da Vinci"…' [lines 710-740]
- 'Tell me, di Credi…' [lines 798-799]

21. 'Volo con le vostr'ale senza piume…' [lines 580-583]

This is the third of the Michelangelo citations, and is once again drawn from the love sonnet which the artist wrote to Tommaso dei Cavalieri in 1534 (see analysis of Fragment 10). It may be translated as:

> Though lacking feathers I fly with your wings; with your mind I am always carried to heaven; on your decision turns whether I am red or pale, cold in the sun, warm in the coldest mists.[81]

Here we see the image of flight as a metaphor for romantic love. The above thereby creates a 'radioactive' counter-voice to Leonardo's scientific treatment of flight in the previous fragment.

22. 'O time…' [lines 586-596]

This fragment, inspired by a passage from the *Codex Atlanticus*, embodies the melancholic strain in Leonardo's personality, reflects his learning of Latin, and identifies the body within the temporal confines of old age and death:

> O Time, consumer of all things! O envious age, thou destroyest all things and devourest all things with the hard teeth of the years little by little, in slow death. Helen, when she looked in the mirror and saw the withered wrinkles which old age had made in her face wept and wondered why she had been twice carried away. O Time, consumer of all things! O envious age, whereby all things are consumed![82]

One of the most interesting features of the above is that it appears to have been directly appropriated from Ovid's *Metamorphoses* (8 CE):

> Helen weeps,
> And wonders why she twice was stolen for love.
> Time, the devourer, and the jealous years
> With long corruption ruin all the world
> And waste all things in slow mortality.[83]

It is easy to see why Ovid's poem would have appealed to Leonardo, for the epic is concerned with 'bodies changed to other forms', something which can be seen reflected in his meditations on force ('a changer of bodies' – see analysis of Fragments 5 and 7), and in his dissection of corpses – an activity which, in effect, metamorphosed the bodies of the dead into a diagrammatic understanding of the living (see analysis of Fragments 8 and 17).[84]

I have divided the fragment into two quatrains and a singlet. In keeping with Leonardo's 'translation' of Ovid I have made the abstract rumination on time the subject of the opening stanza. Here I have stripped away some of the more florid aspects of the language ('thou destroyest', etc) to increase the impact of the passage, which I interpret as reflecting Leonardo's desire for knowledge in the face of a certain, and ever-degenerating mortality. To be sure, I debated whether to change 'all things' to 'me' in the third line, thus making the stanza overtly self-reflexive. However, metrical considerations aside, I decided to retain Leonardo's original sense, as the change would have moved the text away from its Ovidian paradigm, and thus have diminished the passage's potential for multiple significations.

The second stanza focuses the abstract rumination on time onto a single person, Helen of Troy. Indeed, Helen, the dangerously beautiful woman who inspired the Trojan War (hence my description of her beauty as 'violent' [line 592]), seems to be a potent Leonardoesque archetype. Firstly, one must remember Leonardo's general dislike of women. As White observes, Leonardo 'displayed a markedly skewed view of women, especially in a sexual context', and those drawings of *grotesques*,

> in which he places gruesomely ugly male heads upon the shoulders of sumptuously dressed and bejewelled women [demonstrate] a misogynist streak...[85]

All of which accords with Homer's portrayal of Helen in *The Iliad* (c.720 BCE), where the most beautiful woman in the world is often referred to disparagingly as 'bitch' and 'whore'. Secondly, Helen, in her guise as aged whore, subverts the Platonic notion of beauty as both an eternal ideal (the concept of το καλόν) and as being synonymous with a person's inner virtue; something which may put us in mind, both of Leonardo's rejection of conventional wisdom, *and* of his mother, Caterina. Thirdly, it is worth bearing in

mind that Helen was 'hatched' from an egg after Zeus lay with her mother Leda in the guise of a swan, and that this mythological story, rich with the themes of birds and illegitimacy, was the subject of one of Leonardo's lost paintings. Fourthly, we may see, in the person of Helen, Leonardo himself, a man forced to 'prostitute his talents' to powerful patrons and whose own physical beauty as a young man is remarked on by both the Anonimo Gaddiano and Vasari. Thus, I feel it is Leonardo, wearing the mask of Helen, who weeps for what he has lost, and, in a lifetime of beginnings, failed to achieve (line 596).[86]

Key themes: Time; mortality; metamorphosis; Classical learning; reaction against received wisdom; war; melancholy; women; beauty; virtue; self-worth; achievement.

Reflective affinities:

- **'It might be a dream…' [lines 9-24]**
- **'Consider, Salai…' [lines 32-96]**
- **'Force is Spirit…' [lines 107-113]**
- **'…and as well as a musician…' [lines 116-161]**
- **'Force is Spirit…' [lines 164-169]**
- **'Ser Piero, my father…' [lines 205-212]**
- **'And what of the eye?' [lines 221-234]**
- **'Mmm…typical Verrocchio…' [lines 237-349]**
- **'29th January 1494…' [lines 371-384]**
- **'The old man told me…' [lines 387-396]**
- **'And the Great Bird shall rise…' [lines 478-576]**
- **'Ginepro/Ginevra…' [lines 615-616]**
- **'Letter of Authorisation…' [lines 618-634]**
- **'silk tears the air…' [lines 654-665]**
- **'A painter should be solitary…' [lines 668-697]**
- **'A ghost…' [lines 757-764]**
- **'The act of coitus…' [lines 768-773]**

- 'I thought I was learning…' [lines 790-794]

Negative reflections:

- 'Un libro del cazzo!' [lines 27-29]
- 'In me la morte…' [lines 99-104]
- 'It's funny…' [lines 172-202]
- 'Veggio co' be' vostr'occhi un dolce lume…' [lines 215-218]
- 'But when will it be finished…' [lines 352-367]
- 'Welcome to Imola…' [lines 399-419]
- 'Necromancy!' [lines 458-464]
- 'Volo con le vostr'ale senza piume…' [lines 580-583]
- 'As I slumbered in my body…' [lines 599-611]
- 'Nel voler vostro è sol la voglia mia…' [lines 701-706]
- '"Maestro da Vinci"…' [lines 710-740]
- 'Sometimes Heaven…' [lines 778-786]
- 'Tell me, di Credi…' [lines 798-799]

23. 'As I slumbered in my body…' [lines 599-611]

This 'radioactive' fragment is based upon the *Corpus Hermeticum*, a mystical collection of writings that were believed by Leonardo's contemporaries to have been written by the ancient sage, Hermes Trismegistus before the time of Moses. It was, in fact, most probably written in the fourth century of our era, for its doctrines are markedly Neoplatonic in character; something which made them appeal to the Neoplatonic intellectuals of fifteenth-century Florence.

The manuscript first came to prominence in 1460, when a monk by the name of 'Leonardo of Pistoia' presented the work, which was written in Greek, to Cosimo de' Medici, the grandfather of Lorenzo the Magnificent and himself a patron of learning and the arts. During the early Renaissance knowledge of Greek was limited and so

Cosimo handed the manuscript to the scholar Marsilio Ficino. Ficino, who had been engaged on the Herculean task of translating the 'complete dialogues of the divine Plato' into Latin, was told to give the 'new' manuscript priority because, in keeping with the Renaissance belief that the older something was the more important, Cosimo believed the *Corpus Hermeticum* to be 'more significant' than Plato. It was not until the seventeenth century that the age and authority of the work came to be challenged. In Leonardo's day it was at the unassailable pinnacle of intellectual importance.[87]

As one may expect, the work presents a profoundly spiritual and disembodied view of the human condition, and its treatment of 'light', as a mystical form of realisation, is far removed from the scientific understanding of seeing promoted by Leonardo in his notebooks. Thus, it is the extremity of its removal from da Vinci's materialistic, embodied approach to existence which makes the *Corpus Hermeticum* such an excellent 'radioactive' counter-voice; something further enhanced by its status as a piece of received wisdom, and by its close association with the Medicis of Leonardo's first Florentine period.[88]

I have based this fragment on the opening passages of the *Corpus Hermeticum*, in which Hermes Trismegistus describes his first encounter with Poimandres, the *Nous*, or 'mind', of the Supreme Reality, because here the Neoplatonic treatment of the body and light are most succinctly expressed:

> 1. Once, when my mind had become intent on the things which are, and my understanding was raised to a great height, while my bodily senses were withdrawn as in sleep, when men are weighed down by too much food or by the fatigue of the body, it seemed that someone immensely great of infinite dimensions happened to call my name and said to me:

> 'What do you wish to hear and behold, and having beheld what do you wish to learn and know?'
>
> 2. 'Who are you?' said I.
> He said, 'I am Poimandres the Nous of the Supreme. I know what you wish and am with you everywhere.'
>
> 3. 'I wish to learn,' said I, 'the things that are and understand their nature and to know God. O how I wish to hear these things!'
> He spoke to me again. 'Hold in your *Nous* all that you wish to learn and I will teach you.'
>
> 4. When he had thus spoken, he changed in form and forthwith, upon the instant, all things opened up before me; and I beheld a boundless view. All had become light…[89]

Unlike the previous fragment, which sees Helen of Troy trapped in her body, subject to time and decay, here Hermes Trismegistus slumbers in his body and is freed into the light of eternity.

24. 'Ginepro/Ginevra…' [lines 615-616]

This fragment was inspired by the reverse side of a panel painting produced by Leonardo during the late 1470s when, as we have seen, he was a struggling young artist in Florence. The portrait on the front side of the panel depicts Ginevra de' Benci, and was originally thought to have been painted to celebrate her wedding to Luigi de Bernardo Niccolini in 1474. However, more recently, art historians have come to date the painting between 1478 and 1480, and connect the commission not with her husband Luigi, but with the 'brilliant but rackety Venetian diplomat Bernardo Bembo' who, after his arrival in Florence in 1475, 'swiftly threw himself into a highly public "Platonic" affair with Ginevra'. As Nicholl explains,

> Such an affair was permissible: he was, within the conventions of the day, her *cavaliere servente*, though there are suggestions that their relationship strained against the boundaries of chastity...[90]

Indeed, the questionable nature of the relationship was such that the Florentine humanist, Cristoforo Landino, wrote a satirical poem about it

> joking that only two letters of her name needed to be changed for her to become one with her lover, 'and though once she was Bencia, her name will be Bembia.'[91]

It is in this context that the painting on the reverse side of the panel can be best understood, and shows Leonardo indulging in similar wordplay. What we see is 'a juniper-branch surrounded by a wreath composed of laurel and palm' and a scroll bearing the inscription '*Virtutem forma decorat*'. As the art historian Frank Zöllner observes, 'the juniper was a symbol of female virtue [and] the Italian name 'ginepro' was not unrelated to the name of the sitter, Ginevra'. Likewise, 'the laurel branches and palm fronds...are associated with Bernardo Bembo...for both are featured in his own personal arms', thus making it extremely likely that it was Bembo, and not Luigi, 'who commissioned the painting'. The Latin inscription can be translated as 'The form adorns virtue', expressing, as Nicholl explains, 'the Platonic-Petrarchan commonplace that outward physical beauty embodies inner spiritual virtue'.[92]

In light of the circumstances surrounding Ginevra and Bembo's relationship I am inclined to read Leonardo's iconographical game as somewhat ironic, for Ginevra, whilst beautiful, seems to have been of questionable virtue. Consequently, I have composed this fragment of the words 'Ginepro/Ginevra' (line 615) and the Latin inscription (line

616), thereby providing a 'material' counterpart to the Neoplatonic utterances of the previous fragment, and a further reflection of the ideas expressed in the sequence beginning *'O time…'* [lines 586-596].

Key themes: Beauty; virtue; wordplay; ironic subversion of received wisdom.

Reflective affinities:

- 'Consider, Salai…' [lines 32-96]
- 'Ser Piero, my father…' [lines 205-212]
- 'Mmm…typical Verrocchio…' [lines 237-349]
- 'O time…' [lines 586-596]
- 'A painter should be solitary…' [lines 668-697]
- 'Buchi della verità…' [lines 743-754]
- 'A ghost…' [lines 757-764]
- 'The act of coitus…' [lines 768-773]

Negative reflections:

- 'It's funny…' [lines 172-202]
- 'Veggio co' be' vostr'occhi un dolce lume…' [lines 215-218]
- 'Welcome to Imola…' [lines 399-419]
- 'As I slumbered in my body…' [lines 599-611]
- 'Sometimes Heaven…' [lines 778-786]

25. 'Letter of Authorisation…' [lines 618-634]

This fragment provides the 'material' counterpart to Salai's *'Welcome to Imola…'* sequence (lines 399-419), and is set during da Vinci's tour of the Romagna during the summer of 1502. Here I have composed my own version of Leonardo's letter of authorisation (see analysis of Fragment 16), stripping away some of Borgia's excessive list of titles and trying to give the lines a smooth, almost rhythmical cadence. My reason for writing it in 'prose' was that I wanted to distinguish it from Leonardo's voice. The use of a different font is also designed to heighten its 'otherness'. In this fragment Leonardo is presenting his letter of authorisation to the sentry of one of Borgia's fortifications, demanding that they 'open up' (line 634). I imagine that after years of taking orders from his patrons, da Vinci would have rather enjoyed giving them. Indeed, as White observes,

> It seems to have been an immensely satisfying time for Leonardo; his first period of employment in which he was not required to decorate royal chambers or make toys for a fickle ruler...[93]

Salai may not have liked working for Cesare, but Leonardo appears to have found the arrangement most satisfactory. The unusual spelling of 'Borgia' as 'Borges' (line 633) is taken from Leonardo's notebooks, and is most probably a nod to Cesare's French connections.

Key themes: Power/force; military engineering.

Reflective affinities:

- 'Consider, Salai...' [lines 32-96]
- 'Force is Spirit...' [lines 107-113]
- '...and as well as a musician...' [lines 116-161]
- 'Force is Spirit...' [lines 164-169]
- 'Ser Piero, my father...' [lines 205-212]
- 'Mmm...typical Verrocchio...' [lines 237-349]
- '29th January 1494...' [lines 371-384]
- 'The old man told me...' [lines 387-396]
- 'For it is among the horrors...' [lines 423-454]
- 'A riddle, my Lords...' [lines 467-475]
- 'And the Great Bird shall rise...' [lines 478-576]
- 'O time...' [lines 586-596]
- 'silk tears the air...' [lines 654-665]

- 'The act of coitus...' [lines 768-773]
- 'I thought I was learning...' [lines 790-794]

Negative reflections:

- 'In me la morte...' [lines 99-104]
- 'It's funny...' [lines 172-202]
- 'But when will it be finished...' [lines 352-367]
- 'Welcome to Imola...' [lines 399-419]
- 'Necromancy!' [lines 458-464]
- 'As I slumbered in my body...' [lines 599-611]
- 'Tell me, di Credi...' [lines 798-799]

26. 'God's sake!' [lines 638-644]

This fragment concerns how Giacomo got the name 'Salai' but, in effect, forms the 'material' counterpart to Fragment 18, where da Vinci was silenced by the superior power of the Pope. Here it is da Vinci who has the upper hand, and Salai who cannot get a word in edgeways. The fragment also reveals the almost paternal nature of da Vinci's relationship with his servant, who, despite his mischief and lies, forms a very important part of the artist's intellectual and emotional world.

Key themes: Power; paternity; scientific/artistic curiosity.

Reflective affinities:

- 'It might be a dream...' [lines 9-24]
- 'Consider, Salai...' [lines 32-96]
- 'Force is Spirit...' [lines 107-113]
- '...and as well as a musician...' [lines 116-161]
- 'Force is Spirit...' [lines 164-169]
- 'Ser Piero, my father...' [lines 205-212]
- 'Mmm...typical Verrocchio...' [lines 237-349]

- 'For it is among the horrors…' [lines 423-454]
- 'Di Ser Piero…' [lines 648-650]
- 'A painter should be solitary…' [lines 668-697]
- 'Buchi della verità…' [lines 743-754]

Negative reflections:

- 'Un libro del cazzo!' [lines 27-29]
- 'In me la morte…' [lines 99-104]
- 'It's funny…' [lines 172-202]
- 'But when will it be finished…' [lines 352-367]
- 'Welcome to Imola…' [lines 399-419]
- 'Necromancy!' [lines 458-464]
- '"Maestro da Vinci"…' [lines 710-740]
- 'Sometimes Heaven…' [lines 778-786]
- 'Tell me, di Credi…' [lines 798-799]

27. 'Di Ser Piero…' [lines 648-650]

This fragment reflects both Leonardo's delight in wordplay and his negative relationship with his father (see analysis of Fragment 9). It is taken directly from the notebooks (*Codex Atlanticus*) without alteration.

Key themes: Negative relationship with father; melancholy; wordplay.

Reflective affinities:

- 'Consider, Salai…' [lines 32-96]
- '…and as well as a musician…' [lines 116-161]
- 'Ser Piero, my father…' [lines 205-212]
- 'Mmm…typical Verrocchio…' [lines 237-349]
- 'O time…' [lines 586-596]
- 'God's sake!' [lines 638-644]
- 'silk tears the air…' [lines 654-665]

- 'A painter should be solitary…' [lines 668-697]
- 'Buchi della verità…' [lines 743-754]
- 'The act of coitus…' [lines 768-773]
- 'I thought I was learning…' [lines 790-794]

Negative reflections:

- 'Un libro del cazzo!' [lines 27-29]
- 'In me la morte…' [lines 99-104]
- 'But when will it be finished…' [lines 352-367]
- 'Necromancy!' [lines 458-464]
- '"Maestro da Vinci"…' [lines 710-740]
- 'Sometimes Heaven…' [lines 778-786]
- 'Tell me, di Credi…' [lines 798-799]

28. 'silk tears the air…' [lines 654-665]

This fragment is concerned with Leonardo's professed horror of war, which, despite his numerous designs for weapons of mass destruction, he described in his notebooks as 'the most brutal kind of madness there is'. I have based this fragment on a section of his notebooks which Leonardo wrote in 1504, during his preparations for his painting of the *Battle of Anghiari*. The circumstances surrounding this painting form part of the Leonardo legend. The *Signoria* of Florence, perhaps inspired by Leonardo's 'friend' Niccolò Machiavelli, decided to commission 'the two greatest Florentine artists of the day' to paint two frescos on two opposing walls in the Grand Council Chamber of the Palazzo Vecchio. One was, of course, Leonardo da Vinci who, since his painting of the *Last Supper* (c.1495-1498) for Ludovico Sforza in the refectory of Santa Maria delle Grazie in Milan, had secured a pre-eminent reputation for himself in the field of decorative painting. The other was Michelangelo Buonarroti. The animosity between the two artists was well known, and, as Nicholl observes, 'it is hard to believe that [the *Signoria*] did not conceive this as a sort of competition, or indeed a clash of the Titans'. Certainly, the knowledge that his work would be directly compared with that of his archrival seems to have spurred Leonardo to produce a particularly audacious design. Knowing that Michelangelo's fresco, portraying the *Battle of Cascina*, was going to present the soldiers *before* the battle, hurriedly getting into their armour on hearing news of the enemy's advance, da Vinci decided to concern himself with the *action* of his scene; to present the battle of Anghiari in full flight.[94]

In one of his notebooks, now known as *Manuscript A*, he writes:

> First you must show the smoke of the artillery, mingling in the air with the dust thrown up by the movement of horses and soldiers... The air must be filled with arrows in every direction, and the cannon-balls must have a train of smoke following their flight... If you show one who has fallen you must show the place where his body has slithered in the blood-stained dust and mud... Others must be represented in the agonies of death, grinding their teeth, rolling their eyes, with their fists clenched against their bodies and their legs contorted... There might be seen a number of men fallen in a heap over a dead horse.[95]

From the above one gets a sharp picture of what the *Battle of Anghiari* may have looked like; a violent storm of smoke, bodies and blood – a 'brutal kind of madness' indeed. Sadly, like so much of Leonardo's artistic output, the painting remained unfinished. As with the *Last Supper* the artist decided to use 'oils' rather than employ the traditional fresco technique, 'in which powdered pigments mixed in water are applied to wet plaster freshly laid on the wall'; a decision which was to prove his undoing, for, on the 6th June 1505 disaster struck:

> On 6th June 1505, on Friday, at the stroke of the 13th hour [about 9.30am] I began to paint at the Palazzo. At the moment of putting down the paintbrush the weather changed for the worse, and the bell in the law-courts began to toll. The cartoon came loose. The water spilled as the jug which contained it broke. And suddenly the weather worsened, and the rain poured down till nightfall. And it was as dark as night.[96]

The painting began to run and, in a desperate attempt to save the work, Leonardo lit fires beneath the picture, hoping to dry the paint. The idea of using fires to dry an over-moist painting was inspired by Pliny (ironic, when one considers the artist's frequently expressed contempt for received wisdom), however, the technique was not suitable for oil paint. The heat from the fire 'destabilised the pigments, causing them to dissolve', and the *Battle of Anghiari* was left looking like a mutilated corpse on the battlefield. Further attempts to restore the painting proved unsuccessful, and in 1506 Leonardo fled to Milan, much to the chagrin of the *Signoria.* Nevertheless, da Vinci must have drawn some consolation from the fact that Michelangelo did not complete his painting either, for in 1505 he was summoned to Rome by Pope Julius II to 'assist him in his grandiose projects', not least of which was the extravagant 'mausoleum' which Julius wanted built for himself 'within the Vatican basilica'. Thus the epic clash of the Titans, like so much of Leonardo's career, came to nothing.[97]

In this fragment, I have endeavoured to capture something of da Vinci's description of the chaotic violence of war. As we have seen Leonardo makes much of the effect of the 'smoke of the artillery mingling in the air with the dust thrown up by the movement of the horses and soldiers'. To try and communicate this effect I have removed all punctuation from the fragment, thus letting the sense of the lines blur in the wild smoke and dust of the conflict.

Additionally, to try and convey the impression of ragged chaos I have made the typography deliberately frayed. There are no neat stanzas here, but rather a writhing cavalry of words. As ever, form and theme are closely allied, and in the last four lines I have tried to emulate the rhythm of hooves pounding through a tight contraction of stresses and the use of repetition:

steel wounded <u>like</u> flesh,
○ ● ○ ● ○
<u>like</u> tears,
● ○
<u>like</u> hooves pounding
● ○ ● ○
a *sfumato* of pain
● ○ ● ○ ● ○

The word '*sfumato*' in the last line refers to the painting technique often employed by Leonardo and derives from the Italian word '*fumo*', meaning 'smoke'. In the context of painting the term is used 'to describe the blending of tones or colours so subtly that they melt into one another without perceptible transitions', or as Leonardo puts it in his *Treatise on Painting*, so that the image appears 'without lines or borders, in the manner of smoke'. The technique is used to beautiful effect in paintings such as the *Mona Lisa* and the *Virgin of the Rocks*, and thus by speaking of 'a *sfumato* of pain' I have endeavoured to liken the smoky violence of war to something beautiful and thereby express what, in the light of his weapon designs, can only be described as Leonardo's ambivalent attitude to conflict. By way of countering this, and thus expressing the negative aspect of da Vinci's opinion, I have also referred to 'the blind eye of the sun' (line 661). As we have already seen, the eye was very important to Leonardo for, amongst other things, he regarded it as the window of the soul, and thus by speaking of the blind eye of the sun, eclipsed by 'shot and smoke and war-light' (line 660), he is expressing the part of his personality which found war 'the most brutal kind of madness there is'.[98]

Key themes: War; madness; death; beauty.

Reflective affinities:

- 'It might be a dream…' [lines 9-24]
- 'Consider, Salai…' [lines 32-96]
- 'Force is Spirit…' [lines 107-113]
- '…and as well as a musician…' [lines 116-161]
- 'Force is Spirit…' [lines 164-169]
- 'Ser Piero, my father…' [lines 205-212]
- 'And what of the eye?' [lines 221-234]
- 'Mmm…typical Verrocchio…' [lines 237-349]
- 'The old man told me…' [lines 387-396]
- 'For it is among the horrors…' [lines 423-454]
- 'A riddle, my Lords…' [lines 467-475]
- 'And the Great Bird shall rise…' [lines 478-576]
- 'O time…' [lines 586-596]
- 'Letter of Authorisation…' [lines 618-634]
- 'God's sake!' [lines 638-644]
- 'Di Ser Piero…' [lines 648-650]
- 'A painter should be solitary…' [lines 668-697]
- 'Buchi della verità…' [lines 743-754]
- 'A ghost…' [lines 757-764]
- 'The act of coitus…' [lines 768-773]
- 'I thought I was learning…' [lines 790-794]

Negative reflections:

- 'In me la morte…' [lines 99-104]
- 'It's funny…' [lines 172-202]
- 'Veggio co' be' vostr'occhi un dolce lume…' [lines 215-218]

- 'Welcome to Imola…' [lines 399-419]
- 'Necromancy!' [lines 458-464]
- 'As I slumbered in my body…' [lines 599-611]
- 'Nel voler vostro è sol la voglia mia…' [lines 701-706]
- '"Maestro da Vinci"…' [lines 710-740]
- 'Sometimes Heaven…' [lines 778-786]
- 'Tell me, di Credi…' [lines 798-799]

29. 'A painter should be solitary…' [lines 668-697]

This fragment is concerned with Leonardo's almost religious obsession with the eye, and is inspired by several passages from the notebooks. The opening stanza is based on a passage from the *Treatise on Painting* and details Leonardo's belief that a painter should strive to become a second Nature:

> The painter ought to be solitary and consider what he sees, discussing it with himself in order to select the most excellent parts of what ever he sees. He should act as a mirror which transmutes itself into as many colours as are those of the objects that are placed before it. Thus he will seem to be a second nature.[99]

This passage is also revealing about Leonardo's temperament, especially when one considers that an artist's training in a Quattrocento *bottega* was an intensely *communal* activity. Here we can see Leonardo's artistic individualism – something which we have previously encountered in his painting of the angel in Verrocchio's *Baptism of Christ* (see analysis of Fragment 12) – given a theoretical voice.

In my version of the above I have endeavoured to be true to the spirit of what Leonardo has written but have nevertheless made certain changes/aesthetic contractions. For example, the painter's selecting of the 'most excellent parts' of what he sees has become commensurate with the concept of 'beauty', for the fact that something is considered beautiful implies an act of perceptual discernment. Indeed, that 'selecting the most excellent parts' should be identified with 'beauty' is given further credence by the fact Leon Battista Alberti, in his treatise *On Painting*, forwards the argument that a painter should select what is most beautiful from Nature in order to create an ideal composition. Leonardo was a great admirer of Alberti and seems here to have been forwarding the same argument.

In order to highlight the reflective process of light and vision, I have retained Leonardo's concept of mirroring, for, as we have previously observed, the act of artistic creation can indeed be likened to the action of a mirror: the artist absorbs what he sees and reflects an image of beauty in his work, which, in turn, reflects back into the eye, hence the lines, 'whose mirroring of beauty/ gifts beauty to the eye' (lines 671 and 672). I have also placed emphasis on the artist 'absorbing everything he sees' (line 669) rather than merely 'considering'. This is important, and the reason why becomes apparent in the second stanza.

The second stanza is inspired by passages from the *Treatise on Painting* and the *Codex Atlanticus*. As we have previously observed, Leonardo was not a religious man (see analysis of Fragment 4), however here his language takes on an almost religious fervour:

> O marvellous, O stupendous necessity, thou with supreme reason compellest all effects to be the direct result of their causes; and by a supreme and irrevocable law every natural action obeys thee by the shortest possible process. Who would believe that so small a space could contain the images of all the universe? O mighty process! What talent can avail to penetrate a nature such as these? What tongue will it be that can unfold so great a wonder? Verily none!

> This is it that guides the human discourse to the considering of divine things. Here the forms, here the colours, here all the images of every part of the universe are contracted to a point. What point is so marvellous? O wonderful, O stupendous necessity...[100]

For Leonardo, the eye and its operation are supreme, nothing less than the touching point of the Universe. It is the chief informer of the intellect, the '*sensus communis*'; it 'counsels and corrects all the arts of mankind'; 'the sciences founded on it are absolutely certain'; and without it there would be no 'mathematics', 'astronomy', 'architecture', 'perspective', or 'the divine art of painting'. In short the eye is the essential organ by which a man may be transformed into a *Uomo Universale* and thus become a second Nature. It was for this reason that I had the painter in the first stanza absorbing *everything* he sees. Structurally, I have tried to give the second stanza the rhetorical sweep of the above, without indulging in such overt archaisms. Thus the passage has an accumulative, rising quality, punctuated by the repetition of the word 'It' – '*It* is the lord of mathematics./ *It* has measured out the stars' (lines 680 and 681), etc – and climaxing with the image of the eye as 'the touching of the Universe' (line 691). In the light of Leonardo's lack of religion the use of the word 'God' in line 686 may seem strange. However, it must be observed that Leonardo *does* use the word 'God' in the notebooks, and even describes the eye as 'superior to all [other things] created by God'. One explanation is that Leonardo is falling back on an established frame of reference, much the same way as he did when he appropriated Aristotelian terminology to articulate a theoretical conception of force (see analysis of Fragment 5). Another explanation is that Leonardo is not using the term in the Christian sense, but is rather using it as a synonym for his quasi-pantheistic idea of Nature. Alternatively, Leonardo might be adopting the Aristotelian concept of the Prime Mover, a reading which would be consistent with Vasari's statement in the 1550 version of his *Life of Leonardo* that da Vinci 'considered himself in all things much more a philosopher than a Christian'. Whatever the case, it must be remembered that Leonardo was far from being a truly consistent thinker; one merely needs to think of his contradictory position on war to see how paradoxical he could be. Indeed, this was my reason for using the term. I wanted to emphasise his contradictory complexity. His paradoxical nature is also articulated in line 685. Thus when he refers to the eye as 'bright darkness' (line 685), on one level a reference to what he saw as the eye's intricate mystery, he is also referring to himself.[101]

The final stanza is inspired by a passage from *Manuscript A* and is, in effect, a reiteration of what has gone before. The lonely painter should not be pitied because he has become a second Nature, and thus a 'grandchild of God'. The painter sees with his eye and reproduces, or even improves, with his hand. Thus I have endowed the hand with the power of 'vision' (line 695), for it is an essential part of Leonardo's metaphysics of the eye and the journey towards become a *Uomo Universale.*[102]

Key themes: Otherness; the eye; painting; *Uomo Universale*/second Nature; paradoxical personality.

Reflective affinities:

- 'It might be a dream...' [lines 9-24]
- 'Consider, Salai...' [lines 32-96]
- 'Force is Spirit...' [lines 107-113]
- '...and as well as a musician...' [lines 116-161]
- 'Force is Spirit...' [lines 164-169]
- 'Ser Piero, my father...' [lines 205-212]
- 'And what of the eye?' [lines 221-234]
- 'Mmm...typical Verrocchio...' [lines 237-349]
- 'The old man told me...' [lines 387-396]

- ‘For it is among the horrors…’ [lines 423-454]
- ‘O time…’ [lines 586-596]
- ‘Ginepro/Ginevra…’ [lines 615-616]
- ‘Buchi della verità…’ [lines 743-754]
- ‘A ghost…’ [lines 757-764]
- ‘The act of coitus…’ [lines 768-773]

Negative reflections:

- ‘Un libro del cazzo!’ [lines 27-29]
- ‘In me la morte…’ [lines 99-104]
- ‘It’s funny…’ [lines 172-202]
- ‘Veggio co’ be’ vostr’occhi un dolce lume…’ [lines 215-218]
- ‘Welcome to Imola…’ [lines 399-419]
- ‘Necromancy!’ [lines 458-464]
- ‘As I slumbered in my body…’ [lines 599-611]
- ‘Nel voler vostro è sol la voglia mia…’ [lines 701-706]
- ‘“Maestro da Vinci”…’ [lines 710-740]
- ‘Sometimes Heaven…’ [lines 778-786]
- ‘Tell me, di Credi…’ [lines 798-799]

30. ‘Nel voler vostro è sol la voglia mia…’ [lines 701-706]

This is the last of the Michelangelo citations, and is once again drawn from the love sonnet which the artist wrote to Tommaso dei Cavalieri in 1534 (see analysis of Fragments 10 and 21). It may be translated as:

> In your will alone does my will consist, my thoughts spring from your heart, with your breath are my words formed.
> On my own I seem like the moon left to itself, for our eyes can see nothing whatever in the heavens except what is lit up by the sun. [103]

The theme of emotional dependency expressed in the above provides a 'radioactive' counter-voice to the idea of solitude expressed in the previous fragment. Likewise, the statement 'our eyes can see nothing whatever in the heavens except what is lit up by the sun' reveals the eye's limitations, and thus goes someway towards deflating Leonardo's almost hyperbolic rhetoric.

31. '"Maestro da Vinci"...' [lines 710-740]

This is the final 'radioactive' fragment spoken through the voice of Salai. It is set sometime after da Vinci's death and has the feel of a retrospective. In the opening stanza Salai asks himself what he first remembers about 'Maestro da Vinci' (line 710). He is thus thinking back to when he was ten years old, and I have tried to imagine how Leonardo, as an elegant courtier in Milan, might have appeared to a child. Salai mentions a 'flourish of silk' (line 712), a reference to da Vinci's dandyism, and, more revealingly refers to Leonardo as '*Il Moro*'s fool' (line 712). It is important to remember that much of the artist's time at Ludovico's court was spent in devising elaborate spectacles to entertain the Duke and his guests, and thus to the ten-year-old Giacomo, Leonardo may well have appeared more as an entertainer than a painter. The term 'fool' also has negative connotations, reminding us that, for all his genius, Leonardo enjoyed a relatively low social status for most of his career, and was subject to the whims of his patrons. The lines 'The dance of planets at the turn/ of his hand?' (lines 713 and 714), refer to a theatrical performance staged by da Vinci on the 13th January 1490 called the *Masque of Planets*, a spectacle which combined Leonardo's 'artistry, inventive engineering, and...sense of showmanship', and which comprised

> a giant model of the planets in their respective positions, each moving in its course with the signs of the zodiac illuminated by torches placed behind coloured glass...[104]

Considering that Salai did not enter Leonardo's service until 22nd July, this cannot have been a genuine childhood memory. However, the *Masque of Planets* was restaged on the 19th June 1518 for King Francis I as part of a court festival entitled *The Feast of Paradise*, something at which Salai would most likely have been present. Thus, like Leonardo's childhood 'memory' of the kite, so Salai's 'recollection' of the *Masque of Planets* can be interpreted as a retrospective projection (see analysis of Fragment 1). Symbolically, the reference reflects onto the wider cosmological signification of the *Anatomy* sequence, for Leonardo, as the embodiment of matter, has become directly associated with the planets. Nevertheless, the reference is ultimately 'radioactive', for the subject of the *Masque* is astrological rather than astronomical, and the phrase 'The dance of planets at the turn/ of his hand' makes da Vinci seem like the magicians and alchemists he despised. Building on this idea of sorcery, Salai also refers to Leonardo's eyes being 'cold like fire' (line 715), something which emphasises his paradoxical nature, but which also gives him the quality of a myth; of a supernatural being who defies the laws of Nature.

The second stanza sees Salai denying all of the above. What he first remembers is 'the gold' (line 719), a reference to his second day in Leonardo's service in which he stole some of his master's money (see analysis of Fragment 8). In his notebooks, da Vinci lists the sum of money as '4 lire', however here I have given the amount as 'A florin' (line 721). My reason for making this change was twofold. Firstly, the florin was, as the name implies, the currency of Florence and Leonardo was a Florentine. Thus the coin is symbolic of da Vinci, as a foreigner, becoming invested in the interests of Milan (whose main coin was the 'ducat'). Secondly, the florin, as a gold disk, can be seen as being symbolic of the sun, a reference back to the *Masque of Planets* in the previous stanza, and a further identification of the coin with Leonardo, who, by commanding the movement of the planets, has solar implications. Here it is important to remember that Leonardo's astronomical thinking expressed in his notebooks in many ways foreshadows Copernicus' conception of a heliocentric Universe. In terms of authenticity this change is not significant for a florin was worth approximately four to six lire and, because of its high gold content, was valid all over Europe.[105]

The third stanza focuses on the nature of their relationship, which, as we have previously seen, was one of indulgence on Leonardo's behalf, and misunderstanding on Salai's (see analysis of Fragment 8). Line 727 sees Salai mimicking Leonardo's words of chastisement from Fragment 26, thereby linking the two fragments and providing a 'radioactive' counter-voice. Leonardo's indulgence towards Salai is reflected in the latter's almost nonchalant dismissal of the event, 'But I don't think he minded' (line 728). Salai also refers to da Vinci's 'strange smile that/ wasn't there' (lines 729 and 730). This is a reference to the peculiar 'smile' which can be seen in many of Leonardo's paintings, the most notable example being the *Mona Lisa.* It also emphasises the fundamental difference between them, and Salai imagines the smile as saying '"*Fuck you.../You'll never understand*"' (lines 731-732).

The final stanza continues the theme of misunderstanding, and makes reference to da Vinci's habit of leaving his projects unfinished, something which Salai describes as his master's 'endless/ apology of dreams' (lines 734 and 735). The stanza also makes reference to Leonardo's habit of buying birds at the market and letting them go free. In Vasari's biography of da Vinci this is seen as exemplifying his 'wonderful love' for 'animal creation', however here Salai dismisses it as 'Good money for nothing... For a dream...' (line 740). In a negative reflection of Fragment 1, the idea of birds and flight are not interpreted as a symbol of Leonardo's destiny, or metaphors for mental freedom, but rather as a symbol of insubstantial dreams; something which Salai calls 'Wings without birds' (line 736).[106]

32. 'Buchi della verità...' [lines 743-754]

This fragment concerns the circumstances surrounding Leonardo's denunciation for sodomy when he was twenty-three years old. In fifteenth-century Florence there existed a 'strange system' which allowed citizens to

> proclaim their feelings about anything they wished by posting their grievance in writing in specially designed boxes called *tamburi* (drums) or *buchi della verità* (mouths of truth) dotted around the city. Citizens could say what they liked about anything or anybody.[107]

At the beginning of 1476 just such a letter was placed anonymously in one of 'the mouths of truth', accusing Leonardo, 'along with three other men', of committing sodomy 'on the person of one Jacopo Salterelli', a seventeen-year-old goldsmith's apprentice from the neighbourhood of Vacchereccia. Sodomy was a serious offence at this time, and 'although the general mood within Florence...was one of tolerance' – to be sure, the popular word for sodomite in 1470s Germany was '*Florenzer*' – the offence nevertheless 'carried the death sentence'. It is a sobering thought that Leonardo da Vinci, painter of the *Mona Lisa* and dreamer of flight, may have been '[burnt] at the stake' at the age of twenty-three before achieving any of his masterpieces.[108]

The case was heard on the 9th April, 'but no result was proclaimed'. The four men were allowed to return home pending a further hearing 'two months later' on the 7th June. This hearing also passed without a verdict, and the judge once more 'discharged the four men on the condition that the case be heard again'. Fortunately this

> third hearing duly took place a few days later, and this time the case was dismissed altogether. None of the four was charged with any crime.[109]

As White observes,

> Leonardo was affected dramatically by the incident. Not only did he have the threat of the stake hanging over him for two months, but the events surrounding the trial were well publicised throughout the city and he and the others were marked as sexual deviants even after they had been acquitted unconditionally.[110]

Amongst other things this must have caused acute embarrassment for Ser Piero. Not only did he have the shame of being father to an illegitimate son, but now his bastard had been publicly defamed as a sodomite, something which, as White observes, must have 'greatly angered' him, and by extension heightened Leonardo's own sense of 'dishonour'.[111]

Whether Leonardo and his friends were guilty is uncertain. Da Vinci (like the others) had 'proclaimed his innocence' throughout the proceedings, but this is hardly surprising given the severe penalty if the charge were maintained. The fact that the case was dropped in all likelihood reflects the lack of evidence. As Nicholl points out, 'the *denuncia* [appears to be] at the level of a noisy neighbour, scandalised by certain comings or goings' and may have even been 'a competitor'. If the latter is true then the denunciation was as much a business move as a concern to improve civic morality. Alternatively, the case may have been dropped because of powerful intervention. Whilst it might be tempting to see Ser Piero intervening to protect his son (and his own reputation), if intervention did occur then it probably came from a more exulted quarter. One of those accused with Da Vinci was Lionardo Tornabuoni, and the Tornabuoni 'were one of the leading families of the city'. In addition to this, Lionardo Tornabuoni was a 'relative of

Lorenzo de' Medici's mother'; powerful connections indeed. As Nicholl argues, 'the presence of a Medici protégé [among the charged] makes it quite probable that it was influence rather than innocence that got [them] off'.[112]

To be sure, the question of Leonardo's sexual preferences is a problematic one and, as we have previously discussed, must remain a point of conjecture (see analysis of Fragment 10). He certainly expressed distaste for male-female coitus in his notebooks; however, unlike Michelangelo, and the Salterelli trial aside, he is not known to have ever been involved with a man either. Whatever Leonardo's proclivities, the denunciation of 1476 (and its ensuing trauma) may well account for both the artist's obsessive secrecy and his violent expressions of misanthropy. As White argues, the Salterelli trial 'threw [Leonardo] into a paroxysm of anxiety from which he never fully recovered his emotional and sexual equilibrium'.[113]

It is this sense of internal chaos which I have tried to express in the current fragment. The sequence begins with the phrase *'Buchi della verità'* ('mouths of truth') thus identifying it with the Salterelli affair. That this accusation may have been false is expressed in the second line, which juxtaposes 'mouths of truth' with 'the spit of lies' (line 744) – although an alternative reading of the line is that the defendants' protestation of innocence was in fact untrue. To be sure, Leonardo's sexual ambiguity is performed throughout the fragment, and thus the lines are written in such a way as to keep their precise meaning uncertain. As with Fragment 28, I have used what I call '*sfumato* typography'; the absence of punctuation and clearly defined stanzas adding to the fragment's sense of 'smoky' confusion. Indeed, this sense of blurring is heightened by the images of wine and drunkenness. If the incident with Salterelli *did* take place then it is reasonable to assume that it would have occurred after a night on the town. Da Vinci and his friends may well have been drunk, and consequently it may have been their raucousness which aroused the attention of their *denuncia.* To emphasise the impression of drunkenness, I have made the wine slur from laughter into words (lines 745 and 746), rather than from words into laughter – a movement from structured articulation into abstract noise which would have been more logical in the context of drinking and thus ironically more sober. Neither is it clear whether the laughter is friendly or mocking. The images of wine, laughter and words are all connected with the mouth, and consequently reflect back onto the *buchi della verità*. I have also made play with one of da Vinci's later paintings of *John the Baptist* (c.1513-1516), which was altered into a painting of Bacchus sometime after Leonardo's death. Whilst the reference, in the context of the Salterelli affair, is anachronistic, I feel that its inclusion is symbolically valid, for here we are seeing the transformation of a respectable painter of altarpieces into a blasphemous, social deviant. In keeping with the concept of drunkenness I have placed the 'angel of Bacchus' (line 747) before 'St. John of the wilderness' (line 748). To further confuse matters, we do not know whether the 'angel of Bacchus' refers to da Vinci or Salterelli. The line 'St. John of the wilderness' can also be read as pertaining to Leonardo's psychological ordeal during the two months between hearings. If Leonardo were to be identified with St. John, then it would appear that he is innocent, for the Baptist was a celibate ascetic who lived off locusts and wild honey (Matthew 3:4), not wine and boys. The lines 'flesh/ in the torchlight/ swelling the darkness' (lines 749-751) are perhaps sexually suggestive, but also ambiguous, for we do not know whose flesh it is or even if the context is indeed sexual. The lines could equally be referring to a tavern scene, something which would fit with the act of drinking. Additionally, these lines make reference to Leonardo's dramatic use of the chiaroscuro effect in another painting of *St. John the Baptist* (c.1513-1514), where the subject, portrayed as a handsome young man, seems to be pushing out of the darkness. In this context St. John can be identified with Salterelli, the one who brings the wilderness to Leonardo by giving him 'Baptism' – here perhaps a metaphor for sexual initiation – and who thus swells the darkness of scandal around him. The last line, 'Father where are you' continues this ambiguity, for we are uncertain whether he is making a plea to his father, Ser Piero, or, in a moment of crisis, to God. Once again we have a double image (think drunkenness) for the 'hard-playing' Ser Piero can be said to have had bacchic tendencies, whilst God is most definitely associated with St. John. To emphasise this double reading, I have separated the word 'Father' from the rest of the line, thus making one line into two.[114]

Key themes: Sexual ambiguity; drunkenness; truth; lies; the body; relationship with father; problems with authority.

Reflective affinities:

- 'It might be a dream…' [lines 9-24]
- 'Consider, Salai…' [lines 32-96]
- 'Force is Spirit…' [lines 107-113]
- '…and as well as a musician…' [lines 116-161]
- 'Force is Spirit…' [lines 164-169]
- 'Ser Piero, my father…' [lines 205-212]
- 'And what of the eye?' [lines 221-234]
- 'Mmm…typical Verrocchio…' [lines 237-349]
- 'The old man told me…' [lines 387-396]
- 'For it is among the horrors…' [lines 423-454]
- 'God's sake!' [lines 638-644]
- 'Di Ser Piero…' [lines 648-650]
- 'silk tears the air…' [lines 654-665]
- 'A painter should be solitary…' [lines 668-697]
- 'Buchi della verità…' [lines 743-754]
- 'A ghost…' [lines 757-764]
- 'The act of coitus…' [lines 768-773]
- 'I thought I was learning…' [lines 790-794]

Negative reflections:

- **'Un libro del cazzo!' [lines 27-29]**
- **'In me la morte…' [lines 99-104]**
- **'It's funny…' [lines 172-202]**
- **'Veggio co' be' vostr'occhi un dolce lume…' [lines 215-218]**
- **'But when will be it finished…' [lines 352-367]**
- **'Welcome to Imola…' [lines 399-419]**
- **'Necromancy!' [lines 458-464]**
- **'As I slumbered in my body…' [lines 599-611]**
- **'Nel voler vostro è sol la voglia mia…' [lines 701-706]**
- **'"Maestro da Vinci"…' [lines 710-740]**
- **'Sometimes Heaven…' [lines 778-786]**
- **'Tell me, di Credi…' [lines 798-799]**

33. 'A ghost…' [lines 757-764]

This fragment was inspired by Leonardo's famous *Burlington House Cartoon* (1499) which depicts the Madonna, St. Anne, Christ and John the Baptist. Perhaps what is most remarkable about the work is the way in which the infant Christ appears to be emerging out of his mother's body. Indeed, the presence of three generations in a single picture, coupled with the physical intimacy of Mary and Jesus, seems to be a comment on the process of generation and the passage of time. The image, as a cartoon rather than a finished painting, is also reminiscent of Leonardo's other *non finito* works, such as his *Adoration of the Magi* (see analysis of Fragment 13), and is strangely haunting, almost timeless. The bodies appear nearly transparent as though they were composed entirely of light.[115]

Consequently, this fragment behaves somewhat like a prism, and is one of the most reflective fragments of the *Anatomy* sequence. The opening couplet, 'A ghost/ like an image' finds reflective affinities in those fragments

concerned with light and optics, such as *'And what of the eye?'* (lines 221-234), those concerned with painting, such as *'Mmm…typical Verrocchio…'* (lines 237-349), and those which pertain to mortality and the passage of time, such as *'O time…'* (lines 586-596). The second couplet, 'The Madonna/ and St. Anne' (lines 760 and 761), as an image of two mothers, finds a positive reflection in the double entry for *Caterina* in *'29th January 1494…'* (lines 371-384) and a negative reflection in *'It's funny…'* (lines 172-202) in which Salai likens the woman his master is dissecting to the Madonna and St. Anne (Fragment 8, line 195). The third couplet, 'The child/ from the womb' (lines 763 and 764), finds a reflective affinity in *'For it is among the horrors…'* (lines 423-454) where da Vinci discovers that the woman whom he is dissecting is with child (Fragment 17, lines 453 and 454). In light of the above, the relationship of this fragment with the *Burlington House Cartoon* means that it also provides a 'material' counter-voice to the 'radioactive' *'But when will it be finished…'* (lines 352-367) in which the Prior of San Donato berates Leonardo for leaving his work *non finito*.

Key themes: Light; optics; time; mortality; maternity; bodies; painting; leaving works *non finito*.

Reflective affinities:

- 'It might be a dream…' [lines 9-24]
- 'Consider, Salai…' [lines 32-96]
- 'Force is Spirit…' [lines 107-113]
- '…and as well as a musician…' [lines 116-161]
- 'Force is Spirit…' [lines 164-169]
- 'Ser Piero, my father…' [lines 205-212]
- 'And what of the eye?' [lines 221-234]
- 'Mmm…typical Verrocchio…' [lines 237-349]
- '29th January 1494…' [lines 371-384]
- 'The old man told me…' [lines 387-396]

- 'For it is among the horrors…' [lines 423-454]
- 'O time…' [lines 586-596]
- 'Ginepro/Ginevra…' [lines 615-616]
- 'God's sake!' [lines 638-644]
- 'Di Ser Piero…' [lines 648-650]
- 'silk tears the air…' [lines 654-665]
- 'A painter should be solitary…' [lines 668-697]
- 'Buchi della verità…' [lines 743-754]
- 'The act of coitus…' [lines 768-773]
- 'I thought I was learning…' [lines 790-794]

Negative reflections:

- 'Un libro del cazzo!' [lines 27-29]
- 'In me la morte…' [lines 99-104]
- 'It's funny…' [lines 172-202]
- 'Veggio co' be' vostr'occhi un dolce lume…' [lines 215-218]
- 'But when will be it finished…' [lines 352-367]
- 'Welcome to Imola…' [lines 399-419]
- 'Necromancy!' [lines 458-464]
- 'As I slumbered in my body…' [lines 599-611]
- 'Nel voler vostro è sol la voglia mia…' [lines 701-706]
- '"Maestro da Vinci"…' [lines 710-740]
- 'Sometimes Heaven…' [lines 778-786]
- 'Tell me, di Credi…' [lines 798-799]

34. 'The act of coitus…' [lines 768-773]

This fragment was inspired by Leonardo's notebooks and, as we have previously observed, concerns his distaste for male-female coitus (see analysis of Fragment 10). Indeed, it is ironic that a man who was prepared to conduct anatomical investigations in the most horrific of conditions should have found the natural action of living bodies so 'aesthetically displeasing', and is a further example of

Leonardo's complex and contradictory character (see analysis of Fragments 6, 28 and 29). In the wider context of the *Anatomy* sequence, the reference to 'pretty faces' (line 771) can be seen as a passive allusion to unmentioned paintings such as the *Mona Lisa* or the *Portrait of Cecilia Gallerani* ; women whom Leonardo has stripped of their physical, sexual identity, and transformed into objects of contemplative beauty.[116]

Key themes: Sexual distaste; the body; paradoxical personality.

Reflective affinities:

- **'It might be a dream…' [lines 9-24]**
- **'Consider, Salai…' [lines 32-96]**
- **'Force is Spirit…' [lines 107-113]**
- **'…and as well as a musician…' [lines 116-161]**
- **'Force is Spirit…' [lines 164-169]**
- **'Ser Piero, my father…' [lines 205-212]**
- **'Mmm…typical Verrocchio…' [lines 237-349]**
- **'29th January 1494…' [lines 371-384]**
- **'The old man told me…' [lines 387-396]**
- **'For it is among the horrors…' [lines 423-454]**
- **'O time…' [lines 586-596]**
- **'Ginepro/Ginevra…' [lines 615-616]**
- **'Di Ser Piero…' [lines 648-650]**
- **'silk tears the air…' [lines 654-665]**
- **'A painter should be solitary…' [lines 668-697]**
- **'Buchi della verità…' [lines 743-754]**
- **'A ghost…' [lines 757-764]**
- **'I thought I was learning…' [lines 790-794]**

Negative reflections:

- **'Un libro del cazzo!' [lines 27-29]**

- 'In me la morte…' [lines 99-104]
- 'It's funny…' [lines 172-202]
- 'Veggio co' be' vostr'occhi un dolce lume…' [lines 215-218]
- 'Welcome to Imola…' [lines 399-419]
- 'Necromancy!' [lines 458-464]
- 'As I slumbered in my body…' [lines 599-611]
- 'Nel voler vostro è sol la voglia mia…' [lines 701-706]
- 'Sometimes Heaven…' [lines 778-786]
- 'Tell me, di Credi…' [lines 798-799]

35. 'Sometimes Heaven…' [lines 778-786]

This fragment is based on the opening passage from Vasari's biography of Leonardo, and presents the artist in a hagiographic light; something which provides a strong 'radioactive' counter-voice to the flawed materialist revealed by the majority of the 'material' fragments.

36. 'I thought I was learning…' [lines 790-794]

This fragment was inspired by the following passage from the *Codex Atlanticus*:

> While I thought I was learning how to live I have been learning how to die.[117]

and is a further example of Leonardo's melancholic disposition (see analysis of Fragment 22). Given its proximity to the end of the *Anatomy* sequence, and the fact that these lines are the last of those spoken through the persona of da Vinci, the intimation of mortality takes on a heightened significance.

Key themes: Melancholy; mortality.

Reflective affinities:

- 'Consider, Salai…' [lines 32-96]
- 'Force is Spirit…' [lines 107-113]
- '…and as well as a musician…' [lines 116-161]
- 'Force is Spirit…' [lines 164-169]
- 'Ser Piero, my father…' [lines 205-212]
- 'Mmm…typical Verrocchio…' [lines 237-349]
- '29th January 1494…' [lines 371-384]
- 'The old man told me…' [lines 387-396]
- 'For it is among the horrors…' [lines 423-454]
- 'O time…' [lines 586-596]
- 'Ginepro/Ginevra…' [lines 615-616]
- 'Di Ser Piero…' [lines 648-650]
- 'silk tears the air…' [lines 654-665]
- 'Buchi della verità…' [lines 743-754]
- 'A ghost…' [lines 757-764]

Negative reflections:

- 'Un libro del cazzo!' [lines 27-29]
- 'In me la morte…' [lines 99-104]
- 'It's funny…' [lines 172-202]
- 'Veggio co' be' vostr'occhi un dolce lume…' [lines 215-218]
- 'Welcome to Imola…' [lines 399-419]
- 'Necromancy!' [lines 458-464]
- 'As I slumbered in my body…' [lines 599-611]
- 'Nel voler vostro è sol la voglia mia…' [lines 701-706]
- 'Sometimes Heaven…' [lines 778-786]
- 'Tell me, di Credi…' [lines 798-799]

37. 'Tell me, di Credi…' [lines 798-799]

This is the final fragment of the *Anatomy* sequence and it is not spoken by Leonardo da Vinci. My reason for not giving

Leonardo the last word was twofold. Firstly, I wanted to emphasise the *non finito* quality of the sequence, for, as we have previously discussed, this has implications not only for Leonardo's microcosmic mirroring of Nature (something which is in a perpetual state of process) but also in the wider scheme of Book Two's cosmic paradigm. Secondly, having had Leonardo abuse Verrocchio so vociferously in Fragment 12, it seemed fair to let da Vinci's teacher have the last word. The 'scene' takes place before the *Baptism of Christ*, and sees Verrocchio asking his assistant Lorenzo di Credi whether he thinks the angel painted by da Vinci looks strange. Humour apart, the image of the strange angel can also be seen as a metaphor for Leonardo, a man of great complexity, of vision and bitterness, of love and scorn, whose phenomenal gifts, all hagiography aside, enabled him to reach after what is most divine in Man.

NOTES

[1] Anonimo Gaddiano, 'Codex Magliabecchiano' in, Alessandro Vezzosi, *Leonardo da Vinci: Renaissance Man*, tr. A. Bonfante-Warren (London: Thames and Hudson Ltd, 1997), 130.

[2] Giorgio Vasari, 'Life of Leonardo da Vinci' in, *Lives of the Artists (Volume I)*, tr. G. Bull (London: Penguin Books Ltd, 1987), 255.

[3] Michael White, *Leonardo: The First Scientist* (London: Abacus, 2001), 101, 109, 108, 117, 88, 127, 170, 25, 287, 300, 166, 204; Alessandro Vezzosi, *Leonardo da Vinci: Renaissance Man*, tr. A. Bonfante-Warren (London: Thames and Hudson Ltd, 1997), 62; White, 254; Ian Chilvers, *The Oxford Dictionary of Art and Artists* (Oxford: Oxford University Press, 2003), 336; Vasari, 257; Raffaele Monti, *Leonardo*, tr. P. Sanders (London: Thames and Hudson Ltd, 1967), 12; Vasari, 255; Leonardo da Vinci, *St. Hieronymus* (c.1480-82), painted with oil on wood, and measuring 103x75cm, it is housed in the Pinacoteca Vaticana in Rome; Leonardo da Vinci, *The Adoration of the Magi* (c.1481-82), painted with oil on wood, and measuring 243x 246cm, it is housed in the Uffizi in Florence; Elke Buchholz, *Leonardo da Vinci: Life and Work*, tr. P. Barton (Cambridge: Goodfellow and Egan Publishing Management, 2005), 34; White, 303; Charles Nicholl, *Leonardo da Vinci: The Flights of the Mind* (London: Penguin Books Ltd, 2005), 9.

[4] White, 166; Martin Kemp, *Leonardo* (Oxford: Oxford University Press, 2005), 76; Nicholl, 218.

[5] White, 303.

[6] Sigmund Freud, *Leonardo da Vinci: A Memory of his Childhood*, tr. A. Tyson (London: Routledge, 2001), 12; White, 23; Freud, 73, 52, 24, 25.

[7] Freud, 69; White, 18.

[8] White, 164; Kemp, 6, 5.

[9] Kemp, 49, 132; Leonardo da Vinci, 'Macrocosmic Analogy: Codex Leicester (1508)' in, Martin Kemp, *Leonardo* (Oxford: Oxford University Press, 2005), 131.

[10] Kemp, 5.

[11] Kemp, 134; Desmond Lee, 'Introduction' in, Plato, *Timaeus and Critias*, tr. D. Lee (London: Penguin Books Ltd, 1977), 9; Kemp, 133, 7, 49.

[12] Leonardo da Vinci, 'Mathematical Rule: Codex Leicester (1508)' in, Martin Kemp, *Leonardo* (Oxford: Oxford University Press, 2005), 4; Kemp, 49.

[13] Kemp, 48-49.

[14] Irma Richter, ed., *The Notebooks of Leonardo da Vinci* (Oxford: Oxford University Press, 1998), 110, 4, 111; White, 170; Richter, 116, 117.

[15] Richter, 216.

[16] Buchholz, 27; Kemp, 132.

[17] Richter, 2.

[18] Richter, 286.

[19] Richter, 5, 11, 253.

[20] Nicholl, 31.

[21] Maggie Hyde, *Introducing Jung* (Cambridge: Icon Books UK, 1999), 87.

[22] White, 26, 27, 15.

[23] White, 15.

[24] Richter, 1.

[25] White, 16; Richter, 2.

[26] Vasari, 257; White, 118; Leonardo da Vinci, 'On humanity: Codex Forster' in, Michael White, *Leonardo: The First Scientist* (London: Abacus, 2001), 19.

[27] White, 20; Jonathan Barnes, *Aristotle* (Oxford: Oxford University Press, 2000), 102.

[28] Michelangelo Buonarroti, 'Partial Sonnet, 1520s' in, *Everyman's Poetry: Michelangelo*, tr. and ed. C. Ryan (London: J. M. Dent, 1998), 10.

[29] Anonimo Gaddiano, 130; Ross King, *Michelangelo and the Pope's Ceiling* (London: Pimlico, 2003), 249; Anonimo Gaddiano, 131; Nicholl, 126; King, 1; White, 228; Nicholl, 126; Chilvers, 387.

[30] White, 228; Gilles Néret, *Michelangelo*, tr. P. Snowdon (London: Taschen, 2000), 23; Chilvers, 389; White, 229.

[31] Chilvers, 387; Anonimo Gaddiano, 'Codex Magliabecchiano' in, Charles Nicholl, *Leonardo da Vinci: The Flights of the Mind* (London: Penguin Books Ltd, 2005), 379.

[32] Néret, 8; White, 229.

[33] Richter, 62-63.

[34] Kemp, 72; White, 189.

[35] Leonardo da Vinci, 'On War: Codex Urbinus' in, Charles Nicholl, *Leonardo da Vinci: The Flights of the Mind* (London: Penguin Books Ltd, 2005), 348; White, 70, 95, 96, 86, 85; Richter, 2; White, 86.

[36] White, 105, 106; Leonardo da Vinci, 'Draft of Letter to Ludovico Sforza: Codex Atlanticus' in, Michael White, *Leonardo: The First Scientist* (London: Abacus, 2001), 107.

[37] Da Vinci, 'Draft of Letter to Ludovico Sforza: Codex Atlanticus', 108; White, 111; Kemp, 113, 119.

[38] White, 102.

[39] White, 111.

[40] Nicholl, 270; Richter, 311, 312; Nicholl, 270, 271; Kemp, 12.

[41] Ilan Rachum, *The Renaissance: An Illustrated Encyclopedia* (London: Octopus Books Ltd, 1979), 24; White, 265.

[42] White, 265; Rachum, 24.

[43] White, 251; Nicholl, 240; White, 267.

[44] Nicholl, 269-270, 170.

[45] Kemp, 93; Leonardo da Vinci, 'The Centenarian: Codex Leicester (1507)' in, Michael White, *Leonardo: The First Scientist* (London: Abacus, 2001), 269.

[46] White, 14, 27, 73, 19, 94, 96.

[47] White, 18.

[48] Leonardo da Vinci, *Virgin and Child with St. Anne* (c.1502-1516), painted with oil on wood, and measuring 168x130cm, it is housed in the Louvre in Paris; Leonardo da Vinci, *Mona Lisa* (1503-1506), painted with oil on wood, and measuring 77x53cm, it is housed in the Louvre in Paris; White, 19; Leonardo da Vinci, 'Caterina Came: Codex Forster (1493)' in, Michael White, *Leonardo: The First Scientist* (London: Abacus, 2001), 269; White, 146.

[49] Michelangelo Buonarroti, 'Sonnet for Tommaso Cavalieri, c. 1534' in, *Everyman's Poetry: Michelangelo*, tr. and ed. C. Ryan (London: J. M. Dent, 1998), 37.

[50] Néret, 65; White, 71; Jonathan Goldberg, 'Introduction' in, Jonathan Goldberg, ed., *Queering the Renaissance* (New York: Duke University Press, 1994), 5; Leonardo da Vinci, 'On Sex: Manuscript A' in, Michael White, *Leonardo: The First Scientist* (London: Abacus, 2001), 76-77.

[51] Richter, 116.

[52] White, 60.

[53] Chilvers, 619.

[54] Nicholl, 94, 95.

[55] Nicholl, 131; White, 92; Nicholl, 87, 131; Andrea del Verrocchio and Leonardo da Vinci, *The Baptism of Christ* (c.1472-1475/6), painted with oil and tempera on panel, and measuring 177x151cm, it is housed in the Uffizi in Florence.

[56] Vasari, 258.

[57] Nicholl, 103.

[58] Nicholl, 83; Leonardo da Vinci, 'On Painting: Codex Forster' in, Charles Nicholl, *Leonardo da Vinci: The Flights of the Mind* (London: Penguin Books Ltd, 2005), 130.

[59] Leonardo da Vinci, *A Treatise on Painting*, tr. J. F. Rigaud (New York: Dover Publications Inc, 2005), 2.

[60] Da Vinci, *A Treatise on Painting*, 2, 3.

[61] Da Vinci, *A Treatise on Painting*, 3, 46.

[62] Nicholl, 168; White, 80.

[63] Nicholl, 168.

[64] Nicholl, 168; White, 96.

[65] White, 97.

[66] Nicholl, 169.

[67] Vasari, 256.

[68] Sarah Bradford, *Cesare Borgia: His Life and Times* (London: Weidenfeld and Nicolson, 1976), 70; Nicholl, 343.

[69] Nicholl, 343; Bradford, 3; Nicholl, 347; Cesare Borgia, 'Letter of Authorisation: 18th August 1502' in, Charles Nicholl, *Leonardo da Vinci: The Flights of the Mind* (London: Penguin Books Ltd, 2005), 347.

[70] Richter, 347; Nicholl, 344.

[71] Nicholl, 349, 350.

[72] Nicholl, 350.

[73] Richter, 151.

[74] White, 251.

[75] Nicholl, 34.

[76] Richter, 246.

[77] Nicholl, 252; White, 331.

[78] Kemp, 124; Leonardo da Vinci, 'On Flight: Turin Codex ' in, Charles Nicholl, *Leonardo da Vinci: The Flights of the Mind* (London: Penguin Books Ltd, 2005), 32.

[79] Leonardo da Vinci, 'Quaderni, III' in, Michael White, *Leonardo: The First Scientist* (London: Abacus, 2001), 236; Nicholl, 394-395.

[80] Richter, 97, 99, 95, 103-104.

[81] Buonarroti, 37.

[82] Richter, 273-274.

[83] Ovid, *Metamorphoses*, tr. A. D. Melville (Oxford: Oxford University Press, 1998), 359.

[84] Ovid, 1.

[85] White, 19, 20.

[86] Homer, *The Iliad*, tr. R. Fagles (London: Penguin Books Ltd, 1990), 207; Homer, *The Iliad*, tr. L. Janus (London: Berry Books Ltd, 1983), 134; M. C. Howatson, and Ian Chilvers, eds., *The Oxford Concise Companion to*

Classical Literature (Oxford: Oxford University Press, 1996), 252; White, 111.

[87] Gilles Quispel, 'Preface' in, *The Way of Hermes: The Corpus Hermeticum and the Definitions of Hermes Trismegistus to Asclepius*, trs. C. Salaman, D. van Oyen, W. D. Wharton and J-P. Mahé (London: Gerald Duckworth & Co Ltd, 1999), 11.

[88] Hermes Trismegistus, 'The Corpus Hermeticum' in, *The Way of Hermes: The Corpus Hermeticum and the Definitions of Hermes Trismegistus to Asclepius*, trs. C. Salaman, D. van Oyen, W. D. Wharton and J-P. Mahé (London: Gerald Duckworth & Co Ltd, 1999), 19.

[89] Thomas Mautner, ed., *The Penguin Dictionary of Philosophy* (London: Penguin Books Ltd, 2000), 391; Hermes Trismegistus, 19.

[90] Nicholl, 110.

[91] Nicholl, 110.

[92] Nicholl, 110; Frank Zöllner, *Leonardo*, tr. F. Elliot (London: Taschen, 2000), 21; Nicholl, 110.

[93] White, 217-218.

[94] Leonardo da Vinci, 'On War: Codex Urbinus' in, Charles Nicholl, *Leonardo da Vinci: The Flights of the Mind* (London: Penguin Books Ltd, 2005), 348; Nicholl, 376.

[95] Leonardo da Vinci, 'Depicting War: Manuscript A' in, Charles Nicholl, *Leonardo da Vinci: The Flights of the Mind* (London: Penguin Books Ltd, 2005), 373.

[96] White, 233; Chilvers, 220; Leonardo da Vinci, 'Anghiari Disaster: Madrid Codex II' in, Charles Nicholl, *Leonardo da Vinci: The Flights of the Mind* (London: Penguin Books Ltd, 2005), 390.

[97] Vezzosi, 90; Néret, 23, 24.

[98] Chilvers, 548; Leonardo da Vinci, 'Treatise on Painting' in, Ian Chilvers, *The Oxford Dictionary of Art and Artists* (Oxford: Oxford University Press, 2003), 548.

[99] Richter, 216.

[100] Richter, 110-111.

[101] Richter, 108, 110; Giorgio Vasari, 'The Life of Leonardo: 1550 version' in, Charles Nicholl, *Leonardo da*

Vinci: The Flights of the Mind (London: Penguin Books Ltd, 2005), 483.

[102] Leonardo da Vinci, 'Grandchild of God: Manuscript A' in, Alessandro Vezzosi, *Leonardo da Vinci: Renaissance Man*, tr. A. Bonfante-Warren (London: Thames and Hudson Ltd, 1997), 1.

[103] Buonarroti, 37.

[104] White, 127.

[105] Richter, 311; Stella Fletcher, *The Longman Companion to Renaissance Europe* (London: Longman, 2000), 119.

[106] Vasari, 257.

[107] White, 71.

[108] White, 71, 70.

[109] White, 71; Nicholl, 115; White, 71-72, 72.

[110] White, 72.

[111] White, 72.

[112] White, 72; Nicholl, 119, 120.

[113] White, 74.

[114] Leonardo da Vinci, *John the Baptist* (c.1513-1516), painted with oil on canvas, and measuring 177x115cm, it is housed in the Louvre in Paris; Leonardo da Vinci, *St. John the Baptist* (c.1513-1514), painted with oil on wood, and measuring 69x57cm, it is housed in the Louvre in Paris; White, 27.

[115] Leonardo da Vinci, *Burlington House Cartoon* (1499), drawn with chalk on paper, and measuring 139.5x101cm, it is housed in the National Gallery in London.

[116] White, 76.

[117] Richter, 275.

3. Eusebius Hieronymus: Wilderness

Theory

The man who was to become known to history as 'St. Jerome' (c.347-420 CE), the polyglot 'Doctor of the Church' behind the 'Vulgate Bible', scourge of 'heretics', and tireless promoter of the 'ascetic life', was born 'Eusebius Hieronymus' at the small Dalmatian town of Stridon near Aquileia sometime towards the middle of the fourth century CE. Hieronymus' parents were both 'Christians' and, as the Church historian Stefan Rebenich observes, '...[t]he family owned property around Stridon and was well off'. Consequently, the future saint was to receive an excellent education, enjoying the tutelage of such notable didacts as the 'famous grammarian Aelius Donatus', and having the opportunity, coveted by many young men from the provinces, of studying in the capital city of the Western Roman Empire – Rome itself. Indeed, it is probable that Hieronymus' parents, like many of their class, hoped that this impressive, and expensive, education would earn their son a place in the 'imperial bureaucracy'. Certainly, as Rebenich points out, '...[h]is student years in Rome were essential to his intellectual formation...[for] all his later work reveals the brilliant pupil who is proud of his language, style, and dialectic'. However, the course of Hieronymus' life was to take him in a very different direction from the bureaucratic path most probably desired for him by his parents.[1]

Despite coming from a Christian home, and having been, by his own admission, 'nourished on Catholic milk', Hieronymus seems to have undergone a spiritual crisis sometime around the year 370 CE. In his *Letter XXII* (c.384 CE), written to the Roman lady 'Julia Eustochium' some fourteen years later, the future saint recalls a terrifying 'dream' in which his lifestyle and beliefs were called to account:

> Suddenly I was caught up in the spirit and dragged before the judgement seat of the Judge... I was asked to state my condition and replied: 'I am a Christian.' But he who presided said: 'You lie, you are a follower of Cicero and not of Christ (*Ciceronianus es, non Christianus*). For where your treasure is there will your heart be also (cf. Matthew 6:21).' Instantly, I became dumb, and amid the strokes of the lash – for he had ordered me to be scourged – I was even more severely tortured by the fire of my conscience... I began to cry and lament, saying: 'Have mercy upon me, O Lord: have mercy upon me.' Amid the sound of the scourges my voice made itself heard. At last the bystanders, falling down before the knees of him who presided, prayed that he would have pity on my youth and that he would give me the opportunity to repent of my error, on the agreement that torture should be inflicted on me, if I ever again read the works of gentile authors...[2]

The above is revealing in a number of ways, for it amply demonstrates the deep tensions running through Hieronymus' personality. On the one hand there was the brilliant scholar, the avid collector of books, the proud Ciceronian who would have made an excellent imperial bureaucrat. On the other, there was the emergent ascetic, whose penchant for self-mortification is witnessed by his dramatic reference to flagellation; here salvation is equated with suffering, with the seemingly complete renunciation of himself.

Indeed, whilst it is difficult to say with any certainty, it is highly probable that around this time Hieronymus had come into possession of the 'popular Latin version' of Athanasius' *Life of Antony*. An early example of Christian 'hagiography', the *Life of Antony* concerns the adventures of Antony of Egypt, a desert-dwelling, wonder-working 'hermit' who 'gave away all his possessions and devoted himself to a life of asceticism'. To be sure, during the third and fourth centuries there had been a sharp increase in people abandoning the cities and going to live ascetic lives in the desert, devoted to poverty, chastity, and prayer. Although known as 'monakos', or 'monks', they did not initially form the structured communities familiar to us from medieval monasticism, but rather, as the word implies, sought a life of contemplation in solitude, coming together only very occasionally. Athanasius had received personal experience of this radical and arduous lifestyle during his third exile (356-361 CE), and appears to have known Antony personally. Yet the *Life of Antony*, in all its hagiographic glory, is not merely a personal reminiscence of a remarkable man. Rather, it can be seen both as a soteriological paradigm *and* as a theo-political treatise.[3]

The state of the Church in the fourth century was highly complex. Despite having gained social legitimacy during the reign of Constantine I, with Christianity becoming the 'official religion' of the Empire, it had still to defeat the forces of paganism or to satisfactorily reconcile its own internal factions. Athanasius, as an ardent promoter of the Faith, had been an active participant in these disputes, his most notable debacle concerning the teachings of the Alexandrian presbyter 'Arius'. Determined to preserve what he saw as the indivisibility of the Father, Arius promoted the doctrine that 'the Son or Word was a creature, created before time and superior to other creatures, but like them changeable and distinct from the Father'. Athanasius, by contrast, believing that Christ's soteriological power resided in his necessary divinity, argued for the 'consubstantiality of Father and Son'. The extreme tension between these two theologians, and their numerous followers, was one of the catalysts for the famous First Council of Nicaea. Here Athanasius' Christology was declared 'orthodox' and Arius' 'heresy' – the resultant 'Nicene Creed' intended to be a unifying declaration of faith for a single Catholic Church. However, in reality, the tensions between these two rival Christologies, and their devoted adherents, were to remain until the reign of Theodosius I later in the century when Arianism was finally and ruthlessly suppressed.[4]

Works like the *Life of Antony*, written in the post-Nicene era but before the Arian suppression, can thus be seen as part of this spiritual warfare. Athanasius' strategy cannot be described as subtle, but it is certainly rhetorically effective. At every opportunity the theologian seeks to identify his subject with Christ. Like Christ, Antony goes into the desert to be tempted; like Christ, Antony does battle with demons and heals the sick; like Christ, Antony suffers bodily tortures akin to the Passion; and like Christ, Antony undergoes a form of death and resurrection, transforming into a powerful voice of authority, the highly vocal lash of pagans and most pointedly *Arians*. Indeed, the patterns of unity within the text are intriguing, for just as Nicene orthodoxy unites Father and Son through the consubstantial formulation of the Godhead, so Athanasius makes Antony unite with Christ, and through this identification effectively transfigures the Son into the spokesman for the doctrines of a united, Catholic Church. The white heat of the wilderness thus becomes the soteriology of unity.

The apparent influence of the *Life of Antony* on Hieronymus' spiritual development can be seen in two ways. Firstly, he began to write his own hagiographies, such as *The Life of Paul of Thebes* (c.374 CE), which significantly contains an account of Paul's encounter with Antony in the wilderness. Secondly, and even more decisively, Hieronymus decided to put his ascetic beliefs into practice. At sometime around the year 374 CE, he seemingly left the world of the scholar behind him and entered 'the desert of Chalcis,' near Antioch. In his *Letter XXII* he describes the scourging intensity of his experience:

> I used to sit alone because I was filled with bitterness. My unshapely limbs were covered in sackcloth and my skin from long neglect had become as black as an Ethiopian's. Tears and groans

> were every day my portion; and if sleep chanced to overcome my struggles against it, I bruised my bare bones, which hardly held together, against the ground… I remember crying out for days and nights together; and I ceased not from beating my breast till tranquillity returned to me at the Lord's rebuke. I used to dread my small cell as though it knew my thoughts. Stern and angry with myself, I used to make my way alone into the desert. Wherever I saw hollow valleys, rough mountains, steep cliffs, there I made my place of prayer and tortured my unhappy flesh. The Lord himself is my witness, that, after I had shed many tears and had fixed my eyes on heaven, I sometimes found myself among angelic hosts. And in joy and gladness I sang: 'We will run after you because of the savour of your good ointments.' (Song of Songs 1:3).[5]

This is the image of Hieronymus that has seared itself into the iconography of Western art. Dürer's *Penitent Saint Jerome* (c.1497), for example, or Leonardo's *St. Hieronymus* (c.1480-1482), both reveal the saint at once suppurating in his suffering and transcendent in his pain, his eyes fixed on the angelic hosts of heaven. It was certainly an experience which changed Hieronymus' life forever. By living the ascetic life at Chalcis, by suffering in the paradigmatic manner of Antony and Christ, the future saint became endowed with a spiritual authority that would otherwise have been lacking for a young man in his twenties. With only a nominal ecclesiastical rank (he had been ordained 'priest' in Antioch) and lacking Episcopal patronage, Hieronymus needed such credentials to promote himself in the Christian world.[6]

All of which might make Hieronymus sound as much a political opportunist as a devout seeker after God. Certainly, there is evidence to suggest that Hieronymus exaggerated his ascetic experience in the 370s. As Rebenich observes, '…he was never completely secluded from the outside world'. Rather, it appears that he 'maintained his correspondence with his friends', took the opportunity to learn 'Hebrew' from a converted Jew, and entered into heated theological debates with other monks. The tearful penitent was clearly enjoying an active social life, and thus if Hieronymus was not an outright liar then it would seem that he was economical with the truth when he came to write about his ascetic experience to Julia Eustochium in the 380s. Yet it must be remembered that Hieronymus was a gifted writer with a powerful imagination. A man who might see angels might rewrite his life in the light of his faith *and believe it.* That Hieronymus was a devout, if not to say fanatical believer in Nicene orthodoxy, in a single Catholic Church, is not in question, for he gave his adult life to the cause, like Athanasius making numerous enemies and suffering exile. In many ways, the future saint's life can be interpreted as the quest for unity, both personal and ecclesiastical. By identifying himself so strongly in his letters with the soteriological paradigm of the wilderness he was able to fuse Hieronymus the Christian with Hieronymus the Ciceronian, for the rhetoric of *Letter XXII* is worthy of Cicero's own. Despite the dream in which he had to choose between these two identities, Hieronymus found an ingenious way of combining them into a single, powerful voice. Additionally, this identification transformed him into an 'ascetic champion', a divine metamorphosis which enabled him to promote Nicene Christianity to the patrician ladies of Rome. During the 380s Hieronymus acted as guru to many would-be nuns, a position of prominence which secured him Episcopal patronage. This, in turn, put him in a position where he was able to begin work on the Vulgate Bible – itself a unificatory exercise, combining his tripartite knowledge of Hebrew, Greek, and Latin to create a modern translation of the Scriptures – a single Bible for a single Church.[7]

Yet for all his efforts to create unity, Hieronymus was a 'difficult' man, prone to 'cantankerous' outbursts and flashes of 'sarcastic wit'. Indeed, his 'aggressive sarcasm and readiness to equate himself with authentic tradition' alienated many people, old friends among them. 'Rufinus of Aquileia', for example, a childhood friend and fellow Christian, became one of his bitterest enemies. However, one could say that Hieronymus took the wilderness with him into the world, that his true testing in the desert did not take place beneath the Chalcean sun, but in 'Rome', 'Bethlehem' (where he remained in monastic exile from 385 CE until his death in 420 CE), and his own heart. The wilderness never left him – it was the struggle of orthodoxy against heresy, of a man against himself – it was the myth that defined him, and the myth which, through his writings and his actions, he finally became.[8]

Practice

The struggle for unity inherent in the life of Hieronymus, and the soteriological myth of the wilderness which he came to embody, is given dramatic form in the final sequence from Book Two. Following on from the fragmented dynamic of *Anatomy*, which corresponds to the cosmological phase of decoupling, *Wilderness* relates to the next stage of the Matter Era – the 'recombination epoch'. This stage was highly significant for by now the Universe had 'cooled to a temperature of a few thousand degrees', something which allowed 'electrons and protons to form hydrogen atoms'. Indeed, hydrogen is 'the most abundant chemical element in the Universe' and comprises 'some 73% of its mass'. Thus the formation of hydrogen atoms, which have a much heavier atomic weight than other stable atomic nuclei, such as 'neutrinos', led to the formation of regions of varying density. Those with the greater material density, and thus the greater gravitational force, attracted the propagating photons, ultimately causing them to lose some energy and thus be at a lower temperature. During the course of millennia, these photonic areas of material density went on to evolve into the stars and galaxies observable today (see 'Cosmological Paradigm').[9]

In the poem this process is signified through both architectonic and thematic devices. The sequence begins with a passage of Greek and Latin (lines 12-27). The Greek is from St. Paul's *Letter to the Ephesians* (2:14) and may be translated as:

> For he is our peace; in his flesh he has made both groups into one and has broken down the dividing wall, that is, the hostility between us.[10]

The Latin is from Hieronymus' *Letter XLIII* (c.385 CE) and can be rendered:

> For while we were created in God's image and likeness, by reason of our own perversity we hide ourselves behind changing masks.[11]

The desired effect is to create a sense of plurality and confusion, simultaneously mirroring the persona's state of nervous exhaustion in the desert *and* the state of the Universe in the wake of decoupling. The translations also reveal the paradoxical nature of their juxtaposition, for here oneness is also plurality, something which foreshadows the tensions inherent in the forthcoming action of recombination. Another reason for using these languages was, of course, to make reference to Hieronymus' legendary linguistic abilities. Likewise, the Hebrew section which follows (lines 64-70), and which can be translated as 'cease', 'guilt', 'lamb', and 'fracture', offers a further mark of plurality and confusion whilst concurrently making reference to the saint's erudition.[12]

The dynamic of recombination is performed both thematically and architectonically through Hieronymus' battle with himself in the guise of the devil (lines 180-282). Just as the *Anatomy* sequence saw the Caravaggic monologue, *Unstill Life*, 'decouple' into a polylogue, so *Wilderness* sees what is essentially a duologue 'recombine' into a monologue (lines 285-310). As with the *Anatomy* sequence, the body in *Wilderness* is seen to correspond with matter, but here photons and their attraction to areas of material density are characterised through the spiritualising action of light and the metaphor of blindness (e.g. lines 39, 103, 199, etc) versus being able to see (line 310).

NOTES

[1] E. A. Livingstone, *The Oxford Concise Dictionary of the Christian Church* (Oxford: Oxford University Press, 2000), 302; David Farmer, *The Oxford Dictionary of Saints* (Oxford: Oxford University Press, 2004), 270, 613; M. C. Howatson and Ian Chilvers, eds., *The Oxford Concise Companion to Classical Literature* (Oxford: Oxford University Press, 1996), 296; Stefan Rebenich, *Jerome* (London: Routledge, 2002), 7; Howatson and Chilvers, 295; Rebenich, 4, 5, 6.

[2] Jerome, 'Letter LXXXII' in, Stefan Rebenich, *Jerome* (London: Routledge, 2002), 4; Rebenich, 19, 9; Jerome, 'Letter XXII' in, Stefan Rebenich., *Jerome* (London: Routledge, 2002), 8-9.

[3] Rebenich, 7; Livingstone, 254, 29; David Keller, *Oasis of Wisdom: The Worlds of the Desert Fathers and Mothers* (Collegeville, Minnesota: Liturgical Press, 2005), 6.

[4] Chris Scarre, *Chronicle of the Roman Emperors* (London: Thames and Hudson, 2000), 213; Livingstone, 37; Simon Price, ed., *The Oxford Dictionary of Classical Myth and Religion* (Oxford: Oxford University Press, 2004), 55, 68; Livingstone, 400, 36.

[5] Rebenich, 9; Jerome, 'Letter XXII', 19.

[6] Albrecht Dürer, *Penitent Saint Jerome* (c.1497), painted with mixed media on pear-wood, and measuring 23.1x17.4cm, it is housed in the National Gallery in London; Leonardo da Vinci, *St. Hieronymus* (c.1480-1482), painted with oil on wood, and measuring 103x75cm, it is housed in the Pinacoteca Vaticana in Rome; Farmer, 271.

[7] Rebenich, 14, 15, 13.

[8] Farmer, 271; Rebenich, 210, 41.

[9] Ian Ridpath, ed., *The Oxford Dictionary of Astronomy* (Oxford: Oxford University Press, 2003), 381, 220, 314.

[10] St. Paul, 'Ephesians' in, Alfred Marshall, ed., *The Interlinear NRSV-NIV: Parallel New Testament in Greek and English* (London: Zondervan Publishing House, 1993), 560.

[11] Jerome, 'Letter XLIII' in, Jerome, *Selected Letters*, tr. F. A. Wright (Cambridge, Massachusetts: Harvard University Press, 1991), 175.

[12] L. A. Mitchel, *A Student's Vocabulary for Biblical Hebrew and Aramaic* (London: Zondervan Publishing House, 1984), 7, 25.

AFTERWORD

BEYOND THE WILDERNESS

Developing this epic conception has been a journey of refinement, a personal odyssey embodied in a series of artistic metamorphoses. I have learnt a lot; not least that a life's work cannot be condensed into three years. However, perhaps the greatest lesson has been that what one discovers through voyaging is so much more interesting, and surprising, than what one imagined at home. *Silence* has come to speak in ways I could not have anticipated when I began, and it excites me to think that, as a living work, it has the potential to evolve further still.

Upon leaving the wilderness, the question of precisely where to go from here is at once very simple and very complex. As we have seen, the Cosmological Paradigm and the projected action of the apophasis of the singularity provide a clear trajectory for the progression of my epic undertaking. Nevertheless, I am reluctant about saying which personas I will deploy next. Like Leonardo, I have come to value experience over abstract theorising, preferring to define my work empirically through the action of composition rather than restricting myself from the onset with a predetermined blueprint. As we saw in the Preface, predetermined ideas often need to undergo a radical process of transmutation, and thus I have learnt to court spontaneity and move with my rhythms. Suffice it to say that the personas *will* come, and they will be surprising.

Whilst I prefer to remain silent about the linear development of *Silence*, I feel that this would be an opportune moment to briefly discuss my plans for the epic's future dissemination. Its current textual incarnation as a bound book, although personally gratifying as a tangible embodiment of three years hard work, feels, nevertheless, rather restricted. *Silence* is very much an ongoing project and as such the compass of two covers creates an artificial boundary which I feel must, ultimately, be transcended.

The solution would appear to reside in a hypertext/hypermedia website. In such an environment, not only would the reader be able to engage with both textual hemispheres wherever they have access to the Internet, but the liquid quality of cyberspace would enable me to constantly update and expand the work. Additionally, the hypertext/hypermedia format would create the possibility of a more sophisticated artistic experience. For example, I am a great believer that poetry is something to be heard, to be experienced by the ear as well as by the eye. In the context of a website one can, of course, immediately grasp the potential, for the reader could simultaneously become the listener, hearing an audio recording of the text they are reading in front of them.

Indeed, this multimedia approach could be taken even further through the integration of visual texts. Regarding the Caravaggio monologue, for instance, one could have the artist's paintings appearing on the screen concurrent with both the written text and the audio soundtrack. Through such textual immersion the initiation of the reader/listener into the action of the primary negation would become a more sensuous and intense experience. To be sure, in a very Beuysian gesture, the audience could, in fact, become highly active participants, posting comments on a message-board, and perhaps even contributing to the poetry. As the epic of the Universe expands towards its ultimate negation it could swell to embrace numerous poets and critics, to truly become 'one song of many voices'.

Finally, in light of the Zukofskyian sentiment expressed above, I would like to take this opportunity to mention another future textual development. Inspired by the pluralism of Beuys and Barney's oeuvres, and in addition to formulating plans for a hypertext/hypermedia website, I have begun an experimental collaboration with painters, sculptors, filmmakers, photographers, and musicians in order to see whether the epic has the potential to develop into a *gesamtkunstwerk* (total work of art). Thus, as the two written hemispheres of *Silence* create and negate one another as they progress forward from Big Bang to Big Crunch, so these other artists, autonomously playing off the themes and ideas found in my work will move the epic sideways into other dimensions, turning the Universe into a Multiverse. Ultimately, I envision their work complementing the epic's original apophatic dynamic, problematising the reader/listener's interpretation of the epic's written dimensions and, through their diverse, parallel treatments of ideas/themes, problematising each other. Consequently, this artistic Multiverse will contract into a density of connected but contradictory signs. It will become a multi-textual singularity!

This project began inflamed with Promethean hubris…

BIBLIOGRAPHY

Aeschylus, 'Prometheus Bound' in, *Prometheus Bound and Other Plays*, translated with an introduction by P. Vellacott (London: Penguin Books Ltd, 1961)

Ahearn, B., *Zukofsky's "A": An Introduction* (Los Angeles: University of California Press, 1982)

À Kempis, T., *The Imitation of Christ*, translated by L. Sherley-Price (London: Penguin Books Ltd, 1977)

Alberti, L. B., *On Painting*, translated by C. Grayson with an introduction and notes by M. Kemp (London: Penguin Books Ltd, 2004)

Alighieri, D., *The Divine Comedy*, translated by D. H. Higgins and with an introduction by C. H. Sisson (Oxford: Oxford University Press, 1993)

Allen, G., *Intertextuality* (London: Routledge, 2001)

Ames-Lewis, F., *The Intellectual Life of the Early Renaissance Artist* (New Haven: Yale University Press, 2000)

Anatolios, K., *Athanasius* (London: Routledge, 2004)

Andrews Aiken, J., 'The Perspective Construction of Masaccio's *Trinity* Fresco and Medieval Astronomical Graphics' in, Goffen, R., ed., *Masaccio's Trinity* (Cambridge: Cambridge University Press, 1998)

Anonimo Gaddiano, 'Codex Magliabecchiano' in, Vezzosi, A., *Leonardo da Vinci: Renaissance Man*, translated by A. Bonfante-Warren (London: Thames and Hudson Ltd, 1997)

Anonimo Gaddiano, 'Codex Magliabecchiano' in, Nicholl, C., *Leonardo da Vinci: The Flights of the Mind* (London: Penguin Books Ltd, 2005)

Apollonius of Rhodes, *The Voyage of the Argo*, translated by E. V. Rieu (London: Penguin Classics, 1971)
Aristotle, *Poetics*, translated with an introduction by M. Heath (London: Penguin Books Ltd, 1996)
Athanasius, 'The Life of Antony' in, Athanasius, *The Life of Antony and The Letter to Marcellinus*, translated with an introduction by R. C. Gregg (London: SPCK, 1980)
Augustine, *Confessions*, translated with an introduction by R. S. Pine-Coffin (London: Penguin Books Ltd, 1961)
Axelrod, S. G., *Robert Lowell: Life and Art* (Princeton, New Jersey: Princeton University Press, 1978)
Ayer, A. J., *Language, Truth and Logic* (London: Penguin Books Ltd, 2001)
Baglione, G., 'The Life of Michelangelo da Caravaggio' in, *Lives of Caravaggio*, edited and translated by H. Hibbard, with an introduction by H. Langdon (London: Pallas Athene, 2005)
Ball, P., *The Devil's Doctor: Paracelsus and the World of Renaissance Magic and Science* (London: William Heinemann, 2006)
Barasch, M., *Theories of Art 1: From Plato to Winckelmann* (London: Routledge, 2000)
Barnes, J., *Aristotle* (Oxford: Oxford University Press, 2000)
Barnes, J., edits and translates, *Early Greek Philosophy* (London: Penguin Books Ltd, 2001)
Baroni, C., ed., *All the Paintings of Caravaggio*, translated by A. Firmin O'Sullivan (London: Oldbourne, 1962)
Basta, C., *Botticelli*, translated by A. E. Ruzzante (New York: Rizzoli International Publications Inc, 2005)
Bauer, H., and A, Prater, *Baroque*, translated by I. Flett (London: Taschen, 2006)
Baxandall, M., *Painting and Experience in Fifteenth-Century Italy* (Oxford: Oxford University Press, 1988)
Bell, J., 'Color and Chiaroscuro' in, Hall, M., ed., *Raphael's School of Athens* (Cambridge: Cambridge University Press, 1997)
Bellori, G. P., 'On Michelangelo da Caravaggio' in, *Lives of Caravaggio*, edited and translated by H. Hibbard,

with an introduction by H. Langdon (London: Pallas Athene, 2005)

Bellosi, L., *Michelangelo: Painting*, translated by G. Webb (London: Thames and Hudson, 1970)

Berkeley, G., *Principles of Human Knowledge/Three Dialogues*, edited with an introduction by R. Woolhouse (London: Penguin Books Ltd, 1988)

Berman, D., 'Introduction' in, *The World as Will and Idea*, translated by J. Berman with an introduction and notes by D. Berman (London: Everyman, 1995)

Berti, L., *Fra Angelico*, translated by P. Sanders (London: Thames and Hudson, 1968)

Beuys, J., *What is Art?*, edited with essays by V. Harlan, translated by M. Barton and S. Sacks (Oxford: Clairview Books, 2007)

Blunt, A., *Artistic Theory in Italy: 1450-1600* (Oxford: Oxford University Press, 1962)

Boethius, *The Consolations of Philosophy*, translated with an introduction by V. Watts (London: Penguin Books Ltd, 1999)

Borgia, C., 'Letter of Authorisation: 18th August 1502' in, Nicholl, C., *Leonardo da Vinci: The Flights of the Mind* (London: Penguin Books Ltd, 2005)

Bottari, S., *Caravaggio*, translated by D. Goldrei (London: Thames and Hudson, 1971)

Boulter, A., *Writing Fiction: Creative and Critical Approaches* (Basingstoke: Palgrave Macmillan, 2007)

Bower, J., ed., *The Oxford Concise Dictionary of World Religions* (Oxford: Oxford University Press, 2000)

Bradford, S., *Cesare Borgia: His Life and Times* (London: Weidenfeld and Nicolson, 1976)

Braidotti, R., *Nomadic Subjects: Embodiment and Difference in Contemporary Feminist Theory* (New York: Columbia University Press, 1994)

Brown, H., ed., *Hypermedia/Hypertext and Object-Orientated Databases* (London: Chapman and Hall, 1991).

Brown, W. J., *Syphilis a Synopsis* (Honolulu, Hawaii: University Press of the Pacific, 2001)

Browning, R. *Men and Women and Other Poems*, edited by C. Graham with an introduction by J. W. Harper (London: J. M. Dent, 1998)

Bruno, G., *The Ash Wednesday Supper*, edited and translated by E. A. Gosselin and L. S. Lerner (Toronto: University of Toronto Press, 1995)

Buchholz, E., *Leonardo da Vinci: Life and Work*, translated by P. Barton (Cambridge: Goodfellow and Egan Publishing Management, 2005)

Bull, G., ed., *Michelangelo: Life, Letters, and Poetry* (Oxford: Oxford University Press, 1999)

Bull, M., *The Mirror of the Gods: Classical Mythology in Renaissance Art* (London: Penguin Books Ltd, 2005)

Bunting, B., *Complete Poems* (Trowbridge: Bloodaxe Books Ltd, 2000)

Buonarroti, M., 'Partial Sonnet, 1520s' in, *Everyman's Poetry: Michelangelo*, translated and edited by C. Ryan (London: J. M. Dent, 1998)

Buonarroti, M., 'Sonnet for Tommaso Cavalieri, c. 1534' in, *Everyman's Poetry: Michelangelo*, translated and edited by C. Ryan (London: J. M. Dent, 1998)

Burckhardt, J., *The Civilisation of the Renaissance in Italy*, translated by S. G. C. Middlemore with an introduction by P. Burke and notes by P. Murray (London: Penguin Books Ltd, 2004)

Burke, P., *The Italian Renaissance: Culture and Society in Italy* (Oxford: Polity Press, 1991)

Burke, S., *Authorship from Plato to Postmodernism* (Edinburgh: Edinburgh University Press, 1995)

Burkert, W., *Ancient Mystery Cults* (Cambridge, Massachusetts: Harvard University Press, 1987)

Burroway, J., *Imaginative Writing: The Elements of Craft* (New York: Pearson Longman 2007)

Butt, M., *Lipstick* (London: Greenwich Exchange, 2007)

Buttler, J., *Gender Trouble: Feminism and the Subversion of Identity* (London: Routledge, 1999)

Cameron, A., *The Later Roman Empire* (London: Fontana Press, 1993)

Campbell, J., *The Hero with a Thousand Faces* (London: Fontana Press, 1993)

Capra, F., *The Tao of Physics: An Exploration of the Parallels Between Modern Physics and Eastern Mysticism* (London: Flamingo, 1991)

Carlino, A., *Books of the Body: Anatomical Ritual and Renaissance Learning*, translated by J. Tedeschi and A. Tedeschi (Chicago: The University of Chicago Press, 1999)

Carpenter, H., *A Serious Character: The Life of Ezra Pound* (London: Faber and Faber, 1988)

Cashford, J., translates, 'Hymn to Apollo' in, *The Homeric Hymns* (London: Penguin Books Ltd, 2003)

Cashford, J., translates, '1st Hymn to Demeter' in, *The Homeric Hymns* (London: Penguin Books Ltd, 2003)

Cashford, J., translates, '1st Hymn to Dionysos' in, *The Homeric Hymns* (London: Penguin Books Ltd, 2003)

Cashford J., translates, '2nd Hymn to Dionysos' in, *The Homeric Hymns* (London: Penguin Books Ltd, 2003)

Cashford, J., 'Note to The 1st Hymn to Dionysos' in, *The Homeric Hymns* (London: Penguin Books Ltd, 2003)

Cassirer, E., P. O. Kristeller, and J. H. Randall, eds., *The Renaissance Philosophy of Man* (London: Phoenix Books, 1963)

Castiglione, B., *The Book of the Courtier*, translated with an introduction by G. Bull (London: Penguin Books Ltd, 2003)

Cate, C., *Friedrich Nietzsche: A Biography* (London: Pimlico, 2002)

Cellini, B., *Autobiography*, translated with an introduction by G. Ball (London: Penguin Books Ltd, 1998)

Cennini, C., *The Craftsman's Handbook "Il libro dell'arte"*, translated by D. V. Thompson (New York: Dover Publications Inc, 1960)

Chamberlain, L., *Nietzsche in Turin: The End of the Future* (London: Quartet Books, 1996)

Chilvers, I., *The Oxford Concise Dictionary of Art and Artists* (Oxford: Oxford University Press, 2003)

Chomsky, N., *On Nature and Language* (Cambridge: Cambridge University Press, 2002)

Cicero, *The Nature of the Gods*, translated by H. C. P. McGregor with an introduction by J. M. Ross (London: Penguin Books Ltd, 1972)

Cicero, *Selected Works*, translated with an introduction by M. Grant (London: Penguin Books Ltd, 1971)

Clark, K., *Civilisation* (London: John Murray, 2005)

Cohn-Sherbok, L., ed., *Who's Who in Christianity* (London: Routledge, 1998)

Cole, A., *Art of the Italian Renaissance Courts* (London: Weidenfield and Nicolson Ltd, 1995)

Coles, P., *Cosmology* (Oxford: Oxford University Press, 2001)

Coles, P., *Hawking and the Mind of God* (Cambridge: Icon Books Ltd, 2000)

Cook, J., ed., *Poetry in Theory: An Anthology 1900-2000* (Oxford: Blackwell Publishing, 2004)

Cormack, R., *Byzantine Art* (Oxford: Oxford University Press, 2000)

Coupe, L., *Myth* (London: Routledge, 1997)

Culler, J., *Structuralist Poetics: Structuralism, Linguistics and the Study of Literature* (London: Routledge and Kegan Paul, 1980)

Da Vinci, L., 'Anghiari Disaster: Madrid Codex II' in, Nicholl, C., *Leonardo da Vinci: The Flights of the Mind* (London: Penguin Books Ltd, 2005)

Da Vinci, L., *A Treatise on Painting*, translated by J. F. Rigaud (New York: Dover Publications Inc, 2005)

Da Vinci, L., 'Caterina Came: Codex Forster (1493)' in, White, M., *Leonardo: The First Scientist* (London: Abacus, 2001)

Da Vinci, L., 'Depicting War: Manuscript A' in, Nicholl, C., *Leonardo da Vinci: The Flights of the Mind* (London: Penguin Books Ltd, 2005)

Da Vinci, L., 'Di Ser Piero: Codex Atlanticus' in, White, M., *Leonardo: The First Scientist* (London: Abacus, 2001)

Da Vinci, L., 'Draft of Letter to Ludovico Sforza: Codex Atlanticus' in, White, M., *Leonardo: The First Scientist* (London: Abacus, 2001)

Da Vinci, L., 'Grandchild of God: Manuscript A' in, Vezzosi, A., *Leonardo da Vinci: Renaissance Man*, translated by A. Bonfante-Warren (London: Thames and Hudson Ltd, 1997)

Da Vinci, L., 'Macrocosmic Analogy: Codex Leicester (1508)' in, Kemp, M., *Leonardo* (Oxford: Oxford University Press, 2005)

Da Vinci, L., 'Mathematical Rule: Codex Leicester (1508)' in, Kemp, M., *Leonardo* (Oxford: Oxford University Press, 2005)

Da Vinci, L., 'On Botticelli: Codex Atlanticus' in, White, M., *Leonardo: The First Scientist* (London: Abacus, 2001)

Da Vinci, L., 'On Flight: Turin Codex ' in, Nicholl, C., *Leonardo da Vinci: The Flights of the Mind* (London: Penguin Books Ltd, 2005)

Da Vinci, L., 'On humanity: Codex Forster' in, White, M., *Leonardo: The First Scientist* (London: Abacus, 2001)

Da Vinci, L., 'On Painting: Codex Forster' in, Nicholl, C., *Leonardo da Vinci: The Flights of the Mind* (London: Penguin Books Ltd, 2005)

Da Vinci, L., 'On Sex: Manuscript A' in, White, M., *Leonardo: The First Scientist* (London: Abacus, 2001)

Da Vinci, L., 'On War: Codex Urbinus' in, Nicholl, C., *Leonardo da Vinci: The Flights of the Mind* (London: Penguin Books Ltd, 2005)

Da Vinci, L., 'Quaderni, III' in, White, M., *Leonardo: The First Scientist* (London: Abacus, 2001)

Da Vinci, L., 'The Centenarian: Codex Leicester (1507)' in, White, M., *Leonardo: The First Scientist* (London: Abacus, 2001)

Da Vinci, L., 'Treatise on Painting' in, Chilvers, I., *The Oxford Dictionary of Art and Artists* (Oxford: Oxford University Press, 2003)

Davidson, H., *T. S. Eliot and Hermeneutics: Absence and Interpretation in The Waste Land* (London: Louisiana State University Press, 1985)

Davies, P. R. and D. J. A. Clines, eds., *Among the Prophets: Language, Image and Structure in Prophetic Writings* (Sheffield: Sheffield Academic Press, 1993)

Deimling, B., *Sandro Botticelli*, translated by M. Claridge (London: Taschen, 2000)

De Montaigne, M., *The Essays: A Selection*, translated and edited with an introduction by M. A. Screech (London: Penguin Books Ltd, 2004)

Derrida, J., *Positions*, translated and annotated by A. Bass (London: The Athlone Press, 1981)

Derrida, J., *Writing and Difference*, translated by A. Bass (London: Routledge, 2001)

Descartes, R., *A Discourse on Method, Meditations and Principles*, translated by J. Veitch, with an introduction by T. Sorell (London: Everyman, 1994)

Dodds, E. R., *The Greeks and the Irrational* (Los Angeles: University of California Press, 1997)

Duncan, R., *Selected Poems* (New York: Stanza Press, 2000)

Earnshaw, S., ed., *The Handbook of Creative Writing* (Edinburgh: Edinburgh University Press, 2007)

Eckhart, M., *The Essential Sermons, Commentaries, Treatises, and Defence*, translation and introduction by E. Colledge and B. McGinn (New Jersey: Paulist Press, 1981)

Eliot, T. S., *The Complete Poems and Plays* (London: Faber and Faber, 1969)

Eliot, T. S., 'Tradition and the Individual Talent' in, Eliot, T. S., *Selected Essays* (London: Faber and Faber, 1999)

Elliot, S., *Italian Renaissance Painting* (London: Phaidon, 1993)

Euripides, *The Bacchae*, translated by P. Vellacott (London: Penguin Books Ltd, 1973)

Eusebius, *The History of the Church*, translated by G. A. Williamson, edited with an introduction and notes by A. Louth (London: Penguin Books Ltd, 1989)

Farmer, D., *The Oxford Dictionary of Saints* (Oxford: Oxford University Press, 2004)

Fernie, E., ed., *Art History and Its Methods: A Critical Anthology* (London: Phaidon, 2006)

Ficino, M., 'On divine frenzy' in, Ficino, M., *Meditations on the Soul: Selected Letters of Marsilio Ficino*, translated from the Latin by members of the Language Department of the School of Economic Science, London (Rochester, Vermont: Inner Traditions International, 1997)

Field, J. V., 'Masaccio and Perspective in Italy in the Fifteenth Century' in, Cole Ahl, D., ed., *The Cambridge Companion to Masaccio* (Cambridge: Cambridge University Press, 2002)

Finlay. V., *Colour: Travels Through the Paintbox* (London: Hodder and Stoughton, 2002)

Fletcher, S., *The Longman Companion to Renaissance Europe* (London: Longman, 2000)

Flowers, B. S., *Browning and the Modern Tradition* (London: The Macmillan Press Ltd, 1976)

Foister, S., *Dürer and the Virgin in the Garden* (London: National Gallery, 2004)

Foucault, M., *The History of Sexuality: 2*, translated from the French by E. Hurley (London: Penguin Books Ltd, 1992)

Frazer, J. G., *The Golden Bough*, abridged with an introduction and notes by R. Fraser (Oxford: Oxford University Press, 1998)

Freud, S., *Leonardo da Vinci: A Memory of his Childhood*, translated by A. Tyson (London: Routledge, 2001)

Geldard, R., *Remembering Heraclitus The Philosopher of Riddles* (Edinburgh: Floris Books, 2000)

George, A., translates with an introduction, *The Epic of Gilgamesh* (London: Penguin Books Ltd, 1999)

Gibbs, R. W., *The Poetics of Mind: Figurative Thought, Language, and Understanding* (Cambridge: Cambridge University Press, 1994)

Gioni, M., *Matthew Barney*, translated by N. J. Ross (Milan: Electra, 2007)

Goffen, R., 'Introduction' in, Goffen, R., ed., *Masaccio's Trinity* (Cambridge: Cambridge University Press, 1998)

Goffen, R., 'Masaccio's *Trinity* and the *Letter to the Hebrews* ' in, Goffen, R., ed., *Masaccio's Trinity* (Cambridge: Cambridge University Press, 1998)

Goldberg, J., 'Introduction' in, Goldberg, J., ed., *Queering the Renaissance* (New York: Duke University Press, 1994)

Gordon, D., 'The Altarpieces of Masaccio' in, Cole Ahl, D., ed., *The Cambridge Companion to Masaccio* (Cambridge: Cambridge University Press, 2002)

Grant, M., *The Emperor Constantine* (London: Weidenfeld and Nicolson, 1993)

Grant, R. M., *Gnosticism and Early Christianity* (New York: Harper and Row Publishers, 1966)

Graves, R., *The Greek Myths: Volume 1* (London: Penguin Books Ltd, 1960)

Gregg, R. C., 'Introduction' in, Athanasius, *The Life of Antony and The Letter to Marcellinus*, translated with an introduction by R. C. Gregg (London: SPCK, 1980)

Gregory, J., ed., *The Neoplatonists* (London: Kyle Cathie, 1991)

Gribbin, J., *The Future of Cosmology* (London: Phoenix, 1997)

Grömling, A., *Michelangelo*, translated by P. Barton (Cambridge: Könemann, 2005)

Grosz, D., ed., *Barney/Beuys: All in the Present Must Be Transformed* (Berlin: Deutsche Guggenheim, 2007)

Grundlehner, P., *The Poetry of Friedrich Nietzsche* (Oxford: Oxford University Press, 1986)

Guthrie, W. K. C., *Orpheus and Greek Religion* (Princeton: Princeton University Press, 1952)

Hall, J., *Hall's Dictionary of Subjects and Symbols in Art* (London: John Murray, 1996)

Hall, M., 'Introduction' in, Hall, M., ed., *Raphael's School of Athens* (Cambridge: Cambridge University Press, 1997)

Harper, G., 'Creative Writing Doctorates' in, Earnshaw, S., ed., *The Handbook of Creative Writing* (Edinburgh: Edinburgh University Press, 2007)
Harrison, T., *Selected Poetry* (London: Faber and Faber, 2000)
Hawking, S., *A Brief History of Time: From the Big Bang to Black Holes* (London: Bantam Books, 1988)
Hawking, S., *Black Holes and Baby Universes and Other Essays* (London: Bantam Books, 1994)
Hayman, R., *Nietzsche's Voices* (London: Phoenix, 2003)
Heaney, S., trans., *Beowulf* (London: Faber and Faber, 1999)
Heaney, S., *Finders Keepers: Selected Prose, 1971-2001* (London: Faber and Faber, 2002)
Heaney, S., *Seeing Things* (London: Faber and Faber, 1991)
Heath, M., 'Introduction' in, Aristotle, *Poetics*, translated with an introduction and notes by M. Heath (London: Penguin Books Ltd, 1996)
Heaton, J. M., *Wittgenstein and Psychoanalysis* (Cambridge: Icon Books Ltd, 2000)
Heidegger, M., *An Introduction to Metaphysics*, translated by R. Manheim (New Haven: Yale University Press, 1959)
Heidegger, M., *Being and Time*, translated by A. Hofstadter (London: Harper and Row Publishers, 1979)
Heidegger, M., *Poetry, Language, Thought*, translated by A. Hofstadter (London: Harper and Row Publishers, 1975)
Heine, H., *Selected Poems*, translated and edited by D. Cram and T. Reed (London: Everyman, 1997)
Heraclitus, 'Fragment 16' in, Geldard, R., *Remembering Heraclitus: The Philosopher of Riddles* (Edinburgh: Floris Books, 2000)
Heraclitus, 'Fragment 20' in, Geldard, R., *Remembering Heraclitus: The Philosopher of Riddles* (Edinburgh: Floris Books, 2000)
Hermes Trismegistus, 'The Corpus Hermeticum' in, *The Way of Hermes: The Corpus Hermeticum and the Definitions of Hermes Trismegistus to Asclepius*, translated by C. Salaman, D. van Oyen, W. D.

Wharton and J-P. Mahé (London: Gerald Duckworth & Co Ltd, 1999)

Herodotus, *The Histories,* translated by A. de Sélincourt with an introduction and notes by J. Marincola (London: Penguin Books Ltd, 2003)

Hesiod, 'Theogony' in, *Hesiod and Theognis*, translated with an introduction by D. Wender (London: Penguin Books Ltd, 1973)

Heusinger, L., and F. Mancinelli, *All the Frescos of the Sistine Chapel*, translated by R. Fajardo (Firenze: Zincografia Fiorentina, 1973)

Hill, G., *Collected Poems* (London: Penguin Books Ltd, 1985)

Hill, G., *The Orchards of Syon* (London: Penguin Books Ltd, 2002), and Prynne, J., H., *Poems* (Highgreen: Bloodaxe Books Ltd, 2004)

Hölderlin, F., *Hymns and Fragments*, translated with an introduction by R. Sieburth (Princeton: Princeton University Press, 1984)

Hölderlin F., *Selected Poems and Fragments*, translated with an introduction by M. Hamburger (London: Penguin Books Ltd, 1998)

Hollingdale, R. J., 'Note on the Text' in, Nietzsche, F., *Ecce Homo*, translated by R. J. Hollingdale with an introduction and notes by M. Tanner (London: Penguin Books Ltd, 1992)

Hollingdale, R. J., 'Translator's Note' in, *Twilight of the Idols and The Anti-Christ*, translated by R. J. Hollingdale with an introduction by M. Tanner (London: Penguin Books Ltd, 2003)

Homer, *The Iliad*, translated by L. Janus (London: Berry Books Ltd, 1983)

Homer, *The Iliad*, translated by R. Fagles, with an introduction by B. Knox (London: Penguin Books Ltd, 1990)

Homer, *The Iliad*, translated by R. Fitzgerald and with an introduction by G. S. Kirk (Oxford: Oxford University Press, 1984)

Homer, *The Odyssey*, translated by R. Fagles with an introduction by B. Knox (London: Penguin Books Ltd, 2004)

Homer, *The Odyssey*, translated by Walter Shewring and with an introduction by G. S. Kirk (Oxford: Oxford University Press, 1980)

Howatson, M. C., and I. Chilvers, eds., *The Oxford Concise Companion to Classical Literature* (Oxford: Oxford University Press, 1996)

Hughes, T., *Tales from Ovid* (London: Faber and Faber, 1997)

Hume, D., *A Treatise of Human Nature* (London: Everyman, 2003)

Hume, D., *Dialogues Concerning Natural Religion* (London: Penguin Books Ltd, 1990)

Huxley, A., *The Perennial Philosophy* (New York: Harper and Row, Publishers, Inc, 1945)

Hyde, M., *Introducing Jung*, with illustrations by M. McGuinness (Cambridge: Icon Books UK, 1999)

Impelluso, L., *Nature and its Symbols*, translated by S. Sartarelli (Los Angeles: The J. Paul Getty Museum, 2004)

Inwood, M., *Heidegger* (Oxford: Oxford University Press, 2000)

Jabès, E., *From the Book to the Book: An Edmond Jabès Reader*, translated from the French by R. Waldrop with additional translations by P. Joris, A. Rudolf, and K. Waldrop (London: Wesleyan University Press, 1991)

Jarman, D., *Derek Jarman's Caravaggio: The Complete Film Script and Commentaries by Derek Jarman and Photographs by Gerald Incandela* (London: Thames and Hudson, 1986)

Jasper, D., *A Short Introduction to Hermeneutics* (London: Westminster John Knox Press, 2004)

Jaspers, K., *Socrates, Buddha, Confucius, Jesus: The Paradigmatic Individuals*, translated by R. Manheim (New York: Harcourt Brace and Company, 1962)

Jerome, 'Letter XXII' in, Rebenich, S., *Jerome* (London: Routledge, 2002)

Jerome, 'Letter XLIII' in, Jerome, *Selected Letters*, translated by F. A. Wright (Cambridge, Massachusetts: Harvard University Press, 1991)

Jerome, 'Letter LXXXII' in, Rebenich, S., *Jerome* (London: Routledge, 2002)

Jerome, 'Life of Paul of Thebes' in, *Early Christian Lives*, translated, edited, and with an introduction by C. White (London: Penguin Books Ltd, 1998)

Johnson, G. A., *Renaissance Art* (Oxford: Oxford University Press, 2005)

Jones, D., *The Anathemata* (London: Faber and Faber, 1979)

Jung, C. G., *Modern Man in Search of a Soul*, translated by W. S. Dell and C. F. Baynes (London: Routledge, 2001)

Jung, C. G., *On the Nature of the Psyche*, translated by R. F. C. Hull (London: Routledge, 2001)

Kant, I., *Critique of Pure Reason*, a revised and expanded translation based on Meiklejohn edited by V. Politis (London: Everyman, 2002)

Kaufmann, W., 'Translator's Introduction' in, Nietzsche, F., *The Gay Science*, translated with an introduction by W. Kaufmann (New York: Vintage Books, 1974)

Keats, J., 'Letter to Richard Woodhouse, 27th October 1818' in, Gittings, R., ed., *The Letters of John Keats* (Oxford: Oxford University Press, 1970)

Kekewich, L., ed., *The Impact of Humanism* (New Haven: Yale University Press, 2000)

Keller, D., *Oasis of Wisdom: The Worlds of the Desert Fathers and Mothers* (Collegeville, Minnesota: Liturgical Press, 2005)

Kelly, I., *Beau Brummell: The Ultimate Dandy* (London: Hodder and Stoughton, 2005)

Kemp, M., 'Introduction' in, Alberti, L. B., *On Painting*, translated by C. Grayson with an introduction and notes by M. Kemp (London: Penguin Books Ltd, 2004)

Kemp, M., *Leonardo* (Oxford: Oxford University Press, 2005)

Kennedy, I. G., *Titian* (London: Taschen, 2006)

Kenner, H., 'The Broken Mirrors and Mirrors of Memory' in, Leary, L., ed., *Motive and Method in the Cantos of Ezra Pound* (New York: Columbia University Press, 1969)

Kenney, E. J., 'Introduction' in, Ovid, *Metamorphoses*, translated by A. D. Melville with an introduction and notes by E. J. Kenney (Oxford: Oxford University Press, 1986)

Kerényi, C., *Dionysos: Archetypal Image of Indestructible Life*, translated by R. Manheim (Princeton: Princeton University Press, 1976)

King, R., *Michelangelo and the Pope's Ceiling* (London: Pimlico, 2003)

Klossowski, P., *Nietzsche and the Vicious Circle*, translated by D. W. Smith (London: The Athlone Press, 1997)

Knox, B., 'Introduction' in, Homer, *The Odyssey*, translated by R. Fagles with an introduction and notes by B. Knox (London: Penguin Books Ltd, 1996)

Koestler, A., *The Sleepwalkers: A History of Man's Changing Vision of the Universe* (London: Penguin Books Ltd, 1975)

Krauth, N., and T. Brady, eds., *Creative Writing: Theory Beyond Practice* (Teneriffe: Post Pressed, 2006)

Lambert, G., *Caravaggio*, translated by C. Miller (London: Taschen, 2004)

Lane Fox, R., *Alexander the Great* (London: Penguin Books Ltd, 1986)

Laneyrie-Dagen, N., *How to Read Paintings*, translated by R. Elliott (Edinburgh: Chambers Harrap Publishers, 2004)

Langdon, H., *Caravaggio: A Life* (London: Pimlico, 1999).

Langdon, H., 'Introduction' in, *Lives of Caravaggio*, edited and translated by H. Hibbard, with an introduction by H. Langdon (London: Pallas Athene, 2005).

Larkin, P., *Collected Poems* (London: Faber and Faber, 2003)

Larkin, P., 'High Windows' in, Larkin, P., *Collected Poems* (London: Faber and Faber, 2003)

Lee, D., 'Introduction' in, Plato, *Timaeus and Critias*, translated with an introduction by D. Lee (London: Penguin Books Ltd, 1977)

Levey, M., *Early Renaissance* (London: Penguin Books Ltd, 1967)

Levey, M., *From Giotto to Cézanne: A Concise History of Painting* (London: Thames and Hudson, 1997)

Levinas, E., *Alterity and Transcendence*, translated by M. B. Smith (London: The Athlone Press, 1999)

Livingstone, E. A., *The Oxford Concise Dictionary of the Christian Church* (Oxford: Oxford University Press, 2000)

Lowell, R., *Life Studies* (London: Faber and Faber, 2001)

Lucretius, *On the Nature of the Universe*, a verse translation by R. Melville with an introduction and notes by D. and P. Fowler (Oxford: Oxford University Press, 1997)

McGrath, A. E., *Christian Theology: An Introduction* (Oxford: Blackwell Publishers Ltd, 2002)

Macchi, V., ed., *Collins Sansoni Italian Dictionary* (Milan: Rizzoli Larousse, 2003)

Machiavelli, N., *The Prince*, translated by G. Bull with an introduction by A. Grafton (London: Penguin Books Ltd, 1999)

Magnus, B., and K. M. Higgins, eds., *The Cambridge Companion to Nietzsche* (Cambridge: Cambridge University Press, 1996)

Mancini, G., 'On Michelangelo Merisi da Caravaggio' in, *Lives of Caravaggio*, edited and translated by H. Hibbard, with an introduction by H. Langdon (London: Pallas Athene, 2005).

Marini, F., *Caravaggio*, translated by M. Hurley (New York: Rizzoli, 2006)

Marshall, A., ed., *The Interlinear NRSV-NIV: Parallel New Testament in Greek and English* (London: Zondervan Publishing House, 1993)

Matthew, J., ed., *The Holy Bible: New International Version* (Colorado: International Bible Society, 1991)

Mautner, T., ed., *The Penguin Dictionary of Philosophy* (London: Penguin Books Ltd, 2000)

Mesch, C., ed., *Joseph Beuys: The Reader* (London: I. B. Tauris, 2007)

Middleton, C., trans, *Selected Letters of Friedrich Nietzsche* (Cambridge: Hackett Publishing Company, Inc., 1969)

Middleton, P., *Distant Reading: Performance, Readership, and Consumption in Contemporary Poetry* (Tuscaloosa: The University of Alabama Press, 2005)

Milton, J., *Complete English Poems, Of Education, Areopagitica* (London: Everyman, 1990)

Milton, J., *Paradise Lost* (London: Penguin Books Ltd, 2000)

Mitchel, L. A., *A Student's Vocabulary for Biblical Hebrew and Aramaic* (London: Zondervan Publishing House, 1984)

Monti, R., *Leonardo*, translated by P. Sanders (London: Thames and Hudson, 1967)

Monti, R., *Raphael*, translated by C. Beamish (London: Thames and Hudson, 1968)

Motion, A., *Philip Larkin* (London: Methuen, 1982)

Motion, A., *Philip Larkin: A Writer's Life* (London: Faber and Faber, 1993)

Muller, J. E., *Rembrandt* (London: Thames and Hudson, 1968)

Murray, L., *Michelangelo* (London: Thames and Hudson, 1992)

Murray, L., *The Late Renaissance and Mannerism* (London: Thames and Hudson, 1967)

Murray, P., *The Architecture of the Italian Renaissance* (London: Thames and Hudson, 1998)

Murray, P., ed., *The Oxford Dictionary of Christian Art* (Oxford: Oxford University Press, 2004)

Nehamas, A., *Nietzsche: Life as Literature* (Cambridge, Massachusetts: Harvard University Press, 1985)

Néret, G., *Michelangelo*, translated by P. Snowdon (London: Taschen, 2000)

Neruda, P., *Selected Poems*, edited by N. Tarn, translated by A. Kerrigan, W. S. Merwin and A. Reid, with an introduction by J. Franco (London: Penguin Books Ltd, 1975)

Nicholl, C., *Leonardo da Vinci: The Flights of the Mind* (London: Penguin Books Ltd, 2005)

Nietzsche, F., 'An Attempt At A Self-Criticism' in, *The Birth of Tragedy out of the Spirit of Music,* translated by S. Whiteside with an introduction by M. Tanner (London: Penguin Books Ltd, 1993)

Nietzsche, F., 'Appendix: Variants from Nietzsche's Drafts' in, *Basic Writings of Nietzsche*, translated and edited by W. Kaufmann (New York: Random House, 2000)

Nietzsche, F., *Beyond Good and Evil*, translated by R. J. Hollingdale with an introduction by M. Tanner (London: Penguin Books Ltd, 2003)

Nietzsche, F., *The Birth of Tragedy out of the Spirit of Music,* translated by S. Whiteside with an introduction by M. Tanner (London: Penguin Books Ltd, 1993)

Nietzsche, F., *Dithyrambs of Dionysus*, translated with an introduction by R. J. Hollingdale (London: Anvil Poetry Press Ltd, 1984)

Nietzsche, F., *Ecce Homo*, translated by R. J. Hollingdale with an introduction by M. Tanner (London: Penguin Books Ltd, 1992)

Nietzsche, F., *Human, All Too Human*, translated by M. Faber and S. Lehmann (London: Penguin Books Ltd, 1994)

Nietzsche, F., 'Letter to Carl Fuchs: Sils, Sunday, July 29, 1888' in, *Selected Letters of Friedrich Nietzsche*, edited and translated by C. Middleton (Cambridge: Hackett Publishing Company, Inc., 1969)

Nietzsche, F., 'Letter to Franz Overbeck: Postmarked Rapallo, December 25, 1882' in, *Selected Letters of Friedrich Nietzsche*, edited and translated by C.

Middleton (Cambridge: Hackett Publishing Company, Inc., 1969)

Nietzsche, F., 'Letter to Franz Overbeck: Received January 7, 1889' in, *Selected Letters of Friedrich Nietzsche*, edited and translated by C. Middleton (Cambridge: Hackett Publishing Company, Inc., 1969)

Nietzsche, F., 'Letter to Friedrich Ritschl (Basel, January 30, 1872)' in, *Selected Letters of Friedrich Nietzsche,* edited and translated by C. Middleton (Cambridge: Hackett Publishing Company, Inc., 1969)

Nietzsche, F., 'Letter to Jakob Burckhardt: Turin, January 5, 1889' in, *Selected Letters of Friedrich Nietzsche*, edited and translated by C. Middleton (Cambridge: Hackett Publishing Company, Inc., 1969)

Nietzsche, F., 'Letter to Paul Deussen: Sils Maria, September 14, 1888' in, *Selected Letters of Friedrich Nietzsche*, edited and translated by C. Middleton (Cambridge: Hackett Publishing Company, Inc., 1969)

Nietzsche, F., 'Letter to Peter Gast: Postmarked Turin, January 4, 1889' in, *Selected Letters of Friedrich Nietzsche*, edited and translated by C. Middleton (Cambridge: Hackett Publishing Company, Inc., 1969)

Nietzsche, F., 'Letter to Peter Gast: Turin, April 7, 1888, Saturday' in, *Selected Letters of Friedrich Nietzsche*, edited and translated by C. Middleton (Cambridge: Hackett Publishing Company, Inc., 1969)

Nietzsche, F., 'Letter to Peter Gast: Turin, December 2, 1888' in, *Selected Letters of Friedrich Nietzsche*, edited and translated by C. Middleton (Cambridge: Hackett Publishing Company, Inc., 1969)

Nietzsche, F., 'Letter to Peter Gast: Turin, Friday [April 20, 1888]' in, *Selected Letters of Friedrich Nietzsche*, edited and translated by C. Middleton (Cambridge: Hackett Publishing Company, Inc., 1969)

Nietzsche, F., 'Letter to Peter Gast: Turin, Tuesday, October 30, 1888' in, *Selected Letters of Friedrich Nietzsche*, edited and translated by C. Middleton

(Cambridge: Hackett Publishing Company, Inc., 1969)

Nietzsche, F., 'The Anti-Christ' in, *Twilight of the Idols and the Anti-Christ*, translated by R. J., Hollingdale with an introduction by M. Tanner (London: Penguin Books Ltd, 2003)

Nietzsche, F., *The Gay Science*, translated with commentary by W. Kaufmann (New York: Vintage Books 1974)

Nietzsche, F., *Thus Spoke Zarathustra*, translated with an introduction by R. J. Hollingdale (London: Penguin Books Ltd, 2003)

Nietzsche, F., 'Twilight of the Idols' in, *Twilight of the Idols and the Anti-Christ*, translated by R. J., Hollingdale with an introduction by M. Tanner (London: Penguin Books Ltd, 2003)

Nietzsche, F., *The Will to Power*, translated by W. Kaufmann and R. J. Hollingdale (New York: Vintage Books, 1967)

Nonnos, *Dionysiaca*, translated with an introduction and notes by W. H. D. Rouse (Cambridge, Massachusetts: Harvard University Press, 1995)

O'Brien, S., 'Publishing Poetry in Britain' in, Earnshaw, S., ed., *The Creative Writing Handbook* (Edinburgh: Edinburgh University Press, 2007)

Onega, S., and J. A. García Landa, eds., *Narratology: An Introduction* (London: Longman, 1996)

Osborne, R., *Archaic and Classical Greek Art* (Oxford: Oxford University Press, 1998)

Ovid, *Metamorphosis*, translated by A. D. Melville and with an introduction and notes by E. J. Kenney (Oxford: Oxford University Press, 1986)

Parks, T., *Medici Money: Banking and Metaphysics and Art in Fifteenth-Century Florence* (London: Profile Books Ltd, 2006)

Parronchi, A., *Michelangelo: Sculpture*, translated by J. Hale-White (London: Thames and Hudson, 1969)

Peachment, C., *Caravaggio: A Novel* (London: Picador, 2002)

Pfeiffer, R., *History of Classical Scholarship: 1300-1850* (Oxford: Oxford University Press, 1976)

Pindar, 'Second Nemean Ode' in, *The Odes and Selected Fragments*, translated by G. S. Conway and R. Stoneman (London: J. M. Dent, 1997)

Pindar, *The Odes and Selected Fragments*, translated by G. S. Conway and revised with a new introduction by R. Stoneman (London: Everyman, 1997)

Pinker, S., *The Language Instinct* (London: Penguin Books, Ltd, 1995)

Plato, *Early Socratic Dialogues: Ion, Laches, Lysis, Charmides, Hippias Major, Hippias Minor, Euthydemus*, edited with a general introduction by T. J. Saunders (London: Penguin Books Ltd, 1987)

Plato, 'Phaedrus' in, *Phaedrus and Letters VII and VIII*, translated with an introduction by W. Hamilton (London: Penguin Books Ltd, 1973)

Plato, *The Last Days of Socrates: Euthyphro, Apology, Crito and Phaedo*, translated by H. Tredennick and H. Tarrant (London: Penguin Books, Ltd, 2003)

Plato, *The Republic*, translated with an introduction by D. Lee (London: Penguin Books Ltd, 2003)

Plato, *The Symposium*, translated with an introduction and notes by C. Gill (London: Penguin Books Ltd, 2003)

Plato, *Timaeus*, translated with an introduction by D. Lee (London: Penguin Books Ltd, 1977)

Plotinus, *The Enneads*, translated by S. Mackenna, abridged with an introduction and notes by J. Dillon (London: Penguin Books Ltd, 1991)

Poellner, P., *Nietzsche and Metaphysics* (Oxford: Oxford University Press, 2000)

Pope, R., *Creativity: Theory, History, Practice* (London: Routledge, 2005)

Pound, E., *ABC of Reading* (London: Faber and Faber, 1991)

Pound, E., 'A Retrospect' in, Nadel, I. B., ed., *Ezra Pound: Early Writings, Poetry and Prose* (London: Penguin Books Ltd, 2005)

Pound E., *Personae: Collected Shorter Poems* (London: Faber and Faber, 1990)

Pound, E., 'Canto II' in, Pound E., *The Cantos of Ezra Pound* (New York: New Directions Publishing Corporation, 1993)

Pound, E., 'Canto IX' in, Pound, E., *Selected Poems: 1908-1969* (London: Faber and Faber, 1977)

Pound, E., 'Piere Vidal Old' in, Pound, E., *Personae: Collected Shorter Poems* (London: Faber and Faber, 2001)

Pound, E., *The Cantos* (New York: New Directions Books, 1993)

Price, S., ed., *The Oxford Dictionary of Classical Myth and Religion* (Oxford: Oxford University Press, 2004)

Prynne, J. H., *Poems* (Trowbridge: Bloodaxe Books Ltd, 2004)

Pseudo-Dionysius, 'The Mystical Theology' in, *Pseudo-Dionysius: The Complete Works*, translated by C. Luibheid (New York: Paulist Press, 1987)

Pseudo-Dionysius, *The Complete Works*, translated by C. Luibheid with foreword, notes and translation collaboration by P. Rorem, with a preface by R. Roques, and introductions by J. Pelikan, J. Leclercq, and K. Froehlich (New York: Paulist Press, 1987)

Quispel, G., 'Preface' in, *The Way of Hermes: The Corpus Hermeticum and the Definitions of Hermes Trismegistus to Asclepius*, translated by C. Salaman, D. van Oyen, W. D. Wharton and J-P. Mahé (London: Gerald Duckworth & Co Ltd, 1999)

Rachum, I., *The Renaissance: An Illustrated Encyclopedia* (London: Octopus Books Ltd, 1979)

Radice, B., *Who's Who in the Ancient World* (London: Penguin Books Ltd, 1973)

Radke, G. M., 'Masaccio's City: Urbanism, Architecture, and Sculpture in Early Fifteenth-Century Florence' in, Cole Ahl, D., ed., *The Cambridge Companion to Masaccio* (Cambridge: Cambridge University Press, 2002)

Rebenich, S., *Jerome* (London: Routledge, 2002)

Richardson, C. M., K. W. Woods, and M. W. Franklin, *Renaissance Art Reconsidered: An Anthology of Primary Sources* (Oxford: Blackwell Publishing, 2007)

Richardson, N., 'Introduction' in, *The Homeric Hymns*, translated by J. Cashford (London: Penguin Books Ltd, 2003)

Richter, I. A., ed., *The Notebooks of Leonardo da Vinci* (Oxford: Oxford University Press, 1998)

Ridpath, I., ed., *The Oxford Dictionary of Astronomy* (Oxford: Oxford University Press, 2003)

Rifkin, B. A., M. J. Ackerman, and J. Folkenberg, *Human Anatomy: Depicting the Body from the Renaissance to Today* (London: Thames and Hudson, 2006)

Robb, P., *M* (London: Bloomsbury, 2000)

Roberts, P., *How Poetry Works* (London: Penguin Books Ltd, 1986)

Rorem, P., *Pseudo-Dionysius: A Commentary on the Texts and an Introduction to Their Influence* (Oxford: Oxford University Press, 1993)

Rose, G., *The Broken Middle* (Oxford: Blackwell, 1992)

Rosenthal, M., 'Joseph Beuys: Staging Sculpture' in, Braeuer, S., C. Elliot, and J. Watkins, eds., *Joseph Beuys: Actions, Vitrines, Environments* (London: Tate Modern Publishing, 2005)

Rowland, I. D., 'The Intellectual Background of The School of Athens' in, Hall, M., ed., *Raphael's School of Athens* (Cambridge: Cambridge University Press, 1997)

Runciman, S., *A History of the Crusades, Volume III: The Kingdom of Acre and the Later Crusades* (London: Penguin Books Ltd, 1990)

Russell, B., *The Problems of Philosophy* (Oxford: Oxford University Press, 2001)

Safranski, R., *Nietzsche: A Philosophical Biography*, translated by S. Frisch (London: Granta Books, 2002)

Said, E. W., *Orientalism* (London: Penguin Books Ltd, 2003)

Sartre, J-P., *Being and Nothingness*, translated by H. E. Barnes (London: Routledge, 2003)

Scarre, C., *Chronicle of the Roman Emperors* (London: Thames and Hudson, 2000)

Schama, S., *Simon Schama's Power of Art* (London: BBC Books, 2006)

Schmidt, M., *The First Poets: Lives of the Ancient Greek Poets* (London: Weidenfeld & Nicolson, 2004)

Schopenhauer, A., 'On Suicide' in, *Essays and Aphorisms*, selected and translated with an introduction by R. J. Hollingdale (London: Penguin Books Ltd, 1970)

Schopenhauer, A., *The World as Will and Idea*, translated by J. Berman with an introduction by D. Berman (London: Everyman, 1995)

Scruton, R., *Kant* (Oxford: Oxford University Press, 2001)

Sekules, V., *Medieval Art* (Oxford: Oxford University Press, 2001)

Seznec, J., *The Survival of the Pagan Gods: The Mythological Tradition and Its Place in Renaissance Humanism and Art* (New Haven: Princeton University Press, 1995)

Shaffer, P., 'Amadeus' in, Cornish, R., ed., *The Plays of the Seventies* (London: Methuen, 1986)

Singer, P. and R. Singer, eds., *The Moral of the Story: An Anthology of Ethics Through Literature* (Oxford: Blackwell Publishing, 2005)

Sophocles, 'Ajax' in, *Electra and Other Plays*, translated with an introduction by E. F. Watling (London: Penguin Books Ltd, 1953)

Sophocles, 'Electra' in, *Electra and Other Plays,* translated with an introduction by E. F. Watling (London: Penguin Books Ltd, 1953)

Spearing, A. C., trans., 'The Mystical Theology of St. Denis' in, *The Cloud of Unknowing and Other Works*, translated with an introduction and notes by A. C. Spearing (London: Penguin Books Ltd, 2001)

Spector, N., 'In Potentia: Matthew Barney and Joseph Beuys' in, Grosz, D., ed., *Barney/Beuys: All in the*

Present must be Transformed (Berlin: Deutsche Guggenheim, 2007)

Spector, N., 'Only the Perverse Fantasy Can Still Save Us' in *The Cremaster Cycle*, ed. M. Barney (New York: Guggenheim Museum Publications, 2003)

Stamelman, R., 'The Graven Silence of Writing' in, Jabès, E., *From the Book to the Book: An Edmond Jabès Reader*, translated from the French by R. Waldrop with additional translations by P. Joris, A. Rudolf, and K. Waldrop (London: Wesleyan University Press, 1991)

Stevens Curl, J., *The Oxford Dictionary of Architecture and Landscape Architecture* (Oxford: Oxford University Press, 2006)

Stillman, F., *The Poets Manual and Rhyming Dictionary* (London: Thames & Hudson Ltd, 1966)

St. Paul, 'Ephesians' in, Marshall, A., ed., *The Interlinear NRSV-NIV: Parallel New Testament in Greek and English* (London: Zondervan Publishing House, 1993)

Strathern, P., *The Medici: Godfathers of the Renaissance* (London: Pimlico, 2005)

Strawson, P. F., *Individuals: An Essay in Descriptive Metaphysics* (London: Methuen, 1959)

Strawson, P. F., *The Bounds of Sense: An Essay on Kant's 'Critique of Pure Reason'* (London: Routledge, 1995)

Strohmeier, J., and P. Westbrook, *Divine Harmony: The Life and Teachings of Pythagoras* (California: Berkeley Hills Books, 1999)

Stroll, A., *Wittgenstein* (Oxford: Oneworld, 2002)

Tanner, M., 'Chronology of Nietzsche's Life' in, Nietzsche, F., *Ecce Homo*, translated by R. J. Hollingdale with an introduction by M. Tanner (London: Penguin Books Ltd, 1992)

Tanner, M., 'Introduction' in, Nietzsche, F., *Ecce Homo*, translated by R. J. Hollingdale (London: Penguin Books Ltd, 1992)

Tanner, M., 'Introduction' in, Nietzsche, F., *The Birth of Tragedy Out of the Spirit of Music*, translated by S. Whiteside (London: Penguin Books Ltd, 1993)

Tanner, M., 'Introduction' in, Nietzsche, F., *Twilight of the Idols and The Anti-Christ*, translated by R. J. Hollingdale (London: Penguin Books Ltd, 2003)

Tanner, M., *Schopenhauer: Metaphysics and Art* (London: Orion Publishing Group Ltd, 1998)

Taylor, T., trans., *Orpheus: Hymns and Initiations* (Chippenham: Antony Rowe, 2003)

Thoenes, C., *Raphael*, translated by K. Williams (London: Taschen, 2005)

Tisdall, C., *Joseph Beuys* (London: Thames and Hudson Ltd, 1979)

Tusiani, J., 'Introduction' in, Buonarroti, M., *The Complete Poems*, translated by J. Tusiani (London: Peter Owen Publishers, 1986)

Vasari, G., 'Life of Leonardo da Vinci' in, *Lives of the Artists (Volume I)*, a selection translated by G. Bull (London: Penguin Books Ltd, 1987)

Vasari, G., 'The Life of Leonardo: 1550 version' in, Nicholl, C., *Leonardo da Vinci: The Flights of the Mind* (London: Penguin Books Ltd, 2005)

Vernant, J-P., *Myth and Society in Ancient Greece*, translated from the French by J. Lloyd (London: Methuen, 1982)

Vezzosi, A., *Leonardo da Vinci: Renaissance Man*, translated by A. Bonfante-Warren (London: Thames and Hudson Ltd, 1997)

Vigni, G., ed., *All the Paintings of Antonello da Messina*, translated by A. Firmin O'Sullivan (London: Thames and Hudson, 1963)

Virgil, *The Aeneid*, translated by C. Day Lewis and with an introduction by J. Griffin (Oxford: Oxford University Press, 1986)

Virgil, *The Georgics*, translated by L. P. Wilkinson (London: Penguin Books Ltd, 1982)

Waldrop, R., translates, *From the Book to the Book: An Edmond Jabès Reader* (Wesleyan: Wesleyan University Press, 1992)

Weir, D., *Brahma in the West: William Blake and the Oriental Renaissance* (Albany: State University of New York Press, 2003)

West, M. L., translates with an introduction and notes, *Greek Lyric Poetry* (Oxford: Oxford University Press: 1993)

West, M. L., 'Introduction' in, *Greek Lyric Poetry*, translated with an introduction and notes by M. L. West (Oxford: Oxford University Press, 1993)

White, C., 'Introduction' in, *Early Christian Lives*, translated, edited, and with an introduction by C. White (London: Penguin Books Ltd, 1998)

White, M., *Leonardo: The First Scientist* (London: Abacus, 2001)

Whitman, W., *Complete Poetry and Selected Prose and Letters*, edited by E. Holloway (London: The Nonesuch Press, 1938)

Williams, J. P., *Denying Divinity: Apophasis in the Patristic Christian and Soto Zen Buddhist Traditions* (Oxford: Oxford University Press, 2000)

Wilson, P., *A Preface to Ezra Pound* (London: Longman, 1997)

Wilson-Smith, T., Caravaggio (New York: Phaidon, 1998)

Wittgenstein, L., *Tractatus Logico-Philosophicus*, translated by D. F.Pears and B. F. McGuinness (London: Routledge, 2004)

Wolf, N., *Albrecht Dürer: The Genius of the German Renaissance*, translated by K. Williams (London: Taschen, 2006)

Wolf, N., *Giotto: The Renewal of Painting*, translated by K. Williams (London: Taschen, 2006)

Wolf, N., *Hans Holbein the Younger: The German Raphael*, translated by J. Gabriel (London: Taschen, 2006)

Wolf, N., *Diego Velázquez: The Face of Spain*, translated by J. Steinbrecher (London: Taschen, 2006)

Wölfflin, H., 'The School of Athens' in, Hall, M., ed., *Raphael's School of Athens* (Cambridge: Cambridge University Press, 1997)

Wood, P., *Conceptual Art* (London: Tate Publishing, 2002)

Wordsworth, W., *The Prelude, The 1805 Text*, edited from the manuscripts with an introduction and notes by E. De Selincourt, corrected by S. Gill (Oxford: Oxford University Press, 1970)

Wright, F. A., 'Introduction' in, Jerome, *Selected Letters*, translated by F. A. Wright (Cambridge, Massachusetts: Harvard University Press, 1991)

Wundram, M., *Renaissance*, translated by K. Williams (London: Taschen, 2006)

Yates, F., *Giordano Bruno and the Hermetic Tradition* (London: Routledge, 2002)

Yeats, W. B., 'A Packet for Ezra Pound' in, Leary, L., ed., *Motive and Method in the Cantos of Ezra Pound* (New York: Columbia University Press, 1969)

Yonah, M. A., *The Illustrated Encyclopaedia of the Classical World* (Jerusalem: Jerusalem Publishing House Ltd, 1976)

Zöllner, F., *Leonardo*, translated by F. Elliot (London: Taschen, 2000)

Zukofsky, L., *"A"* (London: The Johns Hopkins University Press, 1993)

Zukofsky, L., *Selected Poems* (Boston: Baron and James Ltd, 1998)

Lightning Source UK Ltd.
Milton Keynes UK
30 March 2011

170100UK00001B/5/P